Beautiful upon the Mountains

Studies in Peace and Scripture

Volumes in the Studies in Peace and Scripture series are sponsored by Institute of Mennonite Studies, Elkhart, Indiana, and released by a variety of publishers.

Beautiful upon the Mountains

Biblical Essays on Mission, Peace, and the Reign of God

Edited by
Mary H. Schertz and Ivan Friesen

Institute of Mennonite Studies
Elkhart, Indiana

Co-published with Herald Press
Scottdale, Pennsylvania
Waterloo, Ontario

Copyright ©2003 by Institute of Mennonite Studies
3003 Benham Avenue, Elkhart, Indiana 46517-1999
www.ambs.edu/IMS
All rights reserved

Co-published with
Herald Press
616 Walnut Avenue, Scottdale, Pennsylvania 15683
490 Dutton Drive, Unit C8, Waterloo, Ontario N2L 6H7
www.heraldpress.com

Printed in the United States of America by Evangel Press, Nappanee, Indiana

Institute of Mennonite Studies ISBN 0-936273-35-6

Library of Congress Cataloging-in-Publication Data
Beautiful upon the mountains : biblical essays on mission, peace,
and the reign of God / edited by Mary H. Schertz and Ivan Friesen.
    p. cm. — (Studies in peace and scripture ; v. 7)
ISBN 0-936273-35-6 (alk. paper)
1. Missions—Biblical teaching. 2. Peace—Biblical teaching.
I. Schertz, Mary H. II. Friesen, Ivan. III. Series.
BV2073.B43 2003
266—dc22
                                                         2003024785

Cover design by Mary E. Klassen

Unless otherwise indicated, the Scripture quotations in this book are from the *New Revised Standard Version Bible,* copyright ©1989 by the Division of Christian Education of the National Council of Churches of Christ in the USA, and are used by permission.

The diagram that appears on page 178 is reprinted, by permission of the publisher, from Hendrikus Boers, *Neither on this Mountain nor in Jerusalem: A Study of John 4,* Society of Biblical Literature Monograph Series 35 (Atlanta: Scholars Pr., 1988), 120.

The chart that appears on pages 179–81 is reprinted, by permission of the author, from Linda Oyer, "Interpreting the New in Light of the Old: A Comparative Study of the Post-Resurrection Commissioning Stories in Matthew and John" (Ph.D. diss., Catholic Institute of Paris, 1997), 446.

How beautiful upon the mountains
are the feet of the messenger
    who announces peace,
    who brings good news,
    who announces salvation,
    who says to Zion, "Your God reigns."

Isaiah 52:7

Contents

Foreword

IMAGES OF VIOLENCE HAVE BEEN SEARED INTO OUR SOULS with numbing regularity in recent years, with the collapse of twin towers in New York City and a resulting "global war on terrorism." The present political environment raises issues of justice, retribution, allegiance, and security. A generation ago, global conflicts of the Cold War coalesced (at least in rhetoric) around poles of democracy and communism. With the end of the Cold War, conflicts on several continents now seem to hinge more on ethnic and religious identity than on political ideology.

Today biblical language seeps into the North American body politic through a steady intravenous drip of *Left Behind* books, patriotic "televangelism," and political prayer breakfasts. Bible reading is part of the American president's daily schedule, and those close to him say he "sees the world as a biblical struggle of good versus evil."[1]

No chapter in this volume directly speaks to the specter of a "Christian" West marshalling massive military might against nations of the world where Islam predominates. Nor do these essays offer a critique of the alarming tendency of some western media preachers and politicians to invoke Scripture to justify a foreign policy that fosters empire. But these unsettling realities are the backdrop against which this collection of essays emerges.

When powerful political and military leaders invoke Christian and biblical themes to reinforce policy, the church should demand careful exegesis. Authors of this book do scholarly spadework on biblical themes of mission and peace at a time when those words blaze in the headlines—e.g., "mission accomplished" or "peacekeepers"—usually with meanings far removed from what biblical authors intended.

These essays are not easy reading. They issue from the precise and sometimes technical conversation that academics conduct in seminars and colloquies. Not content to settle for simple analysis or "sound bite" hermeneutics, these authors explore in depth the surprises and

---

[1] Joan Didion, "Mr. Bush and the Divine," *The New York Review of Books* (November 6, 2003), 83.

unresolved tensions conjoining mission and peace as themes in Bible interpretation. Like scientists researching the human genome to understand how genes interplay to shape life, the authors undertake detailed research of Scripture to understand how mission and peace interrelate to shape faithful Christian witness.

Christians in many denominations are familiar with the pattern of "social gospel" advocates marching off in a different direction from the "evangelical" stalwarts. As the following essays verify, no such bifurcation can withstand biblical scrutiny. These scholars are committed church people who in their personal lives integrate a passion for peacemaking and justice with ability to articulate the Good News of salvation in Jesus Christ. I am grateful that, in these pages, they give detailed examples of how such a faithful blend of peacemaking and mission is grounded in careful reading of the sacred texts.

J. NELSON KRAYBILL

President, Associated Mennonite Biblical Seminary

Series preface

VISIONS OF PEACE ABOUND IN THE BIBLE, WHOSE PAGES are also filled with the language and the reality of war. In this respect, the Bible is thoroughly at home in the modern world, whether as a literary classic or as a unique sacred text. This is, perhaps, a part of the Bible's realism: bridging the distance between its world and our own is a history filled with visions of peace accompanying the reality of war. That alone would justify study of peace and war in the Bible. However, for those communities in which the Bible is sacred Scripture, the matter is more urgent. For them, it is crucial to understand what the Bible says about peace—and about war. These issues have often divided Christians from each other, and the way Christians have understood them has had terrible consequences for Jews and, indeed, for the world. A series of scholarly investigations cannot hope to resolve these issues, but it can hope, as this one does, to aid our understanding of them.

Over the past century a substantial body of literature has grown up around the topic of the Bible and war. Studies in great abundance have been devoted to historical questions about ancient Israel's conception and conduct of war and about the position of the early church on participation in the Roman Empire and its military. It is not surprising that many of these studies have been motivated by theological and ethical concerns, which may themselves be attributed to the Bible's own seemingly disjunctive preoccupation with peace and, at the same time, with war. If not within the Bible itself, then at least from Aqiba and Tertullian, the question has been raised whether—and if so, then on what basis—God's people may legitimately participate in war. With the Reformation, the churches divided on this question. The division was unequal, with the majority of Christendom agreeing that, however regrettable war may be, Christians have biblical warrant for participating in it. A minority countered that, however necessary war may appear, Christians have a biblical mandate to avoid it. Modern historical studies have served to bolster one side of this division or the other.

Meanwhile, it has become clear that a narrow focus on participation in war is not the only way—and likely not the best way—to approach the Bible on the topic of peace. War and peace are not simply two sides of the same coin; each is broader than its contrast with the other. In spite of broad agreement on this point, the number of studies devoted to the Bible and peace is still very small, especially in English. Consequently, answers to the most basic questions remain to be settled. Among these questions is that of what the Bible means in speaking of *shalom* or *eirēnē*, the Hebrew and the Greek term usually translated into English as "peace." By the same token, what the Bible has to say about peace is not limited to its use of these two terms. Questions remain about the relation of peace, in the Bible, to considerations of justice, integrity, and—in the broadest sense—salvation. And of course there still remains the question of the relation between peace and war. In fact, what the Bible says about peace is often framed in the language of war. The Bible very often uses martial imagery to portray God's own action, whether it be in creation, in judgment against or in defense of Israel, or in the cross and resurrection of Jesus Christ—actions aimed at achieving peace.

This close association of peace and war, to which we have already drawn attention, presents serious problems for the contemporary appropriation of the Bible. Are human freedom, justice, and liberation—and the liberation of creation—furthered or hindered by the martial, frequently royal, and pervasively masculine terms in which the Bible speaks of peace? These questions cannot be answered by the rigorous and critical exegesis of the biblical texts alone; they demand serious moral and theological reflection. But that reflection will be substantially aided by exegetical studies of the kind included in this series—even as these studies will be illumined by including just that kind of reflection within them.

Studies in Peace and Scripture is sponsored by the Institute of Mennonite Studies, the research agency of Associated Mennonite Biblical Seminary. The seminary and the tradition it represents have a particular interest in peace but, even more so, an interest in the Bible. We hope that this ecumenical series will contribute to a deeper understanding of both.

BEN C. OLLENBURGER   WILLARD M. SWARTLEY
Old Testament editor   New Testament editor

Editors' preface

THE QUESTION OF HOW TO READ THE BIBLICAL CANON IS a common struggle for biblical people and biblical congregations. The truth is that we tend to read the biblical witness in light of our own persuasions and commitments. Those of us who have interests in evangelism, social action, mysticism, liturgy, church structure, and so forth, will organize the canon around our interests and see in the text what we want to see. A degree of subjectivity is present in all our constructions of biblical theology.

There are, of course, ways to test and counteract our biases. Ecumenical discussion is important. Asking people who do not agree with our own theology to comment on our work is vital. Seeking out and incorporating views from people who do not share one's own social location is another way to test one's perceptions. Both of these methods illumine those places where our prejudices may get in the way of our effort to read the Bible well.

The essays in this book represent a third way of testing our readings of texts, a method not so often undertaken because of the rigor it requires. That way is to test the overall assumptions one has about the biblical canon by careful exegesis of pertinent texts. Will our larger theological and ethical commitments stand up to vigorous, hard-headed examination of specific texts within the range of the biblical canon? In this volume, biblical scholars committed to both mission and peace look carefully at the texts they know the best, passages they have spent their lives studying, to see whether the themes of evangelism and social action are as closely intertwined in the biblical witness as they have supposed.

The result of this effort is an impressive array of evidence that in the breadth and depth of the biblical canon there is indeed a unity of evangelism and social action. Isaiah's song about the messenger who announces peace and brings good news is not a lonely voice in the biblical witness. Rather, from Genesis to Revelation, mission and peace are inseparable as the vision of God's reign.

Not casual reading, these carefully researched essays represent the foundational scrutiny and intense self-questioning that are basic to more popular articulations of the relationship between mission and peace.

They are an unprecedented biblical resource for those committed to thinking about and articulating for the church the unity between peace and mission.

We are grateful to the many people who worked together to make this book happen. Appreciation is due, first, to the scholars who invested precious time in this research and writing. We are grateful to Levi Miller of Herald Press, for his assistance in co-publishing this volume. The administrators and Bible department of Associated Mennonite Biblical Seminary were valued consultants. The final form of the book owes much to Barbara Nelson Gingerich's patient and sensitive editing and formatting. Her care for words and the people who write them is evident on every page.

IVAN FRIESEN   MARY H. SCHERTZ
Old Testament editor   New Testament editor

Contributors

Wilma Ann Bailey is Associate Professor of Hebrew and Aramaic Scripture at Christian Theological Seminary, Indianapolis, Indiana. She has authored several sets of Adult Bible Study Guides for the Mennonite Church, as well as articles, book reviews, and essays.

Jacob W. Elias is Professor of New Testament at Associated Mennonite Biblical Seminary, Elkhart, Indiana. He is also co-pastor, along with his wife Lillian, of Parkview Mennonite Church, Kokomo, Indiana. Elias is the author of *1 & 2 Thessalonians*, Believers Church Bible Commentary (Herald Press, 1995).

Reta Halteman Finger is Assistant Professor of New Testament at Messiah College, Grantham, Pennsylvania. She was editor of *Daughters of Sarah* magazine. Besides publishing many articles relating to the New Testament, Christian feminism, and peace and justice issues, she has authored *Paul and the Roman House Churches* (Herald Press, 1993) and co-edited *The Wisdom of Daughters: Two Decades of the Voice of Christian Feminism* (Innisfree Press, 2001).

Ivan Friesen is a pastor at the Hutterthal Mennonite Church in Freeman, South Dakota. He is preparing the Isaiah commentary in the Believers Church Bible Commentary series. He worked in Botswana under the Africa Inter-Mennonite Mission from 1986 to 1992, and is an advocate of a strong Christian peace testimony that is an integral part of the proclamation of the gospel.

Loren L. Johns is Academic Dean and Associate Professor of New Testament at Associated Mennonite Biblical Seminary, Elkhart, Indiana. He is the author or editor of several books and journal articles, including *The Lamb Christology of the Apocalypse of John: An Investigation into Its Origins and Rhetorical Force*, Wissenschaftliche Untersuchungen zum Neuen Testament, 2nd series, no. 167 (Mohr Siebeck, 2003).

Gordon H. Matties is Associate Professor of Biblical Studies and Theology at Canadian Mennonite University, Winnipeg, Manitoba. Matties is author of the Ezekiel commentary in *The New Interpreter's Study Bible* (Abingdon Press, 2003). His article "Can Girard Help Us to Read Joshua?" was published in *Violence Renounced: René Girard, Biblical Studies, and Peacemaking,* edited by Willard M. Swartley (Pandora Press U.S., 2000).

Douglas B. Miller is Associate Professor of Biblical and Religious Studies at Tabor College, Hillsboro, Kansas. His most recent publication is *Symbol and Rhetoric in Ecclesiastes: The Place of Hebel in Qohelet's Work* (Society of Biblical Literature; E. J. Brill, 2002).

Ben C. Ollenburger is Professor of Biblical Theology at Associated Mennonite Biblical Seminary, Elkhart, Indiana. He was previously Instructor in Religious Studies and Philosophy at Tabor College, and Assistant Professor of Old Testament at Princeton Theological Seminary. Among his publications are the commentary on Zechariah in the New Interpreter's Bible (Abingdon Press, 1996), and *Old Testament Theology: Flowering and Future* (Eisenbrauns, 2003).

Willard M. Swartley is Professor of New Testament at Associated Mennonite Biblical Seminary, Elkhart, Indiana, where he has also served as Academic Dean and Director of the Institute of Mennonite Studies. He has edited numerous books, including nine New Testament volumes in the Believers Church Bible Commentary series; *The Meaning of Peace; Love of Enemy and Nonretaliation in the New Testament;* and *Violence Renounced: René Girard, Biblical Studies, and Peacemaking.* He has authored many articles and five books, including *Slavery, Sabbath, War and Women: Case Issues in Biblical Interpretation; Israel's Scripture Traditions and the Synoptic Gospels: Story Shaping Story;* and *Homosexuality: Biblical Interpretation and Moral Discernment.*

Erland Waltner is President Emeritus of Mennonite Biblical Seminary, which became part of Associated Mennonite Biblical Seminary, Elkhart, Indiana. He is the author of the Believers Church Bible Commentary on 1 Peter (1999). Ordained to ministry in 1938, he has served the church pastorally and academically at local, institutional, and global levels. He now serves in a ministry of spiritual direction.

Dorothy Jean Weaver is Professor of New Testament at Eastern Mennonite Seminary, Harrisonburg, Virginia. She is the author of

Matthew's Missionary Discourse: A Literary Critical Analysis (Sheffield Academic Press, 1990) and the compiler/editor of *Bread for the Enemy: A Peace and Justice Lectionary* (Mennonite Church Peace and Justice Committee, 2001).

Gary Yamasaki is Professor of New Testament at Columbia Bible College, Abbotsford, B.C. He is currently working on a book on the relevance of point of view in the exegesis of biblical narratives.

Perry Yoder is Professor of Old Testament at Associated Mennonite Biblical Seminary, Elkhart, Indiana. His most recent book, with coauthor Mary Schertz, is *Seeing the Text: Exegesis for Students of Greek and Hebrew* (Abingdon Press, 2001). His article in the present collection grows out of his work with Leviticus 17 for a commentary on Leviticus. His other writing interest is the Psalms.

Thomas R. Yoder Neufeld is Associate Professor of Religious Studies (New Testament and Peace and Conflict Studies) at Conrad Grebel University College in Waterloo, Ontario, Canada. In addition to teaching, he is director of the Graduate Theological Studies program of the college. His most recent publications are *Ephesians*, Believers Church Bible Commentary (Herald Press, 2002), and "Resistance and Nonresistance: The Two Legs of a Biblical Peace Stance," *Conrad Grebel Review* 21 (2003): 56-81.

Old Testament Essays

1 | *The Noachide covenant and Christian mission*

PERRY B. YODER

G ENESIS 9:1–17 IS A SIGNIFICANT PASSAGE FOR MISSIONS and peacemaking not only because it represents a revision of some Genesis 1 provisions for humankind[1] but also because it represents a new beginning between God and humanity. Following the disaster of the flood, God undertakes a new initiative and a new covenanted relationship. The new era introduced by Gen. 9:1–17 is our era, because from Noah's time onward the universal provisions instituted by God remain in effect. The covenant of the rainbow has not been called back.

This universal and primordial quality of Gen. 9:1–17 gives it significance for understanding the context within which Christian mission and peace building take place today. This beginning is especially pertinent because we usually build from the particular—the claims of the gospel—and work to the universal, rather than beginning with the universal—our understanding of creation and humankind—and working toward the particular. In this passage we find God entering into a covenant relationship with all humankind, a universal relationship that continues to the present.

LITERARY CONTEXT

In its literary context, Gen. 9:1–17 is a continuation of the scene depicted at the end of chapter 8. On leaving the ark (8:18), Noah, like his Mesopotamian counterpart, Utnapishtum, builds an altar and offers sacrifices. God smells the pleasant odor of the sacrifice and promises never again to curse the ground or to destroy all life because of humankind.[2] The words of this pledge, verses 21 and 22, are an internal

---

[1] Both Genesis 1 and 9:1–17 are regarded as P material. In chapter 9 the Priestly writing reflects on and repeats language found in chapter 1.

[2] See the eleventh tablet of the Gilgamesh Epic for a depiction of these events from a Mesopotamian point of view (James B. Pritchard, ed., *Ancient Near Eastern Texts Relating to the Old Testament [ANET]*, 3rd ed. [Princeton: Princeton Univ. Pr., 1978], 93–7).

monologue in the mind of God. They are not addressed to Noah and his sons. God alone undertakes an obligation.

In 9:1 God addresses Noah and his sons. God's direct speech, broken into several separate statements, continues to the end of verse 17. In verse 18 the text shifts to narrative style and a new episode begins with the familiar "And it was . . . "[3] Genesis 9:1–17 is thus marked off from the material around it but is more closely connected to the end of chapter 8, which it continues, than to 9:18 and the following narrative.

Although 9:1–17 forms a compositional unit, it can be divided into two distinct subsections. Verses 1–7 form the first unit, and verses 8–17 form the second. This division is apparent for at least the following reasons. First, these two units have different topics and belong to different formal categories of speech. Verses 1–7 are introduced as a blessing, while verses 8–17 are concerned with making a covenant. Second, the first unit is delineated by an inclusio. Verse 1 is echoed by the repetition of its words in verse 7. The second unit is likewise marked by an inclusio. Verse 9 (verse 8 is narrative introduction to God's direct speech) is echoed in verse 17. In verse 9 the making of the covenant is in the future; in verse 17 it is spoken of as in the past.

Genesis 9:1–17 is not only a continuation of chapter 8, it is also linked closely to Gen. 1:28 by verbal repetition. The first verse, 9:1, tips us off to this horizon of the unit because it echoes the wording of Genesis 1:28a.

וַיְבָרֶךְ אֱלֹהִים אֹתָם וַיֹּאמֶר לָהֶם אֱלֹהִים פְּרוּ וּרְבוּ וּמִלְאוּ אֶת־הָאָרֶץ

(wayĕbārek 'ōtām 'ĕlōhîm wayyō'mer lāhem 'ĕlōhîm pĕrû ûrĕbû ûmil'û 'et-hā'āreṣ)

And God blessed them and said to them, be fruitful and multiply and fill the earth.[4]

וַיְבָרֶךְ אֱלֹהִים אֶת־נֹחַ וְאֶת־בָּנָיו וַיֹּאמֶר לָהֶם פְּרוּ וּרְבוּ וּמִלְאוּ אֶת־הָאָרֶץ

(wayĕbārek 'ĕlōhîm 'et-nōaḥ wĕ'et-bānāw wayyō'mer lāhem pĕrû ûrĕbû ûmil'û 'et-hā'āreṣ)

*And God blessed **Noah and his sons** and said to them, be fruitful and multiply and fill the earth.*

The significance of this duplication is indicated by the fact that it is only in these two verses that we find the expression "be fruitful and multiply and fill the earth." Genesis 9:1 begins with a recapitulation of the divine

---

[3] וַיְהְיוּ (*wayyihĕyû*)

[4] Unless otherwise indicated, translations are my own.

blessing first given at creation[5] and thereby signals its connection with Genesis 1 and creation.

The context of Gen. 9:1–17 is an appropriate one for a renewal of God's original blessing. The blessing of Genesis 1 occurred in the context of creation as ordered by God and inhabited by the first couple. Now the situation is different. First, paradise was lost. Second, in the flood human sin led to the destruction of all life and the partial destruction of God's established order. In the flood we see a reversal, a return of the earth to watery chaos, to a state before God on day two of creation separated the waters above from the waters below and on day three separated the waters below from the land. Only when God had ordered the waters could the fertility of creation be manifested and the blessing of human fertility realized. The death-dealing waters of the flood erased this fertile order.

In the new situation after the flood, God declares that the ground will not again be cursed because of humankind, as in Genesis 3, nor will God strike down all living things, as was done in the preceding flood story (8:21–22). What new thing will God do in this new situation?

RENEWING THE BLESSING

Having placed our passage in its literary context, we turn to an analysis of God's new initiative. The statement of blessing in 9:1 is immediately followed by new regulations that will pertain between humans and the animal world. Humans are now granted a power over animals, and the animals in turn will fear them. However, in contrast to Gen. 1:28, humankind is not again commanded to subdue and rule.[6] Instead, we find simply the descriptive statement that "they have been given into your power."[7]

As opposed to Gen. 1:29ff., where only plants were allotted to humankind and animals for food, the new development in chapter 9 is that God now allows the animals for human food along with the plants.

---

[5] Marc Vervenne, "'The Blood Is the Life and the Life Is the Blood': Blood As Symbol of Life in Biblical Tradition (Gen 9,4)," in *Ritual and Sacrifice in the Ancient Near East: Proceedings of the International Conference Organized by the Katholieke Universiteit Leuven from the 17th to the 20th of April 1991*, ed. Jan Quaegebeur (Louvain: Peeters, 1993), 451–70. Pages 460–62 discuss several parallels between Genesis 9:1–7 and Genesis 1.

[6] I do not have space here to discuss the meaning of these commands. Let it suffice to say that they did not include taking animal life for food. They provided for governance by humans, but as God's representatives on earth. Thus, humans had delegated authority for which they were accountable.

[7] בְּיֶדְכֶם נִתָּנוּ (*bĕyedĕkem nittānû*)

The parallelism of language between Gen. 9:3 and 1:29 brings out the deliberate, innovative quality of the new provision.

> God said, "See, I have given you every plant yielding seed that is upon the face of all the earth, and every tree with seed in its fruit; you shall have them for food." (Gen. 1:29)

> "Every moving thing that lives shall be food for you; and just as I gave you the green plants, I give you everything." (Gen. 9:3)

What follows in verses 4 and 5 are regulations for this new practice.[8] First,

> "You must not, however, eat the flesh with its life-blood in it." (Gen. 9:4, NJPS)[9]

While animals may be killed for food, their blood is not to be ingested.[10]

Second, the taking of animal life allowed in verse 5 is a one-way street. Humans may kill animals, but animals may not kill humans. If they do so, God will require a reckoning. The same is also true for humankind. Whoever takes the life of another human being, God will requite the life of that person. Here we find an absolute prohibition on the taking of human life by either animals or humans. Taking life is only allowed in the realm of animals. If they contravene this principle, God will seek them out.

The emphasis in verse 5 clearly and emphatically falls on God. God's role and prerogative is stressed by the triple repetition of the verb "require,"[11] all in the first person.

> But for your own life-blood I will require a reckoning:
> I will require it of every beast;
> of man, too, will I require a reckoning for human life, of every man for that of his fellow man! (NJPS, arranged)

What follows in verse 6, the most familiar and most often used verse in this section, poses problems both for how it is to be reconciled with its present context, especially verse 5, and for how it should be

---

[8] Verses 4 and 5 begin with the same Hebrew word (אַךְ | 'ak) which can function as an adversative, "however, but" and as a restrictive, "only, except." See D. J. A. Clines, ed., *Dictionary of Classical Hebrew* (Sheffield, England: Sheffield Academic Pr., Ltd., 1993–).

[9] There are several grammatical and exegetical problems in this verse. But in light of Lev. 17:10–14, the above translation is representative of a common construal of this verse. Cf. NRSV, "Only, you shall not eat flesh with its life, that is, its blood."

[10] This verse can be understood to place a high value on all life. Humans may take the flesh of animals for food, but animal life belongs not to humankind but to God. The value and function of the lifeblood is further emphasized in Lev. 17:10–14.

[11] דרשׁ (drš) sometimes translated "seek." The verb does not in itself imply that God will take the life of the murderer. The closest parallels to the use of "requite" here are found in Deut. 18:19; 23:22 (Hebrew versification; 23:21 in English), which need not be construed to mean "to take the life of."

construed. At first glance it seems tacked onto the preceding material, which displayed a parallel pattern: "but" followed by a restriction to what was allowed in verse 3. Verse 6, on the other hand, begins abruptly without a conjunction linking it to what went before.

Second, no subject is stated, although participles in Hebrew normally take one. Third, while verse 5 was in second person, verse 6 is formulated in third person. Fourth, the first half of the verse differs stylistically from the preceding, which seems wordy, while verse 6a is formulated tersely and seems poetic because of its parallelism.[12]

These contextual dissonances of verse 6 are accompanied by difficulties in its construal. Primarily there is the question of the meaning of the word translated "by" in the phrase "by man." Two standard translations are as follows:

Whoever sheds the blood of man,
　　by man shall his blood be shed:
For in His image
did God make man. (NJPS)

Whoever sheds the blood of a human,
　　by a human shall that person's blood be shed;
for in his own image
God made humankind. (NRSV)

These translations represent the normal understanding of this verse. Contextually, however, this understanding of the first half-verse is jarring because the agency of God stressed in verse 5 is now being given into the hands of humankind. This difficulty has been noted by the commentators and has been solved in various ways (see footnote 11).

But it is doubtful that the Hebrew text should be translated this way. The Hebrew text of the first half of the verse reads:

שֹׁפֵךְ דַּם הָאָדָם בָּאָדָם דָּמוֹ יִשָּׁפֵךְ כִּי בְּצֶלֶם אֱלֹהִים עָשָׂה אֶת־הָאָדָם׃

(*šōpēk dam hā'ādām bā'ādām dāmô yiššāpēk kî běṣelem 'ĕlohîm 'āśāh 'et-hā'ādām*)

---

[12] See Claus Westermann (*Genesis 1–11: A Commentary*, trans. John J. Scullion [Minneapolis: Augsburg Publishing Hse., 1984]), who discusses arguments for its being a later insertion. He concludes, however, that the contextual and stylistic grounds are not adequate to consider it a later insertion (464). He further understands the passage as adding nothing new to the previous verses (466). However, because of the form of 6a, many scholars consider this an old saying, perhaps in the form of apodictic law or of a proverb. In any case, verse 6 does not seem organic to its context. It may have been added later, or may be a traditional saying which the author incorporated at this point. Cf. P. J. Harland, *The Value of Human Life: A Study of the Story of the Flood (Genesis 6–9)* (Leiden: E. J. Brill, 1996), 162: "But probably the best solution is to see it as a legal formula which has been expressed in poetic, proverbial style." This assessment seems to cover the majority of views.

It can be translated literally (leaving the preposition in question untranslated) as:

One shedding   the blood   of the human   ב   the human   his blood   will be shed.

A   B   C   C'   B'   A'

It is immediately apparent that this line forms a chiasm. Given this chiastic structure, might not "the human" that ends the first half line be the same "human" which begins the second half line? The standard translations answer this question in the negative, because they introduce a new figure, the agent of the passive verb "be shed." However, the chiastic structure found here has been cited as evidence against this traditional interpretation.[13]

Given these initial surface considerations of context and style, the philological question is, does verse 6 indicate that a human agent is supposed to shed the blood of a murderer?

To answer this question, we begin with a decisive consideration. According to the normal rules of Hebrew grammar, the human mentioned in the second half of the chiasm, C' above, should not be construed as the agent of the passive verb. This is so for the following reasons.

First, when a passive verb is used in Hebrew, the agent is usually not named. Sometimes the agent is unknown; at other times the author does not wish to mention the agent. Rather than putting the agent of the verb in the background, as does the English passive, Hebrew characteristically entirely removes the agent from the picture. Given this feature of Hebrew grammar and style, the initial presumption would be that the agent of the passive verb "will be shed" is not mentioned.[14]

Second, when an agent is mentioned, he or she is usually introduced by the preposition ל *(lāmed)* or, less frequently, by the preposition מִן *(min)*. Rarely, if ever, is the agent introduced by the preposition ב *(bêt)*, the preposition used in our verse.[15] When *bêt* is used with a passive verb, it introduces an instrument rather than an agent (see 1 Kings 1:40 and Deut. 21:3).[16]

---

[13] See Jacob Milgrom, *Leviticus 1–16: A New Translation with Introduction and Commentary* (New York: Doubleday, 1991), 705, who argues for the identity of the two *adams* based on the poetic design of the passage as well as on its grammar.

[14] See for example, Paul Joüon, *A Grammar of Biblical Hebrew,* trans. and rev. T. Muraoka (Rome: Pontifical Institute, 1991), chap. 3, #132c, "Prepositions in General."

[15] In addition to Joüon-Muraoka, see E. Kautzsch, *Gesenius' Hebrew Grammar,* 2nd English ed. (Oxford: Clarendon Pr., 1910), 121f.

[16] It is interesting to note how firmly embedded is the notion that the *bêt* here introduces the agent of the action. Bruce K. Waltke and M. O'Connor, *An Introduction to Biblical Hebrew*

In English we also use two different prepositions to distinguish between agency and instrumentality. We use the preposition "by" to express agency and the preposition "with" to express instrumentality. "He was hit with the bat" expresses instrumentality, but "He was hit by Peter" expresses agency. Of course, sometimes we use "by" in English to express instrumentality, but we do not use "with" for agency—"He was hit with Peter!" This construction would mean that Peter was not the agent. Grammatically the *bêt* in Hebrew parallels our usage of "with"; it indicates instrumentality but not agency. For agency other prepositions were commonly used.

These facts of Hebrew grammar have not gone unnoticed, and recently several scholars have argued that the *bêt* of Gen. 9:6 is not to be translated as introducing the agent of the passive verb. Ernst Jenni, at the end of an exhaustive study of the preposition *bêt*, states that the agentive interpretation "is to be disputed on purely linguistic grounds."[17] Rather, in this context, it is to be construed as a *bêt pretii*, "for, for the price of." Not only is this a frequent meaning of this preposition, but two cases in particular—the *talion* law in Deut. 19:21 and revenge of Joab in 2 Sam. 3:27—have formulations similar to verse 6, and in both cases the *bêt* is to be construed as a *bêt pretii*.[18]

Syntax (Winona Lake, Ind.: Eisenbrauns, 1990), list purported instrumental and agentive uses of the *bêt*. The only example cited in which the *bêt* is followed by a possible actor is Gen. 9:6! A similar phenomenon is found in David J. A. Clines, ed., *Dictionary of Classical Hebrew* (Sheffield, England: Sheffield Academic Pr., Ltd., 1993–), which gives each word exhaustive treatment. Under the entry for *bêt*, 84a, it lists four occurrences of *bêt*'s use as agentive: Gen. 9:6; Num. 36:2; Deut. 33:29; and Isa. 45:17. God, who is considered the agent of the passive verb, is introduced by *bêt* in these verses. These uses are far from certain, however, as Joüon-Muraoka denies an agentive meaning in the Deuteronomy and Isaiah passages and believes the Numbers passage to be doubtful for text-critical reasons. But under a more common meaning of *bêt*, "at the cost of, at the price of" (85b), Gen. 9:6 is listed again and translated "as the price of the (murdered) person will his blood be shed." This would seem the better choice. Ludwig Koehler and Walter Baumgartner, *The Hebrew and Aramaic Lexicon of the Old Testament*, trans. and ed. M. E. J. Richardson (Leiden: E. J. Brill, 1944), does not list Gen. 9:6 under either meaning. The rare attestation for a possible agentive meaning of *bêt*, if it exists at all, makes it seem unlikely that it has this meaning in Gen. 9:6. This is also how the ancient translations understood this construction. See the LXX rendering, ἐκχέων αἷμα ἀνθρώπου <u>ἀντὶ</u> τοῦ αἵματος αὐτοῦ ἐκχυθήσεται (*ekcheōn haima anthrōpou <u>anti</u> tou haimatos autou ekchuthēsetai*).

[17] "Philologische und linguistische Probleme bei den hebräischen Präpositionen," in *Studien zur Sprachwelt des Alten Testaments* (Stuttgart: W. Kohlhammer, 1997), 179.

[18] Ibid. He also points out that one must take into account the strength of the possibilities. *Bêt* is used instrumentally with "sword" 3,000 times in the Hebrew Bible. It is used in the sense "for, in exchange for, at the price of" 300 times. Its possible agentive uses can be counted on the fingers of one hand (ibid., 180). A further important consideration is that, as

Joüon-Muraoka seeks to explain the anomalous use of *bêt* in our clause by arguing that sometimes, although rarely, the preposition *min* is used to indicate the immediate cause of the action, while the true agent of the action is not mentioned, as in Gen. 9:11:

וְלֹא־יִכָּרֵת כָּל־בָּשָׂר עוֹד מִמֵּי הַמַּבּוּל

(wĕlō'-yikkārēt kŏl-bāśār 'ôd mimmêy hammabbûl)
All flesh shall not be cut off by the waters of the flood.

In this verse the waters of the flood are the instrument, while God, who is unmentioned, is the actual agent, the one who sent the flood. In a like manner, Joüon-Muraoka argues, in Gen. 9:6 the human is immediate cause, serving as the instrument of God. It is through the human agent/instrument that God requites the blood of the murderer.

The immediate and obvious objection to this suggestion is that in Gen. 9:6 a *bêt* is used and not a *min* as in Gen. 9:11. Second, the flood was not an agent but an instrument of the action, cutting off all flesh: God (the agent) cut off all flesh by means of the flood (the instrument). Finally, as Jenni indicates, Hebrew does not use *bêt* to express the sense of "through" or "by means of" a human in order to express a human instrument of an action.[19]

By way of summary, we can say that the traditional interpretation and translation of this passage is not the most likely or the natural one.[20] Indeed, it is not likely, because following the normal usage of Hebrew, the most natural understanding is to construe this *bêt* as a *bêt pretii* and to translate the first part of the verse as: "If one sheds human blood, for that human his blood will be shed."

On this understanding, the text also fits with the verses that precede it.[21]

---

discussed above, verse 6 shows close stylistic affinities with apodictic laws such as the *talion* law.

[19] Ibid., 182–3. Jenni argues that usually the expression "by the hand of" is used. Normally this phrase is used with transitive verbs as in Exod. 9:35: "Just as the LORD said through Moses (כַּאֲשֶׁר דִּבֶּר יְהוָה בְּיַד־מֹשֶׁה | *ka'ăšer dibber Yhwh bĕyad-mōšeh*).

[20] P. J. Harland, *The Value of Human Life: A Study of the Story of the Flood* (Genesis 6–9) Supplements to Vetus Testamentum, vol. 64, (Leiden: E. J. Brill, 1996), 161, has suggested that the traditional translation is correct. He cites none of the recent literature, footnoting only *Gesenius' Hebrew Grammar* and Brown, Driver, and Briggs, *A Hebrew and English Lexicon of the Old Testament*.

[21] This non-instrumental use is also the understanding of early translations. Johan Lust, "'For Man Shall His Blood Be Shed': Gen 9:6 in Hebrew and in Greek," in *Tradition of the Text: Studies Offered to Dominique Barthélemy in Celebration of His 70th Birthday*, ed. Gerard J. Norton (Fribourg, Switzerland: Universitätsverlag, 1991), 91–101.

The motive for this rule follows in the second half of the verse, verse 6b:

כִּי בְּצֶלֶם אֱלֹהִים עָשָׂה אֶת־הָאָדָם׃

(kî běṣelem ʾělōhîm ʿāśâ ʾet-hāʾādām)
Because as the image of God he created humankind.

While the meaning of "image of God" has been much debated, there is a growing consensus that the *bêt* preceding "image" is a *bêt* of identification. Humankind is created "as" the image of God rather than "according to" or "in" the image of God.[22] Humankind functions as the representation of God on earth, as the earthly surrogate for the transcendent creator. For the purposes of this essay, whether we understand humankind to be made as God's image or in God's image, human life has a value above all other life. It is for this reason that God will requite the death of a human whether by an animal or by another human.

Ishamel !

COVENANT

The next paragraph, Gen. 9:8–17, can be subdivided into three parts, each introduced by the words "and God said." The first speech comprises verses 8–11; the second speech, verses 12–16; and the third, a single verse, verse 17. What ties these three speeches together is the mention of "covenant,"[23] which occurs here for the first time in the Hebrew Bible.

This initial covenant that God made with humankind has two important characteristics. The first is that it is cosmic in scope. It is made not only with humankind but with the whole of nature. The second is that it is entirely promissory on the part of God. In canonical context, God's understanding of humankind is that humankind has evil inclinations from youth (8:21). Yet God promises not to destroy the earth again because of human evil. Consequently, God makes a covenant that demands nothing on the part of humans or of other living things.[24] It is a covenant founded on God's grace.

---

[22] For a discussion of the interpretation of this verse, see P. J. Harland, "The Image of God," chap. 7 in *The Value of Human Life*, 177–209. Ernst Jenni, *Studien zur Sprachwelt des Alten Testaments*, 183–8, proposes this understanding for the preposition. The primary meaning of "image" in Hebrew Bible is a plastic form, as in Ezek. 16:17; 1 Sam. 6:5, 11. It is also used for the likeness of a son to his father (Gen. 5:3). For a history of the interpretation of "image," see Gunnlaugur A. Jónsson, *The Image of God: Genesis 1:26–28 in a Century of Old Testament Research* (Stockholm: Almqvist & Wiksell, 1988).

[23] בְּרִית *(běrît)*

[24] The stipulations in Gen. 9:1–7 come before the covenant, and the covenant is not conditioned by their observance. The case is different with the rite of circumcision, which is

The language of this paragraph is repetitive, emphasizing the making of the covenant and its key promise, as in verse 11:

וַהֲקִמֹתִי אֶת־בְּרִיתִי אִתְּכֶם
וְלֹא־יִכָּרֵת כָּל־בָּשָׂר עוֹד מִמֵּי הַמַּבּוּל
וְלֹא־יִהְיֶה עוֹד מַבּוּל לְשַׁחֵת הָאָרֶץ׃

(wahăqimōtî 'et-bĕrîtî 'ittĕkem
wĕlō'-yikkārēt kŏl-bāśār 'ôd mimmê hammabbûl
wĕlō'-yihĕyeh 'ôd mabbûl lĕšaḥēt hā'āreṣ)

I will set up my covenant with you;
All flesh will not again be cut off by the waters of the flood;
There will not again be a flood to destroy the earth.

In this poetic formulation the theme of the divine speech reaches its climax.

The second speech introduces the sign of the covenant, the bow, which God places in the clouds. Some have seen in this bow the war bow, which now serves as a sign of peace between God and the world.[25] God has laid the bow aside as a sign that hostilities have ceased and that the world will not again be subjected to total destruction by the flood.

However, we might see here an allusion to the post-flood scene in the Gilgamesh epic. When Utnapishtim comes forth from the ark, he too offers sacrifices. The gods likewise crowd around the altar of sacrifice and repent that they brought about the flood which nearly wiped out humankind. Instead it is declared:

On the sinner impose his sin
On the transgressor impose his transgression!
(Yet) be lenient, lest he be cut off,
Be patient lest he be dis[lodged]![26]

Following these considerations it is stated that lesser forces such as famine, wild animals, or disease should be used to diminish or punish humankind.

---

a sign of the covenant made with Abraham in Genesis 17. Recent scholarship has tended to blur the distinction between promissory and obligatory covenants. Perhaps there is merit in the conflation of these two categories, but it is hard to find a stipulatory element in God's covenant with Noah. What is stipulated of the animals or the earth, for example?

[25] For a discussion of this option as well as a survey of bow technology and the type of war bow that the rainbow would represent, see Udo Ruterswörden, "Der Bogen in Genesis 9: Militärhistorische und traditionsgeschichtliche Erwägungen zu einem biblischen Symbol," in *Ugarit-Forschungen*, vol. 20 (Kevelaer, Germany: Verlag Butzon & Bercker, 1988), 247–63. Others have argued that the war bow is not intended. Since the word "bow" is accompanied by "cloud," it can only mean the rainbow. See the comments of Westermann, *Genesis 1–11*, 473.

[26] *ANET*, 95.

As a preface to these remarks, when the great goddess Ishtar arrives at the sacrifice, she

Lifted up the great jewels which Anu had fashioned to her liking:
"Ye gods here, as surely as this lapis
Upon my neck I shall not forget,
I shall be mindful of these days, forgetting (them) never."[27]

It may be that in the rainbow we have the biblical reflex of the necklace of Ishtar, which likewise was to be a reminder of the flood and that the gods should not again bring such devastation upon the earth.

The last speech, verse 17, gives a closing statement of God's covenant making activity.

"This is the covenant which I have established between me and all flesh which is upon the earth."

This final summary statement emphasizes the universal scope of this covenant: it is between God and all living beings upon the earth. God's concern extends beyond humankind to the future existence of all life. God will not again destroy creation with floodwaters because of human sin.

WHAT DOES ALL THIS HAVE TO DO WITH PEACE AND MISSION?

Let's begin with the value of human life emphasized in the first section. It was not to be shed by either human or beast. Moshe Greenberg has argued that the notion that all humans are created in or as the image of God has had a profound effect on biblical thought and on post-biblical developments.[28] One area where this impact can readily be seen is in the legal material. Life cannot be exchanged for property—life is to be given for life—and material loss cannot demand human life in punishment. In this regard the law of the goring ox, Exod. 21:28–32, which has close cuneiform counterparts, has been illuminated by J. J. Finkelstein as exemplifying biblical law's valuation of human life.[29]

---

[27] *ANET, 95a.*

[28] For a popular treatment of the theme, see "The Biblical Grounding of Human Value," in *The Samuel Friedland Lectures 1960–1966* (New York: Jewish Theological Seminary of America, 1966), 39–52. An earlier article on the same theme is "Some Postulates of Biblical Criminal Law," in *Yehezkel Kaufmann Jubilee Volume: Studies in Bible and Jewish Religion,* ed. Menahem Haran (Jerusalem: Magnes Pr., 1960), 5–28; reprinted, with an additional note, in Moshe Greenberg, *Studies in the Bible and Jewish Thought* (Philadelphia: Jewish Pubn. Society, 1995), 25–41. For a reprise of his position, see "More Reflections on Biblical Criminal Law," in *Studies in Bible, 1986,* ed. Sara Japhet, Scripta Hierosolymitana 31 (Jerusalem: Magnes Press, 1986), 1–17.

[29] J. J. Finkelstein, *The Ox That Gored,* prepared for publication by Maria deJ. Ellis, Transactions of the American Philosophical Society, vol. 71, part 2, (Philadelphia: The

In the end, the value of human life made as God's image on earth became so profound that we find in the Mishnah, in a passage in which instructions are being given to witnesses in a capital case, the following comments:[30]

> It does not say, "the voice of the blood of your brother" but "the bloods of your brother," meaning his blood and the blood of his descendants. . . . Therefore a single man was created in the world in order to teach that anyone who destroys a single life, it is as if he had destroyed the whole world. But everyone who saves a single life, it is as if he had saved the whole world. . . . A man stamps a hundred coins from a single stamp and all of them are exactly alike. The king of kings, the Holy One, blessed be He, stamps every person with the stamp of the first human, and not one of them is exactly alike. Thus each person may say, "for me the world was created."[31]

It is hard to imagine a more emphatic statement of the ultimate value of a single individual. Each individual, as it were, could be a progenitor of the whole human race. Even more important, however, is the fact that to take a human life is to diminish the image of God on earth. This point of view by implication mandates the preservation and enhancement of the life of each individual. In caring for each life, for even the least, we are doing it for God.

Such a mandate would seem to blur the distinction between peacemaking and mission. To go with integrity as a messenger of the God in whose image each person is made is to go as one whose mission is to sustain and enrich the life of others. This sustenance may be physical, it may be emotional or political, or it may be the sustenance of faith in Jesus Christ. But above all, the messenger is focused on the audience, which as God's surrogate presence on earth is approached with the humility and reverence it deserves.

Even when the message and the messenger are rejected, the audience is no less in the image of God and is not of lesser worth. The value of others is independent of whether they accept the message. It is inherent within them. As such, our service to God is in no way diminished when we serve those of other faiths or of no faith.

American Philosophical Society, 1981). In this classic study, Finkelstein examines not only the difference in provision and wording between the biblical laws and cuneiform laws, but also the placement of this law in both the Covenant Code and in the cuneiform law collections. In the Bible the law stands in a section that regulates capital crimes. In the Ancient Near Eastern collections it is found in sections treating property loss.

[30] These comments in the Mishnah are triggered by the "bloods" (plural) of Abel which cried out. Why is the plural used here and not the singular "blood" of Abel?"

[31] *m.Sanhedrin* 4.5, following Rambam's text (*The Mishna, with the Commentary by Rabbi Moshe Ben Maimonides* [Jerusalem: Mossad Harav Kook, 1967]). Greenberg cites this text in "The Biblical Grounding of Human Value," 48, 51.

The Anabaptist-Mennonite tradition has taught the love of enemies, even to the point of one's death. Perhaps the most powerful image in Mennonite collective memory is the figure of a fugitive escaping over the ice who turns back to rescue his drowning pursuer. Likewise, the image of the missionary ingrained in our psyches is of one who continues to serve others even when rejected. Surely the value of others' lives is not diminished by their adherence to another faith; their lives are no less important than an enemy's life. God's emissaries love those they serve.

The second major section, Gen. 9:8–17, also carries several significant considerations for mission and peacemaking. As suggested above, the flood represented a return to disorder, an undoing of the divine order. In day two of creation, the waters above were separated from the water below. On day three, the waters below were separated from the dry ground, which now began to bring forth plant life. The flood erased these distinctions on which life depends. The waters above joined the waters below, and together they covered the dry ground. Life could no longer be sustained.

The covenant that God gives promises that human, animal, and plant life will not again be threatened by the floodwaters. However, while the earth may be safe from the waters of the flood, humankind seems to be working to destroy the world and the life forms with which God has covenanted. Deforestation, erosion, pollution of air and water with chemicals harmful to life, contamination of food with chemicals and disease organisms, destruction of fisheries, and rapid extinction of plant and animal species are all counter to caring for a world with which God has made a covenant and with which humankind is a partner.

Because God has covenanted with the whole world, not only with the human world, our message should also concern the whole world and not only the human world. A healthy ecosystem is a human issue. Without a sustaining environment, human life will be diminished both in quality and quantity. Caring for the fate of the earth as well as for the fate of its people is an issue for Christian mission. Ecological rapacity is also a justice and peace issue because it is the richest who gain and the poorest who suffer.

The figure of Noah, by virtue of the covenant with him, has played a significant role in the development of mission ethics in the New Testament. As has been recognized, the issue facing the early mission conference described in Acts 15 was the status of Gentile Christians. Need they become Jews to be saved, or could they be saved as Gentiles? To put the question in historical context, should Gentile Christians be

treated as proselytes—converts to Judaism, or as Noachides—as righteous Gentiles?[32]

In Second Temple times, a tradition developed regarding the moral
duties of Gentiles. Sirach 17, for example, states that God allotted them
knowledge, established an eternal covenant with them, and gave them
God's judgments. Sirach goes on to write:

> Their eyes saw his glorious majesty,
>   and their ears heard the glory of his voice.
> And he said to them, "Beware of all unrighteousness."
> And he gave commandment to each of them concerning his neighbor.
>   (Sir. 17:13, 14 RSV)

What were the commandments for which the Gentiles were responsible
under the Noachide covenant? There are various permutations in the
tradition, but three commandments were fundamental: Gentiles were
not to worship idols, they were not to eat blood,[33] and they were not to
commit adultery. It is this threefold duty of the Gentiles that the
Jerusalem mission council ratified. In short, Gentile Christians were to
behave as good Gentiles. They need not become proselytes.

Beyond these three commands, what else is required of Gentile
Christians? The answer to this question is not entirely clear in the New
Testament. Paul does not base his ethical pronouncements on the
teachings of Jesus, at least not explicitly, nor does he invoke the doctrine
of justification by faith as the basis for morality, or even the Ten
Commandments (with a rare exception or two). Beyond pointing to the
commandment to love one's neighbor as oneself (perhaps also alluded to
in the Sirach text quoted above), Paul's instructions to Gentile converts
stress avoiding idolatry and sexual immortality. This teaching, of course,
is in line with the pronouncement of the Jerusalem Council.

What is required of Gentile Christians today? In finding our way in
our own mission work, we might do well to begin where Paul and the
early church began: with the basic commandment to love one's neighbor
as oneself and to refrain from idolatry, from the eating of blood as a
symbol of the sacredness of life, and from committing adultery. This
approach may also be a good starting point for peacemaking. Perhaps, it
would also be an appropriate beginning place for all Christians.

---

[32] See the recent discussions of this conference by Markus Bockmuehl, "The Noachide
Commandments and New Testament Ethics: With Special Reference to Acts 15 and Pauline
Halakhah," *Revue biblique* 102 (1995): 72–101; and Terrance Callan, "The Background of the
Apostolic Decrees (Acts 15:20, 29; 21:25)," *Catholic Biblical Quartlerly* 55 (1993): 284–97.

[33] Jewish tradition has understood the prohibition against eating the blood as a command
that protects the value of life, all life. As such, we might paraphrase this command as
"Respect the life of all living creatures."

2 | *God's reign and the missional impulse of the Psalms*

GORDON H. MATTIES

E VERY DAY FOR THE TWO MONTHS OF THE WAR IN THE
Balkans my family prayed at the supper table that the war would
come to an end. We were convinced that our prayers were
grounded in the psalmist's vision of God bringing war to an end: "He
makes wars cease to the end of the earth; he breaks the bow, and shatters
the spear; he burns the shields with fire" (Ps. 46:9 NRSV). Yet every
morning we heard the news of continued bombing. The war continued
in the name of justice. And the pride of nations ran on unabated. As
citizens of the earth we cry out with another psalmist to the sovereign
over all empires, "I am for peace; but when I speak, they are for war"
(Ps. 120:7).

The psalmists of ancient Israel celebrate the majesty and wonder of
a God whose dynamic reign is incomparable, yet they cry out in
unspeakable anguish to the God who apparently refuses to act in the face
of excruciating pain and oppression. These poems mirror the depths of
the human soul, articulate an affirmation of divine sovereignty, and offer
a model for what it means to be truly human within the sphere of that
sovereignty. In articulating the image of a God who reigns, the psalms
participate in "the most comprehensive horizon of hope within the
biblical writings for the history of the world."[1] James L. Mays offers this
summary of the reign of God as a root metaphor in Christian theology:
"The liveliness and actuality of the language of the reign of God supply
an organizing milieu for all the principal topics of the Christian faith. It
constitutes the basis and medium of the three primary functions of our
religion—praise, prayer, and the practice of piety.... It provides a
polemic against the polytheism and paganism that go unnoticed in our
culture. It establishes a critical resistance to the domination of any

---

[1] Jürgen Moltmann, "Theology for Christ's Church and the Kingdom of God in Modern
Society," in *A Passion for God's Reign: Theology, Christian Learning, and the Christian Self,* ed.
Miroslav Volf (Grand Rapids: Eerdmans, 1998), 51.

human politics and the apotheosizing of any ideology, including democracy."[2]

More than supplying resources for our own "praise, prayer, and the practice of piety," the psalms also offer resources for shaping the identity and mission of the people of God. The community discovers, in worship, who it is and what its vocation ought to be in the world. Thus, as Mays suggests, "The praise of psalms as confession is the liturgy for mission."[3] Or, as Walter Brueggemann puts it, when announcements about the reign of God are made in worship, Israel is engaging in "the work of evangelism."[4] This "work" or "vocation," writes Brueggemann, "is to be 'world-makers,' makers of an alternative, evangelical world, a world of news (basar), a world in which the sovereign of truth, equity, and righteousness has just come to power (cf. Psalm 96)."[5]

In this exercise in biblical-theological reflection, I explore how the theme of peace intersects with the motif of the reign of God in the psalms, and how that intersection offers fruitful resources for reflection on the mission of God's people in the world.[6] In other words, I shall seek

---

[2] James Luther Mays, *The Lord Reigns: A Theological Handbook to the Psalms* (Louisville: Westminster John Knox Pr., 1994), 11. Of the 43 times "king" is used of God in the Old Testament, 21 occur in the Psalms. See Tryggve N. D. Mettinger, *In Search of God: The Meaning and Message of the Everlasting Names* (Philadelphia: Fortress Pr., 1988), 116. Among those who suggest divine kingship as the central motif of OT theology, see Mettinger, *In Search of God*, 92; Mays, *The Lord Reigns*; Paul R. House, "The God Who Rules (Psalms)," in *Old Testament Theology* (Downers Grove: InterVarsity Pr., 1998). That metaphor finds expression primarily in the phrase "Yahweh reigns" (יהוה מָלָךְ | *Yhwh mālāk*: Ps. 93:1; 96:10; 97:1; 99:1). On kingship as metaphor, see Marc Zvi Brettler, *God Is King: Understanding an Israelite Metaphor*, JSOT Supplement Series 76 (Sheffield, England: JSOT Pr., 1989).

[3] Mays, *The Lord Reigns*, 68. See also George Peters, *A Biblical Theology of Missions* (Chicago: Moody Pr., 1972), who states: "It is a profound fact that 'the hymn of praise is missionary preaching par excellence,' especially when we realize that such missionary preaching is supported in the Psalms by more than 175 references of a universalistic note relating to the nations of the world. Many of them bring hope of salvation to the nations. . . . Indeed, the Psalter is one of the greatest missionary books in the world" (115–16).

[4] Walter Brueggemann, *Israel's Praise: Doxology against Idolatry and Ideology* (Minneapolis: Fortress Pr., 1988), 38.

[5] Ibid., 124.

[6] Walter Kaiser treats the psalms in chapter 2 of *Mission in the Old Testament*, "God's Purpose for Missions in the Old Testament." He presents an exposition of Psalms 67, 96, and 117. His conclusion suggests that mission is proclamation: "Over and over again the psalmists called on all peoples of all the lands and nations to praise the Lord (Ps. 47:1; 67:3, 5; 100:1; 117:1). Even more directly, these ancient singers of Israel urged their people to tell, proclaim, and make known the mighty deeds of Yahweh (Ps. 9:11; 105:1) and to join in singing praises to God from all the nations (Ps. 18:49; 96:2–3). The psalmists themselves offer to sing God's praises among the nations (Ps. 57:9; 108:3). The expected result would be that all the ends of the earth would turn to the Lord and all the families on earth would

to draw out the missional impetus of the psalms through an integrated theological reading that assumes that worship is the setting in which the psalms sustain and nurture the life of the reading community.[7] The worshiping community hears words and images that shape its identity, direct its imagination, and articulate its vocation. In worship the psalms instruct in the paradigmatic or root metaphors that shape, or lead into, a longed for reality of peace with justice for all. And in worship the community that prays these poems lays bare the full range of its experience in the presence of God and is recreated as the gathered community that bears witness to and anticipates the transforming, sustaining, and always elusive presence of God.[8]

---

bow down in worship to him (Ps. 22:27; 66:4; 86:9)" (Walter C. Kaiser, *Mission in the Old Testament: Israel As a Light to the Nations* [Grand Rapids: Baker Bks., 2000], 37). This essay expands that perspective by arguing that the missional impulse of the psalms links proclamation to speaking an alternative reality into being in worship, anticipating it in praise, and shaping it in the life of the community in the world. Kaiser notes an odd juxtaposition in Ps.67:7, in which the psalmist affirms God's material blessing on Israel, and (but?) a "spiritual increase" on the nations of the earth (ibid., 33). Neither the parallelism nor the motif of cosmic sovereignty in the psalms can support such a dualism.

[7] W. Creighton Marlowe, "Music of Missions: Themes of Cross-Cultural Outreach in the Psalms," *Missiology: An International Review* 26 (1998): 445–56, also explores the theme of mission in the psalms: "As poetry, these passages . . . contain motivational and emotional expressions that reveal how God feels and, consequently, how God's people should feel about missions" (445–6, Marlowe's italics). The heart of the article presents the usage of "terms denoting outreach" in the psalms (particularly Ps. 9:11; 18:49; 33:8; 46:10; 49:1; 57:9; 66:1–4; 67:1–7; 72:8, 11, 17; 83:18; 96:1–6; 105:1–2; 106:8; 108:3; 117:1; 119:46; 145:6, 12, 21). Key words are "proclaim, bring good news" (בשׂר | *bśr*), "declare" (ספר | *spr*) and "tell, make known" (נגד | *ngd*) (447–50). Commenting on Ps. 9:11, Marlowe asks, "How can the nations . . . be reached with this report via Israelite worship?" He takes the parallelism of the verse as sequential: "Praise should precede preaching" (449). I suggest in this article, however, that praise is preaching. Commenting on Psalm 117 Marlowe says as much: "In fact, the Psalm itself is oratorical outreach; it calls and commands the international audience of Israel's day to respond to its obligation as part of created humanity to serve the true and living Creator Yahweh" (ibid., 451). But he does not extend the argument to the larger context of worship as the arena of mission.

[8] It may be important to note that this essay does not draw historical conclusions about Israel's practice of mission from the psalms. What follows is an attempt to reflect on how the psalms offer theological resources to nurture and shape a missional community. As such, rather than attempting to uncover Israel's historical practice, the essay lives in, and in front of, the text to explore what kind of life the psalms evoke. As James Sanders notes, "To theologize in reading a text is to focus on what God can do with the likes of the reader mirrored in the text" (James A. Sanders, *Canon and Community: A Guide to Canonical Criticism* [Philadelphia: Fortress Pr., 1984], 52).

This essay explores the missional impulse of the psalms, which comes to expression first in the metaphor of Yahweh as one who reigns.[9] This missional impulse is formed through acts of allegiance and anticipation. As expressions of worship, the psalms shape our commitments and direct our longings. Second, the missional impulse of the psalms suggests a mission of declaration, announcing and inviting the cosmos and its inhabitants to acknowledge Yahweh's divine kingship. Third, the missional impulse of the psalms entails an embodiment, such that the worshiping, anticipating community shapes its life by the instruction inherent in what is anticipated—the reign of God—and thereby becomes the pilot project of God on earth.

The essay will proceed under three main headings, which correspond to the three missional impulses noted in the previous paragraph: (1) Yahweh's reign and Yahweh's mission as context for missional identity and vocation; (2) Imaging God: Human mission as stewardship; and (3) Embodiment as mission. The essay concludes with a brief reflection on the value of affirming the divine reign in worship, an affirmation that fosters the mission of shalom.

YAHWEH'S REIGN, YAHWEH'S MISSION

The missional identity of the worshiping community is rooted in the theological vision of the Book of Psalms as a whole, that which "transcends the parts to make it more than mere collection."[10] Mays proposes that when the psalms are read as a book, one discovers a convergence of literary and theological features that offers a paradigm for faithfulness.[11] The psalms reflect, through prayer and praise, on the purposes of God which are drawn into focus by the root metaphor of the reign of God, and its associated themes and motifs. "The LORD appears as one who reigns. His reign in the [psalms] is presented by a place and a person. The place is Zion. The person is his chosen king. Zion as city of God and king as the LORD's anointed will themselves be the subject of many particular psalms. What happens to and through them involves the reign of the LORD. And it is this theme of the reign of God that is the

---

[9] For a summary exposition of this "root metaphor," see Mays, *The Lord Reigns*, chapters 1 and 2.

[10] Mays, *The Lord Reigns*, 120.

[11] Most of those observations have been made by others, notably Brevard Childs, Gerald Wilson, and David M. Howard. See J. Clinton McCann Jr., ed., *The Shape and Shaping of the Psalter*, JSOT Supplement Series 159 (Sheffield, England: JSOT Pr., 1993), and David C. Mitchell's summary of recent scholarship, in *The Message of the Psalter: An Eschatological Programme in the Book of Psalms*, JSOT Supplement Series 252 (Sheffield: Sheffield Academic Pr., Ltd., 1997), 56–64.

integrating center of the theology of the entire book. All else is in one way or another connected to and dependent on this divine sovereignty."[12]

Mays's proposal does not claim that divine sovereignty is the only theological rubric in the psalms. He affirms, however, that it is "an organizing center" within a dynamic interplay of other themes and topics.[13] In the orbit of this center, and using a variety of poetic forms, the psalms grapple with the historical and cosmic powers that align themselves against the purposes of that reign. From the beginning of the psalms we see Yahweh's reign as a conflicted and disputed reign that finds partial expression in the figure of Israel's human kings (Psalm 2).[14] Because the Book of Psalms is concerned fundamentally with the outworking of that divine sovereignty, the shape of Israel's worship, as reflected in the psalms, concerns itself not so much with the form of liturgy as with the way those kings, and Israel as a whole, orient themselves within the spheres of Yahweh's sovereignty. The reign of Yahweh calls forth the creation of a people who are oriented around Yahweh's instruction (Torah), and who live toward a world of peace that is sustained by divine justice (89:14). Worship, therefore, is the arena of missional activity. It is both the beginning and the endpoint of mission. Worship offers both an orientation, a perspective from which to live toward a vision of wholeness represented by the shalom of God's reign, and an invitation to the cosmos and all people to acknowledge the sovereignty of Yahweh.

That act of orienting, of getting one's bearings within the uncertainties of life, is an imaginative act that speaks against the chaos of the present; draws on the memory of pain, healing, and liberation from the past; and envisions a hopeful alternative in the future. Above all, Yahweh's reign characteristically shapes a new world in the living hope of the worshiping community. Psalm 146 concludes, for example, with an assertive "The LORD will reign forever." This assertion is not "a private activity"; rather, it is a public declaration of good news.[15] This affirmation is a "destabilizing assertion," as Walter Brueggemann puts it.

---

[12] Mays, *The Lord Reigns*, 122.

[13] Ibid., 13. At the end of the chapter Mays summarizes: "The declaration *Yhwh malak* involves a vision of reality that is the theological center of the Psalter . . . . The organizing role of the declaration does not ignore or obviate the variety and plurality of thought about God in the psalms. It does announce a metaphor that transcends and lies behind the variety. It is what every reader and user of the psalms may know as the code for understanding all of them" (ibid., 22).

[14] Ibid., 9.

[15] Ibid., 69.

It is a "dangerous whisper of an alternative governance that powers Israel's faith."[16]

That dangerous assertion, however, includes a measure of disorienting juxtapositions. On the one hand, the reign of this God is characterized by justice and mercy. On the other hand, the reign of Yahweh is contested by unruly powers, both cosmic (Psalm 29) and historical (Psalm 2), that threaten the stability of the universe and the peaceful intentions of God's rule.

The gods, the nations, and the scope of Yahweh's sovereignty

The conflictual dimension of Yahweh's reign is best set into the context of Israel's "monotheizing" faith,[17] in which, Israel asserts, Yahweh is the supreme sovereign in the universe. The "crucial agenda" for the worshiping community, according to Mays, is to be engaged in "monotheizing, liberating the good realities of life and world from the perversion of divinization."[18] Israel at worship declares that the scope of Yahweh's dominion ranges from the cosmic through the historical, social, and personal spheres of existence.[19]

Missional activity rightly emphasizes the personal sphere of the Lord's sovereignty. The complaint in Ps. 5:2 expresses the personal dimension of Yahweh's sovereignty: "Listen to the sound of my cry, my King and my God." The personal, relational dimensions of Yahweh's protecting and nurturing presence allow the poet to bring all of life's pain into that relationship. Similarly, the royal metaphor embedded in the confession "the LORD is my shepherd" (23:1) assumes that the worshiper is the servant of this king. In both psalms, Yahweh's sovereignty in the personal sphere is the impetus that allows the poet to reflect on the reality of conflict and tension in human experience (see "A world gone awry," below).

The other end of the personal/relational continuum of Yahweh's reign finds expression in the invitation to all peoples and nations to worship by recognizing Yahweh's sovereignty. Psalm 22 declares confidently that "all the families of the nations shall worship before him. For dominion belongs to the LORD, and he rules over the nations"

---

[16] Brueggemann, *Israel's Praise*, 58.

[17] Sanders, *Canon and Community*, 51–2; Mays, *The Lord Reigns*, 68.

[18] Ibid.

[19] Ibid., 8.

(vv. 27b–28). The poet goes on to express a firm hope that even those who have died, as well as those unborn, shall "bow down" (vv. 29–31).[20]

Such sovereignty in the sociopolitical realm is evident in many psalms in which the nations are invited to know and to serve Yahweh (e.g. 67; 96:7; 117). That invitation is warranted by the graciousness of God to those who have experienced that relationship: "For great is his steadfast love toward us" (117:2). Psalm 67:1–2 asks God to "be gracious to us" with the result "that your way may be known upon earth, your saving power among all nations." Yahweh's gracious presence, his shining face (67:1), is to become visible as the community that trusts Yahweh and experiences his care stands as a sign to the peoples of the world. But it is not only because Yahweh is gracious to Israel that the nations are to acknowledge Yahweh. The "saving power" of God is to be known "among all nations" (67:2). The nations are invited to sing not simply because God is good to Israel, but because "you judge the peoples with equity and guide the nations upon earth" (67:4. See also 33:8, 13–15; 24:1; 47:8; 48:10; 66:7; 87; 99:2–3). Psalm 86:9 suggests that "All the nations you have made shall come and bow down before you, O LORD." Perhaps this homage is inevitable because there are no gods like Yahweh and because none can do what Yahweh does (86:8). As creator of the nations (86:9a), Yahweh has a special concern for watching what goes on in the human realm. The peoples of the earth are both audience among whom God's glory and works are proclaimed (57:9; 96:3; 108:3), and also the congregation who, along with all of creation, become the celebrants (96:7–12) as they all pick up the "new song" throughout "all the earth" because "he is coming to judge the world with righteousness, and the peoples with his truth" (96:13; so also 98:9).[21]

This universal expectation makes it possible to interpret the concern for the nations as an eschatological hope, but it cannot be limited to that. One could as readily understand God's particular graciousness to Israel as a singular expression of the larger divine concern for the nations. Johannes Blauw, for example, asserts (commenting on Gen. 12:3) that "here it becomes clear *that the whole history of Israel is nothing but the continuation of God's dealings with the nations, and that therefore the history of*

---

[20] On Psalm 22 see also William Richey Hogg, "Psalm 22 and Christian Mission: A Reflection," *International Review of Mission* 77 (1988): 238–46.

[21] Although Titus Guenther does not draw on the psalms to make his point, as I have done here, I concur with his statement: "The praises of God that should be given by all creatures and all the nations can be heard in Israel. Israel is doing what all the nations should be doing: adoring the Creator of the whole world" (Titus F. Guenther, "Missionary Vision and Practice in the Old Testament," in *Reclaiming the Old Testament: Essays in Honour of Waldemar Janzen*, ed. Gordon Zerbe [Winnipeg: CMBC Pubns., 2001], 154).

Israel is only to be understood from the unsolved problem of the relation of God to the nations."[22] In the psalms, Blauw suggests, "The nations are *witnesses* of Yahweh's deeds in Israel. This is their most prominent function. In God's dealings with Israel, however, they, too, are summoned to recognize the God of Israel as the God of the whole earth."[23] "The active presence of God in Israel is a sign and guarantee of His presence in the world: and the presence of Israel is thus a continuing appeal to the nations of the world."[24] Blauw is surely correct when he emphasizes that "neither the activity of Israel nor that of the nations stands in the foreground of eschatology, but exclusively the activity of Yahweh. His acts happen *to* Israel, in the sight of the nations, and therefore *to* the nations too."[25] Blauw proposes that the universal scope of Yahweh's concern leads to a centripetal sense of mission. The nations come to God *"as a response to God's acts in Israel."*[26] But if the nations are God's ultimate concern, and if the nations are the arena of Yahweh's sovereignty, then Israel understands its identity not so much as passive recipients of Yahweh's gracious sign-acts in the cosmos, but as a community of actors who embody what God has in mind for all. The notion of mission as centripetal is flawed, therefore, by the way it limits how we imagine the psalms participating in the construction of Israel's identity as missional community (see the second and third main sections below).

I have noted that the realm of personal experience and the realm of history (the nations or peoples of the earth) stand within the sphere of Yahweh's sovereignty. Because Yahweh is creator, however, the earth also belongs to him (Ps. 24:1). The psalms sometimes describe this sovereignty as a ruling over the waters. In Psalm 93, Yahweh's kingship is related to the security of the earth. Even the cosmic waters that threaten to undo creation's order are unable to foil the power of Yahweh's creative decrees (93:3–5). The sea and the floods in Ps. 98:7–8 are not threatening entities, but are part of a chorus of praise. Psalm 96 affirms Yahweh's rule, notes the resultant stability of the earth, and invites all of creation to praise God (vv. 11–13) just as the peoples are invited to praise (vv. 7–9). Those are all images of Yahweh's sovereignty in the cosmos where his reign fosters shalom.

---

[22] Johannes Blauw, *The Missionary Nature of the Church: A Survey of the Biblical Theology of Mission* (London: Lutterworth Pr., 1962), 19 (Blauw's italics).

[23] Ibid., 26 (Blauw's italics).

[24] Ibid., 28.

[25] Ibid., 38 (Blauw's italics).

[26] Ibid., 40 (Blauw's italics).

Preserving the moral order, or fostering shalom in the cosmos, however, involves Yahweh in a struggle with all that rises up against the divine project. In this respect the kingship of Yahweh is an embattled kingship. The root metaphor of Yahweh's reign implies that "God asserts sovereignty through battle with the forces of chaos, which continually threaten his creation. This divine activity stretches from creation, across the pages of history, and ahead to the eschatological completion."[27] God's kingship is "asserted and established through battle with evil."[28] Texts such as Ps. 74:12–17 and Ps. 89:9–11 affirm "God's ownership of the created world" (cf. 24:1–2; 95:5).[29] And that ownership is demonstrated in Yahweh's competence to quell the powers arrayed against shalom. To highlight the wonder of it all, the poet in Ps. 104:26 notes that Leviathan is a mere plaything rather than a force to be feared. The ownership motif in Ps. 24:1 is predicated on the taming of the seas and rivers in 24:2 (cf. the exodus motif in 77:16–19). The stability of Zion in Ps. 46:5 depends on the assurance that even a rebellious cosmos cannot thwart the divine project. In fact the goal of that project is the eradication of war and the destruction of weapons (46:8–10; 76:3).[30] That action is contingent on Yahweh reigning (in Psalm 46, as the LORD of hosts). When God is described as king, "the subject is God in confrontation with the chaotic power of the ultimate evil. And this confrontation is not once and for all; rather, it stretches from the creation to the completion of all things. The warring King is the world's Creator and Judge."[31]

We discover, therefore, that divine sovereignty implies both dynamic engagement to create shalom and struggle against the guerrilla tactics of all that is lined up against God's project. Although the monarchical understanding of God is rooted in a hierarchical world view, the metaphor depicts a God who, as liberator, is concerned for the weak and the marginal (see, e.g., 76:9; 146:5–10).[32] This "upside-down" perspective undermines the notion of hierarchical power inherent in the metaphor.

The psalms that celebrate Yahweh's cosmic kingship take the metaphor another step. Yahweh is sovereign even over the gods (95:3). In Psalm 97, the poet imagines that "all gods bow down before him" (v. 7). Yahweh is described as "most high over all the earth" and "exalted

---

[27] Mettinger, *In Search of God*, 115.

[28] Ibid., 97.

[29] Ibid., 99.

[30] Ibid., 102.

[31] Ibid., 150.

[32] Ibid.

far above all gods" (vv. 7, 9). It may seem strange that the next verse of Psalm 97 moves to a reflection on the Lord's attitude toward and action on behalf of "those who hate evil" (v. 10). The poet has linked sovereignty over the gods with human moral conviction.

Yet it is precisely the relationship between divine sovereignty and justice that constitutes the hinge between the cosmic and the historical dimensions of Yahweh's reign. Yahweh's reign hinges on the moral architecture of the universe. When the poet celebrates or anticipates Yahweh's coming to judge with righteousness, to set things right and to bring equity to the peoples, then all creation shares in that joy. In the light of that imagery, Psalm 82 paints a poetic portrait of Yahweh holding court concerning the state of the earth. Only now it is not the nations that are brought before the bar of justice, but the gods.

The psalm begins with a question that implies an accusation. The gods have been supporting the cause of the wicked and empowering them to continue in their injustices (v. 2). Verses 3–4 seem to be an admonition, as though God is reading a job description. To qualify as gods, they must act to assure the well-being of the weak, the lowly, the destitute, and the needy. They are actively to "deliver them from the hand of the wicked" (v. 4b). It is obvious that this divine job description is both an indictment of and the evidence against the gods. The judge turns to the courtroom or to the witnesses in verse 5 and declares his conclusion: "They have neither knowledge nor understanding, they walk around in darkness." What is worse, the poet continues, "all the foundations of the earth are shaken." The gods embody uncreation, a return to cosmic and moral chaos, whereas Yahweh's righteous reign secures the world on its foundations (93:1; 96:10). In fact, as several psalms state, Yahweh's throne is undergirded by righteousness and justice (89:14; 97:2). Psalm 99 summarizes most succinctly the character of Yahweh's rule: "Mighty King, lover of justice, you have established equity; you have executed justice and righteousness in Jacob" (99:4). Not only will Yahweh come to judge the earth, Yahweh has begun to do so in Israel. The gods in the courtroom are now put in their place because they have abdicated their responsibility. Although they are gods, they have no greater status than humans. Like mortals, like אָדָם (ʾādām), they will die. They have no sustaining life in them; they are ephemeral. In a final exuberant cry, the poet calls out from the gallery for God to judge the earth. The nations, after all, belong to this God (v. 8).[33] Since "the present order of the divided world, governed by deputies wielding delegated

[33] See Willem S. Prinsloo, "Psalm 82: Once Again, Gods or Men?" *Biblica* 76 (1995): 219–28; Matitiahu Tsevat, "God and the Gods in Assembly: An Interpretation of Psalm 82," *Hebrew Union College Annual* 40–41 (1969–70): 123–37.

power, is disintegrating because of inner contradictions,"[34] the poet calls on God to assert the divine prerogative and act to set things right.[35]

In the face of these polemical poems against the gods who support the wicked, another psalm portrays Yahweh's alternative governance in exquisite detail. Psalm 146 begins with an intensely personal call to worship as the psalmist vows to sing praises to God as long as life lasts (vv. 1–2). In verses 3–4 the psalmist exhorts others not to trust in princes or in mortals (sons of *'ādām*) who are characterized above all by death. Like the gods and princes of Psalm 82, these sources of human power have no abiding or sustaining resources that one can trust (בטח | *bṭḥ*). By contrast, those whose "hope is in the LORD their God" will experience the benefits of Yahweh's reign, which endures from generation to generation (vv. 5, 10). This one, whom the psalmist wishes to praise all life long, who reigns from generation to generation, is none other than the creator (v. 6) whose work happens to be eternal faithfulness (v. 6b), working justice for the oppressed and feeding the hungry (v. 7). As in the psalms of Yahweh's kingship (93, 95–99) and Psalm 82, which denies kingship to the gods, the job description for divinity links creation with justice. The litany continues in 146:7b–9, with the assertion of Yahweh's eternal reign as the consequence of Yahweh's actions in verses 6–9. Yahweh deserves the title "king" because he faithfully preserves the moral structure of the cosmos and the well-being of its weakest inhabitants.

Because there are no gods that compare with Yahweh (Ps. 86:8, 10; 89:6; 95:3; 97:7), Israel's worship offers participants a way of saying no to the gods and saying yes to Yahweh, whose character and actions fulfill the qualifications of divinity. What Israel is doing by such liturgical wordplay is what James Sanders and James Luther Mays call "monotheizing."[36] The powers of divinity in the ancient world were the real "powers of fertility, weather, warfare, government, and the world itself."[37] In a world of competing allegiances, the gods must be named and found wanting by two criteria: sustaining and revitalizing of creation and active engagement in just peacemaking on behalf of the disenfranchised and poor. The character of the reign of God must be articulated in order to enable worshipers to discern false claims to divinity. This, too, is the work of mission. Whereas mission is rightly

---

[34] Tsevat, "God and the Gods in Assembly," 134.

[35] See also Psalm 58, which reflects a similar concern for justice in the human realm, and an affirmation that there must be an alternative power who makes things right.

[36] Mays, *The Lord Reigns*, 67; Sanders, *Canon and Community*, 51–2.

[37] Mays, *The Lord Reigns*, 67.

seen as God's work, the call to acknowledge the God who is rightfully king is the work of worship and the heart of the community's mission in the world. As Mays notes concerning praise: "monotheizing, liberating the good realities of life and world from the perversion of divinization, is again the crucial agenda. The praise of psalms as confession is the liturgy for mission."[38]

A world gone awry: Lament and shalom

It is against this background that the lament psalms strike a dissonant chord. Embracing divine sovereignty creates a space within which to make sense of suffering, sin, and the brokenness of the world. The dark regions of human experience are not eliminated, but are placed into the care of the one who nurtures all things toward shalom. The lament announces that the promise of God's reign has yet to be realized in all corners of the known world of human experience. Here, too, we can place the imprecations against those who refuse, reject, or rebel against the reign of God. Lament and imprecation make a stand, in the face of the assertion that Yahweh reigns, that reality does not yet embody the promise of the conviction. Yahweh's reign is assured, it is affirmed in worship, it is longed for by those who lament its absence, and it is hoped for in the midst of the fractures in human experience. Lament creates a space for authentic human vulnerability.

Jon Levenson suggests, therefore, that God's covenantal lordship is "fragile," hence "the continual necessity of Israel's active consent" to that lordship.[39] "YHWH's kingship in Israel, like his kingship in the pantheon and his mastery over creation, remained vulnerable and in continual need of reaffirmation, reratification, reacclamation."[40] Levenson notes that "the actualization of the full potential of God requires the testimony of his special people."[41] If that is so, then the assertion of Ps. 22:3, that Yahweh is "enthroned on the praises of Israel," carries much freight. Instead of being "enthroned" as an icon or image in the sanctuary (as one might expect in an ancient temple), Yahweh is made visible in the prayers and praise of God's people. "The throne that bears God forth as presence in Israel's worship is the praises of Israel."[42] Or, as Levenson puts it, "in the covenantal idiom of monotheism, Israel is the functional

---

[38] Ibid., 68.

[39] Jon D. Levenson, *Creation and the Persistence of Evil: The Jewish Drama of Divine Omnipotence* (San Francisco: Harper & Row, 1988), 139.

[40] Ibid., 138.

[41] Ibid., 139.

[42] Mays, *The Lord Reigns*, 66.

equivalent of the pantheon, wisely and joyfully acclaiming their lord and deliverer."[43] Although the psalms assert that Yahweh is undisputed king because he is creator, they also assume that his sovereignty will not be known in the cosmos unless it is declared in worship. Israel's mission, then, is to worship—to declare allegiance by announcing that no other power is suited to sustain creation and to foster shalom in the world.

To announce an alternative imagination governed by passion for peace with justice creates a hopeful way of participating in God's project even in the midst of human suffering and pain. Lament, therefore, is the language of resistance. And, strangely enough, it is also the reality into which "the ends of the earth" are invited to observe the gracious rule of Yahweh (Ps. 22:27–28). "Dominion" and "ruling over the nations" can be acknowledged not because Yahweh is a despot who forces divine rule on all, but because God enters the ambiguity of human experience. The one who has "forsaken me" (22:1), who "does not answer" (22:2), and who was "far from me" (22:11) is also the one who hears (22:24) and in whom the poor are satisfied (22:26). The universalizing of that hope in Ps. 22:27–31 is a way of placing the actions of God with one psalmist into the larger scope of God's purposes for all peoples in all places. The hope at the heart of worship, then, is embedded in the proclamation that even in the darkest of human experiences Yahweh reigns. There is no triumphalism here, nor is there a glossing over of the pain of partial knowledge.[44] The missional hope of such worship asserts that it is possible to live by resistance, trusting that bowing to this sovereign is ultimately life-giving for those who live (v. 26), for those who have died (v. 29), and for those yet to be born (vv. 30–31). As Sally Morgenthaler puts it, "Worship that witnesses makes room for the brokenness in all of us. And it heals by the power of the gospel."[45]

To announce the reign of God in the midst of lament and to long for its reality is, therefore, a political act. As David Bosch suggests, to speak of the reign of God "expresses a profound discontent with the way things are, a fervent desire to see them changed."[46] Oppressive realities do not disappear, but the declaration of God's reign "brings their

---

[43] Levenson, *Creation*, 139.

[44] On this theme see three thoughtful essays by Douglas John Hall, "The Mystery of God's Dominion," "Globalism, Nationalism, and the Reign of God," and "God's Reign and the Metamorphosis of Christendom," in *God and the Nations*, by Hall and Rosemary Radford Ruether (Minneapolis: Fortress Pr., 1995).

[45] Sally Morgenthaler, *Worship Evangelism: Inviting Unbelievers into the Presence of God* (Grand Rapids: Zondervan Publishing Hse., 1995), 113.

[46] David J. Bosch, *Transforming Mission: Paradigm Shifts in Theology of Mission*, American Society of Missiology Series, no. 16 (Maryknoll: Orbis Bks., 1991), 34.

circumstances within the force field of God's sovereign will and thereby relativizes them and robs them of their ultimate validity. It assures the victims of society that they are no longer prisoners of an omnipotent fate. Faith in the reality and presence of God's reign takes the form of a resistance movement against fate and against being manipulated and exploited by others."[47] The lament is a missional act of hope expressed in the liturgical "yes" of "Yahweh reigns," and the struggle for transformation is engaged as the "no" is spoken against the powers that violate and kill and decimate the well-being of the earth and its peoples.

Implications of Yahweh's reign for a missional identity

The affirmation of Yahweh's kingship in Israel's worship is certainly foreign to the language that shapes contemporary life. Yet if worship is about "the formation of an alternative community"[48] then the affirmations of Israel's worship offer clues for the missional identity of a worshiping church. If the celebration of Yahweh's reign is a root metaphor in the "liturgy for mission," then we should consider the implications briefly before exploring the shape and contours of that mission. Mays contends that Yahweh's reign involves two types of activity: "One is the pattern of ordering chaos to bring forth cosmos and world. The other is a scenario of intervening in human disorder by judgment and deliverance. The reign of God is God's activity as creator and maintainer of the universe, and as judge and savior who shapes the movement of history toward the purpose of God."[49]

Those two modes of divine engagement in the world suggest directions for mission. If whom we worship shapes our character and our actions, then we do well to articulate clearly the character of our allegiance. Undergirding and surrounding those modes of divine engagement with the world is the assumption that God's reign nurtures shalom in all relationships, both with the creation and in the human community. As Psalm 29 affirms, the voice of Yahweh is the ordering agent in the cosmos as well as the source of blessing that results in peace (29:11; cf. 99:4).

---

[47] Ibid. We might even say that the lament, and even the imprecatory psalms, function within the liturgy of mission. They are "a form of human struggle against chaos—a struggle simultaneously *against* and *with* God" (Erich Zenger, *A God of Vengeance? Understanding the Psalms of Divine Wrath* [Louisville: Westminster John Knox Pr., 1996], 74). These psalms point out what has gone awry, and cry out for God to renew and to restore a wounded and suffering creation.

[48] Brueggemann, *Israel's Praise*, 28.

[49] Mays, *The Lord Reigns*, 7.

The missional identity of the worshiping community, therefore, will be guided by an orientation toward sustaining and renewing creation as the proper context for praise. To say that Yahweh reigns, and to do so within the language world of the psalms, is to recognize that Yahweh is sovereign of the cosmos. Yahweh's reign is "more majestic than the thunders of mighty waters, more majestic than the waves of the sea" (93:4). All creation is invited to participate (96:1, 11) as the praise of God's people resounds among the nations who are invited to join the song (96:7). "In a glorious way, Psalm 96 and its twin, Psalm 98, remind the believing community that God's purpose with creation is nothing less than a new heaven and a new earth in which justice will be at home."[50] It is not simply naive realism that allows us to make the hermeneutical move from the imagery of creation's praise in Psalms 96 and 98 to creation as the context of mission. It is a recognition of creational praise, however voiceless it may be (Ps. 19:1–4), that suggests that the enterprise of mission may also concern the overlapping and ever more complex worlds of genetics research, global economics, and technology. This awareness is ever more urgent as we acknowledge our mission as agents or stewards of the divine king. If God nurtures the well-being of creation (Psalm 104), perhaps his trustees do well to foster its shalom as well.

The missional identity of the worshiping community will also be oriented toward justice, since divine kingship seeks "to save all the oppressed of the earth" (Ps. 76:9). Worship that celebrates such kingship calls for a politics of justice for the marginalized. Psalm 113 invites all "servants" of Yahweh, those who have pledged loyalty to his reign, to praise him (v. 1). This reign is eternal (v. 2) and global in scope (v. 3). It comprehends the nations and the heavens, the historical world and the cosmic realm (v. 4). Therefore the question arises, "Is anyone comparable?" Verses 5 and 6 suggest that although this transcendent one "is seated on high," he "looks far down on the heavens and the earth" (cf. Ps. 33:13–14). The one who is beyond heaven and earth, and above the cosmic and historical powers, touches and mends, "raises the poor," "lifts the needy," and "gives the barren woman a home" (vv. 7–9). This psalm, along with Psalm 146, articulates without ambiguity the concrete shape of "equity," "justice," and "righteousness" declared in Ps. 99:4. God acts on behalf of the marginal and creates a space in which they can flourish. Those who are his servants, therefore, serve him in worship, but they also act as trustees of his commonwealth.

---

[50] Jannie du Preez, "Reading Three 'Enthronement Psalms' from an Ecological Perspective," *Missionalia* 19 (1991): 127.

Each of the previous two paragraphs lends nuance to the missional identity of God's people as trustees. In that way the psalms place the human vocation within the sphere of Yahweh's sovereignty.

IMAGING GOD: HUMAN MISSION AS STEWARDSHIP

Having said that it is God who judges on earth (Ps. 58:11), there remains a significant role for the human being as agent of divine compassion and justice. Because Yahweh's throne is securely established and the powers have no claim to the royal identity, there remains the matter of managing Yahweh's realm on earth. A variety of psalms transpose the vision for a just social order, governed by Yahweh, into a vision for a just king who works on Yahweh's behalf as a vice-regent. In Psalm 2, for example, the "anointed one," Yahweh's king (vv. 2, 6), "is identified and described in terms of correspondence to and coherence with the character of the reign of God."[51]

At the heart of Yahweh's reign is the vision for a just social order, which we have seen expressed in several psalms (e.g. 58, 82, 96, 113, 146). Psalm 72 echoes the sentiments of those psalms, and illustrates clearly the correspondence between the divine reign and the role of Israel's king.

If the psalms that celebrate Yahweh's reign stand at the center of the "liturgy for mission," we find in Psalm 72 a prayer for the embodiment of that mission. In verses 1–7 the mission of the king mirrors the justice and righteousness of God (v. 1). He exercises justice in behalf of the poor and the needy, and stands firmly against those who oppress (vv. 2, 4).[52] Those sentiments reverberate throughout the psalm, highlighting the mercy of the king, which imitates the mercy of God (vv. 12–14). At the same time, the exercise of justice in behalf of the marginal and the weak yields fruitfulness for creation (vv. 3, 16). Verse 5 calls for the longevity and well-being of the king in outrageous terms—as long as the sun and moon do their work in the sky. Verse 6 continues the odd juxtapositions; now the king is compared to rain and showers. The king, in other words, is to be for creation what he is to the poor—the source of blessing. Verse 7 brings the two images together: righteousness now flourishes so as to create eternal peace. Shalom among humans (v. 7) echoes shalom (prosperity) for creation (v. 3). Patrick Miller writes: "Prosperity and well-being depend upon the maintenance of righteousness and justice by

---

[51] Mays, *The Lord Reigns*, 102.

[52] On this theme, see Walter Houston, "The King's Preferential Option for the Poor: Rhetoric, Ideology and Ethics in Psalm 72," *Biblical Interpretation* 7 (1999): 341–67.

the human ruler. Peace is not possible in a land and system where justice is not nurtured."[53]

Verses 8–14 stretch the imagination to invite God to give the king worldwide dominion. These verses imagine that all kings on earth will acknowledge this one king's reign as worthy of tribute. The picture is hardly credible. Yet the correspondence between this image and the cosmic rule of Yahweh is unmistakable. "All gods bow down" before Yahweh (Ps. 97:7; etc.). Psalm 47 asserts that "God is king over the nations" (47:8). Since all nations belong to Yahweh (82:8), it is within the range of possible imagery for Psalm 72 to extend this language to Yahweh's anointed. The key to the universal rule of this king is in the "for" of verse 12.[54] The king's universal sovereignty is solely dependent on letting go rather than on grasping, on acting on behalf of those who have no helper. Those actions define the meaning of "justice" and "righteousness" in the prayer of verse 1. This king intervenes to create shalom, which "arises from the alliance of the king with the poor against the exploiting class."[55]

Verses 15–17 summarize the hopes for the king in terms of abundance and blessing. Both rural and urban settings will flourish (v. 16). The section ends with an echo of the ancestral promise of Gen. 12:2–3 that links the greatness of the name with the blessing of the nations (v. 17). The psalm links the Abrahamic and the Davidic promises in the one purpose of God: the blessing of the nations. When this promise, now prayed and hoped for, is realized, the whole earth will know the peace that is embodied in justice and righteousness. The psalm has been placed at the end of Book II of the Psalter, with its doxology in verses 18–19. In that doxology all the hope of the monarchic promise is subsumed into the praise of Yahweh, "who alone does wondrous things" (v. 18). It is not the king who, in the end, is able to accomplish this transforming sovereignty. It is Yahweh alone whose glory is celebrated (v. 19) above that of the king's fame (v. 17). Therefore the doxology petitions, "May his glory fill the whole earth" (v. 19).

Since the royal task is to imitate the divine character, there can be no mistaking the correspondences between the hoped-for results of the

---

[53] Patrick D. Miller Jr., "Power, Justice, and Peace: An Exegesis of Psalm 72," *Faith and Mission* 4 (1986): 67.

[54] Miller, "Power, Justice, and Peace," 68.

[55] Houston, "The King's Preferential Option," 360.

king's reign and the character of Yahweh's reign. According to Psalm 72, the just and righteous rule of Yahweh "is embodied in the politics and policies of the Davidic monarchy."[56] It is this imagined and hoped-for reality that causes all creation to rejoice. The ideal king of Psalm 72 becomes the one who models "who[m] and what to look for, the kind of rule God intends."[57]

The king as archetypal human: Stewarding God's resources
Miller rightly reminds us that Psalm 72 "came into being as a prayer for the human ruler of Israel. . . . This means that the psalm was intended to pray for and describe the proper sort of rule for those who govern the human community. . . . One cannot create a kingdom of peace and well-being while one is in constant conflict with neighbor and building up the armaments of war. That is not the shalom God gives. One cannot seek God's kingdom and its righteousness while ignoring the distress and helplessness of the poor."[58] Because the psalm presents an ideal, it also functions as a critique of those who exercise their power inappropriately against the shalom-making project of God. This prayer for the king is also a prayer against the king. Since the king is also the "audience," one who overhears this prayer, the psalm can be read "contrary to reality" and as a manifesto for a state that "truly embodied the rule of God."[59]

The kingship of God, therefore, becomes credible in the visionary portrayal of the Davidic king. Yet the very humanity of Israel's kings also exposes the dangers inherent in the human agent's role as vice-regent of God. Human ideology and desire threaten to undermine the divine rule. The psalms train us in the realism of Davidic rule while awakening in us the desire to live by the vision of justice and peace. The tension between the reality and the vision opens the window to recognizing the embodiment of the vision in the person of Jesus and in the alternative community created by the Spirit. The vision constitutes the horizon toward which we live by grace. This is the vision that fuels the missional community. Yet that vision seems, at times, to be tainted by troubling themes that skew the missional agenda.

---

[56] Brueggemann, *Israel's Praise*, 62.

[57] Miller, "Power, Justice, and Peace," 69.

[58] Ibid.

[59] Houston, "The King's Preferential Option," 361–2.

Sometimes when Yahweh is described as "a great king over all the earth," he is also depicted as the one who subdues the nations on Israel's behalf (Ps. 47:2–3). When David appropriates the role of God's vice-regent, he experiences God's empowerment for warfare and conquest (Ps. 18:31–42). And when the people take on the role of David, acting as children of the king (Ps. 149:2), they imagine themselves as carrying out "vengeance on the nations and punishment on the peoples" (Ps. 149:7). It is a small step from those affirmations in biblical texts to generalized human violence in the name of God. Psalm 149, or example, became a rallying text in the sixteenth century for Thomas Müntzer's aspirations to create a kingdom of God on earth.[60] It becomes difficult to imagine how all nations can be invited to worship Yahweh if that worship depends on their conquest by Israel's king.

Since the monarchic metaphor can be appropriated for violent actions, it is not welcomed by all as a root metaphor that shapes identity and mission of the worshiping community. Many wish for more egalitarian metaphors for God. Even Psalm 72 may convey an ambivalent message. The royal portrait in Psalm 72 implies that the king's identity is inseparable from his mission. Who he is shapes what he is to do. Yet the doing bears with it a temptation. The royal vocation as steward of God's creation is inherently dangerous in that it contains a temptation to mastery and control. Sadly, however, "mastery is the illusion of illusions."[61] Solomon's imperial power, although from some quarters viewed as a fulfillment of Yahweh's dynastic promises, was also problematic. The description of Solomon's reign in 1 Kings 4:20–28 could well be read as a narrative about one who failed to heed the call to care for the weak and the marginal.[62]

Perhaps we, too, have succumbed to the temptation that comes with mastery. As Douglas John Hall writes: "We find ourselves at the end of a process that began with the Renaissance and expressed itself mightily in the Industrial Revolution: the great thrust forward, the bid for sovereignty over nature and history. But just as such sovereignty seems within reach, the whole vision has ceased to charm us. It has in fact turned

---

[60] Robert Davidson, *The Vitality of Worship: A Commentary on the Book of Psalms* (Grand Rapids: Eerdmans; Edinburgh: Handsel Pr., 1998), 476.

[61] Douglas John Hall, *The Steward: A Biblical Symbol Come of Age,* rev. ed. (Grand Rapids: Eerdmans; New York: Friendship Pr., 1990), 85.

[62] Walter Brueggemann, "Vine and Fig Tree: A Case Study in Imagination and Criticism," *Catholic Biblical Quarterly* 43 (1981): 188–204.

sour."[63] The question for us, therefore, is whether the metaphor of Yahweh's reign can become a transforming reality in our lives—in relation to creation, relationships at home and in the workplace, and in all realms of human involvement.

The "theopolitical" scandal

The kingship of God metaphor reflects a "theopolitical" view of reality:[64] Israel lives within the ancient world, using the depiction of gods common in that world. "But Israel made a radical adaptation of this view and its language to faith in one god, the LORD. That adaptation became the historical clothing, the linguistic incarnation of the LORD's self-revelation."[65] As we live our lives from within the biblical poetic prayers and narratives, we learn to inhabit the symbolic world of the root metaphor. We discover as we do so that "the kingship of God involves the opposition and dismantling of every power arrangement and symbol system that employs the politics of violence and self-assertion."[66] Therefore, when we reflect on our missional identity as people of God, we find ourselves driven to acknowledge that "Yahweh's decisive victory over every oppressive power structure inaugurates a reign of justice *and* hope."[67] The mission of God's people is to announce that reign, to embody that justice, and to live in the light of that hope. We do so by God's grace as we discover that we, too, are royal creatures.

Imaging God: The human as royal figure

Psalm 8 is a poetic reflection on human identity and vocation based on motifs from Genesis 1 and 2. The psalm begins and ends with an exclamation about the sovereignty and glorious character of God. Within that framework, the psalm reflects on the heavens, the enemies who threaten, and the place of the human being in the midst of the cosmos. Ironically, it is the weakest of humans whose speech now quells the threat of chaos (v. 2). It is the power of the weakest human voice that now shapes order out of chaos. This frail human being is now celebrated

---

[63] Hall, *The Steward*, 91.

[64] Mays, *The Lord Reigns*, 10; Martin Buber, *Kingship of God*, 3rd ed. (New York: Harper & Row, 1967), 57.

[65] Mays, *The Lord Reigns*, 10.

[66] Louis Stulman, *Order amid Chaos: Jeremiah As Symbolic Tapestry*, The Biblical Seminar 57 (Sheffield, England: Sheffield Academic Pr., Ltd., 1998), 94.

[67] Ibid., 96 (Stulman's italics).

as God's trustee, the one who stands in as God's caretaker. The human has a derivative and limited dominion over creation, dependent on God's dominion over all nations (Ps. 22:28). The language of Psalm 8 is decidedly royal, although its scope is not limited to the Davidic king. It is a reflection on the wonder of human responsibility in the face of God's sovereign majesty.[68]

Like Ps. 72:8, this psalm also honors the dominion of the human being in the "divine project."[69] Whereas Psalm 8 reflects on the human relationship to the creation, Psalm 72 brings the creational dimension into conversation with matters of justice and peace. Whereas Psalm 72 depicts the Davidic king as archetypal trustee in God's pilot project on Zion, Psalm 8 draws the portrait wider. It echoes Gen. 1:26–28 to include the human being (in the "image of God") as royal figure who stands in partnership with God to care for creation on God's behalf.

To understand the image of God not as an inherent characteristic of the human being but as a vocation suggests the missional implications of this democratization of the royal ideal. Robert Davidson writes: "A new sense of stewardship, replacing human greed and irresponsible exploitation, has become a matter of life and death for the human race. Is such a stewardship possible unless we are prepared to accept an authority higher than ourselves?"[70] Hall proposes a verbal reading of the notion of image of God, so that our vocation as image bearer is reflected in relational responsibility through action. "We image God as we are incorporated through grace and faith into the preservational dominion of God in the world. Or, to state the same thing in other words, we mirror the sovereignty of the divine love in our stewardship of the earth."[71]

Although we have affirmed the positive vocation of imaging God, Leonard Sweet raises a concern that "the entire stewardship metaphor is anachronistic and arrogant," since we do not speak about "stewards" any more.[72] In fact, he contends, to claim to "oversee" the working of the

---

[68] See also Ps. 144:3, which asks a similar question in a different context. Both psalms, however, reflect on human frailty.

[69] The expression comes from Sanders, *Canon and Community*, 39–40.

[70] Davidson, *The Vitality of Worship*, 40.

[71] Douglas John Hall, *Imaging God: Dominion As Stewardship* (Grand Rapids: Eerdmans; New York: Friendship Pr., 1986), 200.

[72] Leonard Sweet, *SoulTsunami: Sink or Swim in New Millennium Culture* (Grand Rapids: Zondervan Publishing Hse., 1999), 271.

cosmos is "ludicrous."[73] Like Hall, who transforms the monarchic metaphor by redefining "dominion as stewardship" (the subtitle of his book *Imaging God*), Sweet argues that "God did not call us to 'have dominion' over the earth; he called us to be trustees of his estate":[74] "Whereas 'stewardship' has been stripped of all legal overtones and fiduciary consequences, postmoderns understand that the trustees are the legal guardians of that organization or estate. They do not 'own' it, but they are legally accountable for its health and well-being."[75]

This is not a trusteeship that dominates but one that serves in anticipation of a longed for wholeness. The author of Hebrews cites Psalm 8, suggesting that Jesus' crowning as sovereign is also representative (Heb. 2:6–9). Since human beings are not yet exercising dominion (v. 8), Jesus stands before us as one who signals the way of sacrificial giving for all. Jesus's death defines dominion as self-sacrificial love. Citing Psalm 8 for different reasons, 1 Cor. 15:24–28 notes that Jesus' reign is a reign in process. The enemies are not yet vanquished. "All things," including every hostile power, will one day be tamed and nothing will hinder the life-giving power of God that has been made available through the anticipatory victory of Christ (vv. 20–24).

In the meantime, the human vocation as God's "governer general" continues. That role is reflected both in the representative function of the king in Israel, and in the royal identity and vocation of the human being. All are called to the vocation of bringing cosmos out of chaos, of nurturing peace with justice for all. In this we live in hope, knowing that what God intended as good in the beginning will one day be brought to its goal (Rom. 8:20–25).

Such an interpretation of the human vocation is theocentric, dependent on God for its completion. It is eschatological, but affirms that the firstfruits are already apparent. And it is christological, in that Christ's kingship is "the divinely ordained means of sustaining order and justice."[76] As trustees with a vocation to mirror the dominion of God, we exercise our vocation through preservation of creation and through concern for the vulnerable ones in the world. Hall concludes:

---

[73] Ibid., 272.

[74] Ibid., 276.

[75] Ibid., 273.

[76] Paul Joyce, "The Kingdom of God and the Psalms," in *The Kingdom of God and Human Society: Essays by Members of the Scripture, Theology and Society Group,* ed. Robin Barbour (Edinburgh: T. & T. Clark, 1993), 59.

"As preservers of all life, we have our commission as a sacred trust that inheres in our new identity—or, more accurately, this old identity into which we are newly born through grace and repentance. We are preservers because the creation is intrinsically good, and we are being delivered from the kind of egotism that is able to find goodness only in what is useful to ourselves."[77]

Summary: Mission as royal vocation

Psalms 8 and 72 identify a royal vocation for the human being and offer a critique of human autonomy. Human beings are given the task of nurturing creation as Yahweh's agents, but humanity (including Israel's Davidic kings) abrogates the role and separates itself from the care and protection of the creator and participates in the undoing of creation by acting against the shalom of God's rule. When human beings desire to live inside the reign of God, however, they act as agents of Yahweh by exercising justice and righteousness in all relationships, and when they do that they care for all creation by submitting to the instruction/Torah of the great king.

The royal ideal in the psalms shapes identity and clarifies vocation, just as it serves as a critique of pride, autonomy, and power politics of every kind. We image God as we live to sustain the well-being of others and to nurture the health of all creation. The missional implications of the image of God that we have noted above involve, therefore, both gift and responsibility. Reflecting on the creation stories, John Sanders notes: "God places the responsibility of caring for the world in the hands of humanity. . . . God graciously provides an environment for the sustenance of the humans and calls them into the care of that gift. . . . God sovereignly decides that not everything will be up to God. Some important things are left in the hands of humanity as God's co-creators such that we are to collaborate with God in the achievement of the divine project."[78]

This collaboration does not imply control, but shapes a vocation that is larger than our capacity and is undertaken only by grace as we listen to the instruction of the one to whom all belongs.

---

[77] Hall, *Imaging God*, 200.

[78] *The God Who Risks: A Theology of Providence* (Downers Grove: InterVarsity Pr., 1998), 44.

EMBODIMENT AS MISSION: ZION AND THE PEOPLE OF GOD

Zion, "the city of the great King" (Ps.48:2), is the place from which Yahweh's rule is exercised, first among those who heed his instruction, and then among the nations. And the temple at the heart of Zion is the throne room and instruction hall of Yahweh. Zion represents the paradigm of peace and the hope for the end of violence.[79] As the gathering place of the worshiping community, it is the place in which and from which the mission of God touches the world. It is the symbolic center of God's pilot project on earth.

The missional impulse of Zion is shaped fundamentally by the presence of God. Yahweh dwells as king (in the temple) among his people on Zion (Ps. 132:13–14). As worshipers "speak of the glory of your kingdom" (Ps. 145:11a), they can be assured that "The LORD is near to all who call on him" (Ps. 145:18a). Yet he is also enthroned on high (Ps. 11:4); from there he is able to gain a comprehensive knowledge of wickedness and violence (Ps. 11:5). Yahweh, as king, is known as both protector and judge. Longing to be in Zion, worshipers know that it is a place of blessing and empowerment in the presence of God (Psalm 84). Solomon's temple dedication prayer suggests that the divine presence creates an openness to the foreigner. Worship is the experience of Yahweh's hospitality, both for Israel and for the stranger (1 Kings 8:41–43).[80]

Enemies threaten the city of God (46:6; 48:4; 76:5–6). Although chaotic primeval waters threaten the mountains, they remain firm and creation rests securely (46:3). The powers of chaos appear in historical form: "The nations are in an uproar" (46:6). Neither cosmic forces of chaos nor historical powers that threaten God's project can thwart the secure presence of Yahweh in Zion (46:7, 11). Zion, therefore, cannot be moved (46:5; 125:1), even as creation "shall never be moved," because of Yahweh's reign (93:1–2; 96:10).

---

[79] For comprehensive discussions of Zion in the Old Testament, see Ben C. Ollenburger, *Zion, the City of the Great King: A Theological Symbol of the Jerusalem Cult*, JSOT Supplement Series 41 (Sheffield, England: Sheffield Academic Pr., Ltd., 1987), and Jon D. Levenson, *Sinai and Zion: An Entry into the Jewish Bible* (Minneapolis: Winston Pr., 1985). For a concise summary of the central motifs in the Zion theology, see Hans-Joachim Kraus, *Theology of the Psalms* (Minneapolis: Augsburg Publishing Hse., 1986), 78–84.

[80] Keifert notes: "Since Israel was the recipient of the Lord's hospitality, so Israel's worship was to be hospitable to strangers. As God is host to Israel, so Israel is called to be host to the stranger" (Patrick R. Keifert, *Welcoming the Stranger: A Public Theology of Worship and Evangelism* [Minneapolis: Fortress Pr., 1992], 60).

The pilot project is fueled by the river of life that flows from Zion (46:4, though Jerusalem has no river). The ancient metaphor of the water of life is used to declare the sovereignty of Yahweh, the one enthroned in Zion who intervenes for his people. The waters of chaos have been tamed. Now Yahweh nurtures Zion with water of joyful life (46:4–5; see also Ezekiel 47; Ps. 36:7–9).

Yahweh's nurturing presence transforms Zion into the place of instruction, to which all nations will come. Nations and princes gather to Zion because "God is king of all the earth" and "over the nations" (47:7–9; 48:4; 68:29; 86:9).[81] Psalm 87:4–6 even describes nations being "born" in Zion (Isaiah develops this motif further; see Isa. 56:6–8; 60:3). Those who come to Zion, to the temple, shape their lives by the instruction that comes from the mountain of God (Psalms 15 and 24). Like the earth, and like Zion, those who live by Yahweh's *torah* shall never be moved" (Ps. 15:5). As Zion takes on the instructional motifs of Mt. Sinai, Zion becomes the place where transformation occurs. To orient one's life toward Zion, then, is to "partake of the creative and transforming energy that radiates from the Temple atop Mount Zion."[82]

Zion is therefore a place of presence that calls for the shaping of an alternative community that lives by the instruction of God. Psalm 24, for example, moves from a confession of sovereignty to an invitation to embody *torah* in life. As Levenson writes: "What is clear in the light of covenant theology is the connection between profession of the uniqueness of YHWH and the performance of his commandments. To believe that he alone is lord is to do his will; to do his will is to enthrone him in lordship."[83] To "pledge allegiance to the ideal" in worship is to participate in a catalytic act of transformation.[84] One becomes what one confesses.

Because Zion is the place of moral transformation, it is a place of peace and justice. It is a place where the people pray for, hope for, and wait for shalom for the land and for the whole earth. That shalom will be experienced as fruitfulness, prosperity, and well-being (Ps. 72:6–7;

---

[81] See the recent study by Lynn Jost that explores the belligerent motifs in the Psalm. Jost suggests a hermeneutical priority in the psalms in which "non-bellicose" psalms take priority over those that advocate a violent or militaristic gathering or subduing of the nations.

[82] Levenson, *Sinai and Zion*, 174.

[83] Ibid., 70.

[84] Ibid., 176.

147:14) for the nation (Ps. 29:11; 85:8; 125:5; 128:6) and for Jerusalem (122:6–7). Yet this hoped-for peace is not limited to nationalistic expectation. Zion is the place from which Yahweh makes an end to warfare. The stilling of the cosmic and historical forces of violence evoke the exultant cry, in Psalm 46, that Yahweh "makes wars cease to the end of the earth; he breaks the bow, and shatters the spear; he burns the shields with fire" (46:9; see also Ps. 76:3). As Ben Ollenburger writes: "War and its equipment are recognized as threats . . . not only against the created order established by Yahweh, but against his stature as 'God, exalted among the nations' (Ps. 46:11b)."[85] To affirm that Yahweh is "exalted," therefore, calls for a response, "Be still, and know that I am God!" (46:10). McCann even contends that the call to be still should be understood as "Stop! Throw down your weapons!"[86]

If this interpretation is accurate, the peaceful expectation of the Zion theology is nothing less than a critique of the assumption that political militarism will change the world. Levenson notes: "If God is suzerain, human suzerains are superfluous. If God is lord of the covenant, then political alliances are of no utility and may prove to be a distraction from basic reality."[87] Although the Davidic kings reign from Zion, only Yahweh is "King of Zion."[88] And since God is the one who breaks the weapons, the Zion psalms "do not speak about earthly kings who succeed at battle."[89] Instead, the Zion tradition hopes that God will "scatter the peoples who delight in war" (Ps. 68:30). It is here, then, where we find a critique, internal to the psalms, of the temptation toward militarism inherent in the Davidic monarchy. Although David may be empowered against his enemies (Psalm 18), the worship tradition of Israel asserts that even those weapons in David's hands will ultimately be destroyed (or at least are ineffective; Ps. 33:16–17). God alone remains the one who takes action against the enemy. The worshiping community is called on to "be still." Pleins suggests, in the light of Psalm 46, that "the most politically compelling notion to emerge

---

[85] Ollenburger, *Zion*, 142. Ollenburger cites Hebrew versification; English versification is 46:10b.

[86] J. Clinton McCann Jr., *A Theological Introduction to the Book of Psalms: The Psalms As Torah* (Nashville: Abingdon Pr., 1993), 139.

[87] Levenson, *Sinai and Zion*, 154.

[88] Ollenburger, *Zion*, 64.

[89] J. David Pleins, *The Psalms: Songs of Tragedy, Hope, and Justice* (Maryknoll: Orbis Bks., 1993), 121.

from these psalms is the idea that *critical reflection on Zion's walls ought to lead to the construction of a world beyond war.*"[90]

That peaceful construction begins, however, in Israel, since Zion is the place from which Yahweh rules to bring about justice for the poor and the marginal (Ps. 68:5–6). It is the place of judgment "to save all the oppressed of the earth" (76:8–9).[91]

The missional implication of Zion theology is shaped above all by the question Ollenburger asks: "What kinds of action are appropriate given the nature of Yahweh and his commitment to Zion"? The answer is obvious: "caring for the poor and the practice of social justice" rather than preparations for war.[92] Since Zion theology affirms ultimate security in Yahweh, those who "dwell in Zion" are oriented to an alternative center of gravity, one that initiates peace, justice, and the elimination of all violent and militaristic means of resolving conflict. Zion is God's pilot project; it is not the home of the ancient gods whose fighting brought creation into being. All creation is Yahweh's good work. Therefore to worship in Zion is to be initiated into a people whose vocation is aligned with the one who is bringing an end to the mythic cycle of violence and who cares for the poor and the needy.

Thus, those human beings who trust Yahweh's secure presence are invited to set aside all other allegiances by which they attempt to secure their own destiny. Zion theology relativizes all political power. And it begins to do so as the community, at worship, declares its allegiances and starts to shape its life in the light of those allegiances. That declaration in worship is a public declaration that announces Yahweh's reign to the nations.

Human beings are called, therefore, to live toward the vision of shalom that God's presence initiates. Having no security but God's presence allows us to begin to live now in the light of our hope of a peaceful world in which conflict, violence, war, and abusive relation-

---

[90] Ibid., 121 (Pleins's italics). Remarkably, in Isa. 2:1–4 the place of instruction and the place of gathering of the nations come together. This is the ultimate goal of Zion theology: Now it is not the Lord who makes an end to war, but the peoples themselves who "beat their swords into plowshares." Isaiah also announces "God with us" (Immanuel [7:14], a presence that implies a purifying judgment [1:21–26]), calls for a king who will rule with justice (7:1–17; 9:2–7), and then universalizes the Zion theology for all nations (2:1–4).

[91] Isaiah links the new heavens and new earth to a recreation of Jerusalem (65:17–19), where weeping will be no more. The last verse of that chapter reads: "They shall not hurt or destroy on all my holy mountain" (65:25).

[92] Ollenburger, *Zion*, 139.

ships will be no more. We are called, in the face of the chaos that we see, to trust in the secure and ordering presence of God as we live in the light of divine instruction.

Worship as a political, polemical act[93]

Without being able to announce the reign of God, worship becomes weak and thin, unable to wrestle with the profound ambiguities of our time, and above all, unable to resist the evil, injustice, and violence that continue to stalk the earth. When we are able to say and to sing in our worship that "Yahweh reigns," we tap into an alternative missional imagination that empowers us to resist and to wrestle against all that hinders the prayer "Your kingdom come on earth as it is in heaven." Commenting on the invitation to "all the earth" to "worship/serve the LORD" in Ps. 100:1–2, Mays argues that "the form and style of the activity proposed in the imperative sentences is *political*."[94] "The psalm belongs at the point where mortals publicly assemble to recognize the power to which they will submit their living. Such worshipful activity means opting for one 'power structure' as decisive, and therefore it ought to be the most significant social action that human beings can take."[95]

As a public act, therefore, worship is a missional act. God's people as God's icon "are doing what the whole world may and should do."[96] Worship invites the world to recognize the identity and character of God. Citing Ps. 67:5–7 and 86:9, Morgenthaler suggests that "God not only intends for seekers to *observe* our worship. God intends for seekers to *become* worshipers."[97] And as Mays notes, "Praise is proclamation; it witnesses to the present and coming reign of the LORD. It finds in its very content the motive for its openness and outreach."[98] In worship, those who are partners in God's pilot project announce that God is God of the world and has begun to make all things new in Israel. The cosmos is

---

[93] Without referring to the Psalms, Graham Kendrick, in *Worship* (Eastbourne, U.K: Kingsway, 1984; also published as *Learning to Worship As a Way of Life* (Minneapolis: Bethany Hse. Pubs., 1984]), brings together both missional and political dimensions of worship. Chapter 3, "Dethroning the Gods," includes a subsection called "Worship Is a Political Act."

[94] Mays, *The Lord Reigns*, 76.

[95] Ibid., 77.

[96] Ibid., 65.

[97] Morgenthaler, *Worship Evangelism*, 83 (Morgenthaler's italics).

[98] Mays, *The Lord Reigns*, 68.

God's realm. Worship invites the whole cosmos to participate in what is becoming a reality in the experience of those in Zion, the pilot project of God. And that invitation is first of all an invitation into the hospitality of God who dwells among us.[99]

The ordering impetus of the missional imagination is therefore significant. "The witness to God in the world is possible and hopeful, because Adonai is God of the world. The liturgy calls us to look and listen and think and seek to make sense of the world beyond the church, in terms of God's sovereignty."[100] Thus, according to Mays, praise is an empowering act that speaks against:

a general religiosity that imagines the god it wants;
other religions that say who god is;
a liberal secularity that believes in no god;
a pluralism that says all gods have their rights;
a multiculturalism that relativizes gods as cultural phenomena;
a neopaganism that revives the old gods.[101]

And the most insidious of all, we might add, is the idolatry of consumerism that promises a magic kingdom if only we buy more in order to keep our way of life secure.[102]

Announcing and anticipating the effects of Yahweh's reign

Brueggemann suggests that the liturgical expression "the Lord reigns" is more than a statement of fact and more than an attempt to keep memory of faith alive. It is, rather "an enactment, a making so," since this declaration is a news event.[103] It declares what has come into being, what

holy play

---

[99] For an articulation of worship as a personal yet public act that invites and engages the stranger, see Keifert's theology of "liturgical evangelism," which is rooted in the hospitality of God. Worship is a rhetorical act, suggests Keifert, in which "the rhetorical church has the world as its horizon, and its unique ministry to the world is the gospel. This ministry of public conversation takes place through and on behalf of those who are strangers to each other" (Keifert, *Welcoming the Stranger*, 131). Robert Webber's *Celebrating Our Faith: Evangelism through Worship* (Philadelphia: Fortress Pr., 1985) also deals with the relationship of worship and evangelism.

[100] Mays, *The Lord Reigns*, 70.

[101] Ibid.

[102] Speaking against the idolatries of our time, Brueggemann (*Israel's Praise*, 128) remarks that we are "'summoned' by massive propaganda to this world of consumerism." See also Michael Budde's *The (Magic) Kingdom of God: Christianity and Global Culture Industries* (Boulder: Westview Pr., 1997), and Rodney Clapp, ed., *The Consuming Passion: Christianity and the Consumer Culture* (Downers Grove: InterVarsity Pr., 1998).

[103] Brueggemann, *Israel's Praise*, 34.

has been experienced, and it anticipates a new reality around the corner. The king who restores all things to their intended shalom (Psalm 146) "works justice for *all* who are oppressed" (Ps. 103:6; 76:9).

When such announcements are made in worship, Israel is engaging in "the work of evangelism."[104] If speech has power to create the reality it describes, then to declare an alternative governance is to anticipate and to begin to shape the world in which the worshipers live. If worship is a yes to one allegiance and a no to another, then it also says yes to one kind of world and no to another, yes to one way of being human and no to another, yes to a community of justice and peace and no to a community that is deaf to the cry of the marginal. Israel's worship, and ours as well, "shapes the world so that the old world of inequity, unrighteousness, and falsity is always being defeated, and Yahweh's new world of equity, righteousness, and truth is always freshly emerging."[105] It is in light of such assumptions that the psalmist calls out, "Say among the nations, 'The LORD is king!'" (Ps. 96:10).

Israel's missional liturgy is therefore "characteristically distinctive, polemical, and subversive."[106] When Israel in its worship "tells among the nations" that Yahweh reigns, Israel is announcing also a new hope for the way human community is organized and lived. To imagine a new governance and to declare it in worship creates the possibility of acting out what is being said. Without speaking this affirmation in worship, Israel remains limited to what human structures allow. As Brueggemann puts it, "Without that bold and faithful act of imagination, we are consigned to old governances which are predictably idolatrous about heaven and ideological about earth."[107]

THE MISSION OF SHALOM: A TRANSFORMED ROYAL IDENTITY

I have argued that the worshiping community is summoned to live as stewards of the divine king, embodies that instruction in the world, and proclaims to the nations that Yahweh's reign brings wholeness to all. I conclude by suggesting why affirming the reign of God in contemporary worship is an adequate and necessary impetus for missional identity and vocation in the world.

---

[104] Ibid., 38.

[105] Ibid., 39–40.

[106] Ibid., 158.

[107] Ibid., 158–9.

Even as they herald in their worship that the project of God is underway, God's people are becoming a sign of that project, "God's experimental garden on earth, a fragment of the reign of God."[108] Those who are partners in the divine project live hopefully toward shalom, and as they do so they announce God's reign and seek to live in the light of the alternative character implied by that governance.

In speaking that way we affirm a mystery in the analogy. John Howard Yoder writes that the Bible offers us "a repertory of more or less pertinent paradigms, needing to be selected and transformed transculturally in ever new settings."[109] As part of the canonical memory, the psalms offer us models to imagine, not to imitate. Although a relationship exists between the political and the theological modeling in the psalms, as Joyce notes, it is the function of the modeling that is most significant for the hermeneutical task.

There is a clear "parallelism" or "mirroring" of divine/human rule.[110] More important than the historical priority of one or the other, and more important than searching for "borrowing" or "transforming" of Canaanite imagery, is the function of the model in the context of the literature. Joyce notes that such language "can itself offer a vital *corrective* to the abuse of earthly power, both in the better example of the exercise of just rule which it provides and also through the motif of the earthly king as subordinate 'viceroy,' sitting at God's right hand (cf. Ps. 110:1). Yet we may be sure that the davidic kings would have been as ready to exploit such divine sanction for their often bloody rule as have many more recent despots."[111] Joyce pushes the critique further by asking whether the divine kingship image might not also be "so hierarchical and power-based" as to be inadequate or undesirable.[112] Joyce does not advocate abandoning it: "To stand in a tradition is to be called to work and rework images, many of which may remain potent long after they have begun to feel 'archaic.' Continuity of sorts can be maintained, as long as the most rigorous and radical of critiques is permitted."[113] Joyce

---

[108] Bosch, *Transforming Mission*, 11.

[109] John Howard Yoder, "Is Not His Word Like a Fire? The Bible and Civil Turmoil," in *For the Nations: Essays Evangelical and Public* (Grand Rapids: Eerdmans, 1997), 92.

[110] Joyce, "The Kingdom of God and the Psalms," 45.

[111] Ibid., 53.

[112] Ibid.

[113] Ibid., 54.

notes, for example, that it was "during the period of the great European totalitarian dictatorships of the twentieth century that the Roman Catholic Church instituted and popularized the feastday of 'Christ the King.'"[114] In this way the church refuses to allow "its understanding of those images to be conditioned by the prevailing ethos in which it participates."[115] The metaphor can retain its polemical function.

Although canonical images can easily be subverted by the culture of dominance and control, John Driver notes that the image of kingdom and rule is a way of imagining "the new order" of God.[116] It is the Bible's "primary image for understanding God's saving strategy and for grasping the nature and mission of the church.[117] In an individualistic, consumerist culture it is understandable why the image may have fallen onto hard times. But in situations where people experience conflict and political, religious, or economic oppression and privation, the image of God's reign represents "God's new order of justice, peace, liberation, and covenant community."[118] It is a "hope that sustains" and that offers "encouragement in the pilgrimage and spiritual strength to resist the evil powers which oppress them."[119] The hope is embodied in "healed relationships with the creator, as well as with fellow humans and the rest of the created order. The biblical view of the kingdom of God offers a framework in which to understand more wholistically the nature and mission of a transformed and transforming messianic community."[120]

To affirm that Yahweh reigns, therefore, is shorthand for God's "merciful providence toward the weak and oppressed."[121] It is to say: "God's reign takes these concrete social forms."[122] Commenting on Psalms 145 and 146, Driver concludes: "Someone has aptly said that worship is the most subversive activity in which the people of God can engage."[123] God's reign, as articulated in these psalms "is characterized

---

114 Ibid., n.17.
115 John Driver, *Images of the Church in Mission* (Scottdale: Herald Pr., 1997), 21.
116 Ibid., 22.
117 Ibid., 85.
118 Ibid., 87.
119 Ibid.
120 Ibid.
121 Ibid., 89.
122 Ibid.
123 Ibid., 87–8.

by the concrete practice of those righteous relationships that correspond to life as ordered by God's gracious covenant. The kingdom of God is seen most clearly in the way in which the Lord shows his merciful providence toward the weak and oppressed."[124] "As the ancient psalm reminds us, the kingdom of God is in our midst when the Lord brings justice for the oppressed, food for the hungry, freedom for prisoners, sight for the blind, relief for those bowed down, love for the righteous, care for the strangers, and help for the orphan and widow (Ps. 146:7–9)."[125] This is the mission of God, which becomes the mission of those who do the work of imaging God in the world.

The institution of the church, like the institution of Israel's monarchy and social structure, is not the kingdom of God. The announcement of the reign of God in worship, therefore, is not to baptize the economics and politics of institutional identities. Rather, as Driver suggests, the "vision of God's reign should orient all our evangelizing deeds and words."[126] This will mean interpreting our metaphors in worship by telling stories and singing songs of the subversive and polemical way that this divine project is already underway. When we sing "Yahweh reigns," we will know not only the content of the metaphor, but also the transforming power of God among the weak and marginal among us. And those of us who pretend to be strong and at the center will discover that "it is not by our bow" that God's transforming power is known in the world. Therefore we can invite the entire cosmos to share in God's pilot project because we have begun to experience the shalom-making power of God among us.

---

[124] Ibid., 88–9.

[125] Ibid., 92.

[126] Ibid., 93.

3 | Isaiah 2:2–5 and Micah 4:1–4
Learning the ways of the God of Jacob

WILMA ANN BAILEY

IN DAYS TO COME
the mountain of the LORD's house
shall be established as the highest
of the mountains,
and shall be raised above the hills;
all the nations shall stream to it.
³Many **peoples** shall come and say,
"Come, let us go up
to the mountain of the LORD,
to the house of the God of Jacob;
that he may teach us his ways
and that we may walk in his paths."
For out of Zion shall go forth
instruction,
and the word of the LORD
from Jerusalem.
⁴He shall judge between **the nations**,
and shall arbitrate
for **many peoples**;
they shall beat their swords
into plowshares,
and their spears into pruning hooks;
nation shall not lift up sword
against nation,
neither shall they learn war anymore.
⁵**O house of Jacob,
come, let us walk
in the light of the LORD!"**

(Isaiah 2:2–5)

¹In days to come
the mountain of the LORD's house
shall be established as the highest
of the mountains
and shall be raised up above the hills.
Peoples shall stream to it
²and many **nations** shall come and say:
"Come, let us go up
to the mountain of the LORD,
to the house of the God of Jacob;
that he may teach us his ways
and that we may walk in his paths."
For out of Zion shall go forth
instruction,
and the word of the Lord
from Jerusalem.
³He shall judge between **many peoples**,
and shall decide
for **strong nations far away.**
They shall beat their swords
into plowshares,
and their spears into pruning hooks;
nation shall not lift up sword
against nation,
neither shall they learn war any more;
⁴**but they shall all sit
under their own vines
and under their own fig trees
and no one shall make them afraid;
for the mouth of the LORD of hosts
has spoken.**

(Micah 4:1-4)

The prophetic books of Isaiah and Micah share a vision of a peaceful world, where Jews and Gentiles freely choose to learn the ways of the God of Jacob, to walk in the divine path, and to live in peace. Although scholarship examining these texts is abundant, opinions differ on the meaning and significance of the vision in the context of the two books that carry them. Is this a vision of a universal conversion to Israel's God? What, if anything, does this text have to say about mission as it relates to peace and the reign of God?

A question that will be raised here but set aside is, how did these two books come to contain the same prophecy? Did Isaiah have the vision first? Did Micah get it from Isaiah? Did Micah have it first? Did Isaiah copy it? Did both of them share a third source? Did a later editor add the text to both books? These are not idle questions. The answers have a bearing on how one interprets the texts in the context of the books in which they appear. However, the vision texts are also independent. They have a distinct beginning and end. They may be lifted from the contexts in which they appear without doing undue harm to the thought sequence of the books. It is possible, therefore, to study the content of the vision apart from its connection to the books in which it appears.

Both Isaiah and Micah, prophets of ancient Israel, have generally been assigned a historical date in the eighth century B.C.E. by traditional scholars. During the eighth century there were two Israelite kingdoms, Israel in the north and Judah in the south. The beginning of that century witnessed a time of prosperity and security for the northern kingdom. By the end of the century, Israel ceased to exist as a political entity, having been conquered by Assyria, the superpower of the day. The smaller, weaker kingdom of Judah, with its center at Jerusalem, continued to hold on to a marginal existence for another century and a half in the shadow of a rising Babylonian empire. Isaiah the prophet appears to have been a Jerusalemite, an aristocrat with an entrée into the court. Micah's origins are murkier, though his concern for the plight of the country folk, his anti-urban bias, and his castigation of the leadership of Israel probably place him at the opposite end of the social scale.

As was the case with most of the prophetic writings of ancient Israel, both of these books are filled with oracles of doom softened by occasional insertions of more hopeful material. Isaiah, the longer of the two books, shows evidence of at least three different historical periods and their issues. The first part, Isaiah 1–39, reflects the historical context of the eighth century B.C.E., the period of the prophet. The second, Isaiah 40–55, reflects the exilic period, and the third, Isaiah 56–66, the post-exilic period. In Isaiah, the hopeful "latter day prophecy" appears in the first section and the second chapter. In Micah, it appears in the fourth chapter.

In Isaiah, a literary contrast is set up between current realities (in the first chapter) and what will and should be (in the second chapter, 2:2–4). After the prophet thoroughly excoriates Judah for its sin and rebelliousness, a verbal portrait of a redeemed Zion emerges. The rebellious city becomes the "city of righteousness, the faithful city" (1:26c, d NRSV). Likely, the "latter day" prophecy was set to follow chapter one for two reasons: the redeemed city of 1:26–27 becomes the city of the vision in chapter two; the exilic remnant of 1:7–9 is assured in chapter two that Judah and Jerusalem have not been abandoned by God. In fact, Jerusalem will become a center of moral and ethical teaching, not only for Israel but for the entire world. In Micah, the text is preceded in 3:11 by a diatribe against certain leaders of Israel, rulers, priests, and prophets, who abhor justice and grant their services for a price. It predicts the destruction of Jerusalem. The placement of the text in this book suggests that a grassroots movement of ordinary folk that is not dependent on the leadership of the rulers, priests, and prophets described in 3:9–12 will seek instruction directly from God. In Micah, the prophecy is followed by words of restoration.

A. S. Herbert designates this poem "a hymn of the temple."[1] Ben Ollenburger calls it a "pilgrimage hymn."[2] David Stacey concludes that it "represents the pinnacle of Zion theology."[3] Zion theology, which was not universally adopted in ancient Israel, elevated Zion, Jerusalem in its transcendent form, above other locations on earth. Zion theology developed a powerful symbol of an inviolable city where God was more fully present. Jon Levenson finds allusions to what later emerges as Zion theology in the early ark traditions.[4] According to 2 Sam. 5:7, David captured the "stronghold of Zion," the fortified area of the ancient city of Jerusalem. Then he imported the ark into the city, thereby transforming it into a religious center and giving it a status it had not had in ancient Israel. Solomon made Jerusalem-Zion the focal point of worship when he built a temple in the city, set the ark within it, and redirected prayer toward it (1 Kings 5–8). Jerusalem, however, was primarily a southern

---

[1] A. S. Herbert, *The Book of the Prophet Isaiah, Chapters 1–39* (Cambridge: Cambridge Univ. Pr., 1973), 34.

[2] Ben C. Ollenburger, *Zion, the City of the Great King: A Theological Symbol of the Jerusalem Cult,* JSOT Supplement Series 41 (Sheffield, England: Sheffield Academic Pr., Ltd., 1987), 75.

[3] David Stacey, *Isaiah. Chapters 1–30* (London: Epworth Pr., 1993), 16.

[4] Jon D. Levenson, "Zion Traditions," in *The Anchor Bible Dictionary* (New York: Doubleday, 1992), 6:1101.

shrine and the king's sanctuary until the fall of the northern kingdom and subsequent traumatic events such as the Babylonian exile led to broader ownership by the Israelite people.

The "Songs of Zion" that appear in the Book of Psalms share a focus on Zion-Jerusalem. Otto Kaiser believes that the "latter day" prophecy was composed "under the influence" of the Songs of Zion and dates it to the late fifth or early fourth century B.C.E.[5] Ollenburger summarizes the function of the Zion symbolism in the Songs of Zion in this way: "What we have found in the Zion symbolism of the Jerusalem cult tradition is a constant, pervasive concern for justice, a consistent and radical criticism of royal attempts to pervert justice, a theologically motivated attempt to ground this justice in the action and character of God and a sustained emphasis on the poor."[6] This observation also fits Isa. 2:2–5 and Mic. 4:1–4, except there is no explicit reference to the poor. Moreover, Ollenburger thinks Zion theology is embedded in creation theology. It is therefore universal and stands outside history.[7]

ANALYSIS OF ISAIAH 2:2–5 AND MICAH 4:1–4

The translation of the initial phrase of the poem has been disputed, largely for theological reasons. It may be rendered "in the latter days" (RSV), "in the last days" (NIV), "in days to come" (NRSV), "in the days to come" (JPS).[8] Edward Young finds a parallel in Akkadian writings where the phrase "in future days" appears.[9] The phrase has been used to defend particular stances related to eschatology. For example, according to Robert Wilken, early Christian exegetes such as Eusebius thought the prophecy referred to the church and the calling of the Gentiles during the Pax Romana, even though the terminology in it clearly points to Jewish references such as the temple and the torah.[10] Stacey thinks the language used in the oracle is to be read as metaphor, not as a description of a new cosmology.[11] Likely, however, the phrase simply

---

[5] Otto Kaiser, *Isaiah 1–12: A Commentary* (Philadelphia: Westminster Pr., 1983), 52.

[6] Ollenburger, *Zion*, 154.

[7] Ibid., 161.

[8] The use of "latter day" language in relation to people coming to know YHWH is found in Ezek. 38:16. The phrase is also found in Gen. 49:1; Jer. 49:39; Num. 24:14; Deut. 4:30, 31:29; Jer. 23:20, 30:24, 48:47; Hos. 3:5; Dan. 10:14.

[9] Edward J. Young, *The Book of Isaiah* (Grand Rapids: Eerdmans, 1965), 97.

[10] Robert L. Wilkin, "In novissimis diebus: Biblical Promises, Jewish Hopes and Early Christian Exegesis [Isa 2:1-4; Micah 4:1-7]" *Journal of Early Christian Studies* 1 (spring 1993): 1, 5.

[11] Stacey, *Isaiah*, 16.

designates an unspecified future time and not the end of the age. R. E. Clements notes that this phrase is a "recurrent formula for the introduction of prophetic messages of hope about the future."[12]

The establishing of the mountain of the house of YHWH at the head or top of the mountains, lifted up above the hills, refers the reader to traditional Canaanite and Mesopotamian symbolism that understood high mountains to be the dwelling place of the gods. Jerusalem itself is not located on a high mountain, but its symbolic role elevates it. The Septuagint, an early Greek translation of this text, omits "house" in Mic. 4:1. The phrase "the mountain of YHWH" appears, rather than "the mountain of the house of YHWH." In the second verse, the phrase "the mountain of YHWH" is used. In Isaiah, "the mountain of the house of YHWH" is the terminology used in verse two. In verse three, the phrase "the mountain of YHWH" appears. Hans Wildberger believes that "the mountain of YHWH" is the correct version because the verb that appears there is not typically used in conjunction with the temple.[13] "House of X," when X refers to a god, is a reference to a temple.

Isaiah's nearly universalistic statement, "All nations will flow to it" (but not *all the people in all the nations*), is replaced by the less specific "people(s) will flow to it" in Mic. 4:1. Isaiah 2:4 reports that "many people(s) will come," while Micah claims that "many nations will come" (4:2). Both envision a world beyond Israel, but Micah's vision is not as encompassing as that of Isaiah. The people say, "Come!" (m. imperative) and "let us go up to the mountain of YHWH, to the house of the God of Jacob, and he will teach us his ways and we will walk in his paths." Stacey observes, "Ways and paths provided a certain security and so gave grounds for confidence."[14] Odil Hannes Steck points out that "this prophecy converts the traditional notion of an attack of the nations on Zion into its positive opposite."[15] In the Isaiah and Micah passages, the people come to Zion in peace to learn God's ways. The text does not indicate what prompts these people to do so, though clearly they already have an inkling that something can be learned there that is desirable. One expects that either by observing the deportment, values, standards of justice, and right living of the people of YHWH, or by conversation with them, Gentiles learn enough to know they want more. It is also

---

[12] R. E. Clements, *Isaiah 1–39* (Grand Rapids: Eerdmans, 1980), 40.

[13] Hans Wildberger, *Isaiah 1–12: A Commentary* (Minneapolis: Fortress Pr., 1991), 82.

[14] Stacey, *Isaiah*, 17.

[15] Odil Hannes Steck, "The Jerusalem Conceptions of Peace and Their Development in the Prophets of Ancient Israel," in *The Meaning of Peace: Biblical Studies*, ed. Perry B. Yoder and Willard M. Swartley (Louisville: Westminster John Knox, 1992), 64.

possible that they are just dissatisfied with their lives or feel an inner tug toward something greater than they are. Notice that the destination is not a shrine of spiritual significance in their own religious traditions. They go to a particular place, the mountain of YHWH, where the house of the God of Jacob is located. They expect to learn the ways of YHWH directly from YHWH. YHWH is in the role of teacher in this text. Christopher Seitz understands Israel to be among the nations that seek to learn the ways of YHWH.[16] This is quite possible, but the text may also be implying that Israel is doing the teaching on behalf of YHWH because Zion-Jerusalem is Israel's premier shrine city. As my first Hebrew instructor, Dr. Livia Bitton, pointed out, a remarkable thing in this passage is how naturally people invite one another to accompany them to the house of YHWH to learn the ways and paths of YHWH. It is as natural to them as inviting friends to a feast or recreational event.

"From Zion, instruction *(torah)* goes forth and the word of YHWH from Jerusalem" (2:3f,g). The movement inward to Zion is followed by movement away from Zion. The torah and the word of YHWH go forth from Jerusalem. The text does not say how this happens. Delbert Hillers thinks the "word of YHWH" may be understood to refer to the prophetic word because it is used in that sense elsewhere.[17] Hence, the prophets are taking it forth. It may also be that the people themselves take the teaching from Zion to their home places or perhaps to other places in the world. The emphasis seems to be on the place from which this torah goes out, Zion-Jerusalem. It is a particular vision. In this text, torah is not manifest in other places in the world. Surprisingly, the content of the instruction is not given. It is not said to be the Torah of Moses. It is just torah. Whatever the content of this torah is, it causes people to reorient themselves and redirect the passions of their life.

"He [or perhaps 'it,' referring to the *word of YHWH*] will judge between the nations [Micah: 'many peoples'] and decide for many peoples [Micah: 'mighty nations far away']." YHWH functions as both teacher and judge in this text. As a result of this direct intervention by the deity in human disputes, people will freely choose to recycle their weapons of war into implements of agriculture.[18] They will refrain both

---

[16] Christopher R. Seitz, *Isaiah 1–39* (Louisville: John Knox Pr., 1993), 39.

[17] Delbert R. Hillers, *Micah: A Commentary on the Book of the Prophet Micah* (Philadelphia: Fortress Pr., 1984), 51.

[18] See Joel 4:10 for a reversal of this statement. Hans Walter Wolff explains that this text is to be understood sarcastically. He writes, "The phrase 'plowshares into swords' makes a blunt mockery of the world powers, who think that by completely arming themselves . . . they will have power and superiority over the people of God" (Hans Walter Wolff, "Swords into Plowshares: Misuse of a Word of Prophecy?" in *The Meaning of Peace: Biblical*

from engaging in war and from learning the art of war. As Norman Gottwald points out, war is learned behavior.[19] It is not innate. Notice that YHWH does not force people to give up their warring habits. The people, themselves, choose to do this after their encounter with God. Walking in the way of YHWH precludes both the practice of war and war education. Prior to a change in behavior and practice, however, there must be a change in the thinking of the people, and this is exactly what occurs.

Gottwald thinks the arbitrator (judge) in the text is the prophet, who conveys the word of God,[20] but this is unlikely, particularly in Micah's thought, given the low opinion of prophets evident in Mic. 3:11. Clements has another spin on it. He believes this is a reference to "a tradition of an administration of justice and law through the divinely appointed (Davidic) king."[21] There may be an allusion to such a king in Mic. 5:2–5.

There is a difference of opinion about whether verse five, the call to Jacob to walk in the light of YHWH, belongs to this poem or the next passage. Although the statement probably was not original to the poem, it seems likely that for Isaiah it belongs with it. The call to "Come!" is the same word as that used in verse three. "Let us walk" is the same as the "let us walk" of verse three. It is a call to Israel to begin to live out the vision.

Micah has a different and longer ending for the poem. "Each person will sit under his/her vine and fig tree and no one will make them afraid, for the mouth of YHWH of hosts has spoken." John Oswalt points out that the phrase "the mouth of YHWH has spoken" appears solely in Isaiah except for the Micah text where the variation "the mouth of YHWH of hosts has spoken" appears.[22] In each case, it signals the end of a statement. In light of the diatribe in the preceding chapter, one asks whether the fear of these people comes solely from the foreign nations. Some of their own leaders are also to be feared, those who "build Zion with blood and Jerusalem with injustice" (3:10). In Micah, the people are going to reclaim their own shalom without the help of corrupt leaders.

Studies, ed. Perry B. Yoder and Willard M. Swartley [Louisville: Westminster John Knox, 1992], 112).

[19] Norman K. Gottwald, *All the Kingdoms of the Earth: Israelite Prophecy and International Relations in the Ancient Near East* (New York: Harper & Row, 1964), 202.

[20] Ibid.

[21] Clements, *Isaiah 1–39*, 41.

[22] See Isa. 1:20, 40:5, and 58:14. John N. Oswalt, *The Book of Isaiah: Chapter 1–39* (Grand Rapids: Eerdmans, 1986), 115.

Individual ideas in the vision occur in other prophetic texts. S. H. Widyapranawa combines them in this manner: "The nations go up to Zion to worship the LORD (Zec 8:20–23; 14:16; Isa 66:20); there the nations seek the 'instruction' of the LORD (Isa 42:4); all weapons of war are destroyed (Hos 2:18)."[23] In Isaiah and Micah, the latter two of these three are brought together. There is no reference, however, to the following types of worship in the Isaiah or Micah texts: "bowing down" (Zech. 14:16), "bringing gifts" (Isa. 66:20), "entreat[ing] the favor" or "seek[ing] YHWH of hosts" (Zech. 8:20–23). These are not a part of the agenda of the peoples and nations as they go to Zion. The worship they desire is cognitive. They seek instruction. They want to learn.

Understanding the oracle to date from the eighth century B.C.E., Gottwald concludes that the prophet was frustrated with nations seeking their own national interests while not taking into view the larger picture.[24] In his political reading of this text, Gottwald writes that two things are needed for peace between nations to become a reality, "a common frame of reference for settling differences among nations and . . . a machinery of adjudication which will make war unnecessary."[25] Clements writes that the oracle "expresses a softening and re-minting of the imperialistic notion of a world capital into the more positively religious idea of a center to which the nations come to find truth, justice and peace."[26] If, however, the poem was inserted at a later time, it would seem rather to affirm a continued role for Jerusalem on the world stage. Herbert understands the poem to point to "the fulfillment of the ancient covenant promise that Israel will be the Lord's kingdom of priests, keeping and teaching the divine instruction for all mankind."[27]

A new/old thesis has been articulated by Baruch Schwartz concerning these texts. He vehemently denies that they refer to a universal Gentile pilgrimage to Zion and conversion of the Gentiles. Following the Jewish Publication Society translation, Schwartz translates "see" based on the JPS "gaze" rather than "stream" or "flow" in Isa. 2:2 because, he argues, it does not make sense that people would stream before they call to each other to come. He argues that "streaming" is not a logical

---

[23] S. H. Widyapranawa, *The Lord Is Savior: Faith in National Crisis: A Commentary on the Book of Isaiah 1-39* (Grand Rapids: Eerdmans, 1990), 12.

[24] Gottwald, *All the Kingdoms,* 199.

[25] Ibid.

[26] Clements, *Isaiah 1–39,* 40.

[27] Herbert, *The Book of the Prophet Isaiah,* 35.

translation, because "streaming upwards is patently impossible."[28] He bases this translation on the work of R. Jonah ibn Janah and the translation "light" for the נָהֲרוּ (nāhărû) which he understands to derive from the noun נְהָרָה (nĕhārâ), "light" (the verbal form is "shine, beam"[29] and "be radiant"[30]), rather than נָהַר (nahar) meaning "flow" or "stream." Schwartz concludes that all the nations see, but do not stream to the mountain.[31] Schwartz states that only people who "have disputes to settle" will come.[32] He suggests an emendation of the Masoretic text to support this reading. Instead of "many people," he suggests "disputing peoples."[33] Disputing peoples come to have their conflicts resolved in the Israelite court. Comparing the Isaiah text to Deut. 17:8–11, he reads this text as limited to the legal system of Israel. "Isaiah . . . is expressing . . . the idea that the social and legal system of the Israelites, based on wise and equitable civil laws, is worthy of admiration and of imitation."[34]

Schwartz is correct about conversion of the Gentiles. There is no explicit statement that the Gentiles are converted. They go to learn the ways of YHWH so they may walk in the divine paths. This could be construed as falling short of conversion. Furthermore, there is no reference to putting away other gods, a sign of conversion found in other texts. Micah follows the vision with a statement that "all of the peoples walk, each in the name of its god, but we will walk in the name of the LORD our God forever and ever" (4:5, NRSV). This statement assumes that the people keep their own gods. In reply to his objection to the streaming imagery: metaphors often are illogical (Isa. 55:12) and should not be taken too literally. The point is that people will come in large numbers. The problem with the translation "see" is that it is a leap from the noun "light" or a verb meaning "shine" to the translation "see." Hebrew words that clearly mean "see" are not used here. Swartz stresses that "many nations" but not "all" will come.[35] He writes that all nations

---

[28] Baruch J. Schwartz, "Torah from Zion: Isaiah's Temple Vision (Isaiah 2:1–4)," in *Sanctity of Time and Space in Tradition and Modernity*, ed. A. Houtman, M. J. H. M. Poorthuis, J. Schwartz (Leiden: E. J. Brill, 1998), 15.

[29] Francis Brown, S. R. Driver, Charles A. Briggs, *A Hebrew and English Lexicon of the Old Testament* (Oxford: Clarendon Pr., 1906; reprint, 1951).

[30] Ludwig Koehler and Walter Baumgartner, *The Hebrew and Aramaic Lexicon of the Old Testament* (Leiden: E. J. Brill, 1994).

[31] Schwartz, *Torah from Zion*, 14–15.

[32] Ibid., 21.

[33] Ibid.

[34] Ibid., 24.

[35] Ibid., 21.

will "see" but not all will come. If, however, "stream" is the appropriate translation, then all the nations are streaming to Zion, according to Isaiah. Micah envisions people flowing and many nations coming. Micah does not use "all" language in 4:1–3.

A critical question is, what is the difference between "nations" and "people(s)" in the thought of ancient Israel? The concept of "nation" is a modern one. The use of that word in English translations of the Bible connotes an entity that did not exist in the ancient world. The word עַמִּים ('ammîm) may refer to kin groups or people in general that may or may not be related. The word גּוֹיִם (gôyim) refers to the population of an area. Frequently, it specifies non-Israelite populations (though occasionally it is used for Israel and Judah as well).[36] Isaiah has a large vision, though not a universal one. "All nations" does not necessarily mean all of the people in all of the nations. Furthermore, contra Schwartz, the language of the text suggests that the people are coming not just to settle disputes, but to learn of YHWH's ways so they may walk in YHWH's paths. As Steck says, "They are seeking the wholesome life order of Yahweh."[37] Hillers notes of the Micah passage that a "fundamental change is in mind."[38] They go to Zion because that is where torah and the word of YHWH are. The transformation of the thinking and behavior of these assorted people leads to a decision on their part to stop fighting one another.

CONCLUSIONS

In summary, this reading of the "latter day" texts of Isaiah and Micah understands the vision to apply to both Israel and the Gentiles. Israel, however, has a head start because the destination is the house of the God of Jacob (Israel). Isaiah includes all nations and many people in the vision. Micah's vision is limited to "people" and many nations, though all people benefit when war is no longer a reality. The people wend their way up to a particular place, Zion-Jerusalem, to learn the divine ways so they may be followed. The prompting to go to Zion for education and transformation must come from somewhere, though the text does not indicate from where. It may emanate from the deity, from other people, or from dissatisfaction with life as it is. The movement inward is followed by movement outward. Torah and the word of YHWH do not stay at Zion. They go out from there, perhaps taken out by the pilgrims

---

[36] For a discussion of the terminology, see the Koehler-Baumgartner and Brown Driver Briggs lexicons.

[37] Steck, "The Jerusalem Conceptions of Peace," 64.

[38] Hillers, *Micah*, 50–1.

on their return journey. Either YHWH or the word of YHWH judges between the nations. The judging does not lead to punishment but to transformation. Of their own free will, the people themselves convert their weapons of war to implements for agriculture. The changes in their behavior result from new knowledge and insight.

4 | *Light to the nations in Isaiah's servant songs*

IVAN FRIESEN

THE IDEA OF ISRAEL AS A LIGHT TO THE NATIONS IN Isaiah's servant songs implies two things: that Israel has a light, and that this light ought to be shared rather than kept to itself. Israel's light may be understood to be its covenant relationship with Yahweh, including Yahweh's instruction (*torah*). The sharing of this light with the nations would then signify the distribution of both the relationship and the instruction to the benefit of all.

Whether such a mission carries with it a fundamental commitment to peacemaking depends on how Yahweh's instruction is read. Read through the lenses of the way things are and must always be, the mission's commitment to peacemaking is limited by politics as the art of the possible. Read through the lenses of the reign of God, the mission's commitment to peacemaking is limited only by what is possible with God.

The servant songs of Isaiah are the prism through which Israel's light will be refracted in this essay. Isaiah 49:6 serves as a focus text within the songs. Here Yahweh gives his servant as "a light to the nations" so that Yahweh's salvation "may reach to the end of the earth." The prophet serves as mediator of Yahweh's word to the exiles through the servant so that a remnant of the exiles, in turn, may carry the torch of Yahweh's blessing to the nations.

ISAIAH'S SERVANT SONGS

Four poems in the second part of the book of Isaiah have come to be called servant songs (42:1–4; 49:1–6; 50:4–9; and 52:13–53:12). They are songs only in the general sense that they are poetical compositions available to a musician's artistry. There is general agreement that the songs are distinguishable from the other poetry around them. The debate among scholars is whether the songs should be or can be detached from the surrounding poetry or whether they are integral to it. I take the latter position in the debate. Brevard Childs is right in arguing that the servant songs belong in the literary context where they are found.[1]

There is general agreement that the songs are four in number, although the compass of the songs is debated. The four songs refer to a servant figure (the servant figure is implied in the third song). This servant is presented sometimes as an individual (Israelite) and sometimes as a community (Israel). But precisely when the individual speaks and when the community speaks cannot be easily determined. Opposition to the servant increases from the first to the last song, until in the last song the servant receives the death penalty.

THE NATIONS AND A GREAT NATION IN GENESIS

The origin of the nations receives an explanation in the book of Genesis. Genesis 11 tells the tower of Babel story (11:1–9). The story describes the earth as once inhabited by one people with one language and tells how this one people became scattered throughout the earth into many peoples with many languages. The story provides an explanation of how the family of nations came into being.

Preceding the tower story is the genealogy of Noah and his three sons, the so-called "table of the nations" in Genesis 10. Following the tower story is the genealogy of one of Noah's sons, Shem, the so-called "genealogy of Abraham" in Genesis 11. The tower story interrupts these genealogies to explain the origin of the nations and to provide a context for the origin of a great nation in Genesis 12.

In Genesis 12, then, Abram receives the promise that his offspring will become a great nation. A blessing on Abram and his family and through them a blessing on all the families of the earth lies at the center of the promise. Genesis 18 reaffirms the promise to Abraham and his family and to the nations through him. Abraham is charged to "keep the way of the LORD by doing righteousness and justice" (18:19). In this way the promise to Abraham concerning the great nation and the nations may be fulfilled. The blessing begins with a great nation, but its ultimate goal is the nations as a whole.

Genesis 12 serves as a programmatic text in the Bible. A programmatic text is one that has a trajectory in the larger and longer biblical story. The trajectory takes the text through various transformations as it is reinterpreted for new and different historical situations and needs. In the servant songs of Isaiah, for example, the prophet seeks to persuade the Judean exiles in Babylon that the purpose of the great nation in the

---

[1] Brevard S. Childs, *Isaiah*, The Old Testament Library (Louisville: Westminster John Knox Pr., 2001), 325.

promise to Abraham is now being fulfilled in Israel's mission to the nations.

In the New Testament, to take another example, Paul alludes to Genesis 12 in Galatians 3, where he reasons that those who believe receive a blessing "with Abraham who believed" (3:7–9) and that in Christ Gentiles share in the blessing originally given to Abraham (3:14)

FIRST SERVANT SONG, ISAIAH 42:1–4

> [1]*Here is my servant, whom I uphold,*
>   *my chosen, in whom my soul delights;*
> *I have put my spirit upon him;*
>   *he will bring forth justice to the nations.*
> [2]*He will not cry or lift up his voice,*
>   *or make it heard in the street;*
> [3]*a bruised reed he will not break,*
>   *and a dimly burning wick he will not quench;*
>   *he will faithfully bring forth justice.*
> [4]*He will not grow faint or be crushed*
>   *until he has established justice in the earth;*
>   *and the coastlands wait for his teaching.*

The first song consists of three four-line stanzas.[2] Each stanza has its own topic: 42:1 focuses on the servant's presentation, 42:2–3a on the servant's behavior, and 42:3b–4 on the servant's mission. Yahweh's word is addressed to Jacob-Israel in exile (cf. Isa. 45).

Yahweh has a servant, to whom Yahweh gives his spirit: "I have put [נָתַתִּי | *nātattî*] my spirit upon him" (42:1). The first servant song emphasizes the gift of Yahweh's spirit on his servant. This gift of the spirit works itself out as a mandate to bring justice and to foster Yahweh's teaching among the nations.

The personal character of this servant receives special attention in the song.[3] The servant demonstrates sensitivity to the weak (bruised reed) and empathy with the faint (dimly burning wick). The servant moves about with gentle poise and humility, unhurried in the pursuit of justice.

The production of justice forms the servant's mission. This mission is broadly conceived to include the nations and the earth as a whole. Nations, earth, and coastlands signify the domain of Yahweh's action.

---

[2] I use the NRSV layout for the text of the songs but my stanza divisions usually do not follow the NRSV's poetic structure.

[3] John Barton, "Ethics in the Book of Isaiah," in *Writing and Reading the Scroll of Isaiah: Studies of an Interpretive Tradition*, ed. Craig C. Broyles and Craig A. Evans (Leiden: E. J. Brill, 1997), 1:75.

The servant moves undeterred to establish justice in the earth. The earth's (coastlands') job is to await his teaching.

The language here is similar to the vision of Isa. 2:1–5 and 11:1–9. There the goal of an end to war rests on the teachings of Yahweh (2:1–5), and the spirit of Yahweh guarantees equity "for the meek of the earth" (11:1–9). There Israel (house of Jacob) serves as Yahweh's agent to lead the way to peace on earth. Here the goal of justice to the nations also rests on Yahweh's teaching. But Yahweh's spirit-filled servant engages in the teaching. This servant acts as Yahweh's agent to lead the way to justice in the earth.[4] He does not teach about justice in the usual sense of teaching but models justice by his own behavior and personality.

The immediate context of the song is its sequel in 42:5–9. While third person pronouns in the song describe the servant, the sequel employs second person pronouns to address the servant. In the singular pronoun "you" addressed to the servant, Yahweh appoints a human agent for this work among the nations and in the earth. He gives this agent as "a covenant to the people" and as "a light to the nations." Whether understood as an individual (Israelite) or as a community (Israel), the servant's appointment reads as the celebration of a new day. The relationship of people and nations to the Lord and to each other will be restored. By carrying out his appointment, the servant conveys the blessing promised in Gen. 12:3.[5]

In sum, Yahweh's servant is introduced to Jacob-Israel in exile in the first servant song. The servant, by his gentle behavior and longsuffering persistence, teaches the nations justice by modeling justice in his own life.

SECOND SERVANT SONG, ISAIAH 49:1–6

> [1]*Listen to me, O coastlands,*
>   *pay attention, you peoples from far away!*
> *The LORD called me before I was born,*
>   *while I was in my mother's womb he named me.*
> [2]*He made my mouth like a sharp sword,*
>   *in the shadow of his hand he hid me;*
> *he made me a polished arrow,*
>   *in his quiver he hid me away.*
> [3]*And he said to me, "You are my servant,*
>   *Israel, in whom I will be glorified."*
> [4]*But I said, "I have labored in vain,*
>   *I have spent my strength for nothing and vanity;*

---

[4] Walter Brueggemann, *Isaiah 40–66*, Westminster Bible Companion (Louisville: Westminster John Knox Pr., 1998), 42.

[5] Ibid., 44.

yet surely my cause is with the LORD,
and my reward with my God."

⁵And now the LORD says,
who formed me in the womb to be his servant,
to bring Jacob back to him,
and that Israel might be gathered to him,
for I am honored in the sight of the LORD,
and my God has become my strength—
⁶he says, "It is too light a thing that you should be my servant
to raise up the tribes of Jacob
and to restore the survivors of Israel;
I will give you as a light to the nations,
that my salvation may reach to the end of the earth."

The second song consists of two parts: one part focuses on the servant's calling (49:1, 2), and a second part focuses on the servant's formation (49:3–4, 5, 6). The speaker is the servant, and the servant addresses coastlands and far-away peoples, but he is still speaking to Jacob-Israel in exile.

I take the coastlands and far-away peoples as a poetic allusion to the nation states of what is called, in modern times, the ancient Near East. This area would include nation states on the rim of the Mediterranean as well as the empires on the Nile and Tigris-Euphrates river systems. It is difficult to determine how the servant would have addressed these nations. Perhaps it was to an assembly of exiled Judeans in Babylon that he spoke. I do not assume that the nations were in attendance at this assembly.

We meet the speaker first as an unidentified voice calling the nations to attention (49:1). The nations are made to understand that they have to contend with someone having authority rising out of a divine calling (49:2). The servant's mouth is compared to a sharp sword, indicating a capacity to speak truth to power regardless of consequences.

The unidentified voice recalls how Yahweh addressed him as "my servant" and how he objected to such a calling (49:3–4). Yahweh identifies his servant with Israel, the grandson of Abraham and Sarah. This Israel is meant to be understood as a collectivity of individuals gathered into one people. The servant's despair reflected in 49:4 overlays a fundamental trust that "my cause [מִשְׁפָּטִי | *mišpāṭî*] is with the LORD."

The second servant song emphasizes Yahweh's gift of the servant as a light to the nations: "I will give you [נְתַתִּיךָ | *nĕtattîkā*] as a light to the nations" (49:6). The purpose of this light is to extend Yahweh's salvation to the end of the earth. Salvation means release from the crippling physical circumstances of life as well as deliverance from the spiritual bondage of sin and the forging of a new relationship with God.

The servant's fundamental trust becomes clear in what follows, where the servant describes his formation for servanthood (49:5). This formation includes the servant's calling to bring and gather Jacob-Israel. This means, in particular, reshaping the exilic Jacob-Israel into a new people. The old Jacob-Israel experienced the exodus from Egypt and the calling to be a covenant people at Mt. Sinai. Now a new people will be built up from the old.

In the conclusion to the second servant song, two assignments stand side by side (49:6). First, there is the servant's mission to bring back and gather, to raise up and restore Jacob-Israel. I take this to be the servant's teaching mission to the great nation (Israel). Yahweh declares this mission to be easy! This statement is something surprising in light of the servant's despair about his work in 49:4. Nevertheless, because it is easy, the servant will be given a more challenging assignment: "I will give you as a light to the nations, that my salvation may reach to the end of the earth."

So Yahweh assigns a second task to the servant. As bearer of light and salvation to the nations and beyond, Yahweh gives his servant a mandate to go beyond the frontiers of Jacob-Israel to the Gentiles. "Light and salvation" in 49:6 serve as words with meaning equivalent to "blessing" in the promise to Abraham in Gen. 12:3 that in him "all the families of the earth shall be blessed."

The immediate context of the second servant song is its sequel in 49:7–12. The messenger formula "Thus says the LORD" introduces verse 7 and again verses 8–12. Yahweh addresses his servant first with regard to the nations and their kings and princes (v. 7). While the nations as a whole detest the servant for acting on behalf of Jacob-Israel, those in power (kings and princes) respect him because they respect Yahweh's power enacted through his servant.

Yahweh addresses his servant a second time with regard to Jacob-Israel (8–12). If "prisoners" and "darkness" are understood as images of exile, the servant urges the exiles to leave their captivity and claim their identity as God's people again.[6]

To summarize, the servant gives testimony to his call in the second servant song. In contrast to the first song, where Yahweh commends the servant's behavior in the rendering of justice in the earth, in the second song the servant yields to despair in the rendering of justice in the earth even as he continues his work in the confidence of Yahweh's blessing.

In the second song it becomes clear that the servant's work begins with Jacob-Israel. I take this to mean the redemption of Jacob-Israel as

---

[6] Ibid., 113–14.

Yahweh's mission-inspired people. Such a people will bear the torch of Yahweh's instruction on nonviolence as a light to the nations.

THIRD SERVANT SONG, ISAIAH 50:4–9

> [4]*The Lord GOD has given me*
>   *the tongue of a teacher,*
> *that I may know how to sustain*
>   *the weary with a word.*
> *Morning by morning he wakens—*
>   *wakens my ear*
>   *to listen as those who are taught.*
> [5]*The Lord GOD has opened my ear,*
>   *and I was not rebellious,*
>   *I did not turn backward.*
> [6]*I gave my back to those who struck me,*
>   *and my cheeks to those who pulled out the beard;*
> *I did not hide my face*
>   *from insult and spitting.*
>
> [7]*The Lord GOD helps me;*
>   *therefore I have not been disgraced;*
> *therefore I have set my face like flint,*
>   *and I know that I shall not be put to shame;*
>   [8]*he who vindicates me is near.*
> *Who will contend with me?*
>   *Let us stand up together.*
> *Who are my adversaries?*
>   *Let them confront me.*
> [9]*It is the Lord GOD who helps me;*
>   *who will declare me guilty?*
> *All of them will wear out like a garment;*
>   *the moth will eat them up.*

A word of Yahweh serves as a preface to the song (50:1–3). This word has the form of a disputation but the disputation is not closely connected to the song. The addressee ("you" plural) refers to Israel under discipline.

The third song consists of two parts: one part highlights the servant's gifts of speaking and listening (50:4, 5–6) and one part focuses on Yahweh as the servant's helper (50:7, 8, 9).

Although the word "servant" does not occur in the third song, scholars agree that it belongs with the other servant songs.[7] In this song the servant meditates on how Yahweh helped him in his nonviolent behavior.

---

[7] John D. W. Watts, *Isaiah 34–66*, Word Biblical Commentary (Waco: Word Bks., 1987), 117.

What is the servant's task in the third song? The fourfold reference in the song to what Yahweh does for the servant is instructive. First, Yahweh gives the twin gifts of speaking and listening to his servant (50:4). These gifts are for nourishing the weary, a reference no doubt to the exiles in Babylon. Second, Yahweh opens his servant's ear and the servant listens (50:5). What he hears has to do with patient suffering in the face of brutality. Third, Yahweh helps his servant by instilling in him the courage to face without violence those who abuse him (50:7, 8). Fourth, Yahweh helps his servant by assuring him of his innocence (50:9). This means that the servant operates entirely under the direction and inspiration of Yahweh rather than under his own authority.

The third servant song emphasizes Yahweh's gift of encouraging speech to the servant: "The Lord has given [נָתַן | *nātan*] me the tongue of a teacher" (50:4). His credentials rest on what Yahweh has given him—teaching laced with encouragement. Beyond this the servant's credentials rest on the help and nearness of Yahweh that enable him to accept hostility without retaliation. Through Yahweh's help and nearness the servant gives a promise to the weary that their oppressors will exhaust themselves. The mission of the servant in the third servant song is a teaching mission directed toward Jacob-Israel.

The sequel to the song refers specifically to Yahweh's servant (50:10–11). Here it seems best to understand the speaker as the prophet himself. He exhorts Israel to trust in the Lord (50:10). He addresses those in particular who do not respond to Yahweh's discipline (50:11). Fire is their punishment.[8]

To summarize, the nations do not appear in the preface to the third song, in the song itself, or in the sequel. The servant's entire testimony has to do with his teaching of Yahweh's word to his own people. His teaching (theory) parallels his nonviolence (practice) even as his people reject his testimony.[9]

FOURTH SERVANT SONG, ISAIAH 52:13–53:12

> [13]*See, my servant shall prosper;*
>   *he shall be exalted and lifted up,*
>   *and shall be very high.*
> [14]*Just as there were many who were astonished at him*
>   *—so marred was his appearance, beyond human semblance,*
>   *and his form beyond that of mortals—*

---

[8] Brueggemann, *Isaiah 40–66*, 125.

[9] Millard C. Lind, "Monotheism, Power, and Justice: A Study in Isaiah 40–55," in *Monotheism, Power, Justice: Collected Old Testament Essays*, Text Reader, no. 3 (Elkhart: Institute of Mennonite Studies, 1990), 161.

¹⁵so he shall startle many nations;
    kings shall shut their mouths because of him;
for that which had not been told them they shall see,
    and that which they had not heard they shall contemplate.
¹Who has believed what we have heard?
    And to whom has the arm of the LORD been revealed?
²For he grew up before him like a young plant,
    and like a root out of dry ground;
he had no form or majesty that we should look at him,
    nothing in his appearance that we should desire him.
³He was despised and rejected by others;
    a man of suffering and acquainted with infirmity;
and as one from whom others hid their faces
    he was despised, and we held him of no account.
⁴Surely he has borne our infirmities
    and carried our diseases;
yet we accounted him stricken,
    struck down by God, and afflicted.
⁵But he was wounded for our transgressions,
    crushed for our iniquities;
upon him was the punishment that made us whole,
    and by his bruises we are healed.
⁶All we like sheep have gone astray;
    we have all turned to our own way,
and the LORD has laid on him
    the iniquity of us all.

⁷He was oppressed, and he was afflicted,
    yet he did not open his mouth;
like a lamb that is led to the slaughter,
    and like a sheep that before its shearers is silent,
    so he did not open his mouth.
⁸By a perversion of justice he was taken away.
    Who could have imagined his future?
For he was cut off from the land of the living,
    stricken for the transgression of my people.
⁹They made his grave with the wicked
    and his tomb with the rich,
although he had done no violence,
    and there was no deceit in his mouth.

¹⁰Yet it was the will of the LORD to crush him with pain.
When you make his life an offering for sin,
    he shall see his offspring, and shall prolong his days;
through him the will of the LORD shall prosper.
    ¹¹Out of his anguish he shall see light;
he shall find satisfaction through his knowledge.
    The righteous one, my servant, shall make many righteous,
    and he shall bear their iniquities.

> *12Therefore I will allot him a portion with the great,*
>   *and he shall divide the spoil with the strong;*
> *because he poured out himself to death,*
>   *and was numbered with the transgressors;*
> *yet he bore the sin of many,*
>   *and made intercession for the transgressors.*

The fourth servant song begins with Yahweh speaking about his servant (52:13–15). A "we" passage follows in which the speakers appear to be a remnant of the exiles who understand the servant's suffering (53:1–6).[10] Yahweh's voice responding to the exiles concludes the song (53:7–12).

The song begins by stating that Yahweh's servant shall "prosper" even as he shall "startle" (NRSV) kings and nations (52:13–15). The servant's prosperity describes his royal dominion.[11] His mission to the nations rests on the shock effect of a royal figure submitting to suffering rather than inflicting it. To whom is this word addressed? The word is addressed to kings and nations indirectly through Jacob-Israel's testimony. Kings and nations will come to see an alternative to war and violence because of the suffering servant.

The "we" section of the fourth song portrays the suffering of Yahweh's servant as perceived by Yahweh's people (53:1–6). These people move from disbelief (vv. 1–2), to contrition (v. 3), to dismay (v. 4), to conviction (v. 5), and finally, to belief (v. 6). In some way the servant's distress and disquiet bring healing to the people. His teaching mission is a witness to us, the voice of a remnant of Jacob-Israel. Is it any wonder that Jesus identified himself with this servant? Is it any wonder that the apostolic church saw in the servant of Isaiah a premonition of Jesus' suffering and death?

After the people have spoken, Yahweh's voice is heard in the remainder of the song (53:7–12). Now it becomes clear that while some of the people were convicted of their rebellion through the servant's witness, others were emboldened by their rebellion to see to it that the servant's witness should be extinguished (vv. 7–9).

But Yahweh works even through their rebellion to bring good out of evil intent (10–12). Because of his servant's obedience, Yahweh exalts him. Because the servant "poured out himself to death" rather than inflict death, he was able to bear the sin of all who call on Yahweh out of their rebellion.

The fourth servant song emphasizes the "gift" of a burial with evildoers: "They made [וַיִּתֵּן | *wayyittēn*] his grave with the wicked" (53:9). The beginning and end of the fourth song indicate that through the

---

10 Cf. Childs, *Isaiah*, 413.

11 Lind, "Monotheism, Power, and Justice," 162.

suffering servant's witness the nations will see the power of nonviolence that undergirds God's reign and brings peace on earth. The description of the servant's suffering occupies the center of the song (53:1–9). The servant who is "given" Yahweh's spirit to bring justice to the nations in 42:1 is here "given" a burial with evildoers, though he was no evildoer (53:9). Through it all it is obedience to Yahweh that inspires the servant to accept suffering rather than inflict it. The servant follows with obedience the vision of God's reign, defying both worldly wisdom and human cowardice.[12]

At the end of the song the servant brings blessings to many (53:10–12). Although the many are not precisely differentiated, it seems clear that they are those mentioned at the beginning of the song (52:13–15). There the many are the great nation (Yahweh's people) as well as the nations. Here the many are made righteous by one righteous person who bears their sins.

MISSION, PEACE, AND THE REIGN OF GOD

The servant's mission in the servant songs is a teaching mission moving in two directions: toward the great nation (Jacob-Israel) and toward the nations. The teaching mission to the great nation finds expression in the gathering and restoring of Jacob-Israel in the second servant song (49:5–6). In the third song the weary, understood as Jacob-Israel, are taught (50:4–6), and in the fourth song the witness is to us, the voice of a remnant of Jacob-Israel (53:1–6).

The teaching mission to the nations is demonstrated in the first song by the servant's mandate to establish justice and to promote Yahweh's teaching (42:4). The authorization to be a light to the nations appears in the second song (49:6). The tactic of startling nations by his appearance and bearing their sins occurs in the fourth song (52:15; 53:11–12).

The language of peace does not lie in the foreground of the servant's mission, as it would if the vocabulary of peace were used. Various forms of the Hebrew word שָׁלוֹם | *šalôm* (peace, wholeness, etc.) occur in the second part of the book of Isaiah but only once does this word occur in the servant songs themselves (53:5). Rather, the question of peace arises out of the behavior of the servant. In the first song the servant does not raise his voice in protest but exercises patience (42:2–3). The servant's mouth is compared to a sharp sword in the second song, indicating a capacity to speak truth to power regardless of consequences (49:2). In the third song the servant submits to violence without

---

12 Paul D. Hanson, *Isaiah 40–66*, Interpretation (Louisville: John Knox Pr., 1995), 160.

retaliation (50:5–6), and in the fourth song the servant is silent before his torturers (53:4–7).

Wherever "the nations" appear in the servant songs, they refer to the wider scope of Yahweh's concern for the earth. In particular, they refer to earth's people outside "the great nation." "The nations" refers to those on whom Yahweh intends to extend his blessing.

In the first song, justice flows from Yahweh through his servant to the nations and to the earth. In the second song, light and salvation flow from Yahweh through his servant to the nations and to the end of the earth. In the fourth song, nations and kings are reduced to silence by Yahweh's servant, who appears as exalted and as debased.

In all of the servant songs God's reign is evident in the servant's submission to God's spirit. The servant's faithfulness centers on his endowment with Yahweh's spirit and as Yahweh's choice (42:1). The servant's call and commission define his role as Yahweh's mouthpiece; his mission to Jacob-Israel lies at the forefront of his call. The servant's testimony is that Yahweh has given him a teacher's tongue, has opened his ear, has helped him, and is near him. Yahweh allots his servant greatness in contrast to his oppressors (53:9).

Yahweh's servant is to be light to the nations. The word "light" corresponds to the promise given to Abraham concerning a blessing on all the families of the earth. The servant songs do not use the specific language of blessing, nor does Genesis 12 use the language of light. But the significance of the blessing in Genesis 12 is embodied in the notion of light as good news to the nations in the servant songs.

The light to the nations in Isaiah's servant songs and the blessing to the nations in Genesis find common ground in the biblical notion of righteousness. Abraham "believed the LORD; and the LORD reckoned it to him as righteousness" (Gen. 15:6). Abraham is chosen to keep the Lord's way by doing righteousness and justice. This is Abraham's blessing to the nations. In Isaiah's servant songs, the servant provides an incarnation of righteousness in the sight of the nations. This is Isaiah's light to the nations. The selfless bearing of the sins of many nations stands as a beacon of an alternative to violence.

5 | *Will Jonah be saved?*

DOUGLAS B. MILLER

Or do you despise the riches of his kindness and forbearance and patience? Do you not realize that God's kindness is meant to lead you to repentance? (Rom. 2:4)

THE BOOK OF JONAH, SITUATED AMONG THE BOOK OF the Twelve in the Hebrew canon, presents a text that would seem better nestled among the tales of Elisha and Elijah than between the oracles of Obadiah and Micah. It offers an episode in the life of a Hebrew prophet, a bit of the miraculous in the form of a salvific giant fish, and only a sampling of oracle—a combination more reminiscent of texts involving the nonwriting than the writing prophets.

Its odd location is only one of several unusual features of the book. It is intriguing, for example, to notice that the Ninevites repent ("turned [שׁוב | *šwb*] from their wicked way," 3:10), and even God repents (שׁוב, 3:9; נחם | *nḥm*, 3:9, 10; 4:2). Yet the prophet himself, though disobedient, chastised and rebuked by God, fails to achieve his own repentance. As the book closes, we can only speculate about whether Jonah will persist in his resistance to God's program. Yes, sailors and Ninevites are delivered, but will Jonah be saved?

In this study of the book of Jonah, the method employed is rhetorical criticism of the classical type.[1] The structure and literary devices of the text will be explored to determine the goals toward which it sought to persuade its audience.[2]

---

[1] Aristotle defined rhetoric as "the faculty of discovering the possible means of persuasion . . . in reference to any given subject" (Aristotle, *The "Art" of Rhetoric*, Loeb Classical Library [1926], 1355b).

[2] Helpful introductions to the discipline of rhetorical criticism include Bernard L. Brock, Robert L. Scott, and James W. Chesebro, eds., *Methods of Rhetorical Criticism: A Twentieth-Century Perspective*, 3rd ed. (Detroit: Wayne State Univ. Pr., 1990), and the summaries by Phyllis Trible in *Rhetorical Criticism: Context, Method, and the Book of Jonah*, Guides to Biblical Scholarship: Old Testament Series (Minneapolis: Fortress Pr., 1994), 57–62. The current interest in rhetorical criticism in biblical studies is frequently traced to the work of James Muilenburg, particularly to his presidential address to the Society of Biblical Literature, published as "Form Criticism and Beyond," *Journal of Biblical Literature* 88 (1969): 1–18. Also

Previous interpretations of the book have rightly identified several important themes—such as its depiction of the deity (creator, deliverer, compassionate, free, concerned for Gentiles), the nature of prophecy, repentance, and ecology—although when seeking a central theme, commentators have frequently disagreed. Often, too, interpreters have suggested that the reader is being challenged through the character of Jonah. This essay demonstrates how the appeal to the reader is accomplished and the thematic heart of that appeal. The argument proceeds by two routes: first, that the story's focus is on the conflict between Jonah and God, and second, that the story is instructional, designed to motivate the reader's alignment with God's perspective in the dispute. At the intersection of these two routes, we find the heart of the book's rhetoric: (1) the persuasion of Jonah/the reader in regard to (2) compassion toward all of God's creation, including enemies.

In the final section, two valuable but incomplete readings of the book are assessed: one that focuses on inward dimensions of faith, and one that dwells on the outward call to action. The essay concludes by integrating the book's rhetoric with theological reflections concerning God's invitation to mission, the nature of God's peace, and a strategy for saving the people of God's reign.

Date, Genre, and Literary Integrity

Unlike other canonical works labeled with the name of a prophet, the book of Jonah contains no historical reference. The earliest possible date for the book is the eighth century B.C.E., the time of Jonah son of Ammitai according to 2 Kings 14:25. The reference in Sirach 49:10 to the "twelve prophets" implies its existence in the second century B.C.E. Plausible historical settings have been proposed everywhere in between, and yet the book contains few clues to the character or circumstances of its implied audience. Because of the nature of the book, some have seriously questioned the value of a more specific historical location. This essay will not posit a setting more precise than an Israelite target audience between the eighth and second centuries. Although this essay will not do so, it is interesting to contemplate the impact of the book on an Israelite audience at various points between the eighth and second centuries.

The question of the book's genre is also a difficult one. The story concerns a prophet, yet the term *prophet* is not used, and Jonah's prophetic word is not a major focus. The account has variously been labeled as history, folktale, fable, parable, didactic fiction, satire, parody, farce, allegory, and midrash, among others. The present study, though

---

noteworthy is the work of Edwin M. Good. The second chapter of his *Irony in the Old Testament* (Philadelphia: Westminster Pr., 1965) is devoted to the book of Jonah.

shunning a definitive category, will make a case for Jonah as an instructional narrative with "parable-like" qualities.[3]

Much attention has been paid to the psalm-like prayer of thanksgiving in chapter 2. Some have discounted its existence in the earliest version of the story, arguing that it does not fit Jonah's circumstances, whether spiritual (it includes no acknowledgement of disobedience) or physical (it celebrates deliverance while Jonah remains undelivered inside the fish).[4] However, such assessments fail to recognize that the omission of any reference to Jonah's disobedience is important to the characterization of Jonah, and that the fish itself is the instrument by which Jonah has been rescued from the sea.[5] As a prayer of thanksgiving, chapter 2 parallels the celebration of the pagan sailors for whom the sea was calmed in chapter 1 after they threw Jonah overboard. Within the structure of the book as a whole, chapter 2 represents a shift from the sailors to Jonah, just as chapter 4 will provide a shift from the Ninevites to Jonah.[6]

As for other matters of literary integrity, Jack Sasson in his commentary has helpfully listed aspects of the story that do or do not suggest unity throughout. On the side of discontinuity are differing divine names, variations in language, and reduplications of incidents, among other matters. On the side of unity are such factors as the story's symmetry of structure,[7] the role of God in the story, the parallel rephras-

---

[3] See discussions of date and genre by Jack M. Sasson, *Jonah: A New Translation with Introduction, Commentary, and Interpretation,* Anchor Bible, 24B (New York: Doubleday, 1990), 20–28; 327–40; and Phyllis Trible, *Jonah,* The New Interpreter's Bible, 7 (Nashville: Abingdon Pr., 1996), 467–74.

[4] So Bernhard W. Anderson, *Out of the Depths: The Psalms Speak for Us Today* (Philadelphia: Westminster Pr., 1974), 84.

[5] George M. Landes, "The Kerygma of the Book of Jonah: The Contextual Interpretation of the Jonah Psalm," *Interpretation* 21 (1967): 9–13. Landes also raises and responds to other arguments that the psalm is inappropriate in its placement or inclusion. He points out how the word *dag* is used rather than other terms that would indicate that this was a dangerous sea monster. In addition, the phrase "three days and three nights," in context here or in its occurrences elsewhere, does not suggest a punishment of or threat to Jonah; it simply indicates the time required to transport Jonah back to where he could receive a second chance to obey the divine instruction. See also George M. Landes, "The Three Days and Three Nights Motif in Jonah 2:1," *Journal of Biblical Literature* 86 (1967): 446–50. On the other hand, Trible (*Rhetorical Criticism,* 171–2) notes aspects of the psalm that indicate Jonah's distorted perception of reality (e.g., his protestation of faithfulness, his statement that God has cast him into the deep), so that the fish vomiting him on the shore reflects a bit of divine disgust. His eagerness to fulfill vows may imply his hope to scamper back to the Jerusalem temple, a possibility quickly precluded by the second divine summons in 3:1–2.

[6] So Landes, "Kerygma," 16; Trible, *Rhetorical Criticism,* 110–11.

[7] See Trible, *Rhetorical Criticism,* 110–11, and accompanying discussion.

ing of the divine command to Jonah (1:1–2; 3:1–2), an even distribution of marvels in each section, and various stylistic techniques.[8] In short, while it is plausible that the story developed in stages, there is artistic integrity in the received version. This essay discusses the text synchronically.

THE STORY'S FOCUS: THE CONFLICT BETWEEN GOD AND JONAH

The plot structure of God's action and Jonah's response

The roles played by Jonah and the deity are sustained throughout the story. These two are the only developed characters, the only ones to be named, and the only ones to be suggested in each of the four chapters. They disappear only for brief intervals to allow important aspects of the plot to be presented. The primary pattern of their interaction is that God acts and Jonah responds, a design that runs through the story's plot. This stands in particular relief when we consider a contrasting pattern: divine action and the response of others in the story. All of creation and the pagan world respond to God by cooperating: the storm, the sailors, the big fish, the Ninevites, the plant, the worm, even the lots cast by the sailors! Jonah is the only creature to resist and flee, a significant contrast that serves to develop Jonah's character.

The fate of the disobedient prophet provides one of two major plot tensions as the book proceeds. Jonah, after initial disobedience, reacts to God's discipline by carrying out his mandate. Through chapter 3, God's action and Jonah's response follow this pattern:

> *God calls Jonah*
> > *Jonah flees (chap. 1)*
> *God sends a mighty storm*
> > *Jonah asks to be thrown overboard (chap. 1)*
> *God allows Jonah to sink into the sea*
> > *Jonah prays for deliverance (chap. 2)*
> *God appoints a big fish to swallow Jonah*
> > *Jonah offers a prayer of thanks (chap. 2)*
> *God calls Jonah a second time*
> > *Jonah goes to Nineveh and proclaims a message (chap. 3)*

The threat of Nineveh's destruction—the other plot tension—is resolved when the Ninevites respond to Jonah's oracle of judgment by repenting, and God relents of the destruction initially planned. By the end of chapter 3, then, both tensions have been resolved and it seems time for the story to end.[9]

---

[8] Sasson, *Jonah*, 17–20.

[9] Walter B. Crouch, "To Question an End, to End a Question: Opening the Closure of the Book of Jonah," *Journal for the Study of the Old Testament* 62 (1994): 105.

But the narrator has misdirected us. The first three chapters reveal a strategy of ambiguation regarding Jonah.[10] Now to our surprise comes chapter 4 where the plot tension with Jonah continues on a different level.[11] The prophet, it becomes clear, has obeyed God only grudgingly. We note the subsequent pattern of God's action and Jonah's response:

> *God repents of the plan for Nineveh's destruction*
> > *Jonah becomes angry and angrily prays to God: "Take my life"*[12]
> *God responds with a challenging question: "Do you do well to be angry?"*
> > *Jonah travels outside the city to watch what will happen*
> *God appoints a plant*
> > *Jonah is happy*
> *God sends a worm to destroy the plant, a scorching east wind*
> > *Jonah is angry*
> *God questions Jonah: "Do you do well to be angry for the plant?"*
> > *Jonah replies: "I do well to be angry, angry enough to die"*
> *God questions Jonah: "Should I not pity Nineveh?"*
> > *—and no response is recorded—*

The book ends by breaking the pattern of God's action and Jonah's response.

The primary plot focus of the book is not on God and Nineveh. We might have expected that it would be there when God called a prophet to go to Nineveh in chapter 1, and again in chapter 3. But when Nineveh repents the story does not end. The events of chapter 4 make it clear that this first plot tension serves as the context for the second—and principal—one, the ongoing tension between God and Jonah.

---

[10] Ibid., 103–4. Kenneth Craig comments on the assumption of many commentators that the psalm of chapter 2 cannot be original because it does not match the mood of Jonah at the end of chapter 1. But Jonah's mood on being thrown into the sea is deliberately unclear, as is his motive for fleeing to Tarshish in the first place. His gratitude expressed in the psalm reflects his relief at being delivered from the sea, but no more. His obedient proclamation of judgment is recounted in chapter 3, but no presentation of inner life informs the reader of his thoughts, feelings, or purposes (Kenneth M. Craig, *A Poetics of Jonah: Art in the Service of Ideology* [Columbia: Univ. of South Carolina Pr., 1993], 149–50).

[11] Sasson (*Jonah*, 272) identifies conspicuously paired plays on words that accomplish a reversal of mood in the story, a clue that the narrator is investing much in this reversal. Craig (*A Poetics of Jonah*, 139) notes how the anger of Jonah at this climactic point is confirmed by three voices: those of the narrator (4:1), the Lord (4:4, 9), and Jonah (4:9).

[12] Sasson (Jonah, 273–5, 284–6, 297) makes a case that חרה (ḥrh) without the accompanying term אַף ('ap) need not indicate anger (so most commentators) but dejection or annoyance. He cites, e.g., Gen. 18:30, 32; 31:36; 1 Sam. 20:7; Neh. 3:33; 4:1. Dejection more than anger, he believes, fits Jonah's request that God take his life. This may be compared to Elijah's similar request (1 Kings 19:2–4), and that of a frustrated Moses (Num. 11:10–15). Whatever Jonah's exact emotion, the initial statement in 4:1 (that God's decision not to destroy Nineveh was a "great evil" to Jonah) is phrased as strongly as possible to indicate Jonah's extreme displeasure.

The significance of the story's final scene

Commentators have suggested a variety of themes and issues as the story's central concern.[13] For some, the focus is on the contrast between Israel and the Gentile nations, or the clash between universalism and particularism, or the tension between divine justice and mercy,[14] or the dilemma of false prophecy.[15] For others, the story proclaims the freedom of God or models the concept of repentance.[16] More popularly, the story of Jonah is connected with the outrageous miracle of Jonah's survival in the giant fish, and the driving question has often concerned its historicity. Certainly each of these matters is of some importance in appreciating the book.

One key to discerning the genuineness of a proposed central theme or focus in a story is whether it embraces the end of that story. For example, in the Joseph saga (Genesis 37–50), the prolonged sojourns of the sons of Jacob back and forth to Egypt are often overlooked, and in Jesus' parable of the "prodigal son" (Luke 15), the older brother is often given scant notice. Attention to the endings of these two narratives suggests that family issues, relationships among brothers, are important in both cases. Likewise we must ask the significance of chapter 4 of Jonah, the problem of shade, a plant, a worm, and hot wind.

Here our story ends with a tense exchange between God and Jonah, as well as a final penetrating question to Jonah from the deity. Three controversies in this concluding scene require comment because they affect the character of God's final exchange with Jonah. First, it is significant to determine whether Jonah's rationale for fleeing to Tarshish, (God's compassion, 4:2) is another example of delayed exposition in the

---

[13] See the summary by Alan Cooper, "In Praise of Divine Caprice: The Significance of the Book of Jonah," in *Among the Prophets: Language, Image, and Structure in the Prophetic Writings*, ed. Philip R. Davies and David J. A. Clines (Sheffield, England: JSOT Pr., 1993), 146 (and the literature cited there); the summaries given by Sasson, *Jonah*, 323–5; Trible, *Rhetorical Criticism*, 103; and Uriel Simon, *Jonah*, The JPS Bible Commentary (Philadelphia: Jewish Pubn. Society, 1999), vii–xiii; and the survey by James Limburg, *Jonah: A Commentary*, The Old Testament Library (Louisville: Westminster John Knox Pr., 1993), 99–123.

[14] In this connection, Elmer Martens highlights the creation motifs in the story. God demonstrates compassion on all of the created order. See Elmer A. Martens, "Yahweh's Compassion and Ecotheology," in *Problems in Biblical Theology: Essays in Honor of Rolf Knierim*, ed. Henry T. C. Sun and Keith L. Eades (Grand Rapids: Eerdmans, 1977), 244–8.

[15] Cooper, "In Praise," 146. Cooper believes the book concerns itself with divine freedom; he cites the other positions in summary.

[16] For the former, see Cooper, "In Praise," 150; and Hans Walter Wolff, *Obadiah and Jonah: A Commentary*, trans. Margaret Kohl (Minneapolis: Augsburg Publishing Hse., 1986), 177. For the latter, see the rabbinic texts cited in Simon, *Jonah*, vii–viii.

book (so most commentators),[17] or whether we are to understand that Jonah invented it, perhaps to justify his early (disobedient) action.[18] Reasons to accept the former explanation are several and include the following: (1) No other explanation for Jonah's flight is given, by the narrator or otherwise. (2) It is doubtful that Jonah would attempt pure fabrication expecting impunity when God would surely know the truth (although we may observe some self-serving distortions in the prayer of chapter 2). (3) The insight into Jonah's motives here is consistent with the pattern in the book, which has delayed and misdirected the reader's understanding of Jonah's inner character until this final climactic scene (see below). (4) The explanation Jonah gives strikes at the heart of the theological conflict between Jonah and God, which serves both the development of the plot's second and most important tension (Jonah's response to God) and the deity's final argument and appeal.[19] Thus, I conclude that Jonah is truthful: he fled to Tarshish because he thought God might be merciful to Nineveh (4:2).

However, Jack Sasson, though he accepts that Jonah is making an accurate statement of motivation in 4:2, raises two additional interconnected issues with implications for the story's final scene: the object of Jonah's intense emotion in 4:1–4, and the possible ambiguity of Jonah's message to Nineveh (3:4).

First, Sasson rejects the traditional explanation that Jonah was angry at God out of hatred for the Ninevites. He concludes that Jonah initially fled God's call because Jonah feared God would not adequately safeguard his prophetic credentials when he announced Nineveh's judgment. His later anger (or, as Sasson prefers, dejection) cited in chapter 4 is because God did not allow him a role in announcing the change of divine plans, a situation he anticipates will result in his humiliation and derision.[20]

---

[17] Other examples of delayed exposition include: (1) the comment in 1:5 that Jonah had previously gone below to the inner part of the ship; (2) the information in 1:10 that Jonah had previously told the sailors he was fleeing from the Lord; (3) the sequence in 1:17–2:1 [Heb. 2:1–2] informing us that the mariners offered sacrifices and vows, before the story returns to Jonah's plight and his rescue by the fish; and (4) the mention Jonah makes in his prayer (2:2 [Heb. 2:3]) that he called out for help before the fish rescued him.

[18] For example, Timothy L. Wilt believes Jonah was running to save his life ("Jonah: A Battle of Shifting Alliances," in *Among the Prophets*, ed. Davies and Clines, 165).

[19] Trible (*Rhetorical Criticism*, 199–200) takes this position and notes that Jonah now declares his own "word," given in his homeland, in order to vindicate himself against the Lord's "word" (given in 1:1 and 3:1–2).

[20] Sasson, *Jonah*, 237, 297.

The second part of Sasson's thesis concerns the term הפך (hpk) in the niphal stem (3:4), which may be interpreted either passively ("Nineveh shall be overturned," i.e., destroyed)[21] or reflexively ("Nineveh shall overturn itself," i.e., change or repent).[22] Thus, two possibilities may be seen in Jonah's declaration, something neither Jonah nor the Ninevites realize; they see it as a simple announcement of judgment.[23]

The rabbis who proposed this duality sought to deliver God from self-contradiction. Sasson, who argues similarly to the rabbis on this point, wishes to vindicate Jonah as well as God. As indicated above, Sasson contends that Jonah is dejected (4:1) not because he wishes harm to the Ninevites, but because he thinks God has not safeguarded Jonah's role as a prophet (justifying his decision to flee in 1:3). Yet, says Sasson, God is not being disrespectful to Jonah, as compared, say, to Isaiah, who was given the pleasant task of announcing such a reversal (Isa. 38:1–8; 2 Kings 20:1–6); Jonah has simply missed the ambiguity that made a repeat visit to Nineveh unnecessary. Both the message of hope and the message of judgment were embedded in Jonah's original oracle, according to Sasson.[24]

If Sasson is correct, the story of Jonah turns out to be the tale of a distrustful prophet whose conflict with the deity is actually a happy misunderstanding among friends. However, there are several complications which make the proposal less than compelling. First, it remains unclear why Jonah fled in response to God's initial call. It seems unlikely we are meant to understand that Jonah had a regular habit of rapid flight whenever God sent him on a mission. If it was only in *this* situation where Jonah felt doubtful that God would safeguard his prophetic credentials, it is unclear why that would be the case. Second, the story is completely silent on the means (if any) by which God intends to communicate the news of aborted judgment announced by the narrator in 3:10. If Sasson is correct that Jonah is troubled for not being allowed to announce God's change of plans, it seems the story would make it clear that Jonah did not, in fact, deliver that message. Finally, by Sasson's reading, God in chapter 4 must be coaxing Jonah out of his dejection by reminding him how much Jonah actually cares for the Ninevites. However, it is very hard to understand the intensity of God's

---

[21] The destruction of cities is elsewhere stated using the qal (active) stem of *hpk*, e.g., Deut. 29:22; Gen. 19:21, 25, 29.

[22] The niphal of *hpk* is used in Exod. 14:5 (of Pharaoh) and Hos. 11:8 (of God) with "heart" indicating a change of mind.

[23] Sasson, *Jonah*, 270–9.

[24] Ibid., 234–5, 294–5.

appeal to Jonah regarding compassion in 4:10–11 if, in fact, Jonah has been compassionate toward Nineveh all along.

These complications, along with the absence of other clues in the story to support Sasson's thesis, make it appear strained. A more traditional explanation for Jonah's anger—that he resented God's abandonment of judgment upon Nineveh—makes much more sense. The Scriptures are not silent about other situations in which God reversed direction (e.g., נחם | *nḥm*, Gen. 6:6), and Jonah is not the first to react with anger/dejection (חרה | *ḥrh*, 1 Sam. 15:11). This explanation is supported by several aspects of the book's rhetoric, such as the strong role of foreigners in the story and its pattern of irony. But most significantly, the deity's challenge in response to Jonah (4:9–11)—the conclusion to the entire book—has everything to do with justifying God's compassion on the city and nothing to do with correcting Jonah's alleged misunderstanding, affirming his alignment with God's attitude, or addressing his prophetic call.

To review this discussion of chapter 4: I have argued that Jonah was being accurate in 4:2 about his motivation for fleeing God's initial call (he anticipated that God might show mercy on Nineveh), that his intense anger toward God (4:1; cf. 4:4) was because God did indeed spare these enemies of Israel (the brutal, idol-worshiping Assyrians), and that there was no special ambiguity in his prophetic message—like other messages given by Israel's God, it implied the possibility of forgiveness upon repentance.

Thus, the story's final scene concerns several foci proposed for the story as a whole, such as God's freedom and mercy and concern for non-Israelites. However, we must recognize that these are packaged in the form of a theological controversy between God and Jonah. The exchange between these two clarifies not only the theological distance between them, but also the Lord's determination to win Jonah over to the Lord's position.

Point of view

The story's employment of point of view highlights the events of chapter 4. The narrator develops the overall story largely through the psychological point of view of characters other than Jonah.[25] We learn little of Jonah's inner life in chapters 1 and 3. In the first chapter, God

---

[25] The psychological is one of four point-of-view dimensions proposed by Boris Uspensky. The others are the phraseological, the spatial and temporal, and the ideological. See Boris Uspensky, *A Poetics of Composition: The Structure of the Artistic Text and Typology of a Compositional Form*, trans. Valentina Zavarin and Susan Wittig (Berkeley: Univ. of California, 1973).

calls Jonah, who then flees, sleeps during the storm, and reacts to the decisions of the sailors. We see the action through the eyes of the mariners. We find brief references to Jonah's thought life from his own mouth—I fear the Lord (1:9), I know this storm is because of me (1:12). But we learn more, from the narrator, about the sailors: the seamen were afraid (1:5, 10, 16), greatly afraid (1:10), greatly fearing the Lord (1:16), and knew that Jonah was fleeing from the Lord because he had told them (1:10). Two other bits of information come from the sailors' own mouths: perhaps the gods will give thought to us (1:6), you (Lord) have done as you pleased (1:14).

In chapter 3, Jonah delivers his short oracle. The rest of the chapter presents us with the fervent activity of the Ninevites and their king, and the perspective of God, who relents from the planned destruction. Again the inner life of the other characters is pronounced: the Ninevites believed in God (3:5), the king considers that God may turn from anger (3:9), God repents on account of their actions (3:10).

In chapters 2 and 4 the focus is on Jonah and his point of view. Chapter 2 is part of the narrative misdirection. We learn of Jonah's terror, rescue by God, and gratitude, all through Jonah's eyes. But these words lead us to believe that the plot tension that involves him is about to be resolved. Not a hint is given us about his earlier motives for fleeing God's call.

The explanation for Jonah's initial disobedience comes solely and purposefully in the fourth chapter. This is the first time he responds verbally to God's address to him. It is here that we get Jonah's point of view on the events of the story, hearing both from his own mouth and from the narrator. And what a variety of emotions we find: he is angry (4:2), wants to die (4:3), is extremely happy (4:6), then again asks to die (4:8). These conflicted emotions occur in Jonah as responses to God's actions: repenting from Nineveh's destruction; appointing a shading plant for Jonah; appointing a worm to kill the plant, accompanied by sun and a hot wind.

Also for the first time in the book we find an argument, one drawn out by God's questions to Jonah and Jonah's responses. Though other characters have asked questions, only now do the two lead characters, Jonah and the Lord, begin to ask questions and direct them toward each other. It is the content of these questions and responses that provides the book's climax. Point of view further substantiates the first route of this essay's argument that the focus of the story is on the conflict between God and Jonah.[26]

THE READER INSTRUCTED

We turn now to the second route of the argument: the instructional character of the book. Several aspects suggest a crafting that seeks to persuade the reader to align his or her perspective with that of God.[27]

The pervasiveness of questions

The first indicator of the book's didactic intent is the pervasiveness of questions, as many as fourteen even though the story is a short one. James Limburg summarizes: "In the first part of the story, the questions are all directed at Jonah. The captain questions him (1:6). The sailors interrogate him with seven questions (1:8, 10, 11). In the psalm, Jonah asks a question of the Lord (2:4 [Heb. 2:5]). The king of Nineveh asks a rhetorical question (3:9). In the final chapter, Jonah puts an angry question to the Lord (4:2) and the Lord/God addresses three questions to Jonah (4:4, 9, 11)."[28] As Limburg notes, such questions are characteristic of the instructional wisdom literature both of Israel and of the surrounding cultures.[29] Hans Walter Wolff points out that Jonah is never called a prophet in the book, and is the object of questions (eleven of the fourteen questions) more than a subject who preaches.[30]

---

[26] Terence E. Fretheim, *The Message of Jonah: A Theological Commentary* (Minneapolis: Augsburg Publishing Hse., 1977), 18–19; Crouch, "To Question an End," 106; Paul Kahn, "An Analysis of the Book of Jonah," *Judaism* 43 (1994): 97.

[27] James Limburg (*Jonah*, 24) offers the perspective of many conservative commentators that "the book of Jonah may be described as a fictional story developed around a historical figure for didactic purposes," while he adds that "considering Jonah in this way should not be understood as advocating a general approach to scripture that does not take history seriously." Further, "the message of the story of Jonah ought to be taken as seriously as the message of the parable of the waiting father or the good Samaritan or any other part of the Bible." Craig (*Poetics*, 159–60) insists that Jonah should not technically be categorized in the didactic genre, which subordinates plot, characters, and words to "the exigencies of doctrine," yet it is highly charged ideological literature. According to Meir Sternberg, "Jonah evolves before our eyes into a story of a prophet's education" (*The Poetics of Biblical Narrative: Ideological Literature and the Drama of Reading* [Bloomington: Indiana Univ. Pr., 1985], 320).

[28] Limburg, *Jonah*, 25. There is some uncertainty about those in 1:8a and 2:4 (Heb. 2:5).

[29] Ibid., 26.

[30] Hans Walter Wolff, *Studien zum Jonabuch*, Biblische Studien 47 (Neukirchen-Vluyn: Neukirchener Verlag, 1965), 72.

Parable-like quality of the book

The second indicator of the book's didactic intent is its parable-like quality. This is evident particularly in the exaggeration and irony that also contribute to the book's humor.[31]

Exaggeration is evident throughout. Jonah does not merely resist God's call, he buys passage on a ship and rushes feverishly in the opposite direction. As a result he encounters not slight resistance, but a life-threatening storm. The pagan sailors do not show interest or moderate tolerance, but near-embrace of the Jewish faith (fearing the Lord, offering sacrifice) as a result of the storm's cessation. Jonah does not simply survive the watery threat, but is swallowed whole by a giant fish. He does not merely give thanks to God, but bursts into a psalm worthy of David himself. When in Nineveh, the citizens not only receive his message, but fast and put on sackcloth, from the king down to the animals. When God relents of the planned judgment, Jonah is not simply disappointed, but openly angry. As he sits outside the city, a plant grows up in a day, and a worm destroys it just as quickly. Jonah is "exceed-ingly" glad because of the plant's shade, and "angry enough to die" when it withers and a scorching wind beats down on him. All these not only make for an entertaining story, but also suggest a tale exaggerated for purposes of instruction.

Irony and reversals of expectation in Jonah constitute some of its most enjoyable aspects. The Gentile seamen and Ninevites are models of obedient response to Israel's God, while the Hebrew prophet is not.[32] Yet through his disobedience, a shipload of sailors comes to acknowledge the God of Israel. [33] Jonah claims to fear his God even as he flees dis-obediently from God's call, but when the sailors fear the Lord, they obediently offer sacrifices and make vows. God is so zealous for one particular prophet to give the message to Nineveh that a raging storm threatens the mariners of an entire ship; later the same God demonstrates compassion for both the inhabitants of Nineveh and for the prophet himself. Jonah, who is the actual target of the deity, sleeps peacefully, while the sailors, who soon will be free of danger, are in a complete

---

[31] Some would call the book a comedy in the nontechnical sense, that is, not thereby signifying that it necessarily resolves with a positive ending.

[32] Lorraine Royer, "The God Who Surprises," *Bible Today* 33 (1995): 293–302, notes that the parable-like quality of Jonah is evident in its reversals, e.g., the Gentile sailors and Ninevites are obedient while the Hebrew prophet is not. The message: God is not Israel's exclusive possession, God is unrestricted and free to show mercy to whomever God wishes. God's mercy is pure gift; no one has an absolute claim on it. God's mercy extends to all nations. The story thus shatters the listeners' narrow view of God.

[33] The sailors are said to fear the Lord in 1:16, to the extent of offering sacrifice.

panic. The foreign mariners work hard to save Jonah, who is unrepent-ant, but later Jonah eagerly hopes for the destruction of the foreign Ninevites, who are repentant. Whereas the sailors desperately seek to save their own lives and Jonah's, Jonah willingly assents to being thrown into the sea.

When the scene shifts to Nineveh, "the Ninevites, fearing death, perform actions so that they might live. Jonah, seeing that they have been spared, twice asks that his life might be taken from him."[34] More than half of the book prepares for Jonah's critically important message, which then turns out to be only five words in length. Jonah, who has been the grateful recipient of God's mercy and love, furiously berates God for demonstrating the same qualities toward the Ninevites. Al-though God desires to save Jonah, his apparent death is requisite to the salvation of the sailors, and death to his way of thinking is necessary for the salvation of the Ninevites.

When God repents of Nineveh's judgment, it becomes apparent that Jonah rather than God has sought Nineveh's destruction, and God rather than Jonah has sought their salvation. This is a reversal not in fact but in the reader's awareness, and is accomplished by the narrator withholding information from the reader: the reason, now provided in 4:2, why Jonah fled from God in the first place.[35]

Jonah's anger stands in contrast with that of other prophets in Israel. Instead of anger over the sin of his audience and the destructive nature of their actions, Jonah is angry that the Ninevites have avoided judgment by abandoning these very things (though temporarily, he may suppose), and then is angry because the sun beats on his head.

Finally, Jonah shows concern for a transient plant which provides him fleeting relief, while showing little concern for a city full of people of God's lasting care. As we saw earlier in the book's plot structure, such ironies and reversals are the chief method of developing Jonah's character in the book, and particularly highlight the dissonance between the prophet and his God.[36]

---

[34] Craig, *Poetics*, 61.

[35] At the beginning of the story the reader can only guess at the reasons for Jonah's flight. Jonah's willingness to sacrifice himself for the sake of the sailors may make him seem compassionate in comparison to an apparently wrathful God who announces judgment on an entire city and sends a violent storm on a wayward prophet (Sternberg, *Poetics*, 56, 318–19; see the response by Trible [*Rhetorical Criticism*, 203]).

[36] Athalya Brenner argues that the poem makes Jonah the butt of humor through parody and satire: mercy and grace should be privileged over justice ("Jonah's Poem out of and within Its Context," in *Among the Prophets*, ed. Davies and Clines, 189–92); also Martens

The most important quality of parables is also here: the indirect presentation of the story's ideology. Though Jonah's position is clearly divergent, neither the narrator nor God evaluates it directly. Rather, Jonah (and the reader through Jonah) is prompted to make his own evaluation and to make appropriate choices that follow from that assessment.

Discussion of important theological issues

Presentation of the following important confessional statements about Israel's God, either directly or implied, also reflects the didactic nature of the story:

> *Chapter 1:*   *The Lord is the creator God (a wisdom theology of creation leads to faith as God "saves" the pagan sailors)*
>
> *Chapter 2:*   *The Lord is the delivering God (a psalm of thanksgiving as God "saves" Jonah)*
>
> *Chapter 3:*   *The Lord is the compassionate God (judgment is graciously withdrawn as God "saves" the Ninevites)*
>
> *Chapter 4:*   *The Lord is the questioning God (a wisdom parable of God's mercy as God seeks to "save" Jonah a second way)*[37]

These are important theological truths in the history of Israel's relationship with its God. Here they are integral to the message of the book directed toward Jonah, and through Jonah to the reader. Significantly, the structure of the story is developed so that the foreigners—chapters 1 and 3—are brought into juxtaposition with Israel's confessional tradition—the thanksgiving psalm in chapter 2 and the liturgy of God's mercy in 4:2b.[38] The psalm of chapter 2 is appropriate for both the sailors and Jonah, while the liturgy of chapter 4 is appropriate for both the Ninevites and Jonah.

Final gap, key question

As we consider the book's conclusion, we come to the intersection of this essay's two routes of argument: the story's focus on the conflict between God and Jonah, and the instructional character of the book. From the end of chapter 3 and through chapter 4, several gaps in the story are filled for us: we learn that God's motive for sending Jonah to Nineveh was to preserve the city if possible; we learn of Jonah's motive for fleeing to

---

("Ecotheology," 243) discerns the emphasis in Jonah that the mercy of God takes priority over judgment.

[37] Wolf, *Obadiah and Jonah*, 83; Limburg, *Jonah*, 26. Cf. questions directed to Adam and Eve (Gen. 3:9, 11, 13), Cain (Gen. 4:6–7, 10), Abraham (Gen. 18:9, 14), Job (Job 38:2; 40:2), et al.

[38] Jonah's complaint of 4:2b is an ironic allusion to the liturgical declaration of the Lord's mercy, more completely in Joel 2:13, but also Exod. 34:6; Neh. 9:17; Ps. 86:15, et al.

Tarshish; we learn that God's interest in Jonah goes beyond accomplishing a specific task.

Yet the most important gap remains open. Both the plot structure of God's action and Jonah's response, and the plot shift at chapter 4 direct our attention to the relationship crisis between God and Jonah and raise expectations of its resolution. The book closes, though, by leaving precisely this gap unfilled. We never learn Jonah's response to God's final question, and the book's principal plot tension thus remains unresolved.[39]

The character of God in the story has been crafted to be one of power and authority. God is given both the first and last words. God is the subject of strong verbs: commanding, appointing, hurling, seeing, repenting. The narrator's role (omniscient and also of high authority) diminishes toward the end and the Lord's role becomes more prominent. God's purposes are completely fulfilled in this story, with the significant exception of those regarding Jonah.

Jonah's role as an ideologically authoritative figure is also high. It is only to Jonah that the Lord's word comes, and only Jonah participates in actual conversation with God. The narrator's restraint in revealing Jonah's inner life allows Jonah to remain mysterious so readers cannot evaluate him as easily as they can assess other characters. Only Jonah resists God's commands, a resistance with some depth and substance, as we discover in chapter 4: he actually sits in judgment on God.

Attention to pronouns highlights the polarity between Jonah and God. First, we note that Jonah's prayer in chapter 2 is dominated by the second person *you: you* heard my voice, *you* cast me into the deep, *your* presence, *your* holy temple, *you* brought me up from the pit. The few expressions of first person by Jonah here are all in reverence toward and in compliance with the Lord. Jonah's prayers in chapter 4, however, are more characterized by the first person, which is used to declare his stance in opposition to God: *I* said, *I* made haste, *I* knew, *my* life, *I* beseech, better for *me*, *I* do well. Even the rare second person pronouns in this last episode are used to establish the differences between God and Jonah.

---

[39] Wolff (*Obadiah and Jonah*, 83) concludes that everything in the story moves toward resolving the question of how Jonah will respond to God's provocation and what his fate will be. "Both the composition of the scenes in general and the sentence construction in general are designed to keep the reader in suspense, waiting for the dénouement." Thus, he writes, purpose clauses and chains of consecutive imperfects move the action along. "The reader has been prepared to expect some reaction to the final question."

These two strong characters thus face off in chapter 4 where, for the first time, the book presents two independent points of view.[40] Jonah insists that God is too easy on the violent unrighteous ones who should be judged as announced. God provides for Jonah, or perhaps we should say "provokes" Jonah's anger over a shady plant, then challenges Jonah to care at least as much for the Ninevites, the target of God's concern. Readers must decide whose perspective is worthy of their allegiance, God's or Jonah's.

Although neither God nor the narrator directly evaluates Jonah, the story has been ordered to make us sympathetic to God's position.[41] The exchange in chapter 4 introduces the evaluative term טוֹב (*ṭôb*) (good, right; 4:3, 8) and the related verb יטב (*yṭb*) (4:4, 9 bis) into the discussion. We are led to conclude that Jonah's anger is petty: he cares more for a flimsy plant, simply because it provided him shade, than for a whole city of people.

The determined and stable compassion of God (whom Jonah accuses of changeableness) toward all of creation is strikingly contrasted with the changeableness of Jonah in 4:1–9: anger → death wish → happiness → second death wish. And because the latter pair of dispositions concerns Jonah's personal situation, it seems likely that the former pair reflects an equally self-oriented concern. For this reason, God can use the latter as the analogical basis for the final appeal in 4:10–11.

Craig points out that the Lord here employs new vocabulary, especially the verb חוס (*ḥws*) (pity, concern), rather than the vocabulary Jonah has used to describe the situation.[42] Thereby both Jonah and the

---

[40] Sasson (*Jonah*, 317) notes that the dialogue is balanced as follows:

vv. 2–3	Jonah's monologue	39 words
v. 4	God's query (unanswered)	3 words
v. 8	Jonah's query (sotto voce)	3 words
v. 9	dialogue: God	5 words
	dialogue: Jonah	5 words
vv. 10–11	God's monologue	39 words

Trible (*Rhetorical Criticism*, 224) concludes that this symmetry indicates that Jonah and the Lord "are evenly matched and that each emulates the other."

[41] Likewise, the foreigners do not evaluate Jonah, except for the ship captain, who asks an accusing question in 1:6.

[42] The verb *ḥws* indicates the emotion of sympathy toward its object with the intention of performing a helping act (S. Wagner, "chûs," in *Theological Dictionary of the Old Testament*, ed. G. Johannes Botterweck and Helmer Ringgren, trans. David E. Green [Grand Rapids: Eerdmans, 1980], 4:272). It is striking that of its two dozen occurrences in the Old Testament, most involve a negation. The prophets most often declare that God will *not* have pity on certain ones (Jer. 13:14; Ezek. 5:11; 7:4, 9; 8:18; 24:14) or announce that others did not, should not, or will not have pity (Isa. 13:18; Jer. 21:7; Ezek. 9:5; 16:5), as also in

reader are invited to consider the deity's own presentation of the world rather than the one Jonah has adopted.[43] The Lord then sets up Jonah for a lesser-to-greater argument by asking the question of 4:9, "Do you do well to be angry for the plant?"[44] When Jonah answers in the affirmative, the trap is sprung in 4:10–11. A powerful, surely rhetorical question is left in the air as both challenge and rebuke to Jonah's small and self-centered actions: "You pity the plant. . . . Should I not pity Nineveh?"[45]

Yet the reader may sympathize with Jonah. Although the Ninevites are presented positively in the story (no record of their atrocities is rehearsed), we realize they must deserve Jonah's commission to announce judgment.[46] We might have belittled him as a prophet when he fled for Tarshish (he could seem cowardly compared to Jeremiah and Amos), yet he is a man of faith.[47] His complaint in 4:2 is worthy of consideration: How can one depend on a God who announces one thing yet does another? Why cooperate with a God who is deterred from ridding the world of one of its greatest menaces simply because of some pallor and sackcloth?

As the reader considers whether to take Jonah's perspective, the Lord closes in on Jonah. By the final question in 4:11, the Lord acknowledges that Jonah has been sitting in judgment on divine activity. Does the reader also wish to do so? While inviting Jonah to continue to do so, God challenges him to reconsider his current position. In the process,

---

Deut. (7:16; 13:8 [Heb. 13:9]; 19:13, 21: 25:12). Appeals for the Lord's pity include Neh. 13:22 and Joel 2:17, while Ps. 72:13 declares the king's pity on the poor and needy.

[43] Craig, *Poetics*, 158.

[44] For other examples of this argument style, see Gen. 44:8; Deut. 31:27; 2 Kings 5:13; Matt. 6:30; 10:31; 12:12; Luke 12:24.

[45] Commentators have differed on how to assess the premise of this lesser-to-greater argument. "You pity the plant," God says in verse 10. Trible (*Rhetorical Criticism*, 218–22) argues that the narrator had purposely withheld this particular statement of Jonah's reaction, previously telling us that (1) plant provides shade, Jonah is happy (4:6), (2) worm attacks plant so that it withers (4:7, Jonah's reaction *withheld*), and (3) wind and sun, Jonah is angry enough to die (4:8). The deity announces Jonah's reaction of pity toward the plant in 4:10 (though note 4:9) in order to give greater impact to the argument for which it serves as premise. Irony is another possibility here: perhaps the Lord ironically labels Jonah's attitude toward the plant "pity" to demonstrate that any concern Jonah has for the plant is really for his own well-being. In contrast, God's pity for Nineveh is genuine concern for the well-being of the Ninevites and their animals.

[46] Fretheim, *Message*, 22, emphasizes that it is the wickedness of the Ninevites more than their Gentile-ness that motivates Jonah's rejection of them. He notes that Jonah's attitude toward the sailors is positive, and thus insists that Jonah does not have a radically exclusivistic perspective.

[47] Ibid., 19–20.

"God does not condemn Jonah, but invites the prophet to condemn himself and admit that his anger has no merit."[48]

The unanswered question leaves it to the reader to bring closure to the plot line. The reader must ponder, What *will* Jonah do next?—but then cannot avoid asking, What *should* Jonah do next? And it is the latter question that forces the reader to face the choice with which Jonah is confronted.[49]

CONCLUSION

Inward and outward readings

Among those who agree with the above assessment concerning the book's appeal for compassion, the story raises diverse issues which allow for a significant variation in emphasis. This variation is shaped by the distinctive experiences, values, and questions that each reader and reading community brings to the narrative. A pietistic or inward approach to the story is more concerned with Jonah's personal situation, his experiences in prayer, and the consequences of his choices. In its favor, this approach insists that in attending to our sense of call to action we should not overlook our own need for change.

Matthew Henry, for example, suggests that Jonah's repose during the storm demonstrates the stupefying effects of sin. We must be alert to the causes of the evil around us and seek personal repentance when necessary. The Ninevites cast themselves on the mercy and free grace of God, as should we. God will not despise a broken and contrite heart. The actions of Jonah in chapter 4 challenge us to consider the quality of our hearts. Are we too easily angered? Do we care for others with God's great compassion? We should care more for one soul than for any of our own creature comforts. However much we are willing to keep divine grace to ourselves, God is rich in mercy toward all who call on the Lord.

---

[48] Craig, *Poetics*, 160.

[49] Crouch ("To Question an End," 101), quoting M. Torgovnick, "The test of an ending is the appropriateness of an ending's relationship to the beginning and to the middle—through language, situation, and groupings of characters—not the degree of finality or resolution achieved by the ending." Crouch offers an ending he considers consistent with the characterization of Jonah; in it Jonah accuses God of gullibility, in regard both to Nineveh and to the prophet himself. Simon argues on the grounds that it incorporates the final scene of the story that the central theme of the book concerns compassion (justice versus mercy), whereas other proposed central themes do not embrace the story's ending (Simon, *Jonah*, xii–xiii).

We should be astonished at God's patience toward us in our need for inward change.[50]

The story of Jonah also suggests an outward reading, a call to action in a number of possible directions. Such a call recognizes the danger in becoming too inwardly focused, whether individually or corporately, and ignoring the pain and corruption of the world around. It is because of the wickedness of Nineveh that God calls Jonah to cry out against the city. It is only upon the rejection of their violent life style that God relents of the planned destruction. Likewise are we called to cry out against the injustices around us, and to bring good news to those who are ready to repent. We need to recognize and involve ourselves with the communal complications of sin in our society. God compels us to prophesy against the powerful, and extend compassion to the downtrodden. Because the outward calling is a hard one, we often desire to flee from it. But an inward focus is so easily self-serving, and God calls us to reach out actively to others.[51]

We have much to gain from both the inward and the outward readings of Jonah's story, and the contribution of each will be evident in what follows. Biblical scholars have rightly cautioned against a facile determination of God's will and ways in this story. They have emphasized the freedom of God, lest one suppose, for example, that the Ninevites could manipulate God's compassion toward them by their acts of repentance.[52] Just as it appears that God did not always warn of judgment (note the destruction of Sodom and Gomorrah, Genesis 18–19), neither is God restricted to any formula in meting out grace. Part of Jonah's message is that God may freely choose to be merciful to Israelites and heathen alike.[53]

---

[50] Matthew Henry, *An Exposition of the Old and New Testament,* vol. 4 (1712; reprint, New York: Fleming H. Revell Co., [1910?]).

[51] As Uriel Simon notes regarding those who find the theme of repentance to be central to the book, "The designation of Jonah as the *haftarah* for the Afternoon Service of the Day of Atonement (B. Megillah 31a) reflects the view that this book depicts the concept of repentance so starkly and completely that it can stir hearers to repent of their ways and even modify their conduct" (Simon, *Jonah,* vii). Some rabbinic passages take this theme in a more pietistic or individualistic direction, citing the Ninevites' repentance as an exemplary combination of fasting, prayer, and deeds. But others highlight the dimension of communal justice. B. Ta'anit 16a, for example, cites r. Samuel who interpreted concerning Jonah 3:8 that "Even someone who had stolen a beam and built it into his house destroyed the entire building and returned the beam to its owner" (cited in Simon, *Jonah,* vii).

[52] On God's freedom, Alan Cooper ("In praise," 162) writes, "It is folly to try and justify or rationalize his behavior."

[53] See, e.g., Wolff, *Obadiah and Jonah,* 87–8. Royer ("The God Who Surprises," 298–302) points out interesting connections between the story of Jonah and the Acts 10 story of Peter

God's invitation to mission

Yet let us consider three issues in the story that suggest insights into the ways of God. In the first place, when there is a task God wants accomplished, God typically enjoins one or more human beings to participate in it. Only rarely does it occur otherwise in the Scriptures. It seems that when there is something exciting going on, God wants mortals to be a part of it. God thus initiates the encounter between Jonah and the Ninevites. While part of this involvement of God's people in divine plans is to model a community of righteousness, they are not to be an enclave, set apart by themselves. In particular they are mandated to go forth proclaiming the Lord's name to the nations (Deut. 32:1–3; Isa. 12:4–5; 42:1–4; cf. Matt. 12:18–21).

God's peace

Second, God demonstrates a benevolent care toward all the creation: Israelite, non-Israelite, and nonhuman. Uriel Simon is correct that only the theme of compassion pervades the book in every scene.[54] God's benevolence is indiscriminate, causing the sun to rise on the evil and the good, and sending rain on the just and the unjust (Matt. 5:45; cf. Exod. 33:19). "The author leaves no unambiguous dogma or decree. Just the mystery of divine compassion."[55] This mystery is a reality to which Jonah is being invited to conform. God does not always treat people as they appear to deserve and will not permit Jonah to draw the boundary lines of God's care and concern.

Yet Nineveh and its economy were already prospering under the indiscriminate benevolence of God. If material prosperity is all that constitutes God's generosity, there would have been nothing more to do. And there would have been no story. But neither did God merely strike the Ninevites down because of their violence and insolence. If judgment and destruction are all that constitute God's justice, that might have been summarily arranged.

Rather, God's peace involves both a compassion which does not merely pamper and a justice which does not merely destroy. God intervened so that the Ninevites might repent, and sent Jonah to offer them an opportunity to change and be changed.

---

and Cornelius, the word of God to receive the Gentiles. The two stories have less to say about the conversion of the Gentiles than about the need of Jonah and Peter for conversion from their narrow attitude toward Gentiles.

[54] Simon, *Jonah*, xii–xiii.

[55] Craig, *Poetics*, 165.

Saving the people of God's reign

Third, we can notice that God seeks not only the salvation of pagans but even the salvation of God's people. God is not satisfied with mere messengers. Otherwise Jonah's disobedience (chapter 1) would surely have disqualified him, and when he was given another chance, his subsequent compliance (chapter 3) would have brought the end of his part of the story.

Instead, God motivates Jonah to participate by sending a storm and "appointing" a fish, but remains unsatisfied with Jonah's obedience although it achieved remarkable results. God's call to Jonah was for Jonah's benefit as much as for the benefit of the Ninevites. Jonah's salvation at the deepest level, his God-like wholeness, depended on that call. Thus the Lord pursued him again, this time by "appointing" a plant, a worm, and a hot wind. Only then did Jonah have to face himself, his anger at God, his death wish, and the possibility of his transformation. As with Nineveh, God blessed Jonah without pampering, and judged Jonah without destroying. God sought Jonah's repentance and transformation: a new way of relating to enemies (compassion) and a new understanding of his purpose (to bring hope to the nations).

God demands that Jonah, who is incensed that the brutal Assyrians are left unscathed, consider his own hunger for violence. Jonah would rather seek his own death than accept the failure of his attempts to see the Ninevites destroyed. In Jonah we see the seeds of murder that blossom when the oppressed becomes the oppressor and the cycle of violence repeats itself.

In the case of Nineveh and the case of Jonah, as previously with the sailors, we see the rationale for God's activity. God seeks a change of heart, of character, in those God loves. This will mean a unity of outward action and inward orientation, in what we do and why we do it. Nothing else will suffice. To accomplish this, the deity will invite, even compel human beings to be involved in a process of symbiotic salvation: as they are used to save others, they may also be saved.

Yet note the complication: a storm can get Jonah to Nineveh and even motivate him to give a message, but for a deeper change in Jonah God can only enact a parable, ask pointed questions, and extend an invitation.[56] Jonah gladly received salvation from the sea. Will he also allow God to deliver him from his anger toward Nineveh?

A determination of the book's rhetoric has provided a way to adjudicate among diverse emphases of interpretation as well as to incor-

---

[56] Likewise, we expect that a threat of destruction can motivate an outward change among the Ninevites, but a long-term change of heart may or may not occur.

porate those emphases into a richer understanding of the book's message. And the message of Jonah is not simply a theology in the sense of information about God and humans, as important as that is. It also includes a strategy of God's peace, which offers change both to Jonah and to Nineveh. Simultaneously, God's call to mission provides for the salvation of the mission messengers—the people of God's reign—as well as of the mission recipients.

Our choice is the same as Jonah's, and we may choose to run or to sit with him in anger or frustration. If we do, we had best prepare for seaweed and watery deeps, or perhaps for hot and windy weather. "God's kindness is meant to lead you to repentance."

6 | *Peace as the visionary mission of God's reign*
Zechariah 1–8

BEN C. OLLENBURGER

WHILE I SHALL FOCUS HERE ON ITS FIRST EIGHT chapters, the book of Zechariah has contributed to the inventory of Old Testament peace texts principally by dint of 9:9–10, which we are likely to hear on Palm Sunday. This text promises that YHWH will banish armaments from Ephraim and Jerusalem, and the king who comes on an ass's foal to Zion will "speak peace (דִּבֶּר שָׁלוֹם | *dibbēr šālôm*) to the nations" (KJV). It may be instructive that the Jewish Publication Society's new translation (NJPS) renders this phrase "call on the nations to surrender."[1] Christians, including this one, tend to read the passage with the New Testament and Jesus in the foreground, while NJPS refers us expressly, in a footnote, to Deut. 20:10–12, part of a classic holy war text. Given the literary context, NJPS has a certain point: if Zech. 9:9–10 promises peace, the passage following (9:13–15) envisions war. It will be a war of liberation, but war nonetheless.[2] War has a prominent place throughout Zechariah 9–14, even if it results in universal peace. Mission, insofar as it has a presence in those chapters, assumes war and death as its companions.

Already these few observations beg the question of what we mean by "peace" and "mission," respectively or in combination. It would seem important to avoid begging the question—to avoid, that is, simply (a) assuming agreement among us on what these terms or concepts mean, on one hand; or, on the other hand, simply (b) assuming that the book of Zechariah shares, sponsors, or informs one or more of the meanings we attach to these terms. However, I believe that a certain degree of question

---

[1] *Tanakh: The Holy Scriptures: The New JPS Translation According to the Traditional Hebrew Text* (NJPS) (Philadelphia: Jewish Pubn. Society, 1999).

[2] My interpretation of Zechariah here and in the remainder of this essay reflects my commentary on the book, published in volume 7 of *The New Interpreter's Bible* (Nashville: Abingdon Pr., 1996).

begging is inevitable, and that it can and should be productive rather than pernicious. Let me elaborate on these remarks before proceeding to Zechariah 1–8.

William Alston has dressed up the notion of question begging, in the sense I intend, by giving it the name "epistemic circularity." By this he means that: "in general . . . , the determination of whether we have knowledge in a given sphere is, and must be, an 'inside job.' We are, in general, incapable of showing that we have knowledge in a particular domain without relying on particular bits of knowledge in that very domain, and hence begging the question."[3]

Alston has bigger theoretical fish to fry than any we are likely to catch here, but his point remains instructive. The domain in which we aim to show that we have knowledge, not just as authors but as the church, can be designated "Christian (biblical) theology;"[4] its subdomain that expressly concerns us is "peace and mission." Moreover, the purposes of our inquiries here include acquiring new or better or more certain knowledge in that domain and becoming more self-critical about the knowledge we purport to have. Neither would be possible apart from some prior knowledge in that same domain.

All of this may seem painfully obvious. However, complicating the obvious is the manner in which we, in these inquiries and as Christians, go about "showing" our knowledge and deepening, expanding, or reforming it. In my case, this manner involves studying the book of Zechariah—i.e., studying a Hebrew text that, quite conceivably, betrays no awareness of the domain "peace and mission." Everyone who works in biblical studies and theology is familiar with the "hermeneutical circle," or at least we are familiar with the term. Martin Heidegger provided a succinct definition of it: "any interpretation which is to contribute understanding must have already understood what is to be interpreted."[5] Hermeneutical circularity, as a form of question begging, is inevitable and productive, and not, or not necessarily, pernicious. We would rightly mistrust any proffered interpretation of Zechariah that did not proceed from some kind, or some degree, of *prior* understanding of Zechariah—and of what else? This "what else?" represents a question

---

[3] William P. Alston, "On Knowing That We Know: The Application to Religious Knowledge," in *Christian Perspectives on Religious Knowledge*, ed. C. Stephen Evans and Merold Westphal (Grand Rapids: Eerdmans, 1993), 34.

[4] I put "biblical" in parentheses, as a modifier of "theology," in order (1) to avoid surreptitiously enlisting anyone in some specific project of biblical theology, while (2) acknowledging that the theological inquiries in this volume involve biblical exegesis primarily.

[5] Martin Heidegger, *Being and Time* (New York: Harper & Row, 1962), 194.

about the sort of contextualization we regard as the necessary condition for a properly prior, and hence potentially productive, understanding of Zechariah. Should we contextualize Zechariah within, for example, (1) the larger "canon" of the Hebrew Bible; (2) the corpus of Second Temple Jewish literature; (3) the corpus of ancient and Hellenistic "prophetic" literature; (4) pre-Mishnaic Judaism; (5) the canon of Christian Scripture; (6) a Christian exegetical and theological tradition? Happily, these options and others—there are very many others—are not all exclusive of each other. Even so, the option(s) selected will determine the circumference of the hermeneutical circle.

Because we have to choose which of these options to exercise, and because we tend to do so for reasons that strike us as obvious, I prefer to give logical priority to Alston's notion of epistemic circularity. By this I mean to suggest that certain preinterpretive or noninterpretive understandings—or better, convictions—logically precede and to some extent underwrite interpretive, exegetical, and hermeneutical activities and *their* preunderstandings. As Ludwig Wittgenstein put it, interpretation depends on "some way of grasping . . . which is *not* an interpretation."[6] Let "some way of grasping" stand for "a set of convictions." Among the preinterpretive convictions I bring to the following exegetical work on Zechariah is this: Christian theological knowledge, including as it concerns mission/peace, is shown, gained, shared, disciplined, and reformed by just such exegetical work. Certainly, I would add, it is not *only* by such exegetical work, and perhaps (it may turn out) not at all by *my* exegetical work. Yet the conviction remains—the common conviction that underwrites this project—though I will mount no argument for it. To be sure, arguments in favor of it could be mounted, but all the interesting arguments would fall, most likely, either within or very close to the circumference of the epistemic circle itself.

I am suggesting, then, that the epistemic circle has logical priority over the hermeneutical circle. Christian (biblical) theology has usually assumed, if not in practice, that the reverse is true. It has assumed, for example, that we should seek to discover what the text of Zechariah teaches about peace and mission, or about the domain "peace and mission," and then, having routed our discoveries through the New Testament for refinement, incorporate this teaching within a theology, or offer our discoveries as theological recommendations. But how do we know that Zechariah teaches *anything* about peace and mission? What *is* mission? *The Oxford Dictionary of the Christian Church* suggests that it is

---

[6] Ludwig Wittgenstein, *Philosophical Investigations* (Oxford: Blackwell Pubs., 1958), 201. My quotations of Heidegger and Wittgenstein are taken from Richard Shusterman, "Beneath Interpretation: Against Hermeneutic Holism," *The Monist* 73 (1990): 181–204.

"the propagation of the Christian faith among non-Christian peo-ple. . . ."[7] Nothing much like this will appear in Zechariah or in the Old Testament. In the NRSV, the term "mission" appears but four times in the Old Testament (Judg. 18:5, 6; 1 Sam. 15:18, 20), in each case as a translation of דֶּרֶךְ (derek).[8] "Assignment" would serve equally well as a translation, and none of these four verses bears on however many things, as I presume, we may mean by mission. In 1 Samuel 15, the assignment, or mission, is: "utterly destroy the sinners"—the mission here consists in a punitive military assignment. What about peace? In NJPS's translation, "peace" occurs nowhere in Zechariah, although the word שָׁלוֹם (šālôm) occurs six times (in 6:13, four times in chapter 8, and in 9:10).[9] It would be possible to conclude, then, that Zechariah teaches nothing—has nothing to say to us—about peace or mission. Some critical interpreters of Zechariah would embrace this possibility as a virtual certainty. I do not. My reasons are epistemically circular.

According to what I wrote above, this means that certain pre-interpretive or noninterpretive convictions logically precede and to some extent underwrite my interpretive, exegetical, and hermeneutical work on Zechariah. While these convictions include "that Christian theological knowledge is shown, gained, shared, disciplined, and reformed by exegetical work," they also include convictions specific to the domain "peace and mission." And I strongly suspect that those convictions, or ones roughly compatible with them, are broadly shared among the other authors in this volume. For example, I am treating peace and mission as—rather, as part of—a single domain, not as two separate or independent ones. But now I have mentioned two sets of convictions: one set concerns the relation of exegesis to Christian theological knowledge, and the other set concerns the domain "peace and mission." Both sets are preinterpretive, but they do not occupy the same logical plane: the latter is a subset of the former. That is, specific convictions about the domain "peace and mission" fall within and are subordinate to convictions about Christian theological knowledge. In turn, this means that *Christian* preinterpretive convictions about peace/mission, like the ones we may hold in common, are in principle shown, gained, shared, disciplined, and reformed by exegetical work, i.e., by interpretive work. In other words, it is the odd concomitant of a governing, preinterpretive

---

[7] F. L. Cross, ed., *The Oxford Dictionary of the Christian Church* (London: Oxford Univ. Pr., 1958), s.v. "missions."

[8] It occurs once in the New Testament, at Acts 12:25, where it translates διακονία (*diakonia*).

[9] NRSV does have "peace" six times: at 1:11 it translates a word other than שָׁלוֹם with "peace," and translates שָׁלוֹם in 8:10 with "safety."

Christian conviction that all preinterpretive subsets of that conviction must become, or must become once more, *interpretive*; that they are all potentially interpretive, if they are to count as Christian.

This concomitant does not merely repristinate the common assumption of much Christian biblical theology, mentioned above. Rather, it takes seriously the implicit (or explicit) claims of specific convictions, and employs them—deploys them—as hermeneutical instruments. That is, it describes the contours of a productively circular hermeneutics within a larger epistemic circle. It does so on the assumption, which I hold, that a product of any sound exercise in Christian rhetoric, whether it be ethics or exegesis, theology or preaching, or mission, will be an enriched reading of Scripture.[10] And, by the same token, readings of Scripture thus enriched are themselves, as the product of their enrichment, in the service of ethics, theology, preaching, mission, and all other registers of Christian communal faith and practice, on behalf of their Christian character. This joins Luther's *sola scriptura* to the Anabaptist axiom of Hans Denck: one cannot truly know Christ apart from a life of Christ-following, the possibility of which depends on knowing Christ.[11]

My reading of Zechariah proceeds from and with certain convictions, inchoate as they may be, about the domain "peace and mission." I hope to confirm those convictions, but especially to discipline them, perchance to reform them.

THE VISIONS (AND ORACLES) OF ZECHARIAH, AND A SERMON

As announced above, I will concentrate here on the earlier chapters of Zechariah: chapters 1–8, and, eventually, even more narrowly on chapter 8. These chapters, unlike those that follow, are provided a precise setting. The superscriptions at 1:1, 7; 7:1 date the textual units following them to the year, month, and (except for 1:1), day in the reign of Darius, king of Persia. The dates fall within 520–518 B.C.E., which means that they are situated in the context of empire[12]—an immensely powerful Persian Empire that would extend, on a current map, from India into Greece, and from North Africa into Russia, within which the province of Judah

---

[10] This does not entail, by any means, that any or all of these exercises are merely rhetorical. The reduction of ethics to rhetoric, for example, would be sophistry. But the Sophists had a point, and even ethics is irreducibly (though by no means exhaustively) rhetorical. So is mission.

[11] Clarence Bauman, *The Spiritual Legacy of Hans Denck* (Leiden: E. J. Brill, 1991), 112–13.

[12] I say "situated within" rather than "written in," to avoid debate about the actual date(s) of Zechariah 1–8 or its redaction history. As it happens, I believe that the texts generally reflect a date in the late sixth century, in which they are situated.

was smaller than metropolitan Tokyo, and with a very much smaller population. The historic capital of Judah, Jerusalem, was largely a ruin: according to Nehemiah, no one really wanted to live there; apparently, almost no one did, more than two centuries after its destruction (Neh. 7:4).[13] The book of Zechariah situates its first eight chapters in the early years of Persia's greatest king, Darius, when Jerusalem was a disaster area and its temple rubble.

While the superscriptions in these chapters situate them in close temporal proximity to each other, the literary material that they comprise differs dramatically. Zechariah's first six chapters comprise, in the main, a series of visions, seven or perhaps eight in number, that form the structural framework for oracular material accompanying them (1:7–6:15). Chapters 7 and 8 together form an extended sermon that reiterates and expands some of the themes of the preceding chapters. Reinforcing this internal relation between the visions and the sermon is a briefer sermon, call it a homily, in 1:1–6, which introduces the book and precedes the visions. Its verbal associations with, and formal similarity to, material in chapters 7 and 8 suggest that the contents of this homily are drawn from the sermon. It serves now to frame the visions within the hortatory horizon of the sermon.

Before turning expressly to the domain of peace and mission, and the reign of God, in reference to Zechariah 1–8, I will first survey these chapters, following the broad formal divisions sketched in the preceding paragraph. The survey will capture most of what I have to say about the domain and the reign.

Visions (and oracles): Zechariah 1:7–6:15

The visions of Zechariah follow a general pattern: Zechariah sees or is shown something, a sign; the angel accompanying him in these visions identifies the sign—tells Zechariah what he is looking at but not quite seeing—and then interprets it. This pattern, or a variation on it, occurs in each of seven visions, three in the first two chapters (1:7–2:13),[14] three in chapters 5 and 6, and in what appears to be the pivotal vision of chapter 4. Zechariah 3 departs formally from this pattern and also disturbs the arrangement of 3+1+3. However, chapter 3 does narrate a vision, and like all of the other seven it includes an oracle, or perhaps a pair of

---

[13] I am aware that the date of Nehemiah is uncertain, its value as a historical source controversial, and details of its interpretation problematic. See Joseph Blenkinsopp, *Ezra-Nehemiah: A Commentary,* The Old Testament Library (Philadelphia: Westminster Pr., 1988).

[14] In Hebrew, 1:7–2:17. The versification differs between Hebrew and English in Zechariah 1 and 2; for convenience, I will cite only the English versification. This will hold true for citations of other texts as well.

oracles.[15] In the current arrangement of the book, it is paired with chapter 4, for reasons that we will note below. Its placement also serves to reinforce a division between the material in 1:7–2:13, including the first three visions, and the remainder of the visionary series. This distinction involves both literary differences and ones of content; the former suggest, in my view, that Zech. 1:7–2:13 forms a unit relatively— perhaps also originally, or in one stage of composition—independent of what follows.[16] It is also this material, among the visions, that bears the closest relationship with the sermon in chapters 7 and 8. For that reason the following remarks will concentrate on 1:7–2:13.

Zechariah's first vision includes the notice that it occurred at night. Perhaps we are to take 1:8 as indicating that all of the visions came in the same night, but the night setting is especially appropriate to the initial vision. The scene (1:8–11), has a quality both liminal and numinous, with mythic imagery suggestive of both Eden and the temple, and darkness shrouding the presence of YHWH. Zechariah's access to this shrouded presence is doubly mediated, through his interpreting angel and another, called the angel of YHWH. The latter seems to be identical with the "man" Zechariah sees on a red horse, one of four horses that have returned from a reconnaissance of the earth's four corners or directions. And they have returned to report to YHWH that the whole earth remains quiet. Quiet it may be, but the earth is certainly not at peace (the NRSV not-withstanding). Indeed, the report of the horses(!) provokes the YHWH-angel to an exasperated "How long?" addressed to YHWH. The angel's complaint draws on Jeremiah, who had announced a seventy-year period of Babylonian hegemony to be followed by Judah's restoration (Jer. 25:11–12; 29:10). Taking those seventy years literally, the angel reminds YHWH of divine responsibilities remaining unfulfilled: YHWH continues to withhold mercy from Jerusalem and Judah's cities; they continue to suffer YHWH's anger, and still the world remains undis-turbed.

While the superscriptions (1:1, 7; 7:1) are regarded as secondary and redactional, the date, Darius's second year, provided in 1:7, gives the first vision a context that explains the YHWH-angel's urgency. Darius acceded to the Persian throne in 522, following the sudden and some-what mysterious death of his predecessor, Cambyses. Darius's accession was vigorously contested, and he spent the first two years of his reign

---

[15] An oracle, for these purposes, is the direct address of YHWH through an intermediary, typically introduced by a quotative formula: e.g., "Thus says YHWH." Within Zechariah's visions it is not always clear who is the intermediary, the prophet or his interpreting angel.

[16] Details on this and other matters to follow can be found in my commentary, noted above.

consolidating it and battling other contenders. By the winter of 519, which corresponds to the date of 1:7, Darius and Persia were firmly in control of the empire. Babylon's hegemony was well past, as YHWH had promised through Jeremiah, but Jerusalem remained a ruin, as did its temple and many of Judah's towns. Provoking the angel's exasperated complaint in 1:12 is not only the enduring misery of Judah, understood as the result of YHWH's enduring anger (or curse, זָעַם | zā'am), but also the theological and existential problem that the consolidation of Persian imperial rule represented. It called into question both YHWH's reliability and YHWH's divinity.

YHWH's response comes immediately, in the form of oracles that Zechariah is to proclaim. These oracles (1:14–17) announce YHWH's intention to act on behalf of Jerusalem and Judah, but they also address the theological issue and redefine it: YHWH's undeniable anger—undeniable because of Judah's situation and the prophetic interpretation of its cause—has temporal limits that have been exceeded (1:15). Moreover, the nations who have been the instruments of YHWH's anger have exceeded YHWH's purposes; at contemptuous ease, quiet, they ally themselves with Judah's disaster, serving their purposes, not YHWH's. Hence, YHWH's anger (קָצֶף | qāṣap) now turns toward the oppressing nations. In a more positive vein, YHWH announces, "I am returning to Jerusalem in compassion" (1:16); as a consequence, YHWH's house will be rebuilt. A second oracle expands YHWH's promises: Judah's cities will enjoy prosperity, and YHWH will comfort Zion and will again choose Jerusalem (1:17).

I have attended to this first vision (plus oracles) in some detail, because it lays the groundwork for everything that follows in the successive visions and through chapter 8. Prosaically rendered, that groundwork consists in the declaration that YHWH's anger toward Judah is past, now replaced by anger toward the oppressing nations and compassion toward Jerusalem, and the announcement of YHWH's return to Zion/Jerusalem. However, more must be said, because the declaration and the announcement carry certain implications; the succeeding chapters give them visionary expression. In the second vision (1:18–21), the four oppressing nations are robbed of their power to oppress; they are "de-horned" or pacified.[17] The third vision and its oracles (2:1–13)

---

[17] When Daniel, in chapters 2 and 7, appropriates similar imagery to an apocalyptic genre, the four nations, represented by metals or beasts, have historical identity: Assyria, Babylon, Persia, and Greece (though Daniel seems to omit Assyria and to insert the Medes before the Persians). It is not obvious that Zechariah has anything similar in mind; rather, the four horns represent the totality of international powers whose oppression Judah has suffered and continues to suffer.

reiterate the announcement of YHWH's return, together with the promise of an expanded and unwalled Jerusalem. Walls will be impossible, owing to Jerusalem's vast population, and they will be unnecessary: Jerusalem's enemies have been pacified, and YHWH will be Jerusalem's defense.

The oracles accompanying the third vision address other implications of the groundwork laid in 1:13–17. First, and consistent with what has already been promised and portrayed, YHWH announces punishment for those who have plundered YHWH's people. Second, this provides good reason to flee Babylon, the historic plunderer *par excellence* and the administrative center of Persia's rule over Judah (2:6–9). And third, those fleeing Babylon for Jerusalem, including "many nations," will join themselves to YHWH (2:11). That is, YHWH's people will include foreigners.[18] According to the logic in which Zechariah shares, this is a concomitant of the universal extension of YHWH's reign, which is itself the condition of what YHWH here promises. YHWH's reign is universal, even as YHWH's presence is local—in Zion (1:14, 16; 2:11).

My description of Zechariah's first three visions and their oracles remains static and prosaic, in contrast with the visions themselves. In their form and imagery, the visions are dramatic, even fantastic; they evince a sense of urgency, initiated by the four horses of 1:8–12, and YHWH's response to their report. The picture of four horses patrolling the earth should alert us that something unusual is going on here. However, Job's first two chapters offer an analogous picture: the "sons of God" (בְּנֵי הָאֱלֹהִים | *binê hā'ĕlōhîm*) present themselves to YHWH after patrolling the earth (Job 1:6–7; 2:1–2). In many places the Old Testament portrays YHWH as having a retinue or council, as does Zechariah 3; there and in Job, YHWH's retinue includes "the satan." First Kings 22:19 calls YHWH's retinue the "host of heaven," which elsewhere includes YHWH's messengers/angels and warriors.[19] All of these—the sons of God, the host of heaven, YHWH's host, etc.—are collected in the epithet "hosts," a vigorously martial (Josh. 5:13–15) and also royal metaphor, which Zechariah applies to YHWH more frequently than does any other book of

---

[18] The term "join themselves to" (NRSV) is from the root לוה *(lwh)*—also the root of "Levite." In the niphal stem, as here, it means "devoted." This is the same term and stem Isa. 56:1–8 uses to speak of foreigners who have become devotees of YHWH.

[19] E. Theodore Mullen Jr., "Host, Host of Heaven," in *The Anchor Bible Dictionary* (New York: Doubleday, 1992), 3:301–4. This heavenly host may have been represented by horse figurines in Judean popular religion. See Othmar Keel and Christoph Uehlinger, *Göttinnen, Götter und Gottessymbole: neue Erkenntnisse zur Religionsgeschichte Kanaans und Israels aufgrund bislang unerschlossener ikonographischer Quellen*, Quæstiones disputatæ, 134 (Freiburg: Herder, 1993), 396–8.

the Bible. In his first vision, Zechariah sees these hosts under the image of four horses, but personified by the YHWH-angel who addresses "YHWH of hosts" (1:12). Following that address, action pervades the visions; everything is in motion, stirred by YHWH of hosts. Indeed, the first cycle of visions concludes in 2:13, following a flurry of activity and announcements of dramatic change in international arrangements, with an admonition addressed to "all flesh:" "Silence! For YHWH has stirred from his holy dwelling." YHWH has disturbed the earth's peace.

Zechariah's first vision is set in the dark, literally and metaphorically. Balancing it is the final vision (6:1–8), which once more involves horses. Again the horses present themselves to YHWH who commands them (6:5), but this time the horses have chariots, and this time they are not returning; they are going, as (not *to*, but *as*) the four winds of heaven, to the four (or three of the four) directions. These chariot-equipped horses burst forth from between two bronze mountains like the rising sun. Darkness has passed, and the light has dawned. In between the first and last visions, the world has changed; it has been refashioned, recreated, and YHWH's dominion extends universally.

We can read Zechariah 1–6 as a kind of cosmogony: a creation account similar to the one presented in Ps. 89:5–13.[20] In that text God creates the world, establishing a *cosmos*, by forcibly imposing order on the forces of chaos. As elsewhere in the Old Testament and beyond, those forces are represented mythically by raging waters and the sea (89:9); here they are personified as Rahab, the sea dragon.[21] However, the psalm also carries creation into the political realm, rehearsing YHWH's election of David, whose hands YHWH placed on "sea and rivers." These twin terms have both cosmic and political significance. In Ps. 24:2, YHWH has founded and established—has created—the world on "seas" and "rivers." But the sea and the rivers, in Ps. 89:25, refer also to the great sea, the Mediterranean, and the rivers Tigris and Euphrates; the terms mark out the ideal extent of David's kingdom (cf. Ps. 72:8; Zech. 9:10b). David was thus YHWH's earthly, political agent in maintaining cosmic order. "David," here, refers also to the Davidic royal house (Ps. 89:27–

---

[20] I will not here address the debated question whether the term "creation" is used appropriately in reference to texts such as Psalm 89. See my essay, "Isaiah's Creation Theology," *Ex Auditu* 3 (1988): 54–71.

[21] In Ps. 74:14 and Isa. 27:1 (cf. Job 3:8; 41:1), the sea monster is called Leviathan. On the topic, as related to this symposium, see Ben C. Ollenburger, "Peace and God's Action against Chaos in the Old Testament," in *The Church's Peace Witness*, ed. Marlin E. Miller and Barbara Nelson Gingerich (Grand Rapids: Eerdmans, 1994), 70–88. Rahab the sea monster has nothing to do with the Rahab who entertained spies, in Joshua 2. The words are different in Hebrew, and the sea monster is (grammatically) masculine.

37), and the past tense is appropriate. The point of the psalm's conclusion (vv. 38–51) is that YHWH's promises appear to have failed, there is no king, and chaos threatens—chaos that Psalms 74 and 77 describe with similar creation imagery. Zechariah 1–6, on the other hand, narrates in dramatic visionary fashion, and announces in oracles, the world's re-creation.[22]

Jon D. Levenson, drawing on earlier studies, has shown that the Priestly accounts of creation (Gen. 1:1–2:3) and of sanctuary construction (Exodus 25–40) display a "homology"—a "homology of temple and created world." The Bible depicts "the sanctuary as a world, that is, an ordered, supportive, and obedient environment," and "the world as a sanctuary, that is, a place in which the reign of God is visible and unchallenged, and his holiness is palpable, unthreatened, and pervasive."[23] Zechariah 1:7–6:15 *envisions* such a world, which includes the reconstructed temple at its center—at the center of the world, Jerusalem, and of Zechariah's visions, in chapter 4.[24] Just here, where the visions reduce their scope to what is most local, they refer to YHWH as "Lord of the whole earth" (4:14). At the beginning, in chapter 1, their scope is universal, encompassing the whole earth. From these extremities, the visions move to Judah (chap. 2) and Jerusalem, and finally to the temple itself (chap. 4). And precisely where the visions focus on the temple and YHWH's dwelling, the visions have their focus and pivot. Beginning in chapter 5, the movement is reversed until, in chapter 6, it again encompasses the whole earth whose Lord is YHWH (6:5). In the course of this movement, the "holy land" of Judah (2:12) has been purged of its guilt, injustice, and wickedness (3:9; 5:1–11). The world has been restored to its proper order, with YHWH as its Lord. This order includes the temple as the site of YHWH's presence and rule, symbolized by two olive trees that fuel a golden lampstand. World reconstruction and temple reconstruction form two integrated parts of YHWH's single initiative.

---

[22] See Michael H. Floyd, "Cosmos and History in Zechariah's View of the Restoration (Zechariah 1:7–6:15)," in *Problems in Biblical Theology: Essays in Honor of Rolf Knierim*, ed. Henry T. C. Sun and Keith L. Eades (Grand Rapids: Eerdmans, 1997), 125–44.

[23] *Creation and the Persistence of Evil: The Jewish Drama of Divine Omnipotence* (San Francisco: Harper and Row, 1988), 82, 86.

[24] For Zechariah, Zion/Jerusalem is the symbolic center of the earth, and as the site of YHWH's dwelling it is the real center. Ezekiel makes the notion explicit, in 5:5 and 38:12, where the LXX uses the term ὀμφαλός (*omphalos*, or "navel").

The spatial structure of Zechariah's visions

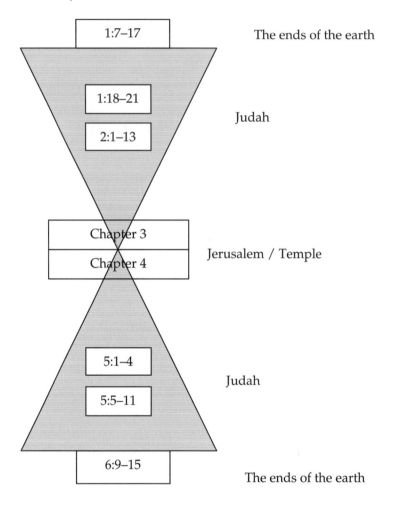

1:7–17	The ends of the earth
1:18–21	Judah
2:1–13	
Chapter 3	Jerusalem / Temple
Chapter 4	
5:1–4	Judah
5:5–11	
6:9–15	The ends of the earth

In the case of temple reconstruction, Zechariah's visions include oracular pronouncements to and about Zerubbabel, identified by Haggai as governor of Judah (Hag. 1:1, etc.). Zechariah 4:7–9 makes clear that Zerubbabel is the temple builder, a role that Israel and other ancient cultures assigned only to kings. That Judah's governor should build YHWH's temple could underwrite messianic expectations of the sort that Haggai attaches to Zerubbabel himself (Hag. 2:4–9, 20–22). If Zechariah's fourth chapter gives rise to such expectations, chapter 3 disarms them. It does so by legitimating the priestly leadership of Joshua against accusations by the satan, and by remanding expectations of royal leadership to the future: Joshua and his priestly colleagues hold a crown in waiting for the royal leader to come (3:8–9; cf. 6:9–15). The addition of chapter 3 to the series of visions pairs it now with chapter 4 at their center. While it disarms any messianic expectations regarding Zerubbabel, it also assigns to the priests a primary role as witnesses, or portents, of what YHWH will do in the future.

Zechariah, in 1:7–6:15, envisions a future dramatically different from current circumstances. The text constitutes a powerful rhetorical performance that envisions a reordered and recreated world. Zechariah's visionary rhetoric creates a counterfactual world that proposes to be taken as eminently real and habitable, intersecting the palpable world of Judean experience and Persian hegemony at a tangent. The radical disjunction between these two worlds takes the form of a disjunction between present and future—between a present that bears the name of Darius, "lord of the whole world," and a future determined by YHWH's initiative. But these two worlds do intersect, at a tangent comprising both Judah's present dismal circumstances and the announced return of YHWH, Lord of the whole earth, to Jerusalem. Zechariah envisions, that is to say, the reign of God.

A sermon: Zechariah 7:1–8:23

Among the remarkable features of Zechariah's visions and the oracles accompanying them is their exclusive emphasis on YHWH's initiative and action, grounded solely in YHWH's own promising self. No one among Zechariah's putative audience is enjoined to do anything, or to respond in any way, except insofar as they are included among the "all flesh" enjoined to be quiet (2:13). This situation changes in the sermon. Here, too, the emphasis falls heavily and decisively on YHWH's initiative, but this initiative is expected to elicit a response from those who hear, or rather who read, the sermon.

Providing the occasion for Zechariah's sermon, some two years after the visions (7:1), is an embassy from Bethel. They ask whether they should continue ritually commemorating the temple's destruction.[25] While they direct their inquiry to unnamed priests and prophets, it is Zechariah who answers—or, rather, who does not immediately answer but first changes the subject and addresses his Judean audience. He addresses them by posing his own rhetorical questions, about fasting and not fasting (7:5–6). He first asks if, when they fasted, it was for

---

[25] Presumably, the commemoration in "the fifth month" was for the temple's destruction in 586. On the fasts mentioned here, in 7:5, and in 8:19, see the essay by Friedman in the following note.

YHWH's sake; and second, if it is not true that, when they did *not* fast, it was *they* who ate and drank. His questions are not indictments, despite our tendency to read them in relation to the indictments of Isaiah 58. Rather, Zechariah regards fasting or not fasting as matters of indifference.[26] Fasting in Israel was a response to adversity, which the Judeans had faced for many years, and an appeal for God's intervention (Isa. 58:3; Joel 2:12–15). Pointedly, Zechariah notes that the Judeans had been fasting for seventy years, a figure that occurs also in 1:12, which inaugurates YHWH's announced return to Zion/Jerusalem. And YHWH's return transfigures everything; it marks a great reversal. Zechariah's sermon pivots on that reversal, and hence on YHWH's return.

The sermon's second section, comprising 7:7–14, speaks of the past, explaining the dire circumstances of the present on the basis of the past. In Zechariah's conception, the past included three interrelated components. First came the preaching of the prophets (7:7–10); second, the ancestors refused to listen to the prophets, which was the same as refusing to heed YHWH (7:11–12a); finally, YHWH reciprocated with wrath, scattering the ancestors among the nations and leaving the land desolate (7:12b–14). Of course, the past has a way of impinging on the present, and it does so here in two ways:

1. The current generation, whom Zechariah addresses, continues to experience, and apparently to rue, the desolation that Zechariah describes.

2. Zechariah's citation and quotation of the prophets serves both to explain the present on the basis of the past, and to address the current generation. Intervening between the citation (7:7) and the quotation (7:8) is a revelation formula: "the word of YHWH came to Zechariah, saying. . . ."[27] The word that comes to Zechariah, and which he proclaims, has as its content the prophetic preaching of the past, which remains the same for the present. Indeed, the prophetic summary quoted in 7:9–10 has its echo in 8:16–17, which Zechariah (speaking for YHWH) proclaims as conduct required in and for the future.

Zechariah does not have to persuade the Judeans that the past impinges on the present. It seems that they perceive a strict continuity between past and present, which is to say, they lack a sense of the *past* and hence

---

[26] My interpretation here follows that of Richard Elliott Friedman, "The Prophet and the Historian: The Acquisition of Historical Information from Literary Sources," *The Poet and the Historian: Essays in Literary and Historical Biblical Criticism*, ed. Richard Elliott Friedman; Harvard Semitic Series 26 (Chico, Calif.: Scholars Pr., 1983), 1–12.

[27] It is important to keep in mind that this sermon is first of all a literary or textual performance rather than an oral one. The reference to Zechariah here is in the third person.

of history. Zechariah's sermon gives them both. It does so by introducing a decisive rupture—YHWH's return to Zion (8:1–3)[28]—between the desolation still in evidence (7:14) and the future to be enjoyed (8:4–8). The announcement of this future, which YHWH's return inaugurates and makes possible, echoes the first and third of Zechariah's visions and their oracles (1:14–17; 2:10–12). But now this announcement and this future are set in contrast with a past that YHWH's return renders truly past, as a *history* that impinges on the present but does not determine it. The homily in 1:1–6, which adumbrates certain points of the sermon and now introduces the visions, reinforces this sense of history. It distinguishes between "you" and "your ancestors:" "Do not be like your ancestors," to whom the prophets preached in vain (1:4). Indeed, the continuity of the prophetic word across the generations forms the only genuine continuity between the past and the present.

As if to stress this very point, Zechariah begins the hortatory section of his sermon (8:9–17, 19) with reference to the prophets. He addresses those who have been hearing the words of the prophets since the temple's foundation was laid (8:9). I take this to be a reference to Zechariah's own proclamation, which both expressly and without citation, in the sermon and in the visions, draws intensively from a prophetic tradition that Zechariah continues. However that may be, the hortatory section of Zechariah's sermon falls into two parts: 8:9–13, 14–17.

Forming an envelope around the first part is the repeated exhortation, "Let your hands be strong" (8:9, 13). The intervening verses proclaim once more the great reversal that YHWH is bringing about. Rather than repeating the announcement of YHWH's return, which inaugurates this reversal, Zechariah points instead to the inauguration of temple reconstruction. Contrary to most interpretations, Zechariah is not here urging the Judeans to keep working on the temple.[29] To the contrary, he points to the temple's founding as a concrete sign of what he has already announced in 8:1–8. In 8:9–13, he exhorts the Judeans to maintain strong hands—that is, to maintain hope and not to fear (cf. Zeph. 3:16)—because YHWH will not deal with "the remnant of this people" as in the former days (Zech. 8:11). In other words, within this

---

[28] The verb in 8:3, as in 1:16, is שַׁבְתִּי (*šabtî*) in the perfect "tense." NRSV translates it as "I have returned" in 1:16, but in 8:3 as "I will return." I take it as a "performative perfect," which both announces and initiates an action (Paul Joüon and T. Muraoka, *A Grammar of Biblical Hebrew*, 2 vols., Subsidia Biblica 14 (Rome: Editrice Pontificio Istituto Biblio, 1991), #112f, g.

[29] That interpretation reads Zechariah in light of Haggai, who does indeed exhort the Judeans to work on the temple.

first part of Zechariah's hortatory section he rehearses the depredations of the past in order to *contrast* them with what has begun: "But now!" (8:11).

One feature of that contrast is especially significant for our consideration. In the past, Zechariah says, there was not shalom; but now there will be a "sowing of shalom" (8:10, 12). The term has different connotations in these two verses. In verse 10, the lack of shalom is associated with economic disaster, affecting both people and livestock. In particular, its absence made any sort of social intercourse so danger-ous—so violently adversarial—as to render it impossible.[30] In verse 12, shalom is associated with agriculture. In particular, its presence will mean agricultural productivity. In these two verses it would be justified to translate shalom as, respectively, "safety" (so NRSV) and "prosperity" (so NJPS).[31] This prosperity depends on the cooperation of earth and sky ("heavens")—that is, on fertility and rain. Perry Yoder has taught us that the term shalom embraces a range of meanings, all of them compre-hended in the notion of well-being—of things as they should be.[32] In Zech. 8:10, this notion refers, as typically, to the social world, while in verse 12 it extends to the natural world. This latter, *natural* conception of shalom does not appear elsewhere in the Book of the Twelve. However, it does appear prominently in Psalm 72.

The psalm is a prayer for the king and for the quality of his reign. Endowed with divine justice and righteousness (v. 1), the king himself shall exhibit those qualities and his reign will reflect them. Indeed, "righteousness shall flourish and an abundance of peace [shalom]" (v. 7). In its context, this is clearly a social conception of shalom, but the verb translated "flourish" (פָּרַח | *pārah*) occurs most often in botanical contexts, with the meaning "to sprout."[33] And Ps. 72:3 clearly employs the natural conception of shalom, praying that the mountains will yield shalom ("prosperity," NRSV). The king is instrumental to the achievement of shalom in both its social and its natural conceptions.[34] He is to deliver the poor and needy and save their lives (vv. 12–14), but also to be like the rain and spring showers, producing both peace and abundant crops (vv.

---

[30] NRSV's "safety from the foe" translates שָׁלוֹם מִן הַצָּר (*šālôm min haṣār*).

[31] NJPS has "what it sows shall prosper" (8:12) for the NRSV's "sowing of peace" (זֶרַע הַשָּׁלוֹם | *zēra' haššālôm*).

[32] Perry B. Yoder, *Shalom: The Bible's Word for Salvation, Justice, and Peace* (Newton: Faith & Life Pr., 1987), 12–16.

[33] As in Ps. 92:12, where the righteous sprout, or flourish, like a palm tree.

[34] Traditionally, the king in this Psalm has been identified as Solomon, whose name in Hebrew is cognate with *shalom*.

6, 16). The psalm also hopes that the king's dominion will be extensive (v. 8), and that kings from subject nations near and distant will bring him tribute (vv. 10–11).[35]

Zechariah's conjunction of both social and natural conceptions of shalom in chapter 8 thus has precedent. In fact, the conjunction may be a matter of cause and effect (David Hume notwithstanding). That is, the absence of shalom in the social world—hence, the presence of pervasive violence (Zech. 8:10)—may have caused the land to be unproductive. Or, to put it positively, the restoration of shalom in the social sphere may be the cause of its restoration in the natural world (8:12). Any number of examples from recent experience could be cited in favor of such a cause-effect relationship. Vineyards, when they are battlegrounds, produce no wine. Earlier, Hosea drew an explicit, causal connection between social non-shalom and ecological disaster—or non-shalom in the natural world (Hos. 4:1–3).[36] Jeremiah makes the same connection, in Jer. 5:23–24.[37] In Zechariah, the connection between shalom's absence in the social and in the natural sphere remains implicit. But strikingly, Zechariah attributes the adversarial social violence of the past to YHWH's own initiative—"I set them all against one another" (NRSV). Literally, "I let them all loose against their fellow-citizens" (8:10). In other words, the absence of shalom was YHWH's punishment—but it was punishment precisely for the ancestors' neglect of shalom-producing social justice (7:8–12). Here, as elsewhere, YHWH's punishment amounts to poetic justice.[38] And the promise of Zech. 8:12, the promise of shalom in the natural world, announces the end of that poetry.

---

[35] The notion of a legitimate, just king whose reign will produce peace and prosperity, fertility and fecundity, and will be universally recognized, is attested in other ancient texts. In some of them, extending from Babylon to the Hellenistic "Potter's Oracle," this ideal king is anticipated in the future. For bibliography see Ben C. Ollenburger, *Zion, the City of the Great King: A Theological Symbol of the Jerusalem Cult*, JSOT Supplement Series 41 (Sheffield, England: Sheffield Academic Pr., Ltd., 1987), 143–4, 233–4, n.305; Shalom M. Paul, *Amos: A Commentary on the Book of Amos*, Hermeneia (Minneapolis: Fortress Pr., 1991), 289, n.11.

[36] I take (false) swearing, lying [bearing false witness], stealing, adultery, and rampant lethal violence to be, for Hosea, examples of non-shalom—of things not as they should be in the social sphere. See Allen R. Guenther, *Hosea and Amos*, Believers Church Bible Commentary (Scottdale: Herald Pr., 1998), 105.

[37] Patrick D. Miller, "Creation and Covenant," in *Biblical Theology: Problems and Perspectives*, ed. Steven J. Kraftchick, Charles D. Myers Jr., Ben C. Ollenburger (Nashville: Abingdon Pr., 1995), 165.

[38] On the theme, see Patrick D. Miller, *Sin and Judgment in the Prophets: A Stylistic and Theological Analysis*, Society of Biblical Literature Monograph Series, no. 27 (Chico, Calif.: Scholars Pr., 1982).

The same verse returns, at its end, to a social matter. Not only will the land again be productive, but YHWH will cause "the remnant of this people" to possess its produce.[39] We should understand this promise on analogy with a contemporary passage, Isa. 62:8–9—"I [YHWH] will never again give your grain to your enemies for food, and neither shall foreigners drink the new wine for which you have labored, but those who harvest it shall eat it . . . and those who gather it shall drink it in my holy courts"—and against the background of oppressive imperial taxation. Shalom, in this instance, includes economic liberation and, by implication, independence.

It may be instructive to refer once more to Psalm 72, which I adduced as precedent for the conjunction of social and natural conceptions of shalom. In that psalm the king is the principal agent of comprehensive shalom, owing to endowments granted by YHWH. And shalom there expressly includes not just independence but dominion—Israel's or Judah's dominion over subject nations who will bring tribute. I first cited Psalm 72, above, in a discussion of Psalm 89, which provided illustrative background to the cosmogonic character of Zech. 1:7–6:15. In that psalm, too, the king is central to the world's divinely constructed order and is YHWH's agent in its maintenance, an order that includes the Davidic king's elevation—hence, his and Israel's dominion—over all adversaries and all rival kings (Ps. 89:23, 27). I also mentioned Haggai's attribution of messianic expectations, redolent of Psalm 89, to Zerubbabel, a Davidide to be sure, but governor of a depressed Persian province, with a capital, Jerusalem, whose population numbered in the hundreds.[40] One of Zechariah's visions (chap. 4), like Haggai's pronouncements, names Zerubbabel the temple-builder; otherwise, the visions postpone any messianic expectations to the future. Neither do they expect Judean (by contrast with YHWH's) dominion *over* other nations. Zechariah's sermon contains no hint whatever of messianism. It adumbrates, in the barest form, a cosmogony—the restoration of social and natural shalom in a reversal of the divinely wrought chaos that reigned for, say, seventy years—but it neither names nor anticipates a regal figure as its symbol or agent. Still, shalom does have agents.

---

[39] "The remnant" here refers to those (literally) left over from the depredations of the past, and who will form, as Zechariah and other prophets hope, the reconstituted houses of Judah and Israel (8:13).

[40] See Carol L. and Eric M. Meyers, "Demography and Diatribes: Yehud's Population and the Prophecy of Second Zechariah," in *Scripture and Other Artifacts: Essays on the Bible and Archaeology in Honor of Philip J. King*, ed. Michael D. Coogan, et al. (Louisville: Westminster John Knox Pr., 1994), 268–85.

Zechariah's sermon assigns the responsibility, the proximate agency, for shalom to the people it addresses.[41] This assignment comes in the context of another recapitulation (Zech. 8:14–17) that stresses YHWH's reversal—a change of intentions from affliction to beneficence. So, again, YHWH says "Do not fear" (8:15, as in 8:9, 13), and then tells the people what to do (8:16–17). In essence, what they are to do is precisely what the prophets had told their ancestors to do (7:9–10). This now takes the form of speaking the truth and issuing legal judgments that are truthful or just and (or which) "make for shalom" (8:16). The people are not to contrive evil toward one another or to **love** false oaths, which YHWH **hates**; instead, they are to **love** truth and shalom (8:19). In light of what YHWH has decided and done, that is to say—in light of YHWH's conversion (transitive and intransitive)—the people are to share YHWH's affectional preferences: a hatred of internecine malevolence and prejudicial judgments that desiccate shalom, and a love of truthfulness and of shalom itself. They are to be shalom's agents.

Intervening between 8:16 and the reference to shalom in 8:19, Zechariah finally answers, in YHWH's voice, the question posed by the embassy from Bethel, which provoked the sermon in the first place (7:3). The fasts, now expanded to three, may indeed be commemorated, but they will be festal occasions of joy. Having answered the provoking question, Zechariah refers again to truth and shalom as things that the Judeans must **love** (8:19c). The concluding clause of 8:19 stands in a disjunctive relationship to the preceding, and the disjunction is probably adversative: "But truth and shalom (you must) **love**."[42] The point is not to oppose love of truth and shalom to celebratory fasting, as though they were incompatible. It is to stress, here as at the beginning, YHWH's indifference to fasting in light of the decisive importance of truth and shalom. That indifference is clear from Zechariah's characterization of the fasts as occasions for joy and celebration, and for delightful convocations (8:19b)—transforming fasts into something quite unlike fasts have ever been.[43]

Zechariah addresses his sermon, not yet concluded, to the Judeans. However, the sermon proceeds from questions posed by delegates from Bethel. The leaders of that delegation have non-Jewish names: Sharezer

---

[41] There is a theological analogy here to the "democratization" of the Davidic covenant in Isaiah 40–55, verbally implicit throughout and explicit in Isa. 55:1–8.

[42] Cf. NJPS; contrast the NRSV's "therefore."

[43] See the characterization of fasting in 7:3, 5.

and Regem-melech.[44] The names alone do not prove anything, but I suggest that Zechariah uses this foreign delegation to illustrate the concluding promise of his sermon, in 8:20–23—a promise that people from many cities and from all the nations will come to seek YHWH of hosts.[45] They will also come to "entreat YHWH's favor" (8:22), which is precisely what the people from Bethel came to Jerusalem to do (7:2; the verbal parallel is exact). That delegation represents the proleptic fulfillment of YHWH's extravagant promises, which conclude Zechariah's sermon.

Those promises echo and expand dramatically Zechariah's oracle in 2:13. There, following the third vision, many nations will devote themselves to YHWH. No motive is given for this devotion, which occurs in the context of international rearrangements spurred by YHWH's anger at the nations (1:15). In Zechariah's sermon, people from all the nations attach themselves to Judeans,[46] saying, "Let us go with you, because we have heard that God is with you" (8:23). How will they have heard?

PEACE, MISSION, AND THE REIGN OF GOD

In my discussion of Zechariah's sermon I have demurred from translating the term *shalom*, and specifically from translating it as "peace." As I noted in the introduction, above, NJPS renders none of Zechariah's six occurrences of *shalom* with "peace." Instead, in the sermon, it has "safe" (8:10), "prosper" (8:12), "perfect" [judgments] (8:16), and "integrity." I have already granted that the translation of *shalom* as "prosper(ity)" in 8:12 has justification: the ground will yield its abundant produce, providing sustenance to the people who work it. Moreover, I grant the appropriateness of each of NJPS's other translations of *shalom* in Zechariah 8. This returns us to the question, also raised in the introduction, whether Zechariah has anything at all to say to us about *peace*. It is difficult, now, to take the question seriously. If

---

[44] The Assyrian king Sennacherib had a son named Sharezer (2 Kings 19:37//Isa. 37:38), which appears also as part of the name of a Babylonian official (Jer. 39:3, 13).

[45] NRSV has "mighty nations," but the adjective (עָצוּם | *'āṣûm*) can also mean "countless" or, in parallel with רַב (*rab*), as here, "all" (Francis Brown, S. R. Driver, Charles A. Briggs, *A Hebrew and English Lexicon of the Old Testament* (Oxford: Clarendon Pr., 1907).

[46] I use the term "Judeans" instead of "Jews" (so NRSV, NJPS, etc.) here with reservations. Some groups have made a distinction between Judeans and Jews in the service of viciously anti-Semitic, and patently specious, historical arguments. By "Judeans" I mean the people—יְהוּדִים "Yehudites"—of whom Zechariah speaks in the Persian province of Yehud. They are in continuity, ethnic, religious, and cultural, with those whom another language and culture will call "Jews."

peace does not comprise safety (freedom from adversarial violence in society), authentic justice, and integrity in social relations, then . . . what?

Historically, among Mennonites and elsewhere, and for understandable reasons, discussions of peace have gathered around war. And we have also learned to insist that "Peace is not . . . simply a negative, the absence of war."[47] Zechariah confirms this common insistence, refusing (unlike the NRSV's translators) to call the cessation of hostilities between international belligerents—i.e., the absence of war—shalom (1:11). Yet peace is *also* the absence of war, and the Old Testament knows very well the contrast, shalom/war (Mic. 3:5; Eccles. 3:8). It does make sense, then, to ask whether Zechariah says anything about peace in contrast to war.

The answer to that question, as it seems to me, is clearly affirmative. And the answer comes where Zechariah broaches the other part of the domain under discussion, mission. Zechariah 8:21 promises that people will go from one city to another saying, "Come, let us go entreat the favor of YHWH." The destination of this international procession, to which people from cities outside of Judah invite each other, is Jerusalem. Their invitation closely echoes that of the peoples similarly quoted in Isa. 2:3//Mic. 4:2—"Come, let us go up to the mountain of the LORD, to the house of the God of Jacob; that he may teach us his ways and that we may walk in his paths" (NRSV).[48] The destination of the international procession in Isaiah and Micah is also Jerusalem/Zion, and its purpose is to hear the *torah* and word of YHWH—YHWH's instruction, by means of which YHWH will judge between nations and adjudicate their disputes. Having no need of them, the nations will transform their armaments into farm implements and forget war. In Isaiah, the medium, or the intermediary, of YHWH's word and *torah* is the prophet (Isa. 1:10; cf. 8:16; 30:8–9).

Zechariah says nothing expressly about the end of war. However, in his sermon—it is technically a prophetic *torah*: responding, on YHWH's authority, to an inquiry (cf. Hag. 2:11–14)—he performs and exemplifies the role of intermediary in the presence of, and as provoked by (on my interpretation), a symbolically international delegation, foreshadowing the future. In the future, all the nations will come to "seek YHWH" and, like the Bethel delegation, entreat YHWH's favor (Zech. 8:22; cf. Amos

---

47 Joseph P. Healey, "Peace: Old Testament," in *The Anchor Bible Dictionary*, 3:206–7. My citation of Healey on this point is not meant to be critical of his article, which I recommend highly. See also Claus Westermann, "Peace (Shalom) in the Old Testament," in *The Meaning of Peace: Biblical Studies*, 2nd ed., ed. Perry B. Yoder and Willard M. Swartley, Studies in Peace and Scripture (Elkhart: Institute of Mennonite Studies, 2001), 37–70; see esp. 37–9.

48 The verbal parallels between Zech. 8:21a, 22a, 23, and Isa. 2:3a//Mic. 4:2a are instructive. Both passages speak of "many peoples who will say, 'come, let us go . . .'"

8:12). Zechariah exemplifies the very prophetic role that Isaiah expects will be instrumental to war's end. But at the end, in 8:23, Zechariah says something dramatically different. In the future, people (or their representatives: "ten men"[49]) from everywhere, speaking every tongue, will reach out, not just to a prophet, but to ordinary Judeans, and indeed to the closest Judean at hand. Their request, "let us go *with you* [plural]," parallels and depends on "God is *with you* [plural]." God's seekable presence, and hence the prophetic role that Isaiah and, differently, Zechariah embody is radically democratized. International and universally representative delegations seeking a divine presence communally embodied bear no swords, and have need of none.

The communal embodiment of shalom—including "peace" in as many senses as the term can plausibly bear—I understand to be one very large part of Zechariah's contribution to our understanding of mission. The other part, perhaps equally large, I understand to be caught up in the notion of intermediation, democratized as Zechariah has it, even if obliquely, at the sermon's end. The sermon, like the visions, is a powerful rhetorical performance, with no fewer than eleven instances of "thus says YHWH," referring to what YHWH said, says, and promises—much of it interpretive of and in continuity with earlier prophetic texts. Mission is also rhetoric, and even hermeneutics.

To this point in a very long essay, I have said almost nothing expressly about the reign of God. It has seemed unnecessary. But let me say that, in Zechariah's sermon as in its visions and oracles, *everything* depends on God's reign, and on the imposition of God's reign against all apparent circumstances. That is to say, "peace," whatever aspect of shalom the term may translate in a given instance, depends utterly and entirely on the regal action of YHWH, which reverses the past and opens the future. Peaceable conduct comes to the Judeans as an obligation precisely on the basis of YHWH's decision *and* action, and it is an obligation to maintain the peace that YHWH desires *and* achieves. They cannot—the Judeans cannot—return the earth to fertility, and neither can they conjure rain from the heavens, nor insure that the produce of a newly restored order will be theirs to enjoy. That is God's doing entirely. They can but bear witness: peace—shalom, if you will—is the shape of their witness, and mission is its concomitant.

---

[49] The locution "ten men" may be shorthand or representative; cf. Judg. 6:27; Jer. 41:1–8; Amos 6:9, etc.

CONCLUSION

The conclusions reached in the preceding paragraphs seem entirely conventional, and well within the epistemic circle I assumed at the beginning. What could be more conventional among contemporary Mennonites than a conclusion that mission is a concomitant of peace—especially if peace, in this instance, includes (social) justice as its defining component? Have we gained no new knowledge at all?

Answers to that question will be forthcoming, I am confident. In the meanwhile, let me suggest that the dependence on God's reign of both peace and mission, as well as their conjunction, is neither incidental nor negligible. Zechariah, in chapters 1–8, goes to massive lengths, rhetorical and theological, to construct a vision of God's reign against equally massive odds. He acknowledges that it will seem impossible to those who hear it (8:6).[50] In other words, his articulated announcement of God's reign, on which everything depends, flies in the face of what passes for reality, controlled as it is by a rigorous Persian administration. In the sermon as in the book's preceding visions and oracles, Zechariah describes and anticipates and proclaims the lineaments of a new world order, consonant with the hilarious notion that YHWH is Lord of the whole earth, including the large part of it claimed for himself by Darius. In that description, Zechariah employs diverse literary forms, all of them part of a prophetic (i.e., biblical) repertoire known to his audience. But he expands those forms and adapts them to a situation in which the *content* of that earlier prophetic corpus seemed inadequate or irrelevant, perhaps even falsified. He goes so far as to employ motifs and imagery from popular religion of a sort that earlier literature condemned. In doing so, he fashions a rhetorical world that is at once counterfactual and habitable: in which what seems literally impossible becomes imaginable and believable, and even, in parts, obligatory. The visionary, artistic, and pastoral way—but also the hermeneutical sophistication with which—Zechariah wrote the new world order into existence forms a part of his essentially missionary task.[51]

It also serves as a laudable example, but not an easily followable one. No missionary, not to mention a seminary professor, can imitate Zechariah's confidence in citing the freshly revealed word of God. Even Zechariah's charismatic exegesis of biblical texts lies beyond our capacity

---

[50] Or perhaps something like, "It would have seemed impossible [to them] in those days . . . "

[51] Samuel Balentine describes similar contemporaneous efforts among those who produced the Psalter and the books of Chronicles, in "The Politics of Religion in the Persian Period," *After the Exile: Essays in Honour of Rex Mason,* ed. John Barton and David J. Reimer (Macon: Mercer Univ. Pr., 1996), 12–46.

and authority. But it is not, finally, the example of the prophet but the creatively formed and world-forming *content* of the book that instructs us. I have tried to show that it instructs us about the single domain, peace and mission, but also that this single domain has both as its presupposition and defining content the reign of God. Peace and mission together depend on, even as they are rendered possible and then obligatory by, the establishment, the imposition, of God's reign.

For Zechariah, the beginning of temple reconstruction is the material sign of that reign's incipience, which does not, however, depend on that material sign. Rather, it depends—all of it depends—on God's own initiative and God's promise, which Zechariah proclaims relentlessly. Of that relentless proclamation we can indeed be imitators, we who believe that the Branch—of whom Joshua and his priestly colleagues were portents, and for whom they held a crown in waiting—has come and has been crowned, though with thorns. That crown, too, is a sign and a witness and an act of God's initiative, making us lovers of integrity and peace. We have grasped the hem of a Judean—a Jew—as the products, proponents, and portents of the *missio Dei* in and against yet always for the world.

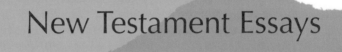

New Testament Essays

7 | *As sheep in the midst of wolves*
Mission and peace in the Gospel of Matthew

Dorothy Jean Weaver

TO EXPLORE THE INTERFACE BETWEEN MISSION AND peace in the Gospel of Matthew is to address an issue that at first glance appears insignificant. While Matthew is clearly concerned with the mission of the church,[1] he employs the vocabulary of peace only five times in the Gospel.[2] And the evidence of these five passages is ambiguous. On one hand, Jesus instructs his disciples to greet the houses they enter with a word of peace (10:12–13a), and he pronounces blessing on peacemakers (5:9). But in the remaining uses of this word group, Jesus speaks about his own mission and that of his disciples in terms not of peace but of its absence (10:13b, 34). Matthew's limited and ambiguous use of the vocabulary of peace suggests that addressing the subject of mission and peace as a central focus of this Gospel is unwarranted.

If one addresses the question of mission and peace to Matthew's narrative, however, the results are quite different. Although Matthew does not give prominence to the vocabulary of peace, he paints a vivid portrait of peace through the events and characters of his story. And this portrait of peace is integrally linked to the motif of mission. Those who are sent to carry out the work of the kingdom of heaven—the prophets,[3] John the Baptist,[4] Jesus,[5] Jesus' first disciples and the disciples to follow[6]—are precisely the ones whose life and calling exhibit a profound commitment to the ways of peace. To pursue the link between mission

---

[1] Note the prominence of Matthew's missionary discourse (9:35–11:1), as it is bracketed within the portrayal of Jesus' ministry (4:23–25; 9:35; 11:1), and the climactic focus on the great commission (28:16–20), with which Jesus both reissues and expands the commission of chapter 10.

[2] "Peace" appears twice in 10:13 and twice in 10:34; "peacemakers" appears in 5:9.

[3] See 23:37; cf. 21:34, 36.

[4] See 11:10.

[5] See 10:40; 15:24; cf. 21:37.

[6] See 10:5, 16; 20:2; 22:3, 4; 23:34.

and peace in Matthew's Gospel, then, we need to examine Matthew's narrative portrayal of those who are sent out, and observe the way they carry out their vocations in behalf of the kingdom of heaven.

"FOR IN THIS WAY THEY PERSECUTED THE PROPHETS"

In the world of Matthew's narrative, the prophets of Jewish history play a crucial role in setting the stage for the events of Jesus' ministry. Throughout the narrative a clear picture of the prophetic vocation emerges. The prophets are those who are sent out (23:37; cf. 21:34, 36) by God[7] to the Jewish people. Their task is primarily verbal: they are the human channels through whom the word of the Lord is first spoken[8] to the people and then written[9] as Scriptures[10] for the continuing instruction of the people. The prophets' vocation also moves beyond the spoken and written word to the level of sign, a word enacted in the life of the prophet.[11] The prophets' entire existence—words, actions, even inner longings—is shaped by their identity as people sent out by God.

Matthew paints a vivid portrait of the fate to which prophets are destined. They are without honor in their own country and in their own house (13:57).[12] They are taken, persecuted, beaten, stoned, killed, murdered, and entombed by others who thereby make themselves responsible for the blood of these prophets.[13] Nor is there any question about the reason for this brutal treatment: the prophets encounter dishonor, persecution, and death precisely because they have faithfully discharged their duties as those who are sent out. In the parable of the wicked tenants (21:33–46), the slaves who are sent out by the vineyard owner to collect his fruits meet their fate at the hands of the wicked tenants precisely as they come to the vineyard to carry out their task. Similarly, Jesus' lament that Jerusalem "kills the prophets and stones those who are sent out to it" (23:37) implies that it is specifically in the

---

[7] The theological passive—"those who are sent" (23:37)—indicates that it is God who sends out the prophets. All Scripture translations in this essay are my own.

[8] See 1:22; 2:15, 17, 23; 3:3; 4:14; 8:17; 12:17; 13:35; 21:4; 24:15; 27:9. Compare 11:13, where Jesus uses the language of prophecy to describe the task of prophets, and 12:38–42, where Jesus speaks of the proclamation of the prophet Jonah.

[9] See 2:5.

[10] See 26:56.

[11] Jesus refers to the sign of Jonah the prophet, who was in the belly of the sea monster for three days and three nights (12:39–40).

[12] Although Jesus is referring to himself in this instance, he does so by appealing to common knowledge about prophetic experience.

[13] See 5:12; 21:35; 23:29–37.

course of their work, and because of it, that the prophets are struck down.

The most striking aspect of this portrait of the prophets is their peaceable response to the brutal reception they encounter. In the story about the wicked tenants, the slaves who are sent out by the vineyard owner to take his fruits instead allow themselves to be taken, beaten, stoned, and killed by those to whom they have been sent. Their mission entails the taking of fruits, not the taking of human life.

But the response of the slaves is not a result of impotence in the face of power greater than their own. Jesus' question to his listeners and their perceptive response (21:40–41) make clear that the vineyard owner has power that will enable him to rain down terrible destruction on his tenants in his own time and way. The vineyard owner could come to the immediate rescue of his beleaguered emissaries. Or he could authorize and empower the slaves to retaliate against the brutalities to which they are repeatedly subjected. Instead, he persistently sends his slaves to the wicked tenants in his vineyard (21:34, 36; cf. 21:37) armed only with the urgent knowledge that the right time for the fruits has arrived and with the certain knowledge that the vineyard owner has commissioned them to take his fruits (21:34).

Nor is the vineyard owner negligent. With clear awareness of what has happened to his first servants, and in direct response to their fate, he renews and even intensifies his efforts to retrieve the fruits of his vineyard. When a second and larger group of slaves meets with the same fate as the first, the vineyard owner finally sends out the most important emissary, his own son, in the hope that the son will meet with the respect that his predecessors did not receive (21:35–37).

The vineyard owner will not let the persecution of his emissaries deter him from his ongoing mission to retrieve the fruits of his vineyard. In the face of all opposition, he will continue to send his slaves to carry out the urgent task of taking his fruits. If their mission is not received, their calling is to suffer brutalities without retaliating. Such is the peaceable mission of the prophets of Jewish history.

But the prophets' mission and their suffering do not go unvindicated. In both the parable of the wicked tenants (21:33–46) and Jesus' lament over Jerusalem (23:37–39), the threat of present, future, and eschatological judgment hangs over those who do not receive the prophets and those sent to them. Already in the present, as Jesus assures Jerusalem, "your house is left to you deserted" (23:38); Jesus' words apparently refer to the spiritual emptiness of the Jewish temple. And in a future both historical and eschatological, the vineyard owner will rain down terrible destruction on those who have rejected his servants and give away to others the vineyard presently under their control (21:41). This word, spoken by Jesus' listeners in unwitting judgment on themselves, points both to the coming destruction of Jerusalem (cf. 22:7; 24:1–2) and to the eschatological judgment on the Jewish leadership from whom the kingdom of God will be taken away (21:43). The prophets of Jewish history, called to face persecution and death peaceably and without retaliation as they carry out their mission to the Jewish people, are assured of ultimate vindication by God, the one who has sent them out to their task.

"BUT THEY DID TO [JOHN THE BAPTIST] WHATEVER THEY WANTED"

The prophets of Jewish history are figures from a former era whose words and lives form the backdrop to Matthew's narrative.[14] In contrast, John the Baptist strides onto the scene as a living, dynamic character in the present-day world of Matthew's story. But much in the portrayal of John the Baptist links him with the prophets of times past.

Like his forebears, John has been sent by God to carry out his task. John is "the one about whom it is written, 'Look, I send out my messenger before your face,'" a prophecy of Malachi spoken in the divine first person (11:10).[15] John also shares with his forebears their prophetic vocation. John appears in the wilderness of Judea proclaiming the word of the Lord, which is at the same time the word of the coming reign of God (3:2): "Repent! For the kingdom of heaven has come near."

John is a prophetic figure, "the voice of one who is crying in the wilderness" (3:3; cf. Isa. 40:3 LXX). John's call to repentance fulfills the prophetic task of calling the people to "prepare [ἑτοιμάσατε | hetoimasate] the way of the Lord"—here a reference to Jesus himself—and to "straighten his paths." Jesus identifies John with the prophetic messenger of Malachi, whose task—in words addressed in this context to Jesus himself—is to "prepare [κατασκευάσει | kataskeuasei] your way before you" (11:10; cf. Mal. 3:1 LXX).

For his part, John prepares the way before Jesus by proclaiming the message of "the one coming after me" (3:11; cf. 11:3) and by inaugurating a ministry of baptism which he carries out at the Jordan river (3:1–17; 21:25), and for which he acquires the label "the Baptist."[16] For their part, the people prepare the way of the Lord by coming to John to confess

---

[14] See, for example, 11:13. See also 23:35, an apparent reference to the historical scope of the Jewish Scriptures.

[15] Cf. Mal. 3:1 LXX; Exod. 23:20 LXX.

[16] 3:1; 11:11–12; 14:2, 8; 16:14; 17:13.

their sins (3:6; cf. 3:11), to receive his baptism,[17] and to hear his proclamation (3:7–12).

John's proclamation is unpolished, uncalculating, and uncompromising. He calls the crowds to repent. He denounces the religious leadership as a brood of snakes seeking to flee the coming wrath, accuses them of unwarranted reliance on their Abrahamic parentage, calls them to bear fruit worthy of repentance, and warns them of impending and fiery judgment if they do not (3:2, 7–12). To Herod the tetrarch, who has married Herodias, the wife of his brother Philip, John's word is blunt and persistent:[18] "It is not lawful for you to have her" (14:4). John's proclamation has all the biting rhetorical character of the proclamation of the prophets of Jewish history.[19]

Because of his words, John acquires a prophetic reputation. Not only do the crowds consider John to be a prophet (14:5; 21:26; cf. 16:14), but Jesus himself labels John "a prophet . . . , and more than a prophet" (11:9). In fact, John fills no less a role than that of "Elijah who is to come,"[20] the final prophet who appears in advance of the "great and glorious day of the Lord" (Mal. 3:22 LXX) in order to restore all things (17:11; cf. Mal. 3:23 LXX). John wears the clothing of Elijah (3:4; cf. 2 Kings 1:8 LXX) and lives a correspondingly righteous (21:32) and ascetic (9:14; 11:18) life. And Jesus announces John's identity as Elijah both to the crowds (11:14) and to his own disciples (17:10–13).

As a prophet, John encounters the fate that befell his forebears. To be sure, John meets with a positive reception from the common people. The crowd reveres him as a prophet (14:5; 21:26). Jerusalem and all Judea and all the surrounding areas of the Jordan go out to receive his baptism (3:5–6), and even the tax collectors and prostitutes witness John's ministry and believe him (21:31–32). But from the leaders, both religious and political, John meets with a different response. The religious leaders accept no aspect of John's prophetic vocation—not his ascetic life style (11:18),[21] his verbal proclamation (21:31b–32; cf. 28–31a), or his baptism

---

[17] 3:5–6, 11; cf. 3:13–14, 16.

[18] The use of the iterative imperfect form ἔλεγεν (*elegen*) suggests that John spoke not once but repeatedly to Herod.

[19] Cf., for example, the rhetoric of Nathan (2 Sam. 12:7–12), Elijah (1 Kings 21:17–24), Amos (Amos 4:1–3), and Ezekiel (Ezek. 34:1–10).

[20] Thus 11:14; 17:10–13; cf. Mal. 3:22 LXX.

[21] Judging from the charges against John (11:18) and Jesus (11:19), Jesus seems to be referring more to the religious leadership than to the common people. Elsewhere it is the Pharisees who accuse Jesus of demon possession (9:34; 12:24) and castigate him for consorting with tax collectors and sinners (9:11); and it is the chief priests and elders of the

(21:25).[22] Instead, they fail to recognize the Elijah in their midst (17:12), accuse him of demon possession (11:18), and do not believe him (21:25, 31, 32) or respond to his ministry (21:30).

At the hands of political powers John faces imprisonment and death. Like the prophets of Jewish history, John meets this fate as the result of his prophetic vocation and in the course of his work. In true prophetic fashion John meddles in the affairs of Herod the king (14:9). Herod responds to the affront by seizing John and binding him (14:3), handing him over (4:12), putting him in prison,[23] killing him (14:5) by decapitation (14:10; cf. 8, 11), and leaving his corpse (14:12) to be buried by his disciples. Such is the fate of the one who comes preparing the Lord's way (11:10).

John meets this fate as one who is physically powerless and peaceable.[24] From the moment of his arrest, John is portrayed not as an actor but as a victim of others' actions. In the accounts of his imprisonment and death (4:12; 11:2–6; 14:1–12), only three active verbal forms refer to John's initiatives: John hears about what the Messiah is doing, he sends his disciples to Jesus, and he says something to Jesus (11:2–3).

By contrast, John appears three times as the subject of passive verbs and nine times as the object of active verbs. John is handed over (4:12), and his head is brought to the daughter of Herodias and given to her (14:11–12). Others seize John, bind him, put him in prison with the intent to kill him (14:3, 5). They then decapitate him, bring his head to Herodias, take his corpse, and bury it (14:10–12). Jesus' comments about John's death portray John in a similar light. Jesus announces to the crowds that "from the days of John the Baptist until now the kingdom of heaven [or John himself!] has been subjected to violence and violent people [or Herod the tetrarch!] have taken it by force" (11:12). Jesus offers his disciples this oblique epitaph for John: "And I say to you that

---

people (21:23) who apparently view themselves over against the tax collectors and the prostitutes (21:31–32).

[22] Elsewhere (3:7, 11) the Pharisees and Sadducees do in fact come out to the Jordan and receive baptism from John, but the harshness of John's rhetorical attack on them ("You brood of vipers" (3:7) clearly suggests that John does not trust the genuineness of their repentance (3:8).

[23] δεσμωτήριον | *desmōtērion* (11:2); φυλακή | *phylakē* (14:3, 10).

[24] For a detailed treatment of Matthew's characterization of John the Baptist in 14:1–12, see Dorothy Jean Weaver, "Power and Powerlessness: Matthew's Use of Irony in the Portrayal of Political Leaders," in *Treasures New and Old: Recent Contributions to Matthean Studies,* Symposium Series, no. 1, ed. David R. Bauer and Mark Allan Powell (Atlanta: Scholars Pr., 1996), 179–96.

Elijah has already come; and they did not recognize him, but did to him whatever they wished" (17:12).

This portrait of John's passion leads to several conclusions. As the vineyard owner sent his slaves, God has sent John to his task (11:10). But God does not intervene in the tawdry and violent affairs of Herod in order to preserve John's life. Rather John, who has worked courageously to prepare the Lord's way (11:10), suffers and dies because of his faithful service. Like the slaves, John does not retaliate against the violence he encounters. The one who called people to bear fruit worthy of repentance (3:8) permits them to do to him whatever they wish (17:12). John's calling, like that of the prophets before him, is a calling to proclaim the word of God. If that word is not received, John's calling—like the prophets'—is to suffer violence without responding in kind.

But suffering and death are not the final word for John. Like his predecessors, John receives ultimate vindication by God for his faithful witness as a prophet of the Lord. Jesus acclaims John on the human level as a prophet, and more than a prophet, and declares that "among those born of women none has been raised up who is greater than John the Baptist" (11:9, 11). Jesus also makes it clear that John's prophetic ministry comes from heaven itself (21:25), directly from God. Further, belief or nonbelief in John's heavenly message of righteousness will determine the eschatological status of John's hearers with respect to the kingdom of heaven (21:31–32; cf. 21:25). John, whose prophetic voice is overpowered by violence in the world of Herod the tetrarch nevertheless speaks a prophetic word, the power of which extends into the eschatological future of the kingdom of heaven. Such is God's vindication of the faithful prophet.

"IN THIS WAY ALSO THE SON OF MAN WILL SUFFER AT THEIR HANDS"

If John the Baptist is the prophet whose task is to prepare the Lord's way (11:10), then Jesus is the Lord whose way John prepares. Jesus appears on the scene immediately after John's announcement of "the one coming after me" (3:13; cf. 3:11–12) to request baptism from John (3:13–16a). Jesus also receives divine confirmation of his identity: the heavens open, the Spirit of God descends on him in the form of a dove, and a voice from heaven, the voice of God, declares him to be "my beloved son, the one in whom I take pleasure" (3:16b–17; cf. 17:5).

Jesus, the Son of God and the one empowered by the Spirit of God, knows himself to be sent by God to a ministry among the Jewish people (10:40; cf. 10:6; 15:24; 21:37). Jesus exhibits a clear sense of how he has come and what he has come to do. By accepting the accolades of the crowds, Jesus acknowledges that he is the one who comes in the name of the Lord (23:39; cf. 21:9). At the same time, he acknowledges that he has come as an ordinary human, eating and drinking, in contrast to the ascetic practices of his predecessor John (11:18–19). Jesus also identifies the tasks to which he has been called. He has not come to destroy the law or the prophets (5:17), to call the righteous people (9:13), to bring peace (10:34), or to be served (20:28). Rather, he has come to fulfill the law and the prophets (5:17), to call the sinners (9:13), to bring the sword that divides families (10:34–36),[25] to serve others (20:28), and to give his life as a ransom for many (20:28).[26]

Throughout Matthew's narrative Jesus works at the tasks for which he has come through a threefold ministry of proclaiming, teaching, and healing (4:23; 9:35; 11:1), a ministry the people acknowledge as one of wisdom[27] and powerful deeds.[28] This ministry of Jesus reaches well beyond that of John, his predecessor (cf. 14:1–2). Like John, Jesus announces the nearness of the kingdom of heaven and calls people to repentance in light of the approaching reign of God (4:17; cf. 3:2). Unlike John, Jesus can cast out demons by the Spirit of God, an act that proclaims that "the kingdom of God has [already] come upon you" (12:28).[29] In addition, Jesus assumes what is widely recognized to be a divine prerogative: proclaiming forgiveness of sins, an act his opponents consider blasphemy. In contrast, the crowds recognize that Jesus, precisely as a human being, extends this forgiveness by God-given authority (9:2–8).

Jesus also carries out a teaching ministry that is mobile, wide-ranging, and prominent throughout his public career. He goes throughout Galilee (4:23), through all the towns and villages (9:35; cf. 11:1), teaching sometimes in their synagogues (4:23; 9:35; 13:54) and at other times on mountains (5:1), beside the sea (13:1–2), in the house (13:36; 17:25), or on the way (20:17). Jesus regularly engages in major teaching sessions, sometimes publicly for his disciples and the crowds,[30]

---

[25] See Dorothy Jean Weaver, *Matthew's Missionary Discourse: A Literary Critical Analysis,* JSNT Supplement Series 38 (Sheffield, England: Sheffield Academic Pr., Ltd., 1990), 112–14.

[26] Cf. 8:29, where demons cry out against Jesus and ask whether he has come to torment them before the time.

[27] 13:54; cf. 11:19; 12:42.

[28] 13:54; 11:20–21, 23; 13:58, 14:2.

[29] Compare the comment of Herod the tetrarch, who attributes the mighty deeds of Jesus to a John the Baptist who has been raised from the dead and is for this reason capable of what he could not previously do (14:1–2).

[30] See 5:1–7:27; 13:1–35; 23:1–39.

sometimes privately for his disciples alone.[31] Jesus' teaching ministry includes sharp and sometimes lengthy controversies with his opponents about the Scriptures.[32]

Authority characterizes Jesus' teaching ministry. He repeatedly offers his own word, "but I say to you," as the definitive response to what his readers have heard in the Jewish Scriptures.[33] The crowds then express astonishment that Jesus is teaching them "as one who has authority and not as their scribes" (7:28–29). Even when Jesus' listeners are not willing to accept his teachings, they grudgingly acknowledge the wisdom of his words (13:54) and bear cynical witness to the truthfulness with which he teaches the way of God (22:16). Jesus' words evoke astonishment and amazement from all his listeners—the crowds (7:28; 13:54; 22:33), his disciples (19:25), and his opponents (22:22).

Jesus also carries out a ministry of powerful deeds.[34] This ministry is all-inclusive, geographically and medically: Jesus goes about through all Galilee (4:23), through all the towns and villages (9:35), and heals all those who are sick.[35] Jesus' healing ministry cures those who are suffering[36] with disease[37] and illness,[38] the sick (14:14) and those with infirmities (8:17), those who are tormented (4:24; 8:6) and demon-possessed,[39] epileptics (4:24; 17:15, paralytics,[40] lepers (8:2; 11:5), those who are burning with fever (8:14), those who are hemorrhaging (9:20, the blind,[41] the deaf and/or mute,[42] the lame,[43] the maimed (15:30–31), and those with withered hands (12:10). Jesus' healing powers extend even to raising the dead (11:5; cf. 9:18).

Jesus' public ministry of proclaiming, teaching, and healing is both authoritative in its origins and dynamic in its outworking. And it takes

---

[31] See 10:1–42; 13:36–52; 18:1–35; 24:1–25:46.

[32] See 12:1–8, 9–14; 15:1–20; 19:3–9.

[33] See 5:21–22, 27–28, 33–34, 38–39, 43–44; cf. 31–32.

[34] See 11:20–21, 23; 13:54, 58; 14:2.

[35] See 4:24; 8:16; 12:15; cf. 14:14; 15:30; 19:2; 21:14.

[36] See 4:24; 8:16; 14:35; 17:15.

[37] See 4:23–24; 8:17; 9:35.

[38] See 4:23; 9:35.

[39] See 4:24; 8:16, 28, 33; 9:32–34; 12:22, 24, 27–28; 15:22; 17:18. See also Matthew's prominent references to Jesus' exorcistic ministry of casting out the demons or spirits (8:16, 31; 9:33–34; 12:24, 26–28).

[40] See 4:24; 8:6; 9:2, 6.

[41] See 9:27–28; 11:5; 12:22; 15:30–31; 20:30; 21:14.

[42] 9:32–33; 11:5; 12:22; 15:30–31.

[43] See 11:5; 15:30–31; 21:14.

on contrasting characteristics depending on the people or groups toward whom it is directed. Toward the crowds and those who come to him in faith, Jesus carries out a ministry of mercy and compassion. Jesus has compassion on crowds who lack effective leadership (9:36), crowds who are hungry (15:32), crowds with sick people in their midst (14:14), and individuals who come to him for healing (20:34). Jesus teaches his disciples about forgiveness by telling them a kingdom parable about a lord who has compassion and forgives the debt of one of his slaves (18:27), a clear allusion to God's own compassionate forgiveness (cf. 6:12, 14–15). Jesus repeatedly characterizes his own ministry in the words of the prophet Hosea, "I desire mercy and not sacrifice" (9:13, 12:7). He grants the requests of all who come to him begging for mercy;[44] castigates the scribes and Pharisees for neglecting the weightier matters of the law, justice and mercy and faithfulness (23:23); and pronounces beatitude on the merciful, who will themselves receive mercy from God (5:7; cf. 18:33).[45]

In contrast, prophetic woes characterize Jesus' interactions with his opponents. Jesus pronounces woes on Chorazin, Bethsaida, and Capernaum, cities that have not repented in spite of the powerful deeds Jesus has done there (11:21–23; cf. 10:15). Similarly, he pronounces generic woes on the world, the one through whom offense comes (18:7), and a specific woe on the one by whom the Son of Man is handed over (26:24).[46] But it is the Jewish religious leaders for whom Jesus reserves his most scathing response, a sevenfold sequence of woes directed against the "scribes and Pharisees, hypocrites"[47] and the "blind leaders" (23:16) for actions Jesus considers hypocritical abuse of their privileged position on the seat of Moses.[48]

Jesus' mission to the Jewish people thus conveys compassion to some and woe to others. And Jesus' ministry evokes sharply divergent responses from those who encounter him. During most of his public career, Jesus meets with an enthusiastic reception from the ordinary

---

[44] See 9:27; 15:22; 17:15; 20:30–31.

[45] See also 6:1–4, in which Jesus assumes that his disciples will participate in the religious practice of giving alms ("merciful deeds").

[46] Note, in a somewhat different vein, the woe Jesus pronounces on pregnant and nursing women at the time of eschatological tribulations (24:19). Here the focus lies not on the failure or sinfulness of the women involved but on the extreme severity of the tribulations that await Jesus' disciples.

[47] See 23:13, 15, 23, 25, 27, 29.

[48] See 23:2; cf. 6:2, 5, 16. See also 12:34, where Jesus refers to the Pharisees as a brood of snakes whose good speech does not correspond with their evil character.

people. He is constantly surrounded by crowds,[49] even great crowds,[50] who come to him (21:14), gather around him (13:2), bring their sick to him (4:24; 14:35), go before him (21:9), and follow him[51] wherever he goes. As people witness his ministry of word and deed, they are amazed,[52] astonished,[53] astounded,[54] shaken up, [55] and awestruck.[56] They acknowledge his wisdom and his powerful deeds (13:54; 14:2),[57] acclaim the uniqueness of his ministry within Israel (9:33), proclaim him prophet (16:14; 21:11, 46) and Son of David (21:9, 15; cf. 12:23), and glorify God because of him (9:8; 15:31). The report about Jesus[58] spreads throughout the countryside, and as Jesus' popularity with the people grows, his opponents fear a riot among the people if they take action against him (26:5; cf. 21:46).

Jesus also meets with sturdy and persistent opposition throughout his ministry. The source of this opposition is sometimes identified with the Jewish people in general: the proverbial "they" (11:19; 9:24); this people (13:15); this evil and adulterous generation (11:16; cf. 12:39; 16:4); the cities in which Jesus has done most of his powerful deeds (11:20); the people of Jesus' hometown (13:54);[59] the crowd at a Jewish wake (9:23, 25). More frequently, however, Jesus' opponents are identified as the religious leadership of the Jewish people: Pharisees, scribes, Sadducees, Herodians, chief priests, and elders of the people.[60]

Jesus' opponents challenge his words and his actions at every turn. They question him about table fellowship (9:10–11), fasting (9:14),[61] sabbath observance (12:2, 10), ritual washing (15:1–2), divorce (19:3), res-

---

[49] See 5:1; 7:28; 9:8, 33; 12:23; 14:13; 15:31; 21:11, 46; 22:33.

[50] See 4:25; 12:15; 13:2; 14:14; 15:30; 19:2; 20:29; cf. 21:8.

[51] See 4:25; 12:15; 14:13; 19:2; 20:29; 21:9.

[52] θαυμάζω *(thaumazō)*: 8:27; 9:33; 15:31; 22:22.

[53] ἐκπλήσσω *(ekplēssō)*: 7:28; 13:54; 19:25; 22:33.

[54] ἐξίστημι *(existēmi)*: 12:23.

[55] σείω *(seiō)*: 21:10.

[56] φοβέομαι *(phobeomai)*: 9:8.

[57] As Matthew makes clear in 13:54–58, however, such acknowledgement does not necessarily lead to faith.

[58] ἀκοή *(akoē)*: 4:24; 14:1; φήμη *(phēmē)*: 9:26; cf. 9:31.

[59] In a similar fashion, note also the reference to the whole city (8:34) of the Gadarenes, which takes a stance of opposition toward Jesus.

[60] Consult a concordance for Matthew's extensive use of these terms.

[61] While the disciples of John the Baptist are not elsewhere portrayed as opponents of Jesus (cf. 11:2–7), their question in 9:14 sets them over against Jesus and his disciples with regard to ritual practices

urrection (22:24–28), and the greatest commandment (22:36). In addition, they ask him for a sign from heaven (12:38; 16:1), question the source of his wisdom and powerful deeds (13:54–56), challenge his acceptance of the accolade "Son of David" (21:15–16), and demand to know on whose authority he acts (21:23). Most cynically of all, they seek to test him (22:35) or to entrap him in words (22:15).

Nor do they stop with questions. Jesus' opponents accuse him of casting out demons through Beelzebul, the ruler of the demons (12:24; cf. 9:34). They castigate Jesus' disciples for transgressing the traditions of the elders (15:1–2). They label Jesus a glutton, drunkard, and friend of tax collectors and sinners because of his nonascetic life style and his scandalous social practices (11:19; 9:10–11). And when Jesus assumes the prerogative to forgive sins, they charge him with blasphemy (9:2–6).

Jesus' opponents reject his ministry in its entirety, word and deed alike. As they had failed to believe John's message of righteousness (21:32), so they now fail to repent in response to Jesus' powerful deeds (11:20). Jesus charges that they do not respond when they are called (11:16–19), that they have closed their eyes to the mysteries of the kingdom of heaven (13:15; cf. 13:11), and that they reject his efforts when he wishes, in the fashion of a mother hen, to gather them (23:37). Instead, they laugh at his words (9:24), take offense at his wisdom and his powerful deeds, and exhibit an attitude of unbelief (13:57–58).[62] Ultimately they take counsel together against him (12:14; 26:4; 27:1) in order to seize (26:4; cf. 21:46) and destroy him (12:14) by killing him (26:4; cf. 21:38) or putting him to death (27:1).

Jesus is keenly aware of this deadly opposition. Throughout his ministry he makes persistent references to the brutal fate that awaits him. Over the course of his public ministry these references create a detailed portrait of his upcoming passion. As Jesus himself announces, he has a cup to drink (20:22; 26:39, 42), which is filled with suffering (16:21; 17:12). He knows that when he arrives at Jerusalem (16:21; 20:18), he will be taken (21:39), seized (26:55), arrested (26:55), and handed over[63] to others. Jesus' opponents will then condemn him to death, mock him, flog him, and kill him[64] by crucifying him (20:18–19; 26:2) on a cross (cf. 10:38; 16:24), after which he will be buried (26:12).[65] In parabolic language Jesus

---

[62] Cf. 8:28–34, where the Gadarenes implore Jesus to leave their territory after he has healed a demoniac and released the demons into a herd of pigs.

[63] See 17:22; 20:18–19; 26:2, 21, 23–24, 45–46.

[64] See 16:21; 17:23; 21:38–39.

[65] Cf. 26:38, where Jesus tells his disciples in the Garden of Gethsemane that his soul is deeply grieved to the point of death.

describes himself as the vineyard owner's son (21:37; cf. 21:33) who will be thrown out of the vineyard and killed (21:39), and as the shepherd who will be struck (26:31). In the metaphorical language of his ultimate prophetic sign, Jesus identifies bread and wine as his body and blood which are poured out for many for the forgiveness of sins (26:26, 28).

But Jesus is not merely aware of the suffering that lies ahead of him. As he tells his disciples, he has come for this very purpose: to give his life as a ransom for many (20:28). Jesus' suffering is as integral to his mission as are his sayings[66] and his powerful deeds.[67] For this reason, Jesus sets out to go up to Jerusalem (16:21; 20:17; 21:1, 10). And when the moment comes, Jesus deliberately moves to accept the suffering that awaits him there.

To be sure, Jesus agonizes in the Garden of Gethsemane, prays repeatedly to his Father for release from the cup that is his to drink, and confesses that the flesh is weak (26:36–44). But when he has submitted himself to the will of his Father, he shows no further hesitation. Jesus steps forward to meet Judas, the one who has come near in order to hand him over (26:45–46). As Jesus does so, he effectively grants Judas permission to carry out his intentions: "Comrade, do what you came to do" (26:50). When one of those with Jesus responds by drawing his sword, Jesus offers him an immediate and sharp rebuke (26:51–52). Then, stunningly, Jesus reveals that he has already renounced the use of violent power far greater and more effective than that of the single sword just drawn in his behalf: "Or do you suppose that I do not have the power to appeal to my Father, who would immediately send me more than twelve legions of angels?" (26:53).

From this moment on, Jesus, whose ministry of authoritative word and powerful action has driven the narrative, becomes the silent and passive recipient of the harsh words and brutal actions of others. From the time of his arrest until the moment of his death (26:46–27:50), Jesus does almost nothing and maintains an almost complete silence, while his religious and political opponents seize the initiative both verbally and physically.[68]

On the verbal level, Jesus' opponents take counsel against him (27:1), say things to him, [69] bear false witness against him,[70] accuse him

---

[66] See 7:28; 11:1; 19:1; 26:1; cf. 13:53.

[67] See 11:20–21, 23; 13:54, 58; 14:2.

[68] Cf. Pilate's question to the crowds: "What then shall I do with Jesus, the one who is called Messiah" (27:22). For a detailed comparison of Matthew's characterizations of Pilate and Jesus in the trial scene, see Weaver, "Power and Powerlessness," 191–5.

[69] See 26:62–63, 68; 27:11, 13, 29, 40–41.

(27:12), pronounce him worthy of death (26:66), condemn him (27:3), mock him (27:29, 31, 41), blaspheme him (27:39), and revile him (27:44). On the physical level, they approach him, kiss him in mock friendship, lay hands on him, and seize him (26:48–50, 57). Then they bind him (27:2), lead him away (26:57; 27:2, 31), take him along and gather people to him (27:27), and hand him over.[71]

When he is bound and within their power, they spit in his face, cuff and slap him, and strike him on the head with a reed (26:67–68; 27:30). They take clothes off him (27:28, 31), put clothes on him (27:31), put things around him (27:28), put things on or over his head (27:29, 37), and bow down before him in mock worship (27:29). Finally they scourge him and crucify him;[72] and in this way they put him to death (26:59; 27:1) or destroy him (27:20). Before he dies, however, they give him something to drink,[73] divide his clothes among them (27:35), and keep watch over him as he hangs on the cross (27:36).

In response to this treatment, Jesus takes few actions and speaks even fewer words. On the level of action, he stands before the governor (27:11), tastes the wine offered to him but will not drink it (27:34), and ultimately gives up his spirit (27:50). On the level of speech, Jesus maintains a total silence in the face of false witness against him,[74] to the amazement of both Caiaphas (26:62) and Pilate (27:13–14b). Only when their questions correspond to the truth does Jesus respond (26:64; 27:11). As he hangs dying on the cross, he cries out to God in his forsakenness (27:46; cf. 27:50).

As did his predecessors, the prophets and John the Baptist, Jesus accepts his sufferings peaceably and without retaliation. He completely renounces his disciples' puny and ineffective efforts to take violent action in his behalf (26:51–52). He also rejects the all-powerful violent option that lies within his reach as the son of his Father (26:53–54). Jesus rejects all violence as means either of saving his own life or for retaliating against his enemies.

As was the case for his predecessors, the story of Jesus' peaceable ministry and his rejection of violent options does not end when Jesus gives up his spirit. Rather, as he predicted,[75] his death at the hands of powerful enemies gives way to the infinitely more powerful act of God

---

[70] See 26:62; 27:13; cf. 26:59–60.

[71] See 26:48; 27:2–4, 18.

[72] See 27:22, 23, 26, 31, 35; cf. 32, 38, 44.

[73] ἔδωκεν πιεῖν (edōken piein), 27:34; ἐπότιζεν (epotizen), 27:48.

[74] See 26:60–61, 63a; 27:12, 14a.

[75] See 16:21; 17:9, 23; 20:19.

in raising him from the dead. To his opponents Jesus speaks in the metaphorical language of Ps. 118:22 about "the stone that the builders rejected [that] has become the head of the corner," an act that has taken place at the Lord's initiative (21:42). In a similar vein he cites Ps. 110:1, which speaks about the Messiah, Son of David (22:42), whom the Lord calls to "sit at my right hand until I place your enemies under your feet" (22:44). God will vindicate the peaceable mission of the beloved Son (3:17; 17:5; cf. 21:37), reversing the sentence of death enacted on Jesus, raising his lifeless body to new life, and granting him authority of the highest order.

In Matthew's biting irony, this reversal is exactly what comes to pass. In an indescribable act of divine power[76] God raises Jesus from the dead[77] and in so doing empties the tomb in which Jesus had been laid (28:6; cf. 27:59–60). Jesus' opponents, who have secured the tomb, sealing the stone and setting a guard (27:66; cf. 27:64), find themselves outwitted and overpowered by this divine initiative. The angel of the Lord descends in a great earthshaking event and coopts their entire security system by rolling back the stone and sitting on it (28:2). The angel then disarms those who are keeping watch over the tomb, instilling such fear in them that they also shake, and fall into a dead faint (28:4). When they recover, they have no explanation to offer for the empty tomb (cf. 28:13–14) which once held the body of Jesus. Ironically, they create and perpetuate the very resurrection fraud they had intended to prevent with their elaborate security measures (28:11–15; cf. 27:62–66).[78]

God, who has vindicated the peaceable ministry of the beloved Son by raising him from the dead, accords Jesus authority of the highest order. When the risen Jesus encounters his disciples on the mountain in Galilee, he announces that "all authority in heaven and on earth has been given to me" (28:18). And he sends them out with a renewed and expanded mission to make disciples not only of the lost sheep of the house of Israel, as before (10:6; cf. 15:24), but of all the nations (28:18). This same risen Jesus, possessing all authority in heaven and on earth, will be with his disciples until the consummation of the age (28:20). As the victorious Son of Man, he also will come[79] to the inhabitants of the

---

[76] Matthew makes no attempt to describe the resurrection of Jesus, contenting himself with pronouncements that Jesus will be raised (16:21; 17:23; 20:19; 26:32; cf. 27:63) and announcements that Jesus has been raised (28:6–7; cf. 27:53, 64).

[77] See 17:9; cf. 16:21; 17:23; 20:19.

[78] For a detailed study of the irony in Matthew's resurrection narrative, see Dorothy Jean Weaver, "Between Text and Sermon: Matthew 28:1–10," *Interpretation* 46 (October 1992): 398–402.

[79] See 10:23; 16:27, 28; 24:30, 44; 25:31; cf. 23:39; 24:42–43, 46; 25:10, 19, 27.

earth on the clouds of heaven (24:30), in kingdom (16:28), power (24:30), and great glory (16:27; 24:30; 25:31), with his angels (16:27; 25:31), in order to sit on his glorious throne (19:28; 25:31) and serve as the judge of all the nations (25:32). As judge he will separate the sheep from the goats (25:32), confess or deny humans before his Father in heaven (10:32–33), and repay all people according to their deeds (16:27; cf. 25:31–46).[80] Jesus, the one who has come to give his life as a ransom for many (20:28) and who has accepted suffering and death peaceably and without retaliation, is now accorded ultimate authority over the eternal destiny of human-kind. Such is the vindication of God's beloved Son, the one who rejects the way of violence.

"AS SHEEP IN THE MIDST OF WOLVES"

In Matthew's view, Jesus' disciples stand at the end of a long and illus-trious line. Like the prophets who went before them, like John the Baptist, and like Jesus himself, the disciples have been sent out by God to a ministry of public proclamation and deeds of power and compassion. They have also been sent out to suffer, peaceably and without retaliation, the persecution brought on by this ministry. The direct correlation between the mission of Jesus' disciples and that of their forebears, especially Jesus, is difficult to overlook in Matthew's narrative.

Jesus' disciples know themselves to be called by Jesus (4:21) to follow (8:22; 9:9) or come after (4:19) him. Jesus sends the disciples out[81] to go[82] and carry forward his ministry (10:1; cf. 9:35), a sending that Jesus equates with the divine sending activities of the Lord of the harvest (9:38) and of the king who gave a wedding banquet for his son (22:3–4). Jesus' disciples know themselves to be both called and sent by Jesus, Son of God, to the same divine vocation that he has claimed.

Initially this vocation sends the disciples to the lost sheep of the house of Israel (10:6), in direct correspondence with Jesus' own mission (15:24), and in clear distinction to any mission to Gentiles or Samaritans (10:5). During his earthly ministry among the Jewish people, Jesus commissions his disciples to join him in his task.[83] After his resurrection

---

[80] Cf. 11:20–24, where Jesus pronounces woes on Chorazin, Bethsaida, and Capernaum—the cities in which he has carried out most of his mighty deeds—because they have failed to repent in response to Jesus' ministry. Jesus warns that on the day of judgment it will be more tolerable for Tyre, Sidon, and Sodom than for these unrepentant cities.

[81] See 10:5, 16; 23:34, 37; cf. 10:2.

[82] See 10:6; 28:19; cf. 22:9.

[83] But Matthew's narrative provides no positive indication that the disciples actually carry out the mission of 10:5b–42 before their arrival on the mountain in Galilee to which the

the risen Jesus expands the mission of his disciples into a global focus on all the nations, and extends their mission temporally to the very consummation of the age (28:19–20). The mission of Jesus' disciples begins with their call by the earthly Jesus to minister here and now to the lost sheep of the house of Israel. But its outward trajectory reaches beyond the Jewish people to all the nations and beyond the present time to the end of the age.

Jesus employs terminology that is both concrete and metaphorical to characterize the identity of his disciples as those sent out into mission. Drawing on imagery from nature and from material culture, Jesus identifies his disciples as salt of the earth whose value lies in its flavor, as the light of the world, the city set on a hill which cannot be hidden, and the lamp on the lampstand which gives light to all in the house (5:13–15). These metaphors focus on the positive influence the disciples exert on the society around them. Drawing on images from human society, Jesus describes them as fishers for people (4:19), workers in the harvest (9:37–38; cf. 10:10), and slaves sent out to call the invited guests into the wedding feast (22:3, 4, 8, 10). These metaphors emphasize the gathering task central to the disciples' mission.

In non-metaphorical language, Jesus calls his disciples prophets,[84] righteous people (10:41), wise people (23:34), scribes (23:34), and little ones (10:42). As such, they have a verbal ministry of proclamation (10:4, 27; 24:14; 26:13), call (22:3, 9), witness (10:18; 24:14), speaking (26:13), and words (10:14). In this ministry the disciples say what they have been given to say.[85] And this ministry is largely invitational in character. The disciples are instructed to greet the houses they enter with a word of peace (10:12–13), to proclaim that the kingdom of heaven has come near (10:4; cf. 3:2; 4:17), and as the slaves of the king to say "See! I have prepared my feast. My oxen and my fatted calves have been slaughtered and everything is now ready. Come to the wedding feast!" (22:2–4).

Jesus' disciples are also called to a ministry of healing and other deeds of compassion. Jesus authorizes his disciples to cast out evil spirits and to heal every disease and every sickness (10:1), the same tasks he had been carrying out among the people.[86] He empowers them to show compassion to the crowds (15:32; cf. 14:14) by giving the disciples enough bread to feed thousands of hungry people (14:19–21; 15:36–38).

---

risen Jesus has called them (28:16). On this point, see Weaver, *Matthew's Missionary Discourse*, 126–53.

[84] See 5:12; 10:41; 23:34; cf. 23:37.

[85] λαλέω (*laleō*): 10:19–20; λέγω (*legō*): 10:27; 22:4.

[86] See 4:23; 9:35; cf. 8:1–17, 28–34; 9:1–8, 18–34.

With this authorization and empowerment Jesus calls his disciples into ministry: "Heal the sick, raise the dead, cleanse lepers, cast out demons, give [the people] something to eat! You have received without cost; give without charge!" (10:8a; 14:16; 10:8b).

But this invitational ministry of proclamation and deeds of compassion will not assure the disciples of a positive reception by those to whom they go. As did the prophets, John the Baptist, and Jesus, the disciples will encounter opposition to their ministry (10:13–39). They will enter houses that are not worthy and encounter people who do not receive them or listen to their words. They will also encounter persecution, the kind of verbal and physical abuse that Jesus has encountered and that will lead to his death.

On the verbal level, people will revile the disciples, say all kinds of evil about them, lie about them, and call them Beelzebul (5:11, 10:25). On the emotional level, the disciples will find their invitation disregarded by those who do not wish to receive it (22:3, 5). They will find themselves separated from members of their family and surrounded by enemies in their own households and beyond (10:35–36; 5:44), who will hate them and rise up against them (10:21–22; 24:9–10). On the physical level, the disciples will be mistreated, slapped on the cheek, sued by those who wish to take their cloaks, and forced to carry burdens for Roman soldiers (22:6; 5:40–41; cf. 27:32). They will be persecuted from town to town,[87] seized (22:6), handed over to councils (10:17, 19), whipped in synagogues (10:17; 23:34), dragged before governors and kings (10:18), and scattered as sheep whose shepherd has been struck (26:31). Ultimately they will lose their lives (10:39; 16:25) as they are handed over to tribulation and death (24:9–10; 10:21), stoned (23:37), crucified (23:34), put to death (10:21), and killed.[88]

This brutal rejection cannot be considered happenstance. It is integral to their mission. Jesus commissions them with these words: "See, I am sending you out as sheep in the midst of wolves" (10:16). The character of their mission is shaped by their identity as those whose lot is suffering at the hands of others. The reason is simple and obvious: Jesus' disciples follow or come after him (4:19–20, 22; 8:22; 9:9; 10:38; 16:24). That is, they must go where Jesus goes. In following Jesus, they have no choice but to take up the cross[89] that Jesus is about to carry (20:19; 26:2) and to drink the cup of suffering (20:22, 23) that Jesus is about to drink (26:39, 42, 44). As they lose their lives, they do so on account of Jesus

---

[87] See 23:34; cf. 10:23; 5:10–12, 44.

[88] See 10:28; 22:6; 23:34, 37; 24:9.

[89] λαμβάνει (lambanei): 10:38; ἀράτω (aratō): 16:24.

(10:39; 16:25). As Jesus indicates, it is sufficient to disciples that they be like their teacher, and the slaves like their lord. If his opponents have called the master of the house Beelzebul, how much more will they malign the members of his household (10:24–25).[90]

As Jesus has come to give his own life (20:28), so he has come to bring the sword that will separate his disciples from members of their families and turn members of households into enemies (10:34–36), a sword that will lead their closest relatives to rise up against the disciples and hand them over to death (10:21). As the divine vineyard owner of Jesus' parable does not spare his slaves or his son from the violence that is sure to be carried out against them (21:36–37; cf. 21:34–35), so Jesus does not promise to spare his disciples from the fate awaiting them. Just before his own death, Jesus tells the Jewish religious establishment in the temple, "See, I send out to you prophets and wise people and scribes! Some of them you will kill and crucify; and some of them you will whip in your synagogues and persecute from town to town" (23:34). The vineyard owner does not allow the inevitable persecution of his emissaries to deter him from his mission to take the fruits from his vineyard (21:33–37), nor will Jesus allow the inevitable persecution of his disciples to halt his mission to the Jewish leadership and their people (10:6, 23). Jesus' disciples follow him into suffering.

As Jesus faces suffering peaceably and without retaliation, he calls his disciples to do the same. With respect to the "evil people" who harass and humiliate them day by day, Jesus challenges his disciples to active nonresistance of the most radical and scandalous sort. He instructs them to turn the other cheek to the one who has struck them, offer their cloak as well to the one who has sued them and taken their tunic, go two miles with the Roman soldier who compels them to go one mile, give to the one who asks for money, and not turn away from the one who wishes to borrow from them (5:38–42).[91] Vis-à-vis their enemies, Jesus calls his disciples to a stance of love; vis-à-vis their persecutors, Jesus exhorts them to prayer (5:44).

To those who reject their ministry, Jesus calls the disciples to a prophetic but nonviolent response. If the house they have entered is not worthy, they are called to let their peace return to them. And if they and their words are not received, the disciples are exhorted to leave that

---

[90] Cf. 9:34; 12:24, 27. On the image/reflection correspondence between the sufferings of Jesus and those of his disciples, see Weaver, *Matthew's Missionary Discourse*, 146–7.

[91] For a detailed exegesis of Matt. 5:38–42, see Dorothy Jean Weaver, "Transforming Nonresistance: From *Lex Talionis* to 'Do Not Resist the Evil One,'" in *The Love of Enemy and Nonretaliation in the New Testament*, ed. Willard M. Swartley (Louisville: Westminster John Knox Pr., 1992), 32–71.

house or town and to shake the dust from their feet as they do so (10:13–14). In this way the disciples dissociate themselves physically and symbolically from the unreceptive house or town and at the same time point prophetically to the divine judgment that will fall on that house or town. For those who reject Jesus' disciples and their mission, the consequence will be severe.[92]

But all such consequences remain the sole prerogative of God, not of the disciples. The disciples are not authorized, empowered, or commissioned to retaliate against those who reject them and their ministry. Jesus calls them to respond to persecution with caution, courage, and confidence. On one hand, Jesus cautions them to be wise as serpents, innocent as doves, and wary of people (10:16–17). When they meet resistance in one town, Jesus urges them to flee to the next one on a journey throughout Israel, and ultimately throughout the world, that will not reach its conclusion before the Son of Man comes.[93]

Jesus calls his disciples to continued courageous proclamation in the face of rejection and persecution. He instructs them not to worry about how they are to speak or what they are to say when they are placed on trial. And he assures them that the words they need will be given to them and spoken through them by the Spirit of their Father (10:19–20). He enjoins them repeatedly not to fear others who have the power to revile them and put them to death (10:26, 28, 31). They are to say in the light and proclaim on the housetops what Jesus has told them in private, and to confess Jesus openly before people (10:27, 32). Even their rejection in one house or town and their flight to the next destination signal not the end but the continuation of a worldwide missionary journey that will occupy their energies until the Son of Man comes at the end of the age (10:23; 24:14; 28:19–20).

In the end God will vindicate the disciples for their faithfulness. They will be rewarded for what they have done (16:27) and saved because of their endurance (10:22; 24:13). Those who lose their life on Jesus' account will find it (10:39; 16:25). Those who acknowledge Jesus before others in hostile settings are assured that Jesus will acknowledge them before his Father in heaven (10:32; cf. 10:17–20). Those who have

---

[92] In the present, they lose their opportunity to hear the disciples' proclamation (10:14). In the historical future (to which Matthew and his congregation look backward), those who have murdered Jesus' emissaries will be destroyed, have their city burned (22:7), have the stones of their temple thrown down (24:2; cf. 24:1) and their house left desolate (23:38)—vivid allusions to the destruction of Jerusalem. In an eschatological future, on the day of judgment, the city that does not receive the disciples will suffer a fate worse than that of the land of Sodom and Gomorrah (10:15).

[93] See 10:23; cf. 24:14; 28:19–20.

left homes, family, and real estate on Jesus' account will receive a hundred times what they have lost and will inherit eternal life (19:29). Those who are vilified and encounter persecution for Jesus' sake are blessed in the present world and will receive great reward in heaven (5:11–12).

Jesus' disciples will also play a crucial role in determining the eschatological status of those to whom they have been sent out. The towns that do not receive Jesus' disciples or listen to their words will find their situation less tolerable on the day of judgment than that of Sodom and Gomorrah (10:14–15), while individuals who receive Jesus' disciples as prophets, righteous ones, and little ones will be granted eschatological rewards (10:41–42).[94] At the renewal of all things, when the Son of Man will be seated on his glorious throne, Jesus' disciples, who have given up everything and followed him, will also sit on twelve thrones, judging the twelve tribes of Israel (19:28; cf. 10:6, 23). Jesus' disciples, whose identity as missionaries is that of sheep in the midst of wolves, and whose life in mission will lead them to unavoidable persecution and death (10:16–19, 21–22; 23:34), will finally receive ultimate authority along with the Lord whose mission they have carried out and whose sufferings they have shared. Such is God's vindication of those sent out unarmed into a violent world to make disciples of all the nations (28:19).

As the narrative evidence of Matthew's Gospel demonstrates, the motifs of mission and peace are closely and consistently linked throughout Matthew's story. In his depiction of those "sent out" on behalf of the kingdom of heaven, Matthew paints a vivid and consistent portrait of the persecution that these messengers will encounter because of their work. And, as the words and example of the Matthean Jesus make clear beyond dispute, God calls these messengers to meet this persecution with love for enemies, prayer for persecutors, and total renunciation of all violent responses. In Matthew's view, the call into mission means not only total engagement on behalf of the kingdom of heaven but also profound commitment to the ways of peace.

Eternal life —
defers the
reward —
still reward+

---

[94] The eschatological character of these rewards is apparent from their juxtaposition to the eschatological judgment of 10:14–15.

punsl

8 | *Shalom for shepherds*
An audience-oriented critical analysis of Luke 2:8–14

GARY YAMASAKI

THE ACCOUNT IN LUKE 2:8–14 OF THE ANGELIC VISITATION to the shepherds on the eve of Jesus' birth is a familiar narrative. In fact, because of its contribution to the Christmas story, it is one of the most familiar passages in all of the New Testament. Even for people not acquainted with the text of this account, prominent motifs from these verses have been disseminated by way of Christmas carols. One, "Christ the Savior is born," appears in the concluding line of "Silent night." Another, "peace on earth," is found in the first verse of "Hark! the herald angels sing." Therefore, for the church and the general public alike, the infant Jesus is depicted every Christmas as the bringer of salvation and the bringer of peace.

Many congregations who heartily sing both of these carols Christmas after Christmas neglect one of these motifs in favor of the other when it comes to their theology and practice. Some focus exclusively on Jesus as the bringer of salvation—understood strictly in terms of his death on the cross—and so have evangelism as a top priority, but have no interest in peace and justice. Others focus exclusively on Jesus as the bringer of peace, and so expend much time and energy in the pursuit of peace and justice, but are uncomfortable with the concept of evangelism. It is my thesis in this study that the salvation and the peace of Luke 2:8–14 are not to be understood as two competing concepts, but rather as two ways of describing the same reality: the nature of God's reign which the infant Jesus is bringing to earth.

Before launching into the analysis of Luke 2:8–14, I will set out the method to be used. This analysis of Luke 2:8–14 adopts a narrative approach to the text. Given the vast array of narrative approaches that have been developed over the past few decades, I need to specify the distinctives of the approach to be used here.[1]

One component of my method in this essay is held in common with most narrative approaches: the bracketing out of historical-critical issues. Unlike historical-critical analyses' interest in such issues as the nature of the "real author's" community or the shape of the real author's theology, narrative approaches are interested in the "implied author" of the narrative—that is, a hypothetical version of the author inferred from the data in the text[2]—and in the "narrator," the voice that the implied author has tell the story to the audience. This commitment to the bracketing out of historical-critical issues does not necessarily require a divorce of the story world of the Gospels from history. Indeed, the narrator of Luke makes a special effort to set his story in a historical context, as is evidenced by the references to Augustus and Quirinius in 2:1–2. Obviously, knowledge of the historical/cultural context of a Gospel narrative will be important to an analysis of the narrative. The point here is that historical-*critical* issues, issues related to factors lying behind the text of the Gospels,[3] are to be bracketed out, leaving the text as it stands as the object of examination.

Another way narrative approaches to the analysis of a Gospel differ from historical-critical approaches is the focus on holism. While historical-critical approaches are inclined to work only with small portions of the text, thus tending to lose sight of the Gospel as a whole, narrative approaches are inclined to stress the unity of the narrative of the Gospel. However, the way this focus on holism is worked out in practice varies among literary critics. A dominant school within the field of narrative criticism would, in the examination of any given passage of a narrative, allow the critic to draw on data from any other passage in the narrative—either prior or subsequent—for the purposes of analyzing the passage under examination. In other words, this school conceives of the task of narrative analysis as being undertaken only on multiple readings of the text.[4] In essence, these narrative critics conceptualize the text of a

---

[1] For a more comprehensive discussion of this approach, see Gary Yamasaki, *John the Baptist in Life and Death: Audience-Oriented Criticism of Matthew's Narrative*, JSNT Supplement Series 167 (Sheffield, England: Sheffield Academic Pr., Ltd., 1998), 33–63.

[2] Wayne C. Booth, *The Rhetoric of Fiction*, 2nd ed. (Chicago: Univ. of Chicago Pr., 1983), 70–1, 74–5. The first edition was published in 1961.

[3] E.g., source-critical, tradition-critical, form-critical, redaction-critical issues.

[4] See, for example, Robert C. Tannehill, *The Gospel According to Luke*, vol. 1 of *The Narrative Unity of Luke-Acts: A Literary Interpretation* (Philadelphia: Fortress Pr., 1986), 6. Note, however, that the position espoused here by Tannehill is significantly different from the position he held earlier in his career; for an example of his earlier position, see his "The

narrative as a static object, existing in space, the whole of which can be examined all at one time. However, research in the field of orality in the ancient world throws into question whether such an approach can be sustained.

Pieter Botha calls the culture within which the New Testament documents were produced a "scribal culture," that is, a "culture familiar with writing but in essence still significantly, even predominantly oral, . . . [in which] reading is largely vocal."[5] Within this culture, individual access to the contents of the New Testament documents would have been severely restricted. First, the documents themselves would have been relatively scarce because of the time and effort required to produce written material in this pre–printing press era.[6] Further, evidence indicates that literacy levels during this era were low,[7] so the contents of the documents would not have been accessible to the vast majority of the members of the early church even if they were fortunate enough to come into contact with them. Owing to these circumstances, the primary mode by which the masses would have had access to the contents of the New Testament writings was through listening to readings from them.

Paul J. Achtemeier's research into the New Testament texts uncovers evidence in support of this assertion. His research reveals features in the texts that appear to be designed to guide a hearer in determining when one unit of thought ends and another begins,[8] thus suggesting that these documents were written with a hearer, not a reader, in mind.

This assessment has profound implications for the way narrative analysis is conducted. Just as narrative criticism posits an implied author, that is, the author presupposed by the text, it also posits an

---

Disciples in Mark: The Function of a Narrative Role," *Journal of Religion* 57 (October 1977): 386–405.

[5] Pieter J. J. Botha, "Mute Manuscripts: Analysing a Neglected Aspect of Ancient Communication," *Theologia Evangelica* 23 (September 1990): 42.

[6] William A. Graham, *Beyond the Written Word: Oral Aspects of Scripture in the History of Religion* (Cambridge: Cambridge Univ. Pr., 1987), 124; Thomas E. Boomershine, "Peter's Denial As Polemic or Confession: The Implications of Media Criticism for Biblical Hermeneutics," *Semeia* 39 (1987): 54; George A. Kennedy, *New Testament Interpretation through Rhetorical Criticism,* Studies in Religion (Chapel Hill: Univ. of North Carolina Pr., 1984), 5.

[7] Werner H. Kelber, *The Oral and the Written Gospel: The Hermeneutics of Speaking and Writing in the Synoptic Tradition, Mark, Paul, and Q* (Philadelphia: Fortress Pr., 1983), 17; Jack Goody, *The Domestication of the Savage Mind* (Cambridge: Cambridge Univ. Pr., 1977), 152–3; Botha, "Mute Manuscripts," 42.

[8] Paul J. Achtemeier, "*Omne verbum sonat*: The New Testament and the Oral Environment of Late Western Antiquity," *Journal of Biblical Literature* 109 (spring 1990): 21–5.

implied reader, that is, the reader presupposed by the text.[9] Further, because the evidence outlined above suggests that the text presupposes a hearer, as opposed to a reader, as the audience, our implied reader should really be conceptualized as an implied hearer. Unlike readers, who have the ability to flip back to earlier passages or even flip forward to check the outcome of the story, hearers do not have the physical words before them; the words are not so much objects existing in space as events existing in time.[10]

For hearers, a narrative is a sequential experience of discovery in which they encounter new detail after new detail while proceeding through the text. If we conceptualize the audience's encounter with the text in this way, we must abandon the presupposition of an audience that is experiencing the narrative for a second or third or fourth time; instead, the audience must be understood as a first-time experiencer of the narrative. This being the case, the literary critic can no longer analyze the text as a static entity; rather, the critic is to engage in a dynamic enterprise, chronicling the ways the text has an impact on the audience at each step throughout the narrative. Stephen Moore calls this a "story of reading," which he describes as follows: "The interpreter, approaching the evangelist's story as if for the first time, narrates a tale of anticipations and reversals, of puzzles, enigmas, and the struggles to solve them, of beliefs and presuppositions challenged and over-thrown."[11]

At first glance, this method appears to resemble "reader-response criticism," a literary approach which also presupposes a first-time audience—conceptualized, obviously, as a "reader"—and also is atten-tive to the dynamic nature of a narrative, tracing a reader's experience of the narrative. However, the method I use here differs from that of reader-response criticism on one crucial point. Stanley Porter provides a concise description of reader-response criticism through summarizing the position of Stanley Fish:[12]

---

[9] Seymour Chatman, *Story and Discourse: Narrative Structure in Fiction and Film* (Ithaca: Cornell Univ. Pr., 1978), 149–50.

[10] Stephen D. Moore, *Literary Criticism and the Gospels: The Theoretical Challenge* (New Haven: Yale Univ. Pr., 1989), 86.

[11] Ibid., 80–1.

[12] Stanley E. Porter, "Why Hasn't Reader-Response Criticism Caught on in New Testament Studies?" *Literature and Theology* 4 (November 1990): 279. These points reflect Fish's method later in his career; earlier, he held a significantly different position. For an example of his earlier work, see his "Literature in the Reader: Affective Stylistics," in *Reader-Response Criticism: From Formalism to Post-Structuralism*, ed. Jane P. Tompkins (Baltimore: Johns Hopkins Univ. Pr., 1980), 70–100.

> *First, reader-response criticism explicitly shifts the centre of authority from the text itself . . . or the author . . . to the reader, not an historical first reader or any particular subsequent reader . . . but a contemporary reader. . . . Second, the reader is involved in a complex interplay with the text, which chronicles his or her struggle to comprehend. Third, meaning is not a single thing—a propositional truth—but the reader's making and then responding to the text. Fourth, the result of the abandonment of independent meaning is that the meaning which one produces cannot be checked against some objective standard but is the product of a reading strategy.*[13]

As this passage makes clear, reader-response criticism sees meaning as subjective in that it comes into existence through a particular reader's interaction with a text. In contrast, the method I use here presupposes that meaning is objective, inherent in the text.

As the foregoing indicates, the method I adopt here is distinguishable from traditional narrative criticism in that it approaches a narrative as a dynamic experience as opposed to a static object. The method is distinguishable from reader-response criticism in that it presupposes an objective meaning inherent in the text. A name for this method should reflect its strong orientation toward the audience's experience of the narrative, yet the word "reader" is to be avoided since this method presupposes a hearer, as opposed to a reader, as the audience. Therefore, I adopt the name "audience-oriented criticism."

This method is, of course, attentive to the story level of the narrative; it scrutinizes developments in such aspects as plot and character. However, this method is also attentive to the discourse level of the narrative, that is, the level of the narrator's crafting of the narrative through the use of various literary techniques and devices.

One area of analysis at the discourse level which is particularly important for the examination of the present passage is the concept of point of view. Moore defines point of view as follows: "Point of view denotes the rhetorical activity of an author as he or she attempts through the medium of a narrator (or more precisely, by an act of narration), and from his or her position within some socially shared system of assumptions, beliefs, and values to impose a story-world upon a reader (or listener)."[14] Among biblical literary critics, the most popular system of analyzing point of view is that of Boris Uspensky who conceptualizes point of view as manifested on five different levels or planes: ideological,

---

[13] Porter includes a fifth point: "Those who hold to similar reading strategies constitute 'interpretative communities.'" While this point is indeed a component of Fish's position, it is not a necessary component of reader-response criticism in general.

[14] Moore, *Literary Criticism and the Gospels*, 26.

phraseological, spatial, temporal, and psychological.[15] For the purposes of the present study, the spatial and temporal planes are the most pertinent.

Point of view on the spatial plane relates to the spatial relation between the narrator and the characters in the story. Point of view on this plane may be analyzed to determine what parts of a passage the narrator emphasizes or de-emphasizes for the audience. For example, by narrating one part of a passage at a distance from the characters, the narrator de-emphasizes the details of that part. But by drawing in close to the characters in another part of the passage—like a movie camera zooming in on the characters—the narrator emphasizes the details of that part.

Point of view on the temporal plane has to do with the position in time, relative to the positions in time of the characters, from which the narrator relates the activities of the characters. The most obvious distinction here is between retrospective narration, by far the most common type of narration, and concurrent narration, evidenced by use of the present tense, as opposed to the more usual past tense.[16] An aspect of point of view on the temporal plane more important for our analysis of the present passage is pacing, the relationship between story time—the time elapsing in the story line—and discourse time—the time required to relate the details of the narrative. Gérard Genette sets out four different paces: "ellipsis," where discourse time halts, but story time continues; "summary," where discourse time is shorter than story time; "scene," where discourse time and story time are equal; and "pause," where story time halts, but discourse time continues.[17] The analysis of a narrator's movement from summary to scene, or vice versa, is another way of detecting points of emphasis and de-emphasis. Genette asserts that summary constitutes "the 'background' against which scenes stand out";[18] therefore, details in summary narrative are being de-emphasized by the narrator, while details in scene narrative are being emphasized.

With this discussion of method as background, we are now ready to examine the present passage.[19] Our passage follows immediately on the

---

[15] Boris Uspensky, *A Poetics of Composition: The Structure of the Artistic Text and Typology of a Compositional Form*, trans. Valentina Zavarin and Susan Wittig (Berkeley: Univ. of California Pr., 1973).

[16] For of discussion of this distinction, see Uspensky, *Poetics of Composition*, 71.

[17] Gérard Genette, *Narrative Discourse: An Essay in Method*, trans. Jane E. Lewin (Ithaca: Cornell Univ. Pr., 1980), 93–5. Chatman, *Story and Discourse*, 72–3, adds a fifth: "stretch," where discourse time is longer than story time.

[18] Genette, *Narrative Discourse*, 97.

[19] All Scripture quotations are the author's own translations.

narrator's presentation of the birth of Jesus; it begins in verse 8 with a description of shepherds guarding their flock nearby on that night. In terms of the pacing of the narrative, this verse is an example of summary narrative; discourse time here is shorter than story time. As we move on to the description in verse 9 of the angel's entry and the shepherd's reaction, we have an example of scene narrative; discourse time now equals story time. With this move from summary to scene, the narrator signals to the audience a move from mere background material toward more central material.

This move is also evident in the way the narrator manipulates point of view on the spatial plane. With the material in verse 8, the narrator paints a picture that is panoramic in scope: shepherds along with flocks in a countryside setting. Clearly, the narrator's spatial point of view here is at some distance from the objects described. For the material in verse 9, however, the narrator's spatial point of view is from a position much closer; here, the countryside and even the flocks have disappeared from the picture as the focus of the narration narrows in on the shepherds and on a new character, the angel. With this narrowing of focus, the narrator leads the audience to sense an approach to the central material of this passage.

The narrator makes a further shift in spatial point of view in verse 10 by moving in even tighter on the angel and the shepherds. In verse 9, the narrator had drawn the audience in to a vantage point close enough to witness even a detail such as the emotional reaction of the shepherds—literally, "they feared a great fear." Note, however, that this vantage point is not yet within earshot; the audience is not yet close enough to hear anything of the shepherds' reaction. This changes in verse 10 as the narrator does draw the audience within earshot; it is made privy to the words of the angel to the shepherds. Through the material of verses 8–10, then, the narrator manipulates point of view on the spatial plane to draw the audience closer and closer to the experience of these shepherds. In this way, the narrator creates a sense of heightening anticipation that the passage is building toward its climax.

Following the angel's exhortation "Do not fear," to address the shepherd's emotional reaction, the narrator inserts the word ἰδού | *idou* ("behold"), a demonstrative particle which functions to draw attention to what follows. This constitutes yet another narrative device, by which the narrator creates a growing sense of anticipation. Therefore, the audience proceeds into the substance of the angel's message anticipating an encounter with the climax of this passage.

The narrator has the angel announce: "I proclaim to you a great joy which will be for all the people" (2:10c). Far from providing a release for the audience's growing sense of anticipation, this statement contributes further to it. This statement speaks of a proclamation of good news (εὐαγγελίζομαι | *euangelizomai*), and uses emphasis—"*great* joy which will be for *all* the people"—to amplify the goodness of the good news of this message. The statement does not, however, stipulate the nature of this good news any more specifically than to say that it involves a "great joy"; the audience is made to wait for the specifics, thus adding to the growing sense of anticipation.

In verse 11, the narrator finally allows the angel to explain the good news, and this explanation begins with the word ἐτέχθη (*etechthē*), most likely to be taken as a dramatic aorist: "is born." With this word, the angel's message dovetails with the immediately preceding passage, the account of Jesus' birth (2:1–7); therefore, it would appear at first glance that the audience is being led to expect this angelic proclamation to the shepherds to consist of a birth announcement for Jesus. If this were the case, the narrator would be guilty of going to great lengths to build up to a prominent climax, only to deliver a feeble one. A mere birth announcement for Jesus at this point would contribute little to the audience's experience of the narrative, for such an announcement would be functioning for the benefit of the characters in the story, and not for the benefit of the audience, because the audience is already privy to this information through the description of Jesus' birth in 2:1–7. However, the word ὑμῖν | *hymin* ("for you") immediately following ἐτέχθη indicates that this proclamation is intended not as a mere birth announcement, but as an announcement of the birth's significance for the shepherds.

The climax of this passage is finally reached in the presentation of three designations outlining the significance of this newborn child: "Savior," "Messiah," and "Lord" (v. 11). However, a closer look at the way the angel presents these three designations suggests that Savior is to be taken by the audience as the most prominent of the three. As outlined above, the narrator has crafted this passage to produce within the audience a sense of growing anticipation while proceeding step-by-step toward the climax. Further, the narrator has led the audience to expect in this climax a declaration of the significance of this child's birth. To an audience in a heightened state of anticipation, waiting with bated breath for an indication of this child's significance, the first designation encountered would have the strongest impact, thus suggesting that Savior is to be taken as the most prominent of the three. This conclusion finds supports in the way the narrator has constructed this statement. The designation Savior is part of the main clause of this statement, functioning as the subject of the verb "is born," while Messiah and Lord are presented only in a relative clause, subordinate to Savior. For these reasons, we conclude that the climax to which the narrator builds in this passage is the declaration of this new-born child as Savior.

What does the narrator want the audience to see in the designation Savior? Rather than examine all references to "savior," "save," "saving," and "salvation" in the whole of Luke/Acts, our analysis will examine only those references in the text leading up to our passage. In this way, we will be able to determine how the audience would take this reference to Savior, given the cumulative effect of the narrative to this point.

Because the reference in our passage to Savior relates to the birth of Jesus, a natural place to start our examination is the point in the narrative where this birth is first mentioned: the report of the angel Gabriel's visit to Mary (1:26–38). This passage does not contain any references to "savior," "save," "saving," or "salvation." Nevertheless, it is highly significant in the determination of how the audience will understand the designation Savior when it gets to 2:11.

The main feature of this visit is, of course, Gabriel's announcement to Mary that she will bear a son. However, Gabriel goes on to speak about the significance of this child who is to be born: "He will be great and will be called the Son of the Most High, and the Lord God will give to him the throne of David, his ancestor. And he will reign over the house of Jacob forever, and of his reign there will be no end" (vv. 32–33). With this proclamation, the narrator establishes the basic significance of the child to be born: he will establish a kingdom, or reign, on earth. Further, this proclamation makes clear that this child will accomplish this task as the "Son of the Most High"—that is, the "Son of God"—and that it is God who is establishing him in this reign. Therefore, this proclamation by Gabriel serves as much more than a birth announcement. It also serves as a proclamation of the establishment of God's own reign on earth.

The narrator provides some elaboration on the nature of this reign through the content of Mary's Magnificat (1:47–55). The song contains several indications of how God deals with those on earth, thus beginning to paint a picture of the reign that God is establishing on earth.

In the opening verse of this song, Mary designates God as her Savior (1:47). By means of this designation, the narrator introduces the theme of God as the provider of salvation, and thus God's reign as a reign characterized by salvation. However, the audience is left to wait for an elaboration on the nature of this salvation.

From verse 51 to the end of the song, Mary enumerates mighty acts of God. The verbs used in this enumeration are in the aorist and are almost invariably translated in the past tense: "has shown strength" (v. 51), "has scattered" (v. 51), "has brought down" (v. 52), "has lifted up" (v. 52), "has filled" (v. 53), "has sent away" (v. 53), "has helped" (v. 54).[20] However, this rendering in the past tense for these aorists has been challenged. Alfred Plummer points out that in this context, in which Mary is speaking about the blessing she has received, she would not likely have in mind past events unconnected to that blessing.[21] F. Blass and A. Debrunner understand these aorists as representing timeless acts, in the same way that the Hebrew perfect can have this sense.[22] Because this understanding of these aorists fits well the context, we conclude that they should be translated in the present, as "shows strength," "scatters," "brings down," "lifts up," "fills," "sends away," and "helps."

A closer look at the nature of these timeless deeds reveals that they all relate to God's interactions with those on earth. More specifically, they relate to God's acting on the side of the downcast in situations of oppression: scattering the proud (v. 51b), bringing down the powerful (v. 52a) and sending the rich away empty (v. 53b), while lifting up the lowly (v. 52b) and filling the hungry with good things (v. 53a). Through this enumeration of these mighty acts of God, the narrator provides an indication of how God as Savior is to be understood. The audience comes to see that God's salvation has a strong sense of *material well-being*; it involves rescue from oppressive conditions as the proud are scattered and the rich are sent away empty. It entails meeting physical needs as the hungry are filled with good things.

Less prominent though still evident in this enumeration is the sense of salvation as *political well-being*. Mary speaks of God as one who brings down the powerful from their thrones (v. 52), connoting a state of political liberation for the people. Therefore, Mary's song of praise not only introduces the theme of God as provider of salvation, it also begins to depict this salvation as a concept that involves more than one dimension.

The audience is provided with a development of the political dimension of God's salvation in Zechariah's Benedictus (1:68–79). In this song, again, the audience encounters a description of God's dealings with the people of God as stated in terms of salvation: "[God] has raised up a horn of salvation for us" (1:69a). In addition, the narrator has Zechariah become more specific with a reference to "salvation from our

---

[20] Cf. NEB, REB, NJB, NKJV, NAB, NIV, TEV, RSV, NRSV, NASB.

[21] Alfred Plummer, *A Critical and Exegetical Commentary on the Gospel According to St. Luke*, 5th ed., The International Critical Commentary, vol. 28 (Edinburgh: T. & T. Clark, 1922), 33; cf. also I. Howard Marshall, *The Gospel of Luke*, The New International Greek Testament Commentary (Grand Rapids: Eerdmans, 1978), 83.

[22] F. Blass and A. Debrunner, *A Greek Grammar of the New Testament*, trans. Robert W. Funk (Chicago: Univ. of Chicago Pr., 1961), 171–2.

enemies and from the hand of all who hate us" (1:71). Here, we have the word "salvation" used clearly in the sense of political well-being, a state resulting from the elimination of enemies.

Later in this song, the narrator provides further exposition on the specifics of God's salvation, but in a different sense. Zechariah prophesies that his son will prepare the Lord's ways (1:76), and then that he will "give knowledge of salvation to his people" (1:77), a clause epexegetical to the preceding one.[23] Therefore, the audience is informed that this child's preparation of the Lord's ways will entail providing knowledge—with the sense of experience[24]—of salvation. What is most significant for our purposes is the following phrase, for it specifies the means by which this salvation is to be experienced: "by the forgiveness of their sins."[25] Here, then, the narrator provides a third sense in which the audience is to understand the concept of God's salvation: the sense of spiritual well-being.

The narrator closes Zechariah's song by having him speak of the consequences for those who experience salvation in the form of forgiveness of sins:[26] they are given light and are guided in the way of peace (εἰρήνη | *eirēnē*). In this way, peace is stipulated as a resulting state for those experiencing God's salvation. To put it another way, God bestows salvation on the people in the form of peace.

From this analysis, it is evident that the audience is to understand the concept of salvation as tied to the concept of peace. The connection between these two concepts is reinforced in 2:12–14, the second half of the passage under examination. Recall that as the audience proceeds through this passage, a climax is reached in the angel's proclamation of the birth of a Savior (2:11). After that, the angel's message recedes to less momentous details: the fact that the child is to be found "wrapped in bands of cloth and lying in a manger" (2:12). With these directions, the intensity of the passage falls off markedly. These details lead the audience to expect this scene to wind to a close with the shepherds' heading off to find the child. In this atmosphere of diminishing intensity, the impact of the adverb "suddenly" in verse 13 is especially jolting; it injects a fresh intensity into the narrative. Having been let down from a

---

[23] Marshall, *Luke*, 93.

[24] Raymond E. Brown, *The Birth of the Messiah: A Commentary on the Infancy Narratives in Matthew and Luke* (New York: Doubleday, 1979), 373.

[25] Plummer, *St. Luke*, 42; Marshall, *Luke*, 93.

[26] Joseph A. Fitzmyer, *The Gospel According to Luke (I-IX)*, The Anchor Bible, vol. 28 (Garden City, N.Y.: Doubleday, 1981), 388.

climax, the audience appears now to be launched toward a second climax.

This movement is confirmed in how the narrator crafts the following text. Note how the narrator handles the angelic presence. With the conclusion of the proclamation at the end of verse 13, the angel's usefulness is exhausted; the audience would expect the angel simply to fade from the spotlight. Instead, the narrator has the angelic presence grow, as the angel is joined by "a multitude of the heavenly host" (v. 13). It should be noted, though, that it is not only the massive increase in the angelic presence that serves to heighten this scene toward a second climax; the narrator's word order also contributes to this end. The narrator states: ἐγένετο σὺν τῷ ἀγγέλῳ πλῆθος στρατιᾶς οὐρανίου; the verb ἐγένετο | *egeneto* ("appeared") comes first, followed by the prepositional phrase σὺν τῷ ἀγγέλῳ | *syn tō angelō* ("with the angel"), and then the subject πλῆθος στρατιᾶς οὐρανίου | *plēthos stratias ouraniou* ("a multitude of the heavenly host"). By referring to the sole angel first, and only after that drawing in the heavenly host, the narrator creates an image in which the focus is first on the sole angel and then shifts to the heavenly host. To put it in visual terms, the camera begins with an initial tight shot on the sole angel, and then pans to take in the spectacle of angels filling the sky in behind the sole angel. The resulting glorious display serves to heighten the intensity of the narrative flow.

The intensity continues to build until it reaches a second climax in an angelic outburst: "Glory in the highest heights to God . . ." (v. 14a). This climax is not restricted to how the birth of this child is significant "in the highest heights." It continues by including a reference to how this birth is significant "on earth," and that significance is epitomized in the word "peace" (v. 14b). Therefore, while the first climax highlighted this newborn child as the bringer of salvation, the second climax highlights the child as the bringer of peace. As a result, the concepts of salvation and peace are again tied together.

How is this usage of the term "peace" to be understood? The basic feature of the Greek concept of εἰρήνη is "a state, i.e., 'time of peace' or 'state of peace,' originally conceived of purely as an interlude in the everlasting state of war."[27] However, we have seen that peace in our passage represents the outcome of experiencing God's bestowal of a multifaceted salvation, so this basic Greek conception of peace is obviously too narrow.

---

[27] Werner Foerster, "εἰρήνη," in *Theological Dictionary of the New Testament*, ed. Gerhard Kittel (Grand Rapids: Eerdmans, 1964), 2:400–1.

A more fruitful avenue of pursuit is the Hebrew thought underlying the Greek term εἰρήνη. Donald Gowan and Ulrich Mauser assert that the semantic range of εἰρήνη is almost identical to that of the Hebrew word *shalom*, though also noting that their respective usages in the New and Old Testaments bear significant differences in emphasis. [28] Despite these differences, it is still helpful to examine the nature of the Hebrew concept of shalom to see its impact on the way we understand the references to εἰρήνη in the Lukan birth narrative.

Gerhard von Rad points out that the root meaning of shalom is "'well-being,' with a strong emphasis on the material side."[29] Still, the semantic range of shalom expands far beyond material well-being, as von Rad's own treatment of this concept reveals. Before exploring the full semantic range of the word, however, I must first address the issue of whether it can be used to denote either a state or a relationship, or only a state. A determination on this issue will dictate the breadth of the term's semantic range open for our consideration.

Von Rad's treatment of shalom clearly shows him to be in the first camp. He starts by speaking about shalom as material well-being—clearly a state—but then goes on to assert that shalom can also signify a relationship, pointing to an example such as 1 Kings 5:26 (Hebrew versification; 5:12 in English) where shalom is used to denote "a relationship of friendly alliance between Solomon and Hiram."[30] Claus Westermann, on the other hand, argues: "Shalom can never represent something that exists between two entities, such as between two groups, two parties, two persons, and so forth."[31]

What does Westermann do with the occurrences of shalom as the opposite of war, such as 1 Sam. 7:14, which clearly pertain to the relationship between two nations? He contends that "this is not the original usage of the Hebrew word. Our most obvious and self-evident meaning of the word 'peace' represents a major shift to a specialized meaning in Hebrew. . . . In the Hebrew this was an inappropriate and derivative use of shalom."[32] For Westermann, it is the original usage of

---

[28] Donald Gowan and Ulrich Mauser, "Shalom and Eirene," in *The Peacemaking Struggle: Militarism and Resistance,* ed. Ronald H. Stone and Dana W. Wilbanks (Lanham: Univ. Pr. of America, 1985), 124–5.

[29] Gerhard von Rad, "שָׁלוֹם in the OT," in *Theological Dictionary of the New Testament,* ed. Gerhard Kittel (Grand Rapids: Eerdmans, 1964), 2:402.

[30] Ibid.

[31] Claus Westermann, "Peace (*Shalom*) in the Old Testament," in *The Meaning of Peace,* ed. Perry B. Yoder and Willard M. Swartley (Louisville: Westminster John Knox Pr., 1992), 19; see also 43–5, n. 2.

[32] Ibid., 30–1.

shalom that is normative for a proper understanding of this concept, so much so that later, derivative usages, even ones found in the Old Testament itself, can be ignored. Our inquiry affords us no such luxury. Our goal is to gain an appreciation for how the concept of shalom was understood in the New Testament era, and this goal requires us to consider all senses in which the concept was used, not just the original one. Therefore, because Old Testament passages do bear witness to the use of shalom in connection to relationships, our understanding of this concept must include the sense of relational well-being. Further, because some passages, such as 1 Sam. 7:14, do use shalom in the context of peace between nations, this idea of relational well-being must include the sense of well-being in political relationships in addition to well-being in interpersonal relationships.

Westermann and von Rad agree that shalom does not carry the spiritual sense of inner peace,[33] and Westermann adds that it also does not carry the sense of peace with God.[34] Westermann comes to this conclusion because peace with God involves a relationship and, as we have seen, central to Westermann's position is the contention that shalom does not apply to relationships. However, we have already determined that Westermann's contention is suspect. For this reason, his position on whether shalom carries the sense of peace with God is also suspect.

On this issue of a spiritual side of shalom, von Rad notes references to a covenant of peace between Yahweh and the people of God.[35] And even Westermann, despite his disavowal of any relational sense for the concept of shalom, points out that Isa. 27:5 does speak of peace between God and people, though he dismisses it as a late modification of the concept.[36] This usage is admittedly rare, but it does suggest that in the Old Testament, shalom is used to indicate well-being even in the relationship of the people with Yahweh. Therefore, the concept of shalom does also carry the sense of spiritual well-being, although this sense is definitely underdeveloped in the Old Testament.

One final dimension of the concept of shalom remains to be considered: its role in Old Testament eschatological expectations. Von Rad notes the expectation of "a final state of eternal peace" in many passages using the term shalom, but also in passages containing the idea

---

[33] Westermann, "Peace," 20; and von Rad, "שָׁלוֹם," 406.

[34] Westermann, "Peace," 20.

[35] Von Rad, "שָׁלוֹם," 403, points to Ezek. 34:25; 37:26; and Isa. 54:10 as examples.

[36] Westermann, "Peace," 40.

of shalom, though not using the actual term.[37] Further, Jürgen Kegler points out that this state of peace would come in the form of a reign of peace to be brought about by a new king.[38] So prophetic writings of the Old Testement looked forward to a coming reign characterized by shalom.

It now remains to compare the concept of shalom developed here with the narrator's use of εἰρήνη in the Lukan birth narrative. Recall that both usages of εἰρήνη (1:79, 2:14) are tied to the concept of salvation; clearly, the narrator intends that the audience see the two as related. Further, the birth narrative depicts this peace-related salvation as multifaceted—including material well-being (1:51–53), political well-being (1:71), and spiritual well-being (1:77)—a depiction very similar to the Jewish concept of shalom.[39] For these reasons, we conclude that the highlighting of Jesus as Savior in 2:11 should be understood as a depiction of Jesus' being the bringer of shalom.

It must be noted, however, that the narrator's understanding of salvation is not completely coterminous with the Jewish concept of shalom. As we have seen, forgiveness of sins is clearly included in the narrator's understanding of salvation (cf. 1:77), but is not part of how the term shalom is used in the Old Testament. Nevertheless, forgiveness of sins is not necessarily incongruent with the concept of shalom; in fact, in that forgiveness of sins results in well-being in the people's relationship with God, it could be considered a part of spiritual well-being which, as we have seen, is a recognized component of shalom. Therefore, the narrator's inclusion of forgiveness of sins as part of his understanding of salvation does not necessarily preclude consideration of shalom as the concept underlying that understanding. To the contrary, the narrator's inclusion of forgiveness of sins may constitute a logical expansion of the existing concept of shalom in light of the narrator's understanding of the role Jesus is to play as the bringer of shalom.

In conclusion, this analysis has found that the birth narrative of Luke depicts the establishment of God's reign on earth through the birth of Jesus who is portrayed as the bringer of salvation understood largely in terms of the Jewish concept of shalom. This finding, in turn, goes a long way toward addressing the issue set forth at the outset: should

---

[37] Von Rad, "שָׁלוֹם," 405–6, gives Isa. 2:2ff.; 11:1ff.; Hos. 2:20ff.; Amos 9:13ff.; and Zech. 9:9f. as examples.

[38] Jürgen Kegler, "Prophetic Speech about the Future," in *The Meaning of Peace*, ed. Perry B. Yoder and Willard M. Swartley (Louisville: Westminster John Knox Pr., 1992), 101, points to Isa. 9:2–7 as evidence of this expectation.

[39] Cf. Foerster, "εἰρήνη," 412–13, and Perry B. Yoder, *Shalom: The Bible's Word for Salvation, Justice, and Peace* (Newton: Faith & Life Pr., 1987), 120.

Being

evangelism on the one hand, or the pursuit of peace and justice on the other hand, occupy the efforts of Jesus' followers today? The answer is: the two cannot be seen as alternatives, but rather as two components of the same enterprise. Shalom involves spiritual well-being, so working toward bringing people into a right relationship with God is a key ingredient in following the bringer of shalom. At the same time, shalom also involves material well-being, so working toward the alleviation of suffering and the elimination of oppression should also be a part of the vision of one who follows the bringer of shalom. And finally, shalom involves political well-being, so participation in peace activism fits the agenda of a follower of the bringer of shalom.

The angelic announcement to the shepherds in Luke 2:8–14 proclaims a message that transcends the barrier separating the factions in the peace and justice/evangelism debate. The shalom announced by the angels is wide enough to encompass the concerns of both sides. Indeed, shalom requires both sides, so the world may know the full breadth of the salvation that Jesus offers.

9 | *Peace and mission in John's Gospel*
Jesus and the Samaritan woman (John 4)

WILLARD M. SWARTLEY

SCHOLARS HAVE MINED JOHN'S GOSPEL FOR ITS MISSION paradigms and theology, but have made little effort to understand its peace emphasis.[1] Although John uses the word "peace" (εἰρήνη | *eirēnē*) more frequently than Matthew and Mark, few researchers have studied the use of the term in the Gospel.[2] Two key texts in John blend emphases on peace and mission. The linking of these themes merits attention to their place in John's overall literary and theological purposes.

The first of the two peace and mission texts is John 4:1–42. In it, "peace" is not explicit; the term does not occur. Here the mission action, directed by the Spirit-anointed Jesus (1:32–34), is the foundation and possibility for peacemaking between alienated peoples, Jews and Samaritans. In the second text, John 20:19–23, the *Sendung* text of the Gospel, εἰρήνη occurs twice (and again at the end of v. 26). This passage portrays peace as Jesus' gift that, together with receiving the Holy Spirit, foundationally empowers the disciples to carry out the mission charge.

The literature on mission in John is extensive, as Martin Erdmann's recent article, "Mission in John's Gospel and Letters," indicates.[3] An entire monograph has been devoted to the topic, with its locus for

---

[1] In an extensive article on "War and Peace in the New Testament," I have discussed the secondary work done on John's peace teaching. See Willard M. Swartley, "War and Peace in the New Testament," in *Aufstieg und Niedergang der römischen Welt* II.26.3, ed. Wolfgang Haase and Hildegard Temporini (Berlin, New York: Walter de Gruyter, 1996): 2365–9.

[2] Luke's emphasis on peace is significant but rarely discussed in scholarly literature, as my articles on the topic note. See "Politics and Peace *(Eirēnē)* in Luke's Gospel," in *Political Issues in Luke-Acts*, ed. Richard J. Cassidy and Philip J. Scharper (Maryknoll: Orbis Bks., 1983), 18–37. See also my analysis in *Israel's Scripture Traditions and the Synoptic Gospels: Story Shaping Story* (Peabody, Mass.: Hendrickson Pubs., Inc., 1994), 134–9.

[3] This article appears in William J. Larkin Jr., and Joel F. Williams, eds., *Mission in the New Testament: An Evangelical Approach* (Maryknoll: Orbis Bks., 1998), 207–26; see n. 7.

research the very text of this paper's exposition, John 4:1–42.[4] Most recently Linda Oyer has completed a dissertation (in French) on the mission *Sendung* text of John, comparing it with Matthew's commission, 28:16–20.[5]

Although John 4 has received widespread attention for its mission impulse, few authors make the connection to the inherent peacemaking impact of the text. Ben Witherington's recent commentary on John is an exception. He comments, in criticizing the "target audience" emphasis in the church growth movement:

> The story of Jesus and the Samaritan woman is extremely potent to use as a tool for sharing the Gospel across socioeconomic, ethnic, and racial barriers and for exhorting Christians to get on with doing so. Jesus in this story not only rejects the notion that he shouldn't associate with Samaritans, he also rejects the notion that he shouldn't talk with a "strange" woman in public, and furthermore rejects the idea that one shouldn't associate with notoriously immoral people. Besides that, Jesus' act involves witnessing to a person that many of his fellow Jews would have written off as both unclean and theologically out of bounds, a hopeless case.[6]

Even in this commentary, however, Witherington does not speak about the degree of enmity, historical and ethnic, that had developed between the Samaritans and Jews. The potential of the text for peacemaking has not been sufficiently exploited.

Judith Gundry-Volf does pick up on the peacemaking dimension. She pairs the narrative about the Samaritan woman in John 4 with that of the Syrophoenician woman in Mark 7:24–30, and identifies them as paradigmatic for Christian mission-peacemaking:

> The Gospel stories of Jesus' encounters with the Samaritan woman (Jn. 4:1–42) and the Syrophoenician woman (Mk. 7:24–30; Matt. 15:21–28) can both be read as tales about the inclusion of the "other," about crossing the boundaries caused by ethnic, religious, social and gender otherness and bringing about a new, inclusive community of salvation. Exclusion is overcome in two radically different, but complementary models for dealing with a problem both urgent and complex in our own world. In John 4, the divine gift of the Spirit breaks down barriers between peoples and leads to reconciliation and fellowship. In Mark 7 and Matthew 15, human insistence

---

[4] Teresa Okure, *The Johannine Approach to Mission: A Contextual Study of John 4:1–42*, Wissenschaftliche Untersuchungen zum Neuen Testament, 2nd series, no. 31 (Tübingen: Mohr Siebeck, 1988).

[5] Linda Oyer, "Interpreting the New in Light of the Old: A Comparative Study of the Post-Resurrection Commissioning Stories in Matthew and John" (Ph.D. diss., Catholic Institute of Paris, 1997).

[6] Ben Witherington III, *John's Wisdom: A Commentary on the Fourth Gospel* (Louisville: Westminster John Knox Pr., 1995), 124.

on divine mercy, which is blind mercy, dramatically reverses a pattern of exclusion.[7]

Gundry-Volf thus identifies the contribution this narrative of Jesus and the Samaritan woman makes to understanding the socioethical dimensions of the gospel: the good news of salvation is the breaking down of racial and cultural barriers. Mission and peacemaking are not two separate ideas that are integrally linked. What in our conception is a dual entity is, in Scripture, ontologically one, as other texts (Luke 2, Acts 10, Ephesians 2) also explicitly show. As Krister Stendahl rightly perceived, what is usually regarded as Paul's conversion is his call to announce Jesus Christ's peace to the Gentiles, and to make peace with the enemy.[8]

LITERARY ANALYSIS OF JOHN 4:1–42

Peter Ellis seeks to unlock meaning in all units in John's Gospel by showing their concentric structure. His analysis of the John 4 narrative is as follows:

a   *Jesus,* **wearied** (kekopiakos), *sits at the well (4:4–6)*

   b   *The Samaritan woman is* **surprised** *(4:7–18)*

      c   *Worship is in spirit and truth (4:19–24)*

   b'   *The apostles are* **surprised** *(4:25–34)*

a'   *Others have* **labored** (kekopiakasin), *and you have entered into their* **labor** (kopon)—*4:35–38)*[9]

This analysis highlights the connection between Jesus' *weariness* in *a* and the mission-*labor* in *a'*: both use the same verb root in Greek, though different grammatical forms and shades of meaning occur. The *surprise* element in both *b* and *b'* is also notable. Ellis's analysis, however, is fundamentally flawed because it does not include the final paragraph of the narrative (4:39–42), the climax, in which "many *Samaritans*" [italics added] believe in Jesus and confess that he is "the Savior of the world." One might rectify the deficiency in Ellis's analysis in part, at least, by beginning the narrative to be analyzed at verse 3, so that verses 3–6 parallel verses 39–42 structurally in this concentric analysis, framing 4:4–38, as the real *a* and *a'*:

---

[7] Judith Gundry-Volf, "Spirit, Mercy and the Other," *Theology Today* 51 (1995): 508.

[8] *Paul among Jews and Gentiles* (Philadelphia: Fortress Pr., 1976), 7–22.

[9] Peter F. Ellis, *The Genius of John: A Composition-Critical Commentary on the Fourth Gospel* (Collegeville, Minn.: Liturgical Pr.), 65–6.

> *a   Jesus deliberately goes through **Samaria**, to the historic Jacob's well (4:3–6)*
>
> *a'   The **Samaritans** come to believe that Jesus is the Savior of the world through the **Samaritan woman's testimony** (4:39–42)*

This correction to Ellis's schema surely accentuates the mission element intended by the story itself. The center of the chiasm still focuses on the topic of the right place to worship, the issue that separated the Jews and the Samaritans at a fundamental level (see below). The topic of proper worship mediates the mission and peacemaking themes in that alienating ideologies of cult are transcended by the cult of "spirit and truth" that knows no worship wars, specifically none of geography or edifice. Here also is a vital perspective: mission and peace are crucially linked to worship. The common worship of formerly alienated people testifies that mission and peacemaking are accomplished. Indeed, worship is often the first casualty in alienation arising from ethnic, gender, or racial barriers. We will return to this point later, but register it here as arising from the text itself.

Using A. J. Greimas's work on discourse structure and semio-narrative structure, Hendrikus Boers undertakes a book-length structural and semiotic analysis of John 4.[10] After analyzing each pericope on a "need/preparedness/performance/sanction" grid, with syntactic and semantic components, Boers explicates the whole text with the motifs of life, integration, and solidarity overcoming alienation and death. See one of Boers's many diagrams in Attachment 1.[11]

Arising from this structural semiotic analysis, Boers's commentary discloses keen insight about how the story generates meaning at the deep structural level. It is a story of overcoming factional security with human solidarity, and partisan salvation with universal salvation. Boers's analysis correlates the life-giving dimensions with Jesus' salvific initiatives and the woman's receptivity:

> *What may be the most important thing to note is that Jesus' "engaging in discussion with the woman," and "staying with the Samaritan villagers" occurs under "life" and the value /obedience/, as well as under "integration" and the value /human solidarity/. That once more underlines the integrity—in the deep structure of our text—of life and integration, and of the existential value /obedience/ and the social value /human solidarity/. . . .*
>
> *The realization of worship of the Father in spirit and truth, in opposition to either on this mountain or in Jerusalem, when the Samaritan villagers, having invited Jesus to stay with them, recognize him as the savior of the world,*

---

[10] Hendrikus Boers, *Neither on this Mountain nor in Jerusalem: A Study of John 4,* Society of Biblical Literature Monograph Series 35 (Atlanta: Scholars Pr., 1988).

[11] Ibid., 120.

reinforces the integration of the values /human solidarity/ and /universal salvation/. These values, in turn, are integral to /obedience/ in the overall structure of the story. Everything that happens in it is a transformation of the value /obedience/ into a concrete figure of the story, represented at the most general level by Jesus "doing the will of the one who sent him and completing his work" for which the woman is his indispensable co-worker. . . .[12]

Boers's concluding emphasis is that we can recognize "all the figures in the story as transformations of values into concrete reality."[13] In short, the story *performs* transformation.

From another angle of analysis, Gail R. O'Day, focusing on the Johannine narrative as revelation, appeals to this narrative to demonstrate that it not only mediates revelation but *is* revelation. It not only reports Jesus as revealer, but also "allows the reader to *experience* Jesus' revelation for himself or herself."[14] The experience of revelation and transformation centers specifically in the mission of salvation, crumbling structures and prejudices of partitioning, alienation, and enmity. To understand this experience adequately, some investigation of the historical background to the key phrases in verse 9 is necessary:

> Woman: *"How is it that you, a Jew, ask a drink of me, a woman of Samaria?"*
> Narrator: *For Jews have no dealings with Samaritans.*

HISTORICAL BACKGROUND OF JOHN 4:1–42: SHARPENING THE MEANING

One of the most demeaning and hostile representations of Samaritans comes from the lips of Jews in John's Gospel who say in accusing Jesus: "Are we not right in saying that you are a Samaritan and have a demon?" If John's Gospel in chapter 4 seeks to show that Jesus transforms the enmity between Jews and Samaritans into salvation and solidarity in faith, the same Gospel narrator in 8:48 has Jewish lips voicing the prevailing hostility between the two groups: to Samaritanize is to demonize. This rhetoric is a war-making and ethnic cleansing strategy that dehumanizes and simultaneously demonizes the opponent. The vitriolic interchange voices bitterest enmity.

This particular enmity developed and festered over centuries. Probably originating at the time of the exile of the northern kingdom (721 B.C.E.), the hostility is clearly evident in the post-exilic period of Ezra and Nehemiah's leadership (ca. 464–438 B.C.E.). The returned Babylonian Jewry regarded itself as the "holy seed" (Ezra 9:2) or faithful remnant

---

[12] Ibid., 119, 200.

[13] Ibid., 200.

[14] Gail R. O'Day, "Narrative Mode and Theological Claim: A Study in the Fourth Gospel," *Journal of Biblical Literature* 105 (1986): 668.

(9:15), in contrast to those who had stayed in Israel, intermarried and practiced pagan worship, and thus became "unclean with the pollutions of the peoples of the lands, and with their abominations" (Ezra 9:11). The Samaritans under Sanballat, their Persian governor, resisted Ezra and Nehemiah's program to rebuild the temple in Jerusalem (Neh. 6:1–14). Post-exilic Jewry sought vigorously to protect itself from this "pollution" by forbidding marriage to foreigners and building a wall around Jerusalem. Through these post-exilic decades and centuries, two contesting ideologies prevailed in Jewry: one, more self-protective against outsiders (represented above) and another, more inclusive of outsiders (Isa. 52–53; 56:6–8; Jonah, Ruth).

Their conquest by Alexander the Great and the rule of the Ptolemies exacerbated the tension between the two peoples. According to Josephus *(Antiquities)* the schism and separation arose when Alexander gave the Samaritans permission to build their own temple on Mount Gerizim.[15] A text from Sirach (ca. 180 B.C.E.) shows the depth of Jewish antipathy toward the Samaritans, whom they considered semi-pagan: "Two nations my soul detests, and the third is not even a people: Those who live in Seir, and the Philistines, and the foolish people that live in Shechem" (50:25–26). The Septuagint renders the last part: "those dwelling on the mountain of Samaria."

The final split between the Jews and Samaritans occurred during the Maccabean revolt (165 B.C.E.) and was a consequence of the brutal destruction of Samaritans under John Hyrcanus (134–104 B.C.E.). John's policy was to burn Hellenistic cities to the ground, but to extend sympathy toward most circumcised peoples. Although Samaritans were circumcised, they fell under the axe destroying the pagan peoples. In 128 B.C.E. John burned the temple on Mount Gerizim, and in 107 B.C.E. he destroyed Shechem. Little wonder that Samaritans sought retaliation. In 6–9 C.E. some Samaritans scattered human bones in the Jerusalem temple during the Festival of Unleavened Bread. About twenty years later, close to the time of Jesus' ministry in Samaria, an atrocity occurred against the Samaritans, apparently perpetrated by some Jews in cohort with Pilate. According to Josephus, a man persuaded a group of Samaritans to go

---

[15] Scholars contest whether a temple was ever built because no archeological remains have been found, but Josephus narrates that the temple was burned in the period of John Hyrcannus' rule. John R. Donahue notes that Menachem Mor, a respected scholar of this period, regards Josephus as reliable enough to accept his report that a temple was built and destroyed (see Donahue, "Who Is My Enemy? The Parable of the Good Samaritan and the Love of Enemies," in *The Love of Enemy and Nonretaliation in the New Testament*, ed. Willard M. Swartley [Louisville: Westminster John Knox Pr., 1992], 154, n. 21). See Mor's article, "The Persian, Hellenistic, and Hasmonean Period," in *The Samaritans*, ed. Alan D. Crown (Tübingen: Mohr Siebeck, 1989), 16.

with him to Mount Gerizim to view some sacred vessels preserved there. Some of the men in the group were armed and when Pilate forbade ascent of the mount, fighting broke out and some Samaritans were killed or taken prisoner. Pilate then executed some of the Samaritan leaders, presumably blaming them for the "concocted uprising."[16]

Against this background of hostility, it is only natural that the two communities avoided contact, as verse 9 explains: "for the Jews had no dealings with the Samaritans."[17] The shared beliefs of the two communities faded in importance, and differences were magnified. Both communities looked forward to the coming of an eschatological figure who would restore their community's autonomy, so they could live in peace and worship according to their beliefs. The Samaritans expected a Restorer *(Taheb)* to fulfill the prophecy of Deut. 18:18: a prophet like Moses would reinstate worship on Mount Gerizim with a new undefiled temple. Jews expected a messianic figure who would free them from Roman oppression and purify (or rebuild) the temple in Jerusalem so they could worship the Lord in unhindered freedom (see Zech. 6:12; Mal. 3:1).[18] In John 4:25, the woman sounds more Jewish than Samaritan, because she says, "I know that Messiah is coming (he who is called Christ); when he comes, he will show us all things."

In addition to this history that bears on Jesus' encounter with a Samaritan woman, two other religious and cultural enforcers figure into the situation. In Jewish and Samaritan custom, women were not to hold conversation with men in public. For a woman to do so would reflect negatively on her character, classifying her with the loose, immoral women.[19] This woman also carries a moral burden or societal oppression

---

[16] This information comes from Josephus, *Antiquities* 18.4.1–2, Sect. 85–89. I have used John R. Donahue's article for recounting this narrative of hostilities (ibid., 138–43). One of the more definitive studies of the Samaritans is by Menachem Mor (ibid.). See also other essays in the Crown volume and Nathan Schur, *History of the Samaritans* (Frankfurt am Main: Verlag Peter Lang, 1989). Other secondary sources are cited by Donahue, "Who Is My Enemy?" 153.

[17] Some early manuscripts lack this clause (א* D it cop), but the evidence for its inclusion is comparatively much stronger (p63, 66, 75, 76 אa A B C K L Wsupp Δ Θ Π f1 f13 28 33 565 700 892, et al.)

[18] An Isaiah Targum on 53:5 says, "He will build the temple which was profaned for our transgressions and delivered up because of our sins." See Donald Juel, *The Messiah and Temple: The Trial of Jesus in the Gospel of Mark* (Missoula: Scholars Pr., 1977), 181, and my discussion in *Israel's Scripture Traditions*, 158–70, 195.

[19] Charles Talbert cites two primary rabbinic texts (m. Pirke Aboth 1:5 and b. Kiddushim 70a), advising against and forbidding a man to hold public conversation with a woman, even to greet a woman: "It is forbidden to give a woman any greeting" (in *Reading John: A*

of her own. She has had five husbands, and the man she is living with is not her husband.[20] Jesus in his prophetic role perceives this, discloses that he knows her situation, and yet continues to engage her in conversation in order that she and her fellow Samaritans, rejected as they have been by Jews, might come to know him as "the Savior of the world." What a marvel!

For Jesus it is necessary (δεῖ | *dei*)[21] to go through Samaria. Why? To meet the woman at the well, initiate significant "salvation" conversation with her—in public—and welcome her to the living water. Even when her moral condition is mutually acknowledged, he continues to engage her in theological conversation about the proper place of worship, a key point in the ethnic enmity. The mission of Jesus is clearly depicted as shattering boundaries of religion, gender, and moral stigma. The movement of the text is from exposing the boundaries, to shattering and transcending them, to extending the living water of salvation, to welcoming the alienated community of Samaritans—not just the woman—into the solidarity of messianic salvation.

Literary and Theological Commentary on the Fourth Gospel and the Johannine Epistles [New York: Crossroad, 1992], 112).

[20] Many commentators allegorize the Samaritan woman as representing the five religious idolatries that characterized Samaritan worship, as delineated in 2 Kings 17:24–41. For this view, building on the form of the narrative as a betrothal-type (cf. Genesis 24), see Sandra M. Schneiders, who contends that the main point of the narrative is the "incorporation of Samaria into the New Israel . . . a 'wooing' of Samaria to full covenant fidelity in the New Israel by Jesus, the New Bridegroom" (*The Revelatory Text: Interpreting the New Testament As Sacred Scripture* [San Francisco: Harper San Francisco, 1991], 190–1).

Another recent and novel interpretation argues that we should not ascribe to this woman the moral guilt of adultery, either literally or allegorically. Rather, she is not a loose woman or a type of something else, but the victim of levirate-type practices, forced economically to be attached to one man after another. Further, she is doubly victimized because her present partner will not give her marriage status; thus she is "stigmatized." For this view see Luise Schottroff, "The Samaritan Woman and the Notion of Sexuality in the Fourth Gospel," in *Literary and Social Readings of the Fourth Gospel*, vol. 2 of *"What Is John?"* ed. Fernando Segovia, SBL Symposium Series, no. 7 (Atlanta: Scholars Pr., 1998), 157–81.

While these interpretations are engaging, the woman's climactic word to her townsfolk, "'He told me everything I ever did'" (4:39) gives one pause. Is this also part of the allegory, revealing the Samaritans' idolatries, or does it disclose her oppression, as in Schottroff's interpretation? The astounding element of the story is that the woman does not appear as a victim, nor as "morally loose" and crushed by her experience. In Jesus' encounter with her, she is first and finally a human being expressive of human dignity, a trusted hearer, and then the bearer of Jesus' salvation news.

[21] Note that this term "it is necessary" (δεῖ in Greek) occurs here climactically in a series of four uses: *it is necessary* to be born from above (3:7); *it is necessary* that the Son of Humanity be lifted up (3:14); *it is necessary* for Jesus to increase (3:30); and *it is necessary* for Jesus to go through Samaria (4:4).

As Clifford W. Horn notes in a mission essay based on this text, this story is a model for cross-cultural communication. The meeting place is a well, a point of common human need, providing a natural opportunity for encounter. In this narrative, it is also a place of discovery. The woman discovers who Jesus is, and Jesus discovers receptivity in the Samaritans. Mission is accomplished in a simple but profound manner.[22]

JOHN 4:1–42 AND JOHN 20:19–23

John 20:19–23 is here considered alongside John 4:1–42 because it also contains a strong call to mission: "As the Father has sent me, so I send you." This missional charge is given under the umbrella of Jesus' peace-greeting. "Peace be with you" prefaces the commission (v. 21), and is distinct from the same word in the original greeting when Jesus first came and stood among the disciples (v. 19d).

It is striking, first, to note the verbal connection between 4:38 and 20:21. For the disciples, the significance of Jesus' encounter with the Samaritan woman is explicated in a brief homily concerning Jesus' vocational food: to complete the work of the Father and to call, or perhaps by calling the disciples to see the fields ripe for harvesting (v. 35d). Jesus concludes the homily with his sending commission: "*I sent you* to reap that for which you did not labor" (v. 38a, italics added).

Expositions of John 4 regularly slight the impact of Jesus' encounter on the disciples, and understandably so. The narrative is constructed in a way that interchanges the disciples and the woman in narrative space. When the disciples leave to buy bread, Jesus meets and talks with the woman. When the disciples return, the woman takes her water jar and goes back to the city (though verse 27 indicates that the disciples were astonished that Jesus was speaking with a woman). But the story does portray Jesus in dialogue with, indeed presenting a mini-discourse, to his disciples. The discourse clearly focuses on mission. For that reason, mission should remain as the primary focal point of John 4, and thus be seen as precursor to this famous sending text in John 20. If we consider John 3:16 and 20:31 together, we cannot maintain, as some scholars do, that John's Gospel and community represent a community turned in on itself, with concern only for intracommunal welfare.[23]

---

[22] "Communicating the Gospel Cross-Culturally," *Missio Apostolica* 2 (1994): 42–3.

[23] While the text is clear that the world hates the believers, nowhere does it say that the Johannine Christians hate the world (to deduce this from 1 John 2:15 is not necessary). See Wayne Meeks' description of the ambivalence between hating and loving the world in *The Origins of Christian Morality: The First Two Centuries* (New Haven: Yale Univ. Pr., 1993), 58–61.

Another intratextual connection is significant, in grasping the peace dimension of 20:19–23. Talbert helpfully shows the integral connection between themes directed to the disciples in Jesus' farewell discourse and 20:19–23, as follows:

I am coming back to you (14:18; 16:22)	*1. Jesus came to them (20:19)*
Peace I leave with you (14:27) [16:33]	*2. Peace be with you (20:21)*
Then your hearts will rejoice (16:23)	*3. Then the disciples were glad (20:20b)*
As you have sent me,	*4. As the Father has sent me,*
I have sent them (17:18)	*even so I send you (20:21)*
If I go, I will send the Spirit to you	*5. Receive the Holy Spirit (20:22)*
(16:7b) [14:16, 26; 15:26]	

Clearly, the gift of peace, which Jesus alone can give, is linked integrally to the sending theme in John's presentation of what Jesus has to say directly to his disciples.

The Holy Spirit (advocate, comforter, empowerer) is also a key player in this post-resurrection reality, envisioned by the text. In 20:22 Jesus breathes the Spirit on his disciples, as the empowerment for the sending task. As noted by numerous commentators, the term "breathe" (ἐμφύω | *emphyō*) is a singular New Testament use, and harks back to the LXX version of Gen. 2:7 where the LORD God breathed into humans the spirit-breath that made the human a "living soul." Is it too much to infer that in both narratives, Gen. 2:7 and John 20:22, the God-Jesus breath is the source of true *shalom* and *eirēnē* the peace of God's gospel manifest in Jesus Christ?

Regarding the Johannine stance toward the Jews, sometimes described as hatred (a judgment arising from the vituperative language used against the Jews, most extreme in 8:48), Adele Reinhartz, a Jewish scholar, challenges the Martyn/Brown/Rensburger "consensus" that holds that John's Gospel reflects the alienation of those excommunicated from the synagogue (9:22; 12:42c; 16:2). She reminds us that chapter 11 portrays the Jesus community together with Jews. See her excellent article, "The Johannine Community and Its Jewish Neighbors: A Reappraisal," in Segovia, ed., *Literary and Social Readings of the Fourth Gospel*, vol. 2 of *"What Is John?"* 111–38. Further, 11:45 and 12:42 clearly declare that *many* Jews, even the authorities, believed in Jesus. Thus the text does not show a uniformly hostile relationship between Jesus and the Jews.

Granted, John's repeated use of the term "the Jews" in a negative tone reflects hostile relations. It is incumbent upon us—for the sake of the salvation of all people—not to one-sidedly interpret the text and thus empower it to foster racist enmity or anti-Semitism. To explain the situation by means of a specific historical situation, excommunication from the synagogue that is speculatively linked with the Jews adding the *Birkat ha-minim* "malediction" in the "Eighteen Benedictions," as Martyn proposes, does not alleviate the problem of the text. Rather, it unfortunately places the blame for the alienation on the Jews. It would be better, as Reinhartz proposes, and textually more responsible, to propose that the *dual* portrait of *both* hostile and amicable relationships between Jesus/the Johannine community and the Jews is part of the Christian "community's ongoing struggle for self-definition rather than as an external, Jewish act of expulsion . . ." (ibid., 138).

It is essential to locate Jesus' gift of peace within the context of John's larger conflictual ethos. Some commentators of these texts contend that the peace Jesus bestows on his disciples refers specifically to inner peace, which relieves anxiety and fear.[1] But the conflicts that bedevil the disciples in the entire narrative and the persecution predicted in the farewell discourse require a different conclusion. The conflictual reality exists in at least three dimensions: *cosmic*, in which Jesus and his followers are in combat with the prince of this world (12:31, where victory is triumphantly declared); *religious*, between Jesus and some—at times many—of the Jews; and *political*, where Jesus knows that his not-of-this-world kingdom will clash with the world empires (both Jewish and Roman authorities, see chapters 18–19). Given this context, it seems more correct to hold that the peace bestowed by Jesus on the disciples, in chapters 14, 16, and 20, is a peace that not only grants relief from fear and anxiety, but promises victory amid the tribulation of these conflicts. As Brandenburger and Foerster hold,[2] this peace belongs to the Old Testament royal messianic hope, which anticipates victory over all evil. It is the eschatological victory—hence Jesus' triumphant word from the cross, "It is finished" (19:30). This word is spoken in the context of the trilingual proclamation of Jesus as king of the Jews—truth in irony.

The joining of the greeting bestowing peace and the commission in John 20 is significant, because the earlier two strands of emphasis, from John 4 and chapters 14 and 16, indicate that the peace and mission of John's Gospel are cross-cultural and break racial boundaries.[3] The ripe fields (4:38) include Samaritans and others as well. The sequel account in John 4 portrays the splendid faith of the Roman official, which brings Jesus' healing to his son. As a result, this man and his household become believers. In both cases, ethnic, religious, and national enmities are dis-

---

[1] So I. John Hesselink, "John 14:23–29," *Interpretation* 43 (1989): 174–7, and Richard L. Jeske, "John 14:27 and 16:33," *Interpretation* 38 (1984): 403–11.

[2] Egon Brandenburger, *Frieden im Neuen Testament: Grundlinien urchristlichen Friedensverständnisses* (Gütersloh: Gütersloher Verlagshaus Gerd Mohn, 1973), 48–50, and Werner Foerster, "εἰρήνη," in *Theological Dictionary of the New Testament*, ed. Gerhard Kittel; trans. and ed. Geoffrey W. Bromiley (Grand Rapids: Eerdmans, 1999), 2:400–2.

[3] To what extent does this feature of the mission-commission set forth a normative conviction, that the mission charge stands under the umbrella of the peace greeting? Luke 10 bears eloquent testimony to this conviction, in that the peace greeting of the seventy initiates and extends the gospel of the kingdom of God. The seventy go out on the gospel mission with the greeting "Peace be to this house." The result is that the demons lose their power: Jesus saw Satan falling from heaven like lightning, when the disciples' mission was being accomplished (10:17–18). Paul, in Ephesians and more broadly, affirms the same point, as Tom Yoder Neufeld's essay demonstrates; see "'For He Is Our Peace': Ephesians 2:11–22," pages 215–33 in this volume.

empowered and transformed by the power of Jesus, the Savior of the world. The sending of 20:21, then, has the whole world as its horizon.

The authority bestowed on the disciples in this "peace-breath-word" enables them to release people from sin's bondage, and to grant freedom to live, and live abundantly (10:10b). As Marianne Meye Thompson has noted, Jesus as the Son is one with his Father precisely in authority to give life (5:26).[4] This unity is also the foundation of the so-called high priestly prayer: "And this is eternal life, that they may know you, the only true God, and Jesus Christ whom you have sent" (17:3). This gift of God through Jesus is extended in 17:20 to all "those who will believe in me through [the disciples'] word."

The specific part of the mission charge that gives authority to forgive or retain sins is significant also in relation to John 4. Nothing is ever said in John 4 that indicates explicitly that Jesus forgave the sins of the woman. The emphasis falls on the gift of living water, so that she will never thirst again. This metaphor is never fully explained, but in John's overall narrative strategy it coheres with other metaphors describing the gift of salvation: born from above, bread of life, seeing clearly, branches abiding in the vine, and light of the world. All these metaphors illumine Jesus' offer of the gift of eternal life, which for John is not so much future as an experience here and now of newness and transformed living, liberated from sin (cf. John 8:1–12). The overall tone of the Gospel narrative leads us to expect that the Samaritan woman was forgiven of her sins, and thus she received the gift of life that led her and her community to declare Jesus "savior of the world."

Moreover, this particular confession of the Samaritan community has political significance, as does the trial narrative. Several authors have pointed out that "savior of the world"—in variant forms—was a title applied to Roman rulers from Julius Caesar to Hadrian. For Hadrian this precise form was used (σωτήρ τοῦ κόσμου | sōtēr tou kosmou). Craig Koester contends that the text intends to evoke in the reader imperial associations and, in keeping with David Rensberger's treatment of John 18–19,[5] to show that the Samaritan confession places them beyond "a form of worship tainted by charges of idolatry to true worship of God, and beyond national identity defined by colonial powers to become true people of God."[6] Richard Cassidy likewise acknowledges the alternative

---

[4] Marianne Meye Thompson, *The Promise of the Father: Jesus and God in the New Testament* (Louisville: Westminster John Knox Pr., 2000), 135, 141–8, 152–4.

[5] David Rensberger, *Johannine Faith and Liberating Community* (Philadelphia: Westminster Pr., 1988), 87–100.

[6] Craig R. Koester, "The Savior of the World (John 4:42)," *Journal of Biblical Literature* 109 (1990): 667, 680.

political option, but also stresses another point, arising from his extensive study of the theme of persecution in John, especially in Jesus' farewell discourse. Through this Samaritan confession, and Jesus' teaching more pervasively in the Gospel, John seeks "to encourage his readers not ever to be swayed or intimidated by the aggrandizing claims of the Roman emperors who styled themselves as saviors."[7] In my judgment, this point is correct, and it need not discount from but may add to Rensberger's contribution.

Precisely within this context of the Gospel's political realities, especially the certainty that believers will be persecuted by the world— i.e., the authorities (15:20; 16:33; 17:14–15; chap. 18–19; 21:18–19), the bestowal of peace (also in 16:33) and the sending charge to bear the presence of Jesus and the Father in the hating world take on new depth of meaning. The bearers of this unique mission of peace will be known by their love for one another (13:35), for their love incarnates God's love for the world (3:16), even though the world does not receive the one whom God sent (1:11; 5:40–44; 15:18–21). Within the fabric of the Gospel as a whole, the Samaritan woman with her community and the community empowered by the commission represent the light of salvation, transformation, peace, and reconciliation in a world of hate, blindness, and persecution. Peacemaking is the mission; the mission is peacemaking—through the transforming power of the one who is the savior of the world.

JOHN 4:1–42, JOHN 20:19–23, AND JOHN'S LARGER NARRATIVE PURPOSE

John 4:1–42 and 20:19–23 connect to the explicitly stated purpose of the Gospel: "to believe that Jesus is the Christ, the Son of God, and that believing, you might have life in his name" (20:31). A textual variant in this statement of purpose had generated much discussion. The manuscript evidence is divided between the present and aorist tenses for the word *believe* (πιστεύητε | *pisteuēte* or πιστεύσητε | *pisteusēte*). If the present tense is considered original, then we might translate: "continue to believe." The Gospel's purpose then is that of strengthening and deepening the faith of believers, at a time when it is being tested. But if the aorist tense is accepted, we would translate it: "come to believe." Then the Gospel is intended to be unequivocally missionary in posture and purpose. Although a few strong and early manuscripts read with the present tense (πιστεύητε), the greater manuscript support is for the aorist (πιστεύσητε). Because this reading has manuscript support from a wide

---

[7] Richard J. Cassidy, *John's Gospel in New Perspective: Christology and the Realities of Roman Power* (Maryknoll: Orbis Bks., 1992), 84–5.

geographical range in the early church,[8] it is clear that most of the early church understood the Gospel evangelistically (but this need not exclude nurturing and spiritual formation functions of the Gospel).

The pervasive use of "sent" language in the Gospel, more than fifty uses of various forms of ἀποστέλλω (apostellō), presents strong internal evidence that the Gospel is to be understood in this evangelistic way. As part of her dissertation work on John 20:19–23, Linda Oyer tabulated and analyzed all uses of ἀποστέλλω and πέμπω (pempō) in John.[9] Her conclusions from this study emphasize that the Father's sending of the Son into the world to save the world is the predominant emphasis, and that Jesus' sending of the disciples is to be understood as extending the work of the sent one. Whatever view of mission we attribute to John's Gospel, it is clear that "having been sent" is the empowering muscle of mission, based in prior action of the Father and the Son.

Andreas Köstenberger amplifies this point by showing that Jesus' work in John is viewed pervasively as the work of the sent one:

bring glory and honor to the sender (5:23; 7:18)
do the sender's will (4:34; 5:30, 38; 6:38-39) and works (5:36; 9:4)
speak the sender's words (3:34; 7:16; 12:49; 14:10b, 24)
be accountable to his sender (chapter 17)
bear witness to his sender (5:36; 7:28 = 8:26)
represent him faithfully (12:44-45; 13:20; 15:18-25)
exercise delegated authority (5:21-22, 27; 13:3; 17:2; 20:23)
know the sender intimately (7:29; cf. 15:21; 17:8, 25)
live in a close relationship with the sender (8:16, 18, 29; 16:32)
follow the sender's example (13:16)[10]

Not only is the entire work of Jesus grounded in the *sending* of the Father, but the mission of Jesus is often governed by a purpose statement that flows out of this reality, as Teresa Okura in her extensive study of mission in John, and specifically of John 4, describes:

All the major statements on mission in the Gospel have or presuppose a purposeful ἵνα-clause: Jesus is sent by the Father "so that" those who believe in him may have eternal life (3:15, 16) or "so that" the world be saved through him (3:17); he comes "so that" all may have life to the full (10:10). John the

---

[8] Textual support, from all text types, for the aorist, πιστεύσητε, is: א^c A C D L W X Δ Π Ψ f¹ f¹³ 33 565 700. et al. Syr^s, p, h, pal; support for the present, πιστεύητε, is: p^66vid א* B Θ 892.

[9] Oyer, "Commissioning Stories," 446; reprinted as Attachment 2 on pages 179–81of the current volume.

[10] Andreas J. Köstenberger, "The Challenge of a Systematized Biblical Theology of Mission: Missiological Insights from the Gospel of John," *Missiology: An International Review* 23 (1995): 449. See also his monograph, *The Missions of Jesus and his Disciples According to the Fourth Gospel: With Implications for the Fourth Gospel's Purpose and the Mission of the Contemporary Church* (Grand Rapids: Eerdmans, 1998), 107–11.

Baptist is sent "so that" he may bear witness to the light (1:7a, 8), that Jesus
may be revealed to Israel (1:31) and that all may believe through him (1:7b).
Though no purposeful clause is explicitly attached to the missions of the Holy
Spirit and of the disciples, it is understood that the whole purpose of their
witnessing mission to Jesus (14:26; 15:26, 27) is "so that" the world may
believe that the Father sent Jesus (17:21, 23; cf. 16:13–14; 17:17–20).
Moreover, since their mission is portrayed as an integral aspect of Jesus' own
mission, both necessarily share the same purpose.[11]

Commenting on 4:38, she says, "In the Johannine conception, every missionary endeavor of every age means essentially and fundamentally a harvesting, a reaping of the fruit of the work of salvation accomplished definitively by Jesus and the Father."[12] Köstenberger also notes that "the sending of the Spirit occurs with reference to the missions of Jesus and the disciples."[13]

The inclusion of the Samaritans into the Johannine community of faith, which John 4 affirms, demonstrates the mission of the Son, and also serves as a model for instruction to the disciples whom Jesus has *sent* to reap in fields ripe for harvest (4:38).

This mission emphasis of the Gospel serves further the attainment of Jesus' purpose as the sent one: to glorify God, and that God will also glorify him (17:1–5). In John, the mutual interdependence of Father and Son is depicted not only in the common *work* of giving life, mission, and love, but all also in mutual glorification. The Son glorifies the Father, and also asks for the Father to glorify him "in your own presence" (v. 5a).

That the accomplishment of mission as the sent one is so crucial to the actualization of this glorification is demonstrated clearly in John 12:20–32. Until this point in the Gospel, the narrator paces and interprets Jesus' mission with the arresting phrase, "my hour has not yet come." But here in 12:23, the mantra changes to "the hour has come." Why so? What triggered the change is the news from Andrew and Philip, who tell Jesus the Greeks are there and wish to see him. Jesus' way of "answering the door" is to announce a strategic shift in ministry emphasis: "'The hour has come for the Son of man to be glorified." Clearly, the cross is now in view, in Jesus' teaching about a grain of wheat falling into the ground and dying in order to bear fruit; in his cry to be saved from this hour; in the voice from heaven that answers his announcement, "I have glorified it, and will glorify it again"; and in Jesus' pronouncement that "Now is the judgment of this world; now the ruler of this world will be cast out." The Greeks coming to see Jesus rings the alarm on the sent

---

[11] Okure, *Johannine Approach*, 5.

[12] Ibid., 164.

[13] Köstenberger, *Missions of Jesus*, 192.

one's clock. Symbolically, it functions in the narrative as the ringing that sets in motion Jesus' glorification through death, so that "I, when I am lifted up, will draw all people to myself" (12:32).

USING JOHN 4 IN WORSHIP AND CATECHESIS FOR MISSION-PEACEMAKING

Appropriating John 4 for the life of the church could take many turns. My students have noted that this narrative illumines many ministry themes and challenges. They have suggested that it provides resources for:

> *lifting women from oppression to apostolic witness;*
> *a model of counseling that is nonjudgmental, inviting, and life-giving;*
> *a spirituality meditation on Jesus as the living water;*
> *a redemptive approach to divorce and remarriage;*
> *understanding dimensions of Christology, from prophet to Messiah to savior*
> *of the world;*
> *understanding the nature of true worship;*
> *evangelism and mission;*
> *peacemaking and reconciliation.*

All these are hermeneutically legitimate and empowering uses of this rich text. The last three, however, are not only explicit in the text itself, but connect directly to larger themes in the Gospel, as shown above. Further, the interlinking of these three—worship, mission, and peacemaking—cuts to the heart of the gospel and to crucial dimensions of religious life. To probe still deeper, one might contend rightly that unless these three emphases are all vitally present in a community of faith, any of them alone may be arid, pretentious, or phony.

It is beyond the scope of this essay to explicate each of these topics, as they might shape contemporary church life. As indicated at the beginning of this essay, Ben Witherington, in his commentary on John, speaks persuasively to at least two of these dimensions, in a way that edifies and calls the church to faithfulness:

> *Finally, at the climax of the story Jesus is portrayed as the savior of the world, which means the savior of all races, ethnic groups, sexes, and ages, regardless of one's socio-economic status, health, or previous theological orientation. While it is true that no local church can be all things to all people, and that there is nothing wrong with sharing the faith with those sorts of people with whom one has various things in common, there is something wrong with an evangelism strategy that deliberately tries to avoid crossing lines, and ignores the mandate to reach out across social barriers as Jesus does in this story. We too easily forget that the community of Jesus is not intended to be a museum for a particular kind of saints, but rather is to be a hospital for sick sinners in a broken and divided world full of hate, prejudice, and discrimination. If one is going to preach or teach this text adequately, it will be necessary to stress the intentionality of Jesus and of God in reaching across lines, and to stress the*

way Jesus enables even despised and disfranchised people like Samaritans and women to become disciples and able witnesses for the Savior of the world. The question becomes, is the food that satisfies Jesus also the food that satisfies us, or are we settling for the more material fare that the disciples brought back from town? The fields are ripe for harvest, but the laborers are few.[14]

Indeed, John 4, especially when it is understood within the larger narrative dynamic of the Gospel—especially 20:19–23—is an exceedingly rich text instructing the church in holistic mission and peacemaking action. It reminds us that the two themes are not two, but inherently one: without mission, there is no peace that reconciles and makes whole; without peacemaking, there is no mission that is authentic and worthy of the gospel of Jesus Christ. The sent one sends us, and beckons us *to go through Samaria*, offering the water of life that quenches the thirst of the human soul, and like an artesian spring, wells up unto eternal life.

Finally, the Johannine emphasis on glorification reminds us that both the mission and peacemaking emphases stand in the service of true worship of God. The chiastic structuring of John 4 regularly puts the worship pericope in the center of the chiasm. The empowering *dei* of Jesus' journey into "enemy" land—sent from the heart of God—culminates in Jesus presenting the gospel to the Samaritans, who then confess Jesus as the savior of the world. This opens up the new strategic breakthrough: the true worship and glorification of God, in which neither Jerusalem nor Gerizim is prescriptive. Rather, the one who came as the light of the world, with authority to give life, inviting us to worship God in spirit and in truth, and empowering us to love one another, becomes for us living water, bread of life, model shepherd, peace-giver, and finally "My Lord and my God!"

---

[14] Witherington, *John's Wisdom*, 125.

Boers
p.196

THE ENTIRE SEMANTIC COMPONENT OF JOHN 4 ON A SINGLE SQUARE

Death =
/sustenance/ =

(Jesus asking the woman for a drink of water)
(the disciples offering Jesus food to eat)

(Jesus passing through Samaria because he had to)
(Jews and Samaritans do not associate)
(Jesus a greater miracle worker than Jacob)
(Jesus a prophet)
(worshiping either on "this mountain" or in Jerusalem)
(Samaritans do not know what they worship, but Jews do)
(salvation is from the Jews)
(Jesus the messiah in a Samaritan sense)

$\overline{\text{Life}}$ =
$\overline{\text{/obedience/}}$ =

$\overline{\text{Solidarity}}$
$\overline{\text{/universal salvation/}}$
$\overline{\text{/human solidarity/}}$

(the woman reminding Jesus of the impropriety of him, a Jew, asking her, a Samaritan woman, for a drink of water)

Alienation
/partisan salvation/
/factional security/

macro-function move toward negation

MF$_2$

MF$_1$

macro-function move toward affirmation

Solidarity
/universal salvation/
/human solidarity/

(Jesus engaging in conversation with the Samaritan woman)
(the woman participating in the discussion with Jesus)
(true believers worshipping the Father in spirit and truth)
(Jesus the messiah in a universal sense)
(the Samaritans inviting Jesus to stay with them)
(Jesus staying with the Samaritans)
(the villagers recognize Jesus as the savior of the world)

$\overline{\text{Alienation}}$
$\overline{\text{/partisan salvation/}}$
$\overline{\text{/factional security/}}$

(Jesus ignoring the convention of nonassociation between Jews and Samaritans)
(worship neither on "this mountain" nor in Jerusalem)
(the villagers reject the woman's testimony)

= Life
= /obedience/

(water of life = the woman witnessing about Jesus)
(Jesus' other food = engaging in discussion with the woman, and staying with the Samaritan villagers = doing the will of the one who sent him, and completing his work)
(the sower and the reaper rejoicing together in the fruit of the harvest)

$\overline{\text{= Death}}$
$\overline{\text{= /sustenance/}}$

(the woman leaving her water behind)
(Jesus refusing the disciples' food)

SENT IN THE GOSPEL OF JOHN

Verse		Verb	Sender	One sent
1:6	a man was sent from God, whose name was John	A	God	John B.
1:19	the Jews sent priests and Levites	A	Jews	priests
1:22	have an answer for those who sent us	P	Jews	priests
1:24	they had been sent from the Pharisees	A	Pharisees	priests
1:33	the one who sent me to baptize with water	P	God	John B.
3:17	God did not send the Son into the world to condemn	A	Father	Jesus
3:28	I am not the Messiah, but I have been sent ahead of him	A	God	John B.
3:34	he whom God has sent speaks the words of God	A	Father	Jesus
4:34	my food is to do the will of him who sent me	P	Father	Jesus
4:38	I sent you to reap that for which you did not labor	A	Jesus	disciples
5:23	does not honor the Father who sent him	P	Father	Jesus
5:24	believes him who sent me	P	Father	Jesus
5:30	I seek to do the will of him who sent me	P	Father	Jesus
5:33	you sent messengers to John	A	Jews	priests
5:36	the works testify that the Father has sent me	A	Father	Jesus
5:37	the Father who sent me has himself testified on my behalf	P	Father	Jesus
5:38	you do not believe him whom he has sent	A	Father	Jesus
6:29	the work of God → that you believe in him whom he has sent	A	Father	Jesus
6:38	I have come to do the will of him who sent me	P	Father	Jesus
6:39	and this is the will of him who sent me	P	Father	Jesus

For verb: A=*apostellō*; P=*pempō*.

SENT IN THE GOSPEL OF JOHN

Verse	Verse text	Verb	Sender	One sent
6:44	Father who sent me	P	Father	Jesus
6:57	just as the living Father sent me	A	Father	Jesus
7:16	my teaching is not mine but his who sent me	P	Father	Jesus
7:18	the one who seeks the glory of him who sent him is true	P	Father	Jesus
7:28	the one who sent me is true	P	Father	Jesus
7:29	I know him, because I am from him, and he sent me	A	Father	Jesus
7:32	chief priests and Pharisees sent temple police	A	priests	officers
7:33	I am going to him who sent me	P	Father	Jesus
8:16	I and the Father who sent me	P	Father	Jesus
8:18	the Father who sent me testifies on my behalf	P	Father	Jesus
8:26	the one who sent me is true	P	Father	Jesus
8:29	the one who sent me is with me	P	Father	Jesus
8:42	I did not come on my own, but he sent me	A	Father	Jesus
9:4	We must work the works of him who sent me	P	Father	Jesus
9:7	pool of Siloam, which means Sent	A	Father	Jesus
10:36	the one whom the Father has sanctified and sent into world	A	Father	Jesus
11:3	the sisters sent a message to Jesus	A	Martha/Mary	unnamed
11:42	that they may believe that you sent me	A	Father	Jesus
12:44	whoever believes in me believes in him who sent me	P	Father	Jesus
12:45	whoever sees me sees him who sent me	P	Father	Jesus
12:49	the Father who sent me has told me what to say	P	Father	Jesus
13:16	messengers are not greater than the one who sent them	P	general	Jesus
13:20	whoever receives one whom I send receives me	P	Jesus	disciple

SENT IN THE GOSPEL OF JOHN

Verse	Verse	Verb	Sender	One sent
13:20	and whoever receives me receives him who sent me	P	Father	Jesus
14:24	the word not mine but from the Father who sent me	P	Father	Jesus
14:26	the Holy Spirit, whom the Father will send in my name	P	Father	Spirit
15:21	they do not know him who sent me	P	Father	Jesus
15:26	Paraclete, whom I will send to you from the Father	P	Jesus	Spirit
16:5	I am going to him who sent me	P	Father	Jesus
16:7	the Paraclete, I will send him to you	P	Jesus	Spirit
17:3	Jesus Christ whom you have sent	A	Father	Jesus
17:8	they have believed that you sent me	A	Father	Jesus
17:18	as you have sent me into the world	A	Father	Jesus
17:18	so I have sent them into the world	A	Jesus	disciples
17:21	that the world may believe that you have sent me	A	Father	Jesus
17:23	that the world may know that you have sent me	A	Father	Jesus
17:25	these know that you have sent me	A	Father	Jesus
18:24	Annas sent him bound to Caiaphas	A	Annas	Jesus
20:21	as the Father has sent me	A	Father	Jesus
20:21	so I send you	P	Jesus	disciples

10 | "Reconciled to God through the death of his Son"
A mission of peacemaking in Romans 5:1–11

RETA HALTEMAN FINGER

PAUL WRITES TO THE ROMANS, "THEREFORE, SINCE WE are justified by faith, *we have* peace with God through our Lord Jesus Christ" (Rom. 5:1). Or perhaps Paul's words should be translated, "Since we are justified by faith, *let us have* peace with God." In either case, to what kind of peace is Paul referring? Is it primarily personal, the reward of trusting Christ for one's salvation and the relief of a troubled conscience? Is it communal, the fruit of unity and reconciliation in Christian community? Or does it extend to the Christian community's relationships with the broader society, even to opponents and enemies?

When I was teaching an upper-level college course on Romans, this question arose. We were simulating the squabbling house churches of Rome. It seemed natural to me to think that Paul, after finishing his first proof that Jews and Gentiles are equally sinful and equally accepted by God, would urge the Roman Christians to put their theology into practice: "Therefore, since we are all made righteous by faith, let us have *peace with each other* through our Lord Jesus Christ." But Paul doesn't say that, and many students were skeptical of this reading. Indeed, the traditional interpretation does not hint at communal peacemaking. Rather, it assumes that Rom. 5:1–11 concerns the individual: Christ died for me, a sinful person (v. 6), washed away my sins, and now I have an inner sense of peace and am reconciled with God.

I will argue in what follows that the mission of making sinful people righteous before God through Jesus Christ and the mission of peacemaking—among Christian communities and beyond to an antagonistic world—are inseparable in Paul's mind in this text and throughout Romans.

We begin by looking at this passage in the broader historical and literary contexts of the letter.

Pax Romana or Pax Judaica?

The Roman Empire had no trouble understanding its mission in terms of peacemaking. During the centuries before Paul, Roman armies trekked hither and yon, subduing tensions and stopping skirmishes among various ethnic groups in the Mediterranean region. The more peace the Roman armies made, the more Rome dominated the world militarily and politically. By the time of the empire under Augustus (37 B.C.E–14 C.E.), the poet Virgil identified and promoted the great destiny of Rome. The gods were on her side, willing Rome to rule the whole world and thus provide peace to all nations. Augustus himself began to be worshiped by many as "the son of a god," the savior of the world, the one who brings peace.

Though pious Jews at that time chafed under the peace of Rome, their vision of God's mission in the world was just as broadly corporate and political. One version declared that with God's help the Jewish people would throw off their oppressors: "You shall break them with a rod of iron, and dash them in pieces like a potter's vessel" (Ps. 2:9). Another saw the day when all nations would peacefully submit to Yahweh and warfare would be eliminated (Isa. 2:2–4, Mic. 4:1–3).[1] In either case, earnest, law-observant Jews (such as Saul in Acts 8:1–3)—and Zealots, in particular—saw mission and world peace as inseparable.

Had Paul not met Jesus on the road to Damascus, he probably would have been among those who promoted a Pax Judaica through military means. Instead, he came to see himself as one called to promote the vision of Isaiah and Micah. Galatians 2:1–10, Rom. 1:5, 13–16, and many other texts reveal Paul's self-understanding. He believed God had given him a unique call to bring the good news of peace and reconciliation to the Gentiles. For Paul, mission and world peace were inseparable.

The purpose of Romans

The purpose of Romans has long been argued, though today scholars generally agree that, like all of Paul's letters, it is an occasional letter, directed toward a particular situation. It was written from Corinth to Rome in 56 or 57 C.E., at the end of Paul's third missionary journey, and at a turning point in his career. He had established churches throughout the eastern part of the Roman Empire and believed his work was finished in those parts (15:19). He wanted to move west to evangelize

---

[1] A detailed discussion is found throughout N. T. Wright, *The New Testament and the People of God* (Minneapolis: Fortress Pr., 1992), but especially on pages 299–301.

Spain, but first he had to take the collection from the Gentile churches he had founded to the Jewish Christians in Jerusalem (15:25–27).

The symbolic significance of this gift in ancient Greco-Roman context should not be underestimated. Not only did Paul aim to fulfill his promise to help the poor (Gal. 2:10), but he reasoned that the Gentiles owed the Jerusalem Christians a great debt because they had received the gospel through Jewish believers. But in that culture, to receive a gift from another party was to acknowledge that party as an equal.[2] Could Jewish believers accept as Christian brothers and sisters former pagans who did not first become circumcised and law-observant Jews? Paul was anxious about this, so he asked the Roman Christians to pray for his safety and success (15:30–31). From Paul's perspective, the unity of the worldwide church was at stake. The outcome of Paul's mission to Jerusalem would be either peaceful unity or growing conflict.

Though Paul mentioned his trip to Jerusalem to explain why his visit to Rome was further delayed, his underlying reasons for writing to the Roman Christians were both practical and theological. They beautifully demonstrate how integrated was his vision of mission and peacemaking. Because Rome was on the way to Spain, it made sense for Paul to stop and visit these churches: to "share with you some spiritual gift— or rather so that we may be mutually encouraged by each other's faith" (1:11–12). No doubt Paul was also hoping for logistical support for his mission. Because no Jews lived in Spain at that time, and no Greek was spoken there, he would need to develop new methods for evangelism. Roman Christians could help by providing Latin translators or smoothing out legal tangles.

Clearly, however, a deeper reason occasioned this extended theological letter. The reason, I believe, relates to issues of peace and conflict. Stitching together facts from the political scene at the time, we conclude that the house churches and cell groups in Rome must have been in turmoil.

One can infer from Acts 2:10 that the gospel was probably brought to Rome very early by law-observant Jews some time after Pentecost. In the years that followed, some Gentiles also became attracted to the good news about Jesus circulating in the Jewish synagogues. Conflict arose between Jesus-believers and Jews who rejected his messiahship. The

---

[2] Robert Jewett, *Romans,* Cokesbury Basic Bible Commentary, vol. 22 ([Nashville]: Graded Pr., 1988), 141; James D. G. Dunn, *Romans 9–16,* Word Biblical Commentary, vol. 38B (Dallas: Word Bks., 1988), 881–3; Jacob Jervell, "The Letter to Jerusalem," in *The Romans Debate,* rev. ed., ed. Karl P. Donfried (Peabody, Mass.: Hendrickson Pubs., Inc., 1991), 58–9.

resulting disturbances led the emperor Claudius to issue an edict expelling Jews from Rome in 49 C.E. (cf. Acts 18:1–2).[3]

With many Jewish Christians gone, leadership probably passed to Gentile adherents, and the cell groups probably moved into homes for their corporate worship and study. The character of these Christian groups changed as those present had less knowledge of or concern for the Torah.[4]

By 54 C.E., Claudius was dead, and the new emperor, Nero, who was more pro-Jewish than Claudius had been, allowed the expulsion edict to lapse. Jewish refugees began to return, among them the Christian Jews who had earlier led Roman cell groups. By the time Paul wrote to these groups in 56 or early 57 C.E., serious conflict had apparently arisen between the returning refugees and those who had stayed in Rome.[5]

In addition to power struggles over leadership of the house churches, basic theological issues were at stake. Do Gentiles have to become Jews in order to become Christians? If they do, what is Jesus' role in salvation? If they do not, is God no longer honoring the eternal covenant God made with Israel, according to the Scriptures? Or, in theocentric terms, can God be trusted within the new covenant in Jesus Christ if God is no longer faithful to God's original covenant with Israel?

Marshaling all his persuasive powers, Paul wrote a nonpolemical, diplomatic letter to both sides of the conflict and to all the house churches or cell groups in Rome. Not only was his mission to Spain at risk, not only did he need their prayerful support for his dangerous trip to Jerusalem, but the heart of his gospel was at risk. Jesus' life, death, and resurrection prove the faithfulness and love of God for all people, apart from national identity. And if God, through Jesus, loves and accepts equally all the children who come to God (see 3:21–31), those children

---

[3] There had apparently been political disturbances at the instigation of "Chrestus," which may be a misspelling of Christus, or, less likely, may refer to a messianic pretender present in Rome at the time (Wolfgang Wiefel, "The Jewish Community in Ancient Rome and the Origins of Christianity," in *The Romans Debate*, ed. Donfried, 85–101). Wiefel, "The Jewish Community in Ancient Rome, 92–3, quotes Seutonius *Claudius* 25.4: "*Judaeos assidue tumultuantes impulsore Chresto Roma expulit*" (since the Jews constantly made disturbances at the instigation of Chrestus, he [Claudius] expelled them from Rome).

[4] Wiefel, "The Jewish Community in Ancient Rome," 94.

[5] This reconstruction has been challenged by Mark D. Nanos in *The Mystery of Romans: The Jewish Context of Paul's Letter* (Minneapolis: Fortress Pr., 1996), 41–84. Nanos rejects this interpretation of Claudius's edict and believes both Jewish and Gentile believers were still meeting in Jewish synagogues when Paul wrote to them. Nanos's view has been taken seriously by scholars but is not yet generally accepted. In either case, the relationship of Jews and Gentiles is at stake.

only demonstrate God's love and acceptance when they relate to each other impartially (see 15:1–3).

Thus, in the context of the Romans letter as a whole, evangelism and peacemaking make up two sides of the same coin, inextricably united for the goal of God's reign on earth.

THE CONTEXT OF ROM. 5:1–11 IN THE ARGUMENT OF ROMANS

Although traditional interpretive practices do not see Romans as a single argument, the letter should be read as a cohesive speech to be delivered in one sitting. It is Paul's sustained effort to explain righteousness to both Jews and Gentiles, and thus to heal the divisions between them. Robert Jewett has shown how carefully crafted are the introduction (1:1–17) and the closing (15:14–16:24).[6] Paul states the thesis of his letter in Rom. 1:16: The gospel is "the power of God for salvation to everyone who has faith, to the Jew first and also to the Greek" (NRSV). Traditional interpretations have highlighted the faith part of this statement and underplayed the power of God in bringing Jew and Greek together.

Romans 1:17–4:25, then, elaborates two important parts of this story. First, Paul discusses the wrath of God (1:18–3:20). God's wrath is revealed against sin—the sins of Gentiles and the sins of Jews equally. Paul first describes typical Gentile sins (1:18–32), then uses a diatribe technique to squash Jewish pretensions that they are more righteous than Gentiles (2:17–29). Jews are not keeping the law any better than Gentiles, and the fact is, there is none righteous, no not one! (3:9–20).

But God is righteous! Paul's brief phrase in 1:17—"the righteousness of God is revealed through faith"—receives elaboration in 3:21–26. In a ringing conclusion to his first major proof, Paul insists that the righteousness of God has now been shown, not by Jews keeping the works of the law, but by the faithfulness of Jesus Christ. This is for all who believe. Since all have sinned (3:23), all are "justified [made righteous] by his grace as a gift, through the redemption that is in Christ Jesus" (3:24).[7]

Paul clinches this main idea in 3:27–4:25 by appealing to Abraham. He sidesteps the law of circumcision given to Abraham and renewed in

---

[6] Robert Jewett, "Ecumenical Theology for the Sake of Mission," in *Romans,* vol. 3 of *Pauline Theology,* ed. David M. Hay and E. Elizabeth Johnson (Minneapolis: Fortress Pr., 1995), 89–108.

[7] The English noun "righteousness" and the verb "to be justified" are translated from the same root word in Greek: δικαι- *(dikai-).* Unfortunately, justification is often limited to the legal or forensic sense of being declared forgiven although we have sinned. Being made righteous, however, means in this context "a transformation in which humans come to reflect the righteousness of God" (Jewett, *Romans,* 24).

Moses by showing that Abraham himself was made righteous before God while he was still outside the law, an uncircumcised Gentile. Only because of his trust in a trustworthy God was Abraham considered righteous.

The next section might be summarized, in J. Paul Sampley's words, as "all share the same story from peace to parousia."[8] Chapter 5:1–11 serves as a bridge into this section, still using terms like "being made righteous" but now moving into "peace" and "reconciliation." Implications for righteous living are explored in chapters 5 and 6. In chapter 7, Paul wrestles with the relationship of the law to sin. This section closes with the awesome apocalyptic picture of God's redemptive purposes. Since none can bring anything against God's elect, how can Gentile or Jewish Christians condemn each other?

Since God's grace and love through Jesus Christ are so great, Paul must then address, in chapters 9–11, why the majority of Jews have not accepted it, and how God remains faithful to the original covenant and has not rejected the true Jews—the remnant. Paul then warns arrogant Roman Gentile Christians not to scorn the observant Jews for their obedience to the law, for it is by grace alone that Gentiles remain grafted onto the olive tree. They have not done anything to deserve it, either (11:13–24).

Finally, in chapters 12–15, Paul discusses how the reconciliation introduced in 5:1–11 is worked out on the horizontal level. Reconciliation happens as Christians appreciate each other's gifts (12:3–8), as they extend hospitality (contributing to the Jewish refugees: 12:9–13), as they love enemies and do good to them (12:14–21). Reconciliation also comes about as Christians accept and welcome each other without despising or judging, despite their differing traditions about whether some foods are forbidden and some days are set aside for special observances (14:1–15:6).

EXEGESIS OF ROMANS 5:1–11

Romans 5:1–11 is a clearly defined text unit, although scholars argue about whether it belongs to chapters 1–4 or 5–8.[9] The discussion about Abraham's faithfulness reaches its conclusion in 4:24–25, where it is connected to that of the Roman believers. The use of first person pro-

---

[8] J. Paul Sampley, "Romans in a Different Light: A Response to Robert Jewett," in *Romans,* ed. Hay and Johnson, 122.

[9] The older Protestant view included chapter 5 with chapters 1–4, under the topic of justification. Chapters 6–8, then, discussed sanctification. This view is not generally promoted in recent scholarship.

nouns in these two verses is carried through 5:1–11, while 5:12–21 shifts to the third person.

The content of 5:1–11 is also distinct, though intimately tied to Paul's first major proof of his thesis: God's righteousness is revealed through the faithfulness of Jesus Christ to all who believe, both Jew and Gentile. The proof concerns the benefits or blessings that flow from this experience of being made righteous, as the two participles in verses 1 and 9—δικαιωθέντες | *dikaiōthentes* ("having been made righteous")— make clear: Paul draws his conclusions from the fact of having been made righteous.[10]

Following is a visual layout of Rom. 5:1–11:[11]

5:1a	*Therefore, having been made righteous out of faithfulness,*
5:1b	*let us have peace with God*
5:1c	*through our Lord Jesus Christ,*
5:2a	*through whom (also) we have gained access to this grace*
5:2b	*in which we are standing.*
5:2c	*And let us boast in the hope of the glory of God.*
5:3a	*And not only, but also let us boast in the sufferings,*
5:3b	*knowing that the suffering works patience,*
5:4a	*and the patience proven character,*
5:4b	*and the proven character hope,*
5:5a	*and the hope does not let us down,*
5:5b	*because the love of God has been (and continues to be) poured out in our hearts through the Holy Spirit who has been given to us.*
5:6a	*For to what purpose did Christ die at the right time for the ungodly,*
5:6b	*while we were yet helpless?*
5:7a	*(One would scarcely die on behalf of a righteous person,*
5:7b	*though perhaps one might dare to die on behalf of a good person.)*
5:8a	*But God introduced God's own love to us,*
5:8b	*because while we were sinners Christ died on behalf of us.*
5:9a	*Therefore, much more having been made righteous now by means of his blood,*
5:9b	*we shall be saved through him from God's end-time wrath.*
5:10a	*For if while we were enemies,*
5:10b	*we were reconciled to God through the death of his Son,*
5:10c	*much more, having been reconciled,*
5:10d	*we shall be saved by his life.*
5:11a	*And not only, but also let us boast in God*
5:11b	*through our Lord Jesus Christ*
5:11c	*through whom we have received reconciliation.*

In our individualistic culture, the plain sense of the text seems obvious: Paul must be referring to our individual relationships with God. We

---

[10] Pre-publication manuscript of John E. Toews, *Romans*, Believers Church Bible Commentary (Scottdale, Waterloo: Herald Pr., forthcoming), 81.

[11] Adapted from Toews, *Romans*, 82.

have all been ungodly (v. 6), sinners (v. 8), enemies of God (v. 10). Through the death of Jesus we are now reconciled to God and have a clear conscience, a peaceful relationship with God. This gospel should be proclaimed throughout the whole world. It is implicit throughout Paul's letter, and he must have preached it hundreds of times to people who were not yet believers.

However true that sense of the text is, I do not think it is Paul's main point here. Paul is writing to people in Rome who already believe in Jesus but who are not getting along with each other. Each group thinks the other group's theology is deficient. Those (mostly) Jews who observe the Mosaic law cannot believe a holy God, who ages ago set up a permanent covenant with their people, would accept Gentiles who do not uphold this covenant. Gentiles who think belief in Jesus is sufficient and have experienced the Holy Spirit in their lives are scornful of those who believe God still demands observance of food laws, circumcision, and holy days.

The switch Paul makes from third person to first person plural in 4:24–5:11 is critical. "We," "us," and "our" (used 24 times here) refer to Jews and Gentiles together. The one God is God of both Jews and Gentiles (3:29–30). Abraham, traditionally called "father of the Jews," is also father of the Gentiles because years before he was circumcised he was made righteous before God by his faithful trust in God (4:1–12). On these grounds, Paul contends that reconciliation and peace with God cannot be had without reconciliation and peace among the diverse house church believers.

Let us now examine some key phrases in greater depth. A better understanding of the rhetorical nature of this passage, its textual variants, and the background understanding of words such as "peace" and "reconciliation" may shed light on this issue.

Having been made righteous out of faithfulness (Rom. 5:1a)

The phrase "out of faith" (ἐκ πίστεως | ek pisteōs) in 5:1a is unusual. Πίστις (pistis) can mean faith as assent to some truth (the verb form in English is "to believe"), or faithfulness, which implies an active trust in someone. Since this phrase follows the example of Abraham's active and continuing trust in and obedience to God in chapter 4, the second meaning is the obvious one.

The genitive form ἐκ πίστεως can be either an objective genitive (faith *in* someone) or a subjective genitive (the faith[fulness] *of* someone). Although most scholars still hold to "faith in Christ," Richard Hays has made a convincing case for the subjective genitive.[12] Thus, in 1:17 and 3:26, ἐκ πίστεως refers to the "faithfulness of Messiah Jesus," in 3:30 it describes the faithfulness of Gentiles, and in 4:16 "the faithfulness of Abraham."

The implication for the phrase of 5:1a is that "we"—Paul and all the Jewish and Gentile believers in Rome—have been made righteous through their active trust in and obedience to God, not by keeping the Mosaic law.

Let us have peace with God through our Lord Jesus Christ (Rom. 5:1b)

There is a textual problem in this phrase. Is the main verb, ἔχομεν *(echomen)*, in the indicative *(we have* peace with God) or ἔχωμεν *(echōmen)*, in the hortatory subjunctive *(let us have* peace with God)? Most commentaries and translations, including the United Bible Society Greek New Testament (UBSGNT), read "we have peace with God." Reading this entire sentence from the majority perspective, then, gives the effect of passivity, as in the NRSV or NIV. "Since we are justified [declared righteous] by faith [head belief], we have peace with God." Thus we are declared to be righteous, whether or not we experience ourselves to be at peace with God.

However, the external evidence for "let us have peace" is much stronger.[13] Paul is saying, in effect: "Now that we have been made righteous before God, let us take advantage of it and enjoy it by experiencing peace with God."

The association of peace with righteousness is not a new one, especially for Jews familiar with the Psalms and Isaiah (see especially Isa. 32:17: "The effect of righteousness will be peace").[14] Peace was an inte-

---

[12] Richard Hays, "ΠΙΣΤΙΣ and Pauline Christology: What Is at Stake?" in *Society of Biblical Literature Seminar Papers*, no. 30 (Atlanta: Scholars Pr., 1991), 714–29.

[13] Consequently, some older commentaries, such as those by Lightfoot, Dodd, and Sanday and Headlam, prefer the subjunctive, as does Ralph P. Martin. However, although Bruce Metzger of the UBSGNT translation committee acknowledges the strong external support for ἔχωμεν, a majority of the translation committee "judged that internal evidence must take precedence." They assume Paul is not exhorting here, but simply stating facts. See the third and fourth editions of the UBSGNT, or Bruce M. Metzger, *A Textual Commentary on the Greek New Testament* (London: United Bible Societies, 1975), 511. So also J. B. Lightfoot, *Notes on Epistles of Saint Paul from Unpublished Commentaries* (London: Macmillan and Co., 1895), 284; C. H. Dodd, *The Epistle of Paul to the Romans* (London: Hodder & Stoughton, 1932), 74–5; William Sanday and Arthur C. Headlam, *A Critical and Exegetical Commentary on the Epistle to the Romans,* 5th ed., The International Critical Commentary, vol. 32 (Edinburgh: T. & T. Clark, 1902), 129; Ralph P. Martin, *Reconciliation: A Study of Paul's Theology* (Atlanta: John Knox Pr., 1981), 135, 148.

[14] James D. G. Dunn, *Romans 1–8*, Word Biblical Commentary, vol. 38A (Dallas: Word Bks., 1988), 262.

gral part of God's covenant and connoted more than the cessation of war. It related to material prosperity and everything that makes for well-being and harmony. But by first saying "peace with God," rather than "peace with each other," Paul implies that unless peace exists between the creator and the created, complete harmony is impossible among human beings. James Dunn also observes that by using the first person plural throughout this passage, Paul denationalizes peace. Often, as in Zech. 9:10, Old Testament peace was a peace imposed by Israel on other nations. But the "we" who are addressed in this passage includes both Jews and Gentiles equally.[15]

The ethnic conflicts among the house churches and cell groups of Rome are evidence that to have peace in the comprehensive Hebrew sense of the word, these Christians needed to appropriate Paul's message.

Let us boast in the hope of the glory of God. And not only, but also let us boast in the sufferings (Rom. 5:2c–3a)

The same textual issues arise here. If the first verb in 5:1 is a hortatory subjunctive, in these parallel phrases καυχώμεθα *(kauchōmetha)* will be. Because Paul has excluded boasting on the basis of law observance in 3:27, it make sense that he would encourage his listeners to boast in a hope that depends entirely on the initiative of God, rather than saying they are already boasting.

The NIV translates καυχώμεθα as "we rejoice." However, this is the same word used for boasting in 3:27, where such boasting is excluded. John Toews comments, "Boasting about a salvation and identity that excludes some people is rejected. Boasting about end-time hope that depends entirely on the initiative and power of God is encouraged. The object of boasting is the glory of God."[16]

Additional support for the use of the hortatory subjunctive comes from a detailed rhetorical analysis of this passage by Stanley Porter.[17] Porter demonstrates that Paul uses the rhetorical technique of diatribe off and on from 1:18 through chapter 14. A diatribe's basic orientation is not doctrinal but dialogical, a framework that includes the introduction of questions or objections by a hypothetical interlocutor.[18] This conversa-

---

[15] Ibid., 263.

[16] Toews, *Commentary on Romans,* 84.

[17] Stanley E. Porter, "The Argument of Romans 5: Can a Rhetorical Question Make a Difference?" *Journal of Biblical Literature* 110 (1991): 655–77.

[18] This is most obvious in 2:3–4, 21; 3:1–9; 4:1–3, 9–10; 6:1–3, 15; 7:1, 7, 13; 9:14, 19–23; 10:6–8, 14–18; 11:1–7, 11, 15; 14:4.

tional partner can speak as an opponent, as a helper, or even for the author him/herself.[19] In this case, Paul is urging his conversational partner to boast.

And not only, but also, let us boast in the sufferings (Rom. 5:3a)

The use of "and not only, but also" in 3a intensifies what follows it, which is that Paul and the Roman Christians are to boast in suffering. Suffering is not a popular concept in our western culture today, where relief of suffering is a top priority. But in a stratified, honor/shame culture like that of the ancient Mediterranean world, suffering is not only personal and often physical but also publicly shameful. The person who can publicly humiliate another by verbal put-downs or physical strength is considered superior; the loser is inferior. In a society where men related to other men antagonistically for the sake of public honor, boasting in suffering was wildly counter-cultural. Men, more than women (who were assumed to be inferior to men and who belonged mostly in the private sphere), would have found this activity difficult to embrace. Fighting for one's honor was instinctive for males in that antagonistic society, yet Paul's vision of peace evidently precluded it.

Let us boast in the sufferings, knowing that the suffering works patience, and the patience proven character, and the proven character hope (Rom. 5:3a–4b)

Another feature of the diatribe style is the use of a catalog of vices or hardships that the wise person must face (see also 2:8, 21–23). Paul promises that embracing suffering and humiliation will strengthen character and drive one to hope for a different future.

And the hope does not let us down, because the love of God has been (and continues to be) poured out in our hearts through the Holy Spirit given to us (Rom. 5:5)

"The love of God" is subjective genitive, referring to the character of God. God is loving. Usually the term "poured out" (ἐκκέχυται | *ekkechutai*) is used with God's wrath, not God's love. But here the Holy Spirit, sometimes represented as a fluid, is poured out. The verb is in the perfect tense, suggesting an ongoing state resulting from a life-changing event.[20] This reference recalls the descent of the Spirit at Pentecost and its implications in Peter's sermon for the radical inclusion of both genders, all classes—including slaves, and all ethnic groups.

---

[19] Porter, "The Argument of Romans 5," 661.

[20] Toews, *Commentary on Romans*, 85.

For to what purpose did Christ, while we were yet helpless, die at the right time for the ungodly? (Rom. 5:6)

This sentence also contains a textual problem and is translated by the NRSV as a declarative sentence: "For while we were still weak, at the right time Christ died for the ungodly." In the UBSGNT the preferred reading is ἔτι γὰρ ... ἔτι *(eti gar ... eti)*, which is a very difficult reading and receives only a "D" rating. However, the translation committee chose this rating because they could not see how the text could have accidentally been changed to such a strange reading.[21] But Porter suggests that the original reading was εἰς τι γὰρ ... ἔτι *(eis ti gar ... eti)*, with the first ἔτι resulting from accidental deletions from εἰς τί. Such a reading could then be translated into the above question, a form appropriate to the dialogical diatribe Porter sees carried through in this passage.

Rather than interrupting the flow of the text, as they usually seem to, the next two lines carry on the statement of shock posed by the interlocutor's question.

One would scarcely die on behalf of a righteous person, though perhaps one might dare to die on behalf of a good person (Rom. 5:7)

This comment is not an interpolation but is part of the interlocutor's argument. If one can scarcely imagine someone dying for a good person—meaning one's benefactor, to whom one owes a personal obligation—one cannot conceive of giving up one's life for the ungodly! But Paul reiterates what he has just said. God's love is so great that "while we still were sinners," Christ died on our behalf (5:8). He concludes his train of thought in verse 9.

Therefore, much more having been made righteous now by means of his blood, we shall be saved through him from (God's end-time) wrath (Rom. 5:9)

This assertion can be seen as a simple evangelistic statement: the blood of Christ saves sinners from God's judgment. Though this is entirely true, in its context here Paul implies horizontal reconciliation as well. A Jewish audience familiar with blood sacrifice under Mosaic law would connect with the idea of being saved by Jesus' blood. But Paul's next sentence reiterates in even stronger language what he has just said in verses 6–9.

For if while we were enemies, we were reconciled to God through the death of his Son, much more, having been reconciled, we shall be saved by his life (Rom. 5:10)

Here Paul uses different language with slightly different meanings in order to appeal to a different group of Roman Christians. He is doing the

---

[21] Metzger, *A Textual Commentary*, 512.

same thing here that he does in 1:2–6 and especially in 3:24–26.[22] Jewish believers can easily understand the images used in 5:6–9. "Sinners" are those who transgress the commandments and laws of God. Christ dying on behalf of us "by means of his blood" clearly refers to the Jewish cultic-sacrificial system where an animal dies on behalf of the sinner, in order for the sinner to be made righteous.

But for Gentiles less familiar with and/or rejecting Jewish practices, verse 10 will connect. Unlike "sinners," "enemies" is not a theological term, but it is even stronger language. Gentiles, regarded as enemies of the biblical God, were traditionally viewed as worse than Jewish sinners. Now Paul writes that these enemies are "reconciled to God through the death of his Son." "Death" is a more neutral term than "blood" and can connote one person giving up life for another, without cultic overtones. Καταλλάσσω | *katallassō* ("reconciliation") is a common Greek word used by many pagan writers in various contexts.[23] Reconciliation is what happens when enemies lay down their hatred, fear, and desire for revenge, and become friends.[24]

And not only, but also let us boast in God through our Lord Jesus Christ through whom we have received reconciliation (Rom. 5:11)

The last sentence of this passage forms a fitting and rhetorically satisfying conclusion. It picks up terms and phrases from previous verses. "And not only, but also" intensifies Paul's declaration of this good news as in 5:3a and the "much more" of 5:10c. "Let us boast," is another reminder of what it is appropriate to boast about (5:2, 3). "Through our Lord Jesus Christ" (5:1) identifies the key reason for making peace among Jews and Gentiles, because he died even for his enemies. "Reconciliation" parallels "peace" (5:1). Verse 11, then, forms an *inclusio* with verses 1–2, twin pillars holding up the gate of truth between them. The peace with God through Jesus Christ spoken of in verse 1 brings about relational reconciliation in verse 11.

SUMMARY AND CONCLUSION

The final goal of even the most militarily-oriented mission—such as that of the Roman Empire or of the USA today—is world peace. Religious Jews also perceived Yahweh's ultimate mission—and theirs—as effecting

---

[22] On 1:2–6, see Robert Jewett, "Ecumenical Theology for the Sake of Mission," 93–4. On 3:24–26, see Jewett, *Romans,* 52.

[23] Stanley Porter, *Katallasso in Ancient Greek Literature, with Reference to the Pauline Writings* (Cordoba: Ediciones el Almendro, 1994), 23–75.

[24] In a typical usage, Aristotle *Rhetoric* 1367a (1.9.24) cites an instance in which an angry party gives up its anger against another; cited in Porter, *Katallasso,* 37.

world peace, whether through fierce judgment or by national conversions. But Paul, who once would have supported Jewish domination, came to see himself as an apostle to bring non-Jews on an equal basis with Jews into God's realm. A major purpose of his Romans letter was to reconcile believers—Jew and Gentile, conservative and liberal—with each other, so the mission of proclaiming the gospel would not be hindered.

Romans 5:1–11 demonstrates that peace and reconciliation are not only concessions that must be made for practical reasons in mission, they are benefits of having been made righteous. They lie at the very heart of the gospel. Practically, mission cannot be accomplished if people do not work in harmony toward a goal. But deeper than practical necessity is the truth that the gospel itself breaks down walls between groups of people, because God accepts every person and every group on exactly the same basis—through the grace of God expressed in the faithfulness of Jesus Messiah, and not by works of the law or any other badge of ethnic identity.

Yet this text pushes Christians to go beyond the reconciliation of believers, such as those in the Roman house churches. They can also look at the way God acts through Christ Jesus toward enemies. At the center of this passage so attuned to salvation through the blood of Christ is the question, How does God treat enemies? The answer, of course, is, Not by killing them but by dying for them (5:10). That Christians are called to follow Jesus' example of loving enemies is clear from the ethical instructions in Rom. 12:20–21 (which result from Paul's theology articulated in Romans 1–11): "If your enemies are hungry, feed them; if they are thirsty, give them something to drink. . . . Do not be overcome by evil, but overcome evil with good."[25]

Christian mission and peacemaking are warp and woof of the same cloth. As proclamation and reconciliation merge, we begin to live out the reign of God, where "righteousness and peace will kiss each other" (Ps. 85:10).

---

[25] This injunction is consistent with Jesus' instructions to love enemies in Matt. 5:38–48 and Luke 6:27–36.

11 | *The new has come!*
An exegetical and theological discussion of 2 Corinthians 5:11–6:10

JACOB W. ELIAS

IN 2 CORINTHIANS 5:17, PAUL POETICALLY INVITES HIS hearers to enter with awe into the mystery of the new thing God has launched in Jesus Christ: "Therefore, if anyone is in Christ, there is a new creation: everything old has passed away; see, everything has become new!" This NRSV rendering leaves open the question whether the new creation now seen as emerging is the individual believer, the Christian community, or the cosmos as a whole. Many other translations, however, leave no doubt that the new creation that has come is considered to be the transformed individual: "Therefore if any man be in Christ, he is a new creature; old things are passed away; behold all things are become new" (KJV). "When someone becomes a Christian he becomes a brand new person inside. He is not the same anymore. A new life has begun!" (Living Bible).

Evangelists and pastors have frequently used this text in their evangelistic invitations to people needing to be redeemed or renewed. Even the rhetoric of reconciliation in the verses following has often been viewed as pertaining mainly to the individual in his or her relationship to God. Any social, corporate, or cosmic implications of this new creation have then been seen at best as the secondary outcome of the changed lives of individuals whose impact on society brings social transformation as well.[1]

Concurrent with this ongoing evangelical emphasis on the ontological transformation of the individual person has been a growing scholarly

---

[1] See John Reumann, *Creation and New Creation: The Past, Present, and Future of God's Creative Activity* (Minneapolis: Augsburg Publishing Hse., 1973), 89–99, and 100–8, for a vigorous articulation of the view that καινὴ κτίσις *(kainē ktisis)* refers to the converted believer. Similarly, a recent commentary by Paul Barnett, *The Second Epistle to the Corinthians*, The New International Commentary on the New Testament (Grand Rapids: Eerdmans, 1997), 296–9, and Moyer V. Hubbard, *New Creation in Paul's Letters and Thought* (Cambridge, U.K.: Cambridge Univ. Pr., 2002).

consensus supporting a social and cosmic understanding of the new creation. Any inner transformation of the individual through conversion is then considered a parallel development, a byproduct of this systemic change.[2]

The argument of this paper is that Paul's pastoral intervention relative to the situation in Corinth supports a holistic view of the gospel as addressing individual, social, and cosmic realities. Evangelistic mission and social, political, and ecological initiatives all receive theological support from Paul's exultant celebration of the dawning of a new age. Both evangelism and peacemaking gain impetus within Paul's vision of the new creation unveiled in Christ.

Our focus will be on 2 Cor. 5:11–6:10. Because this study is part of a collection of studies on the themes of mission, peace, and God's reign, the question might be raised, Why this text? After all, neither peace nor the reign of God appears explicitly as a theme in this part of the letter.[3] The rationale for including an exposition of this text will emerge, but a preliminary comment is in order.

Paul's pastoral and theological agenda in this letter is driven by the need to work at both evangelism and reconciliation. Even a casual reading of this passage in its context reveals that Paul is not just crafting a gentle evangelistic tract. He is engaged in battle. Paul's appeal to the Corinthians to align themselves unwaveringly with his understanding of the gospel barely conceals his indignation at rival preachers who have apparently won the minds and hearts of some new believers in Corinth. Here is a missionary apostle with a fight on his hands. Called by God to proclaim the gospel, Paul also finds himself summoned to seek peace.

In this examination of how Paul's evangelistic and peacemaking agendas intersect, I first trace briefly the story of Paul's relationship to the Corinthian congregation. Then I will explore the relevant highlights

---

[2] See John Howard Yoder, *The Politics of Jesus*, 2nd ed. (Grand Rapids: Eerdmans, 1994), 221–3, for a discussion of the way καινὴ κτίσις has traditionally been understood individualistically within the Pietist heritage. Yoder urges that this passage be viewed as referring primarily to a new social reality. Similarly, Victor P. Furnish, *II Corinthians*, The Anchor Bible, vol. 32A (Garden City, N.Y.: Doubleday, 1984), 314–15, 329–33.

[3] The term εἰρήνη *(eirēnē)* appears a total of 38 times in the Pauline letters (if one includes all the letters of the Pauline corpus, but not the Pastoral Epistles). The theme of βασιλεία τοῦ θεοῦ *(basileia tou theou)*, God's dynamic reign, shows up explicitly in Paul's writings only in Rom. 14:17; 1 Cor. 4:20; 6:9, 10; 15:24, 50; Gal. 5:21; Eph. 5:5; Col. 1:13; 4:11; 1 Thess. 2:12; 2 Thess. 1:5. In Rom. 14:17, the reign of God is linked with "righteousness and peace and joy in the Holy Spirit." See George Johnston, "'Kingdom of God' Sayings in Paul's Letters," in *From Jesus to Paul: Studies in Honour of Francis Wright Beare*, ed. Peter Richardson and John C. Hurd (Waterloo: Wilfrid Laurier Univ. Pr., 1984), 143–56.

of our focus text. The conclusion is a theological commentary about implications for the church's ministries of mission and peacemaking.

PAUL AND THE CHURCH AT CORINTH

The Corinthian correspondence yields a lively picture of the ongoing interaction between the missionary pastor Paul and the newly established congregation in Corinth, a relationship that unfolded over a period of several years.[4] In 1 Corinthians, Paul rehearses aspects of his initial evangelistic visit, which likely occurred in 51 or 52 (2:1–5; 3:1–15; 4:15). He also recalls his first letter to the church (5:9, 11). This first letter is now lost, unless a fragment of it survives in 2 Cor. 6:14–7:1.[5] References to oral reports from Corinth (1:11; 5:1; 11:18) and a letter addressed to Paul (7:1; see also 8:1; 12:1; 16:1, 12) show that later communication flowed in both directions.

After sending Timothy back to Corinth (4:17; 16:10–11), Paul also returned to Corinth. This return visit turned out to be difficult, both for the apostle and for the church, because of the need to deal with an offending individual (2 Cor. 1:23–2:11). Paul left Corinth and later sought to intervene in the congregational situation by means of yet another letter, one that was written "with many tears" (see 2:4). During a subsequent rendezvous in Macedonia, Titus reported to Paul that, likely in response to Paul's severe letter, the Corinthian believers had turned from their earlier recalcitrance and were again feeling kindly disposed toward Paul and receptive toward his understanding of the gospel (7:5–16).

In Macedonia, Paul pens 2 Cor. 1:1–7:16 in response to this good news conveyed by Titus. This pastoral communication to the Corinthian church may be called the "letter of reconciliation," because Paul both celebrates the resolution of troubling issues and expresses the hope that

---

[4] It is not possible here to rehearse the details of this relationship, or to define the sequence and chronology of the various underlying events. The description here is based broadly on Ralph P. Martin, *2 Corinthians,* Word Biblical Commentary, vol. 40 (Waco: Word Bks., 1986), see especially p. xlvi; cf. Barnett, *The Second Epistle to the Corinthians,* 14–15. Calvin J. Roetzel, *The Letters of Paul: Conversations in Context,* 4th ed. (Louisville: Westminster John Knox Pr., 1998), 93–6, considers 2 Cor. 1–9 (minus 6:14–7:1) to be Paul's fourth letter to Corinth (following 2 Cor. 10–13, the "severe letter").

[5] Commentators are divided on this question and on the larger issue of the unity of 2 Corinthians. Some literary analyses of 2 Corinthians propose that the epistle is a canonical unity: Frances Young and David F. Ford, *Meaning and Truth in 2 Corinthians* (Grand Rapids: Eerdmans, 1987). Others, such as Roetzel, suggest that 2 Corinthians in its present form is the result of an editing and collecting process. Roetzel, *The Letters of Paul,* 202, n. 7, notes that some argue that 6:14–7:1 is a fragment of the "lost letter," but he believes that the language here is more like Qumran than Paul.

the Corinthian believers will fully identify with his message of reconciliation (5:18–19). Evidently, the ongoing activity of rival missionaries in Corinth continues to be upsetting to Paul. In this letter, which may have been written in the year 55, there are a variety of apostolic moods. Prominently, one hears a sigh of relief concerning a resolution of the crisis: "Thanks be to God, who in Christ always leads us in triumphal procession!" (2:14). However, one can also sense Paul's passionate desire to shore up the Corinthian congregation's commitment to his theological and missional agenda.

In 2 Cor. 5:11–6:10, Paul unleashes a vigorous summary of the ministry reflections that make up the first part of this letter. Paul's "therefore" in 5:11 is more than a literary formality. Paul seems to have reached a climax in his extended personal and theological reflections concerning his relationship with the Corinthian church.

In the exegetical discussion that follows, I will examine 2 Cor. 5:11–6:1 with some care, but give special attention to 5:16–6:2, where Paul's recollection of his earlier ministry and his reflections on that ministry give way to a series of hearty appeals addressed to the Corinthian church. Interpreters often comment on the theological density of 5:16–6:2.[6] Later readers, who may find the rich interplay of vivid images and metaphors both compelling and bewildering, need to try to hear Paul's appeals through the ears of the original hearers of this letter.

COMPELLED BY CHRIST'S LOVE (2 COR. 5:11–15)

Paul articulates his apologetic deliberately with reference to the Christ event. Having noted that "all of us must appear before the judgment seat of Christ" (5:10), Paul speaks candidly about the transparent nature of his ministry among the Corinthians. Rooted epistemologically in "the fear of the Lord" (5:11), Paul's persuasive activity, whether considered to be ecstatic or ordinary, is both "for God" (before whom all are known) and "for you" (the Corinthians) (5:13). Even when he expresses himself in terms of what Christ has done and will do, Paul sees God as the primary actor. Paul views the role of Jesus Christ from within a theological perspective. The God whom Paul blesses in the opening of the letter is "the God and Father of our Lord Jesus Christ" (1:3). The divine enterprise initiated in Christ is described as being "to the glory of God" (1:20; 4:6) and as evidence of "the grace of God" (6:1). But Paul not only views Jesus' ministry theologically, he also describes his own ministry

---

[6] Charles B. Cousar, *A Theology of the Cross: The Death of Jesus in the Pauline Letters* (Minneapolis: Fortress Pr., 1990), 76–82, 87, writes about the interplay of various metaphors for the atonement in this passage and urges that the expressive categories of this text not be sacrificed for the sake of any one neat atonement theory.

and the life of the congregation from within the framework of God's grand intention.

Paul's understanding of the scope of God's enterprise is expressed programmatically in terms of his conviction about the compelling impulse of Christ's love.[7] Paul declares, "One has died for all; therefore all have died" (5:14). This cryptic assertion helps us glimpse Paul's central conviction about God's gracious gift and invitation in Christ. Paul understands Christ's death as a watershed event with universal implications: Christ died "once for all" and Christ is "the one who died for all."[8] Strikingly, however, Paul also regards Christ's death, though once for all, and one for all, as an invitation for the beneficiaries to participate in the way of Christ. Here Paul's understanding could be summarized with the words, "All in one!" All participate in the death and the resurrection of the one.[9]

Here lies the key: God's love in Christ, expressed supremely in Christ's self-giving on the cross, impels the recipients into a responsive giving of themselves to God and to each other. The ἵνα (hina) statement in 5:15 clearly announces this intention: "that those who live might no longer live for themselves but for him who died and was raised for them." Those now alive because of Christ's sacrificial love for them share in the self-giving and loving mission of their crucified and risen Lord.

Christ's death therefore has both individual and social implications. Paul himself and the community being addressed in this letter are beneficiaries of and participants in the graciously inviting and compelling love of Christ.

NEW CREATION! (2 COR. 5:16–17)

Two purpose statements (with ὥστε | *hōste*) elicit the reader's awareness of the cosmic consequences of this individual and corporate participation

---

[7] There are several translation judgments to be made here. The reference to "love of Christ" is best understood as subjective, as a reference to Christ's love. The meaning of συνέχει (synechei) is debated, but it is best to see this verb as conveying both the sustaining grace of God's love in Christ and the resulting drive or obligation to share that love with others. For discussion of the issues, see Martin, *2 Corinthians,* 128; and Furnish, *II Corinthians,* 309–10.

[8] The preposition ὑπέρ (huper) sometimes is understood to have substitutionary or sacrificial implications ("in place of"), but the larger context of Paul's treatment here suggests the notion of representation ("in behalf of" as representative or proxy): Cousar, *A Theology of the Cross,* 55, 56, 77; Martin, *2 Corinthians,* 129–31; V. George Shillington, *2 Corinthians,* Believers Church Bible Commentary (Scottdale, Waterloo: Herald Pr., 1998), 123.

[9] J. Christiaan Beker, *The Triumph of God: The Essence of Paul's Thought* (Minneapolis: Fortress Pr., 1990), 101, refers to Paul's interpretation of the death and resurrection of Christ using these categories of "once for all," "one for all," and "all in one."

in the way of Christ. The first ὥστε introduces Paul's conviction, which is rooted in his theological assessment of the coming of Jesus Christ into the world, especially Jesus' self-giving death on the cross. A woodenly literal translation of this assertion might read as follows: "Therefore we from now no longer know according to flesh; although we knew according to the flesh Christ, now we no longer know." It is evident that Paul's train of thought here needs to be discerned beyond what he has actually said. Is Paul talking about his changed perspective concerning Jesus, or about a new way of viewing all reality?

This passage has frequently been cited as Paul's personal testimonial, in which he contrasts his understanding of Christ before and after his conversion. Seyoon Kim says that when Paul as a Pharisee was persecuting the church, he had judged Christ according to fleshly conceptions of the Messiah, but after his conversion he no longer viewed Jesus as a blasphemous pretender to messiahship.[10] Other interpreters understand Paul to be talking not about his personal acquaintance with or opinions about the earthly Jesus, but about the corporate and cosmic implications of what God has done in Christ. In other words, Paul is here concerned not about Christology but about epistemology. According to J. Louis Martyn, with the coming of Christ, Paul recognizes a whole new way of perceiving reality (5:16).[11] Viewing the Christ event, especially Jesus' death and resurrection, from within an apocalyptic framework, Paul describes life at the juncture of the overlapping epochs in the eschatological drama introduced by God through Christ. The present evil age (cf. Gal. 1:4) continues, although the new age has already been inaugurated. In the meantime, while awaiting the consummation of the new age, the community of believers already knows what is the assured outcome of God's dramatic intervention into history through Christ.

The second ὥστε statement has also been interpreted in individual, social, and cosmic ways. A straightforward literal rendering of this passage reads as follows: "So if anyone in Christ, new creation! The old has passed away; see, the new has come!" (5:17). An anthropological

---

[10] Seyoon Kim, The Origin of Paul's Gospel (Tübingen: Mohr Siebeck, 1981), 14–15. Similarly, Christian Wolff, "True Apostolic Knowledge of Christ: Exegetical Reflections on 2 Corinthians 5:14ff," in Paul and Jesus: Collected Essays, ed. A. J. M. Wedderburn, JSNT Supplement Series 37 (Sheffield, England: JSOT Pr., 1989), 87–8. Also Barnett, The Second Epistle to the Corinthians, 293–6.

[11] J. Louis Martyn, "Epistemology at the Turn of the Ages," in Theological Issues in the Letters of Paul (Nashville: Abingdon Pr., 1997), 89–110, argues that the prepositional phrase κατὰ σάρκα | kata sarka ("according to the flesh") in 5:16b is adverbial, modifying ἐγνώκαμεν | egnōkamen ("we know"), rather than adjectival, modifying Χριστόν | Christon ("Christ"). Paul is therefore not differentiating between Jesus in the flesh and Christ the risen one. Rather he is describing the new way of looking at reality made possible through Christ.

reading of καινὴ κτίσις *(kainē ktisis)* as "new creature" (so KJV) seems to be invited by the impersonal pronoun τις | *tis* ("anyone"). Seyoon Kim regards this declaration as Paul's unambiguous testimonial to his own radical transformation on the Damascus road: "Paul, who had estimated Jesus in a fleshly way and persecuted his followers, has now become a new creature in Christ."[12] Representatively, Paul also speaks for other believers who are transformed in Christ, whose impulses are no longer centered on the flesh but on God's Spirit. Christian Wolff makes this explicit: "As a 'new creation' the believer (τις, 'anyone') walks in newness of life (Rom. 6:4), and his or her life is no longer centred on the σάρξ, 'flesh' (v. 16; cf. Gal. 6:14–15), but on God's Spirit (πνεῦμα)."[13]

However, many scholars have abandoned this individualized understanding of new creation. Ralph P. Martin argues for an eschatological and salvation-historical reading: "The accent falls on a person (τις) entering a new order in Christ, thus making καινὴ κτίσις an eschatological term for God's age of salvation. . . . Paul is talking of a 'new act of creation,' not an individual's renovation as a proselyte or a forgiven sinner in the Day of Atonement service."[14] Similarly, Cousar examines Paul's two references to καινὴ κτίσις (2 Cor. 5:17; Gal. 6:15) and concludes that Paul views the new creation as "an eschatological reality, a community reconciled to God and to one another, in which the customary social distinctions are not observed and the dynamic of faithful love is operative."[15] Richard B. Hays proposes the new creation theme as one of three New Testament focal visions (along with "community" and "cross") that provide normative moral guidance for the Christian community.[16]

What is at stake here? Anthropological notions of new creation tend to provide warrants for an evangelical view of missions, which is understood as appealing to individuals to experience personally God's gracious forgiveness of sin through the redemptive love of God in Christ.

---

12 Kim, *The Origin of Paul's Gospel,* 18; see 15–20.

13 Wolff, "True Apostolic Knowledge of Christ," 91.

14 Martin, *2 Corinthians,* 152. Note also his comments earlier: "Paul is not describing *in this context* the personal dimension of new birth; rather he is announcing as a kerygmatic statement *the advent of the new creation 'in Christ,'* the dramatic recovery of the world, formerly alienated and dislocated, by God who has acted eschatologically in Christ, i.e., the world is placed now under his rule" (146).

15 Cousar, *A Theology of the Cross,* 146; see 144–6.

16 Richard B. Hays, *The Moral Vision of the New Testament: Community, Cross, New Creation: A Contemporary Introduction to New Testament Ethics* (San Francisco: Harper San Francisco, 1996), 19–27; 198–200. See also Hays, *Echoes of the Scriptures in the Letters of Paul* (New Haven: Yale Univ. Pr., 1989), 223, n. 15.

Cosmic interpretations generally undergird mission strategies of peace-making and reconciliation among conflicted parties and with the natural world itself. Which is more in harmony with Paul's language here?

Paul's exultant coda in 5:17b may not decide the issue, but a study of its Old Testament allusions offers a direction.[17] Second Isaiah, with its hopeful and promising vision of God's new redemptive initiative in behalf of Israel in Babylonian exile, seems to have shaped Paul's language here. Echoes of Isa. 43:18–19 are clearly perceptible in this acclamation:

> *Do not remember the former things,*
>   *or consider the things of old;*
> *I am about to do a new thing;*
>   *now it springs forth, do you not perceive it?*
> *I will make a way in the wilderness*
>   *and rivers in the desert.*

God's reassuring promise of the restoration of a covenant people from their exile is narrated as a new creation, although the accompanying imagery of the way in the wilderness also suggests a new exodus. This redemptive initiative leads to the creation, or re-creation, of the people of God as "my chosen people, the people whom I formed for myself, so that they might declare my praise" (43:20–21). In exile because of her disobedience, Israel hears the exhortation that they should no longer reflect on their past sin and the resulting judgment and exile but rather on God's promise of restoration.

Similarly, the apocalyptic visions of Third Isaiah appear to have provided inspiration for Paul's celebration of the new creation, the new thing God is doing. The prophet is addressing people who, though they have returned to their homeland from their exile in Babylon, are still experiencing despair and unrealized dreams. In a significant sense, they are still in exile. To these people the prophet promises new heavens and a new earth. Hear Isa. 65:17–18:

> *For I am about to create new heavens*
>   *and a new earth;*
> *the former things shall not be remembered*
>   *or come to mind.*
> *But be glad and rejoice forever*
>   *in what I am creating;*

---

[17] For a helpful and stimulating treatment of the Old Testament background to this passage, see G. K. Beale, "The Old Testament Background of Reconciliation in 2 Corinthians 5–7 and Its Bearing on the Literary Problem of 2 Corinthians 6:14–7:1," in *New Testament Studies* 35 (1989): 552–9.

for I am about to create Jerusalem as a joy,
    and its people as a delight.

Particularly instructive here is the parallelism between the cosmic (new heavens and a new earth) and the social or corporate dimensions (Jerusalem, its people) promised in God's future redemptive initiative. A people longing to be released from their exile hear that the time of their forsakenness will finally end. God the creator is now engaged in a redemptive re-creation of the people into a restored and renewed community whose trespasses, which had led to their experience of exile, have now been forgiven.

In harmony with these hopeful visions in Isaiah, Paul views the new creation ushered in by Christ as a renewed social reality that God has now launched. The church is the community whose existence in Christ is itself a witness to a cosmic transformation which has begun and is still unfolding. The social, eschatological, and cosmic dimensions of the new creation in Christ are dominant. Yet individuals, including Paul himself, are incorporated in Christ within God's dynamic movement unleashed into the world. This movement encompasses both the individual in community and the corporate reality made up of individuals who commit themselves through baptism to the way of Christ, "who died for us so that we together might live for him!" This results in a community giving witness to God's reconciling activity in the world.

RECONCILED RECONCILERS (2 COR. 5:18–19)

In 2 Cor. 5:18–19, Paul clarifies and grounds his poetic outburst concerning the passing of the old and the dawning of the new. The generative source of the new creation is God, from whom are "all things" (τὰ πάντα | *ta panta*). Here τὰ πάντα refers both to the created universe generally (as in 1 Cor. 8:6; 11:12; Rom. 11:36; Eph. 3:9; 4:15; Col. 1:16–17) and specifically to the new creation which God has made possible through Christ.[18] In Romans 8, Paul in similar fashion testifies to God's redemptive concern both for the creation as a whole and for the new community that has emerged through the regenerative power of the Holy Spirit. Paul acknowledges that "the creation waits" (Rom. 8:19), and "the whole creation has been groaning in labor pains until now" (8:22). Paul also quickly adds, "but not only the creation, but we ourselves, who have the first fruits of the Spirit, groan inwardly while we wait for adoption" (8:23). The newness that Paul envisions as a

---

[18] See Beale, "The Old Testament Background of Reconciliation in 2 Corinthians 5–7," 559, n. 1; also Martin, *2 Corinthians*, 152–3; Furnish, *II Corinthians*, 316.

consequence of what God has done in Christ has both cosmic and personal implications.

Having noted that God is at work in Christ to bring about a new creation, Paul enlarges on the subject of God's recreating strategy by employing the metaphor of reconciliation (5:18–19). God has acted "through Christ" (διὰ Χριστοῦ | *dia Christou*). In this way, Paul says, God "reconciled us to himself" (5:18). Paul emphasizes this point through repetition: "That is, in Christ God was reconciling the world to himself" (5:19).

Paul also amplifies this theological claim by adding the phrase "not counting their trespasses against them" (5:19). In the story of Israel, God's grace initiatives toward these people during their exile demonstrated God's willingness to restore them from the circumstances that had resulted from their unfaithfulness. Climactically in Christ, God offers both Jews and Gentiles a new possibility of restoration, a possibility borne through God's readiness not to continue to count their sin against them. Paul's language echoes the Septuagint language of Psa. 31:1 (32:1 in MT), literally, "Blessed is the one against whom the Lord will not charge sin" (a text quoted in Rom. 4:8). In Romans 5, Paul elaborates on how Christ's death on the cross provides the way for humanity to be reconciled by God. Christ died, Paul says, "while we still were sinners" (5:8). God's reconciling initiative through Christ came "while we were enemies" (5:10). In Rom. 5:15–21, Paul follows through by comparing and contrasting human sinfulness in Adam with the gracious legacy of the obedience of Christ even unto death on the cross.

In 2 Cor. 5:18–19, following each of the declarations of God's restorative and reconciling initiatives in Christ, Paul describes the desired response as the ministry (5:18c) and message (5:19c) of reconciliation. Those who have been reconciled to God through Christ are assigned a reconciling ministry. As reconciled reconcilers, they are entrusted with a reconciling message. Though definitely speaking about himself ("us"),[19] Paul also broadens the scope to include the Corinthians, as the subsequent appeal in 5:20ff. clearly shows.

Is Paul here simply piling up images willy-nilly? Or might there be a discernible link between his new creation imagery in 5:16–17 and the reconciliation metaphor in 5:18–19? Again, scholars tend to suggest divergent answers, with some emphasizing the personal, others the corporate and cosmic. Wolff proposes that Paul probably found a connection between new creation and reconciliation in the Jewish

---

[19] Kim, *The Origin of Paul's Gospel*, 18–19, views Paul as primarily referring to his own Damascus Road encounter and call.

understanding of the forgiveness of sins, in particular the New Year and the Day of Atonement, when a person was made a new creation, no longer burdened by past sin.[20] Paul understood Christ's self-giving love, as made known to him personally on the Damascus road, to be the means by which God's reconciling grace enrolled a persecutor of the church to be an apostle proclaiming the message of reconciliation. According to Wolff, then, the "us" in 5:18–19 refers to Paul himself personally as new creature, though representatively also to other individuals rescued from their sin by God's reconciling work on the cross.

Scholars have made several other suggestions regarding the background of Paul's new creation and reconciliation themes. In his extensive study of the scriptural argument in 2 Corinthians 3, Scott Hafemann includes frequent references to what he considers to be a connection between the theme of new covenant (2 Cor. 3:6; cf. Jer. 31:31–34) and new creation.[21] According to Hafemann, Paul views the new covenant people of God as the gathered eschatological community in which Israel's sin with the gold calf (Exodus 32–34) is being overcome:

> For at the very center of the "new creation" as a "second Exodus" redemption is the manifestation of the glory of God in the midst of his people, both Jew and Gentile, and among his creation. The ultimate result of this revelation of God's glory in the new creation is a life of faithful obedience among the people of God, in contrast to Israel's present rebellion and the wickedness of the nations, and the reign of peace throughout the newly created order. In this sense, the "end" is like the "beginning," since God's people are freed from slavery to the power of sin so that they may fulfill the Law by their love for God and mutual acceptance of one another.[22]

Hafemann also suggests that Paul views the vision of new creation as having implications for humanity's fall into sin. Paul understands his ministry, and that of the community of the faithful, to participate in the salvific impact of Christ's death and resurrection, thereby bringing about the reversal of the effects of the fall of humanity into sin (Genesis 3).[23]

Another proposal comes from Beale, who believes that the new creation and reconciliation motifs derive from Paul's theological reflection on Isaiah 40–66, especially 43 and 65. God as creator of Israel, both

---

[20] Wolff, "True Apostolic Knowledge of Christ," 92–3.

[21] Scott J. Hafemann, *Paul, Moses, and the History of Israel: The Letter/Spirit Contrast and the Argument from Scripture* (Peabody, Mass.: Hendrickson Pubs., Inc., 1996), 119–28; his summary, 429–36.

[22] Ibid., 431.

[23] Ibid., 434; similarly C. Marvin Pate, *Adam Christology As the Exegetical and Theological Substructure of 2 Corinthians 4:7–5:21* (Lanham, Md.: Univ. Pr. of America, 1991), 33–76.

in the original act of creation and in the restorative exodus event, also acts to recreate this people through restoring them from their exile. In Isaiah 43, "Israel is exhorted not to reflect on her former condition of exile when she experienced divine wrath (43:18; cf. 65:16b–19) but on God's imminent new creation of her as His 'chosen people' whom He 'formed' for himself (43:19–21)."[24] Reconciliation in Christ is, therefore, the inaugurated partial fulfillment of Isaiah's promises of restoration from the alienation of exile. Paul's appeal to the Corinthians in 5:20 is based on the premise that if they are to be truly participants in the new creation, the new relationship with God made possible through Christ, they will live and behave like renewed and reconciled people.

N. T. Wright presents a similar analysis of the new creation and reconciliation themes in 2 Corinthians 5. According to Wright, the story of Jesus, which is narrated in the Gospels and glimpsed in Paul's pastoral communications to the churches, needs to be viewed from within Israel's still unfolding story. As Israel's Messiah, Jesus died and was raised in a representative capacity in behalf of the people, thereby ending their captivity as exiles. Wright's framing of the story of Jesus within the narrative of Israel deserves to be cited extensively:

> The end of this exile, and the real 'return,' are not now future events to be experienced in terms of a cleansed Land, a rebuilt Temple, an intensified Torah. The exile came to its cataclysmic end when Jesus, Israel's representative Messiah, died outside the walls of Jerusalem, bearing the curse, which consisted of exile at the hands of the pagans, to its utmost limit. The return from exile began when Jesus, again as the representative Messiah, emerged from the tomb three days later. As a result, the whole complex of Jewish expectations as to what would happen when the exile finished had come tumbling out in a rush. Israel's god had poured out his own spirit on all flesh; his word was going out to the nations; he had called into being a new people composed of all races and classes, and both sexes, without distinction. These major features of Paul's theology only make sense within a large-scale retelling of the essentially Jewish story, seen now from the point of view of one who believes that the climactic moment has already arrived, and that the time to implement that great achievement is already present. Paul fitted his own personal narrative world into this larger framework. His own vocation, to be the apostle to the Gentiles, makes sense within a narrative world according to which Israel's hopes have already come true.[25]

This narrative approach to Paul's assertion regarding the new creation makes sense of the data. The God who created the world and called Israel into a covenant relationship also intervened in the exodus

---

[24] Beale, "The Old Testament Background of Reconciliation," 555.

[25] N. T. Wright, *The New Testament and the People of God*, vol. 1 of *Christian Origins and the Question of God* (Minneapolis: Fortress Pr., 1992), 406.

and now climactically in Christ to redeem Israel from their exile and to form a renewed people from both Jews and Gentiles. In this story, now climaxed in Christ, the reassuring message of comfort and hope in Isaiah plays a crucial role.[26] Especially pertinent here is the quotation from Isaiah 49 to which Paul turns as he moves into his vigorous appeal.

A GRACEFUL APPEAL (2 COR. 5:20–6:2)

Although Paul has used the language of appeal elsewhere throughout his apostolic apologia, his hortatory intent is made explicit in 5:20–6:2.[27] Grammatically, there is a shift from the indicative mood to the imperative, and at 5:20 and 6:1 the stock language of entreaty (δεόμεθα | *deometha* and παρακαλοῦμεν | *parakaloumen*) is deployed.

In 5:20, Paul uses ambassadorial language to portray his ministry. The apostolic task resembles that of an emissary who represents her nation abroad. As ambassador, Paul speaks ὑπὲρ Χριστοῦ *(huper Christou)*, not merely as representative of Christ but also with Christ's authorization. The ambassador speaks as though God were making an appeal in person. The content of this appeal is now recapitulated from Paul's earlier use of the reconciliation metaphor: "Be reconciled to God!" The dative τῷ θεῷ *(tō theō)* could appropriately be conveyed: "Be reconciled by God." The reconciliation metaphor does not imply that a wrathful God needs to be reconciled to sinful humanity; rather the wounded love of a gracious God motivates God's initiative made manifest in Christ's death. God graciously initiates; the covenant people are being wooed to recognize the new thing God has done, and all humanity is invited also to respond to God's grace.

The language of 5:21 is often seen as traditional, perhaps a citation from an early church credal statement: "For our sake he made him to be sin who knew no sin." Some link the themes of this passage to Isa. 53:10, depicting Jesus' death as an offering for sin,[28] or to the cultic sin offering in Leviticus (e.g., 4:8, 20, 24).[29] Morna D. Hooker emphasizes instead the representational aspect of Jesus' life, death, and resurrection: "Paul

---

[26] See Richard B. Hays, "'Who Has Believed Our Message?' Paul's Reading of Isaiah," in *1998 Seminar Papers*, Society of Biblical Literature Seminar Papers Series, 0145-2711, no. 37 (Atlanta: Scholars Pr., 1998), 205–24.

[27] In agreement with Furnish, *II Corinthians*, who suggests that the paraenesis section begins at 5:20 (cf. Martin, *2 Corinthians*, and others, who see 5:20–21) as the conclusion of the apostolic apologia.

[28] Martin, *2 Corinthians*, 157.

[29] N. T. Wright, "On Becoming the Righteousness of God," in *1 and 2 Corinthians*, ed. David M. Hay, vol. 2 of *Pauline Theology* (Minneapolis: Fortress Pr., 1993), 207.

might well have said, with Irenaeus, that Christ became what we are, in order that we might become what he is."[30]

The ἵνα statement in 5:21b introduces the outcome or intent of God's salvation initiatives in Jesus Christ: "so that in him we might become the righteousness of God." Clearly, Paul envisions God's identification in Christ with sinful humanity as being replicated in the character and activity of the community of faith. But what does Paul mean by the phrase δικαιοσύνη θεοῦ *(dikaiosunē theou)*, "the righteousness of God"?

Exegetical and theological debates on this question have been extensive, and cannot adequately be reviewed here. However, the fundamental question is whether the righteousness of God refers to the status conferred by God on humans on the basis of their faith or whether it points to God's dynamic saving activity. The former view (righteousness as imputed to humans) has been championed classically by Augustine and Luther and their theological progeny; the latter view (God's righteousness as God's salvation-creating activity) has been argued by Ernst Käsemann and is increasingly accepted. On the basis of "the overwhelming weight of Jewish evidence, including many passages in Scripture that Paul either quotes or alludes to," Wright opts decisively for the position that the righteousness of God is to be understood as God's own righteousness. Wright suggests that the genitive θεοῦ, "of God," needs to be seen as both possessive (righteousness as a moral quality of God, namely, God's covenant faithfulness) and subjective (righteousness as God's salvation-creating activity, namely, God's acts of covenant faithfulness).[31] Indeed, δικαιοσύνη θεοῦ, "the righteousness of God," can best be viewed in this latter dynamic sense, as God's power to establish covenant and to remain faithful to it, as demonstrated dramatically in God's rectifying activity in Jesus Christ. As recipients of God's gracious gift in Christ, the church participates in this reconciling and justice-creating mission.

In 6:1, speaking as God's ambassador (implied in the participle συνεργοῦντες | *synergountes*, "working together with [God])," Paul reiterates and emphasizes his appeal: "We urge you not to accept the grace of God in vain." In 1 and 2 Corinthians, the phrase τὴν χάριν τοῦ θεοῦ *(tēn charin tou theou)* seems to be shorthand not only for the gospel with its message of grace but also for Paul's apostolic ministry of proclaiming

---

[30] M. D. Hooker, "Interchange in Christ [Gal 3:13, 2 Cor 5:21, et al]," *Journal of Theological Studies*, n.s., 22 (1971): 360.

[31] Wright, "On Becoming the Righteousness of God," 202–3; also helpful for chart and discussion is Wright's *What Saint Paul Really Said: Was Paul of Tarsus the Real Founder of Christianity?* (Grand Rapids: Eerdmans, 1997), 101–3.

this gospel (1 Cor. 1:4; 3:10; 15:10; 2 Cor. 1:12; 4:15). Paul seems concerned both that the Corinthians might have received the gospel in vain and that they might yet turn their backs on the apostolic missionary who had preached the gospel to them. The message and the messenger are irrevocably intertwined.

Paul moves immediately to the citation of a text from Isa. 49:8, interpreted as God's reassuring word of favor and salvation to the exiles, a reality now declared to have been accomplished: "See, now is the acceptable time; see, now is the day of salvation!" This quotation from Isa. 49:8 provides a strong clue that throughout this section of the letter he has been recalling the biblical story of God's redemptive engagement in the past. In particular, the message of hope from the prophet in Isaiah 49 to the exiles in Babylon has been articulated as being potentially realized in Corinth in the new creation. Indeed, "the new has come!" And Paul appeals to these believers to live within the reality that is now breaking in.

THE APPEAL MODELED (2 COR. 6:3–10)

Paul reinforces his emphatic declaration of the arrival of "the acceptable time, the day of salvation" (6:2) in paradoxical fashion. He abruptly introduces an extended recital of some of the hardships he has personally experienced in his ministry (6:3–10). In this way, he resumes the direct apologetic defense of his ministry, which preoccupies him in so much of his letter of reconciliation (2 Cor. 1–7). In particular, Paul's catalog of his traumatic experiences and his ministry posture seem to reconnect with what he asserts as his agenda at the beginning of the section under consideration: "We are not commending ourselves to you again, but giving you an opportunity to boast about us, so that you may be able to answer those who boast in outward appearances and not in the heart" (2 Cor. 5:12). In 6:3–10, Paul appears to be giving the Corinthian believers something they can say in their interactions with rival missionaries. But how does this list cohere with the new creation theme that has been the center of Paul's reflections here?

In 5:14–15, Paul reminds his hearers about "the love of Christ," which was expressed in his willingness to die. The anticipated outcome of Christ's sacrificial love, Paul says, is the believers' participation in the self-giving and loving mission of their crucified Lord. That same message is underscored in 6:3–10. Paul shares candidly with the Corinthians ("We have spoken frankly to you" [6:11]) about the paradoxical fact that Christian ministry and discipleship call for a life style that conforms to the way of the cross. "As servants of God," Paul and his co-workers endured "afflictions, hardships, calamities, beatings, imprisonments, riots, labors, sleepless nights, hunger" (6:4–5). Yet, just as Christ who died was raised back to life, so for ambassadors of Christ, suffering and death paradoxically become the entrée to joy and life:

> We are treated as imposters, and yet are true;
>   as unknown, and yet are well known;
>   as dying, and see—we are alive;
>   as punished, and yet not killed;
>   as sorrowful, yet always rejoicing;
>   as poor, yet making many rich;
>   as having nothing, and yet possessing everything. (6:8–10)

These contrasts between outward appearances and deeper reality are reminiscent of Paul's earlier emphases in 2 Corinthians. Paul had had a near-death experience in Asia, but God rescued him (1:8–10). Paul describes himself metaphorically in 2:14 as a prisoner of war being paraded as the winner's trophy in the streets of the victorious capital, but the parade turns out, ironically, to be a triumphant celebration for the one defeated. In 4:7–12, Paul enumerates his experiences in some detail, and he summarizes: "For while we live, we are always being given up to death for Jesus' sake, so that the life of Jesus may be made visible in our mortal flesh" (4:11)

In his defense against his critics and in his appeal to the Corinthians to side with him in his understanding of the gospel, Paul emphasizes that Christ's death and resurrection demonstrate that genuine power comes through weakness. Jesus was crucified, but his weakness turns out to be the supreme manifestation of God's power. Similarly for those who follow Jesus, as Paul states succinctly later in this letter, weakness for the sake of Christ paradoxically leads to strength: "I will boast all the more gladly of my weaknesses, so that the power of Christ may dwell in me. Therefore I am content with weaknesses, insults, hardships, persecutions, and calamities for the sake of Christ; for whenever I am weak, then I am strong" (12:9–10). Those who in Christ have gained a whole new way of perceiving reality (5:16) know that in the new creation strength comes through the apparent weakness of living not only for oneself but for others, even to the point of giving one's life.

RELEVANCE FOR PEACEMAKING AND MISSION?

One goal of this exploration into the poetic and polemic thicket of the climax of Paul's letter of reconciliation in 2 Corinthians has been to investigate the convergence between evangelism and peacemaking. What is the relationship between mission and peace in God's unfolding reign?

Paul's poetic celebration of the new creation is embedded in a section of the letter in which he appeals vigorously to people who have been influenced by the contrary vision of his opponents. Paul passionately desires the Corinthian believers to be restored to his vision of the community of faith. His evangelistic ministry led to the emergence of a new congregation, yet a reconciling ministry of peacemaking was also needed for the church to survive and grow. Announcing the good news parallels naming the bad news and then working toward reconciliation. Mission and peacemaking are of one piece.

What God has done in Christ leads not only to changed individuals but also to a renewed social reality, a new creation. Through Christ, God initiates in grace the supreme and climactic manifestation of God's saving and empowering justice. As apostolic witness, Paul views himself as authorized representative announcing the *now* of God's favor, urging that God's grace not be received in vain but that it bear fruit in the life of the Christian community. This community, the church, consists of saved individuals who are recipients of God's grace, but in a primary way the church as corporate entity, as social reality, is the recipient of God's gracious saving activity. The church, as recipient of God's righteousness, God's covenant faithfulness, also embodies that righteousness, engaging in reconciling ministry in a broken world. And the church identifies with the groaning of the physical world in its longing for the cosmic newness of life in the new created order which is still being birthed.

Paul's overall pastoral approach derives from his theological understanding of the unfolding story of God's reign. One needs to tune in to Paul's narrative structures, the various stories that echo throughout his correspondence. One needs to listen to the ways Paul recalls the story of God's redemptive activity, in the past and present, and as anticipated in the future. In this way the themes and images such as "new creation, " "message of reconciliation," and "righteousness of God" yield a clearer picture of Paul's theology and his pastoral and missional strategy. Later readers who read this letter as part of the scriptural canon can then seek to discern the relevance of these themes for their time.

12 | *"For he is our peace"*
Ephesians 2:11–22

TOM YODER NEUFELD

W ITHOUT DOUBT EPHESIANS 2:11–22 IS ONE OF THE MOST important peace texts in the Bible.[1] Its central image of the broken wall enjoys wide currency even among those who have no idea about its origin. The crumbling wall of division might serve just as well as a central motif of the church's mission efforts at spreading the good news of reconciliation in Christ.[2] After all, the one who broke down the wall of enmity is none other than the Christ who gave his life on the cross to create a new humanity at peace with God.

The conclusions reached in the following analysis of Eph. 2:11–22 are as follows: First, peace is not fully the peace of *Christ* unless it implies

---

[1] I discuss this text much more thoroughly in *Ephesians,* Believers Church Bible Commentary (Waterloo, Scottdale: Herald Pr., 2002), 106–37. In addition to the major commentaries by, among others, Markus Barth, *Ephesians: Introduction, Translation, and Commentary on Chapters 1–3,* and *Ephesians: Introduction, Translation, and Commentary on Chapters 4–6* (Garden City, N.Y.: Doubleday, 1974); Ernest Best, *A Critical and Exegetical Commentary on Ephesians,* International Critical Commentary on the Holy Scriptures of the Old and New Testaments (Edinburgh: T. & T. Clark, 1998); Joachim Gnilka, *Der Epheserbrief* (Freiburg: Herder, 1971); Andrew T. Lincoln, *Ephesians,* Word Biblical Commentary, vol. 42 (Dallas: Word Bks., 1990); Heinrich Schlier, *Der Brief an die Epheser: Ein Kommentar,* 7th ed. (Düsseldorf: Patmos-Verlag, 1971); and Rudolf Schnackenburg, *Ephesians: A Commentary,* trans. Helen Heron (Edinburgh: T. & T. Clark, 1991)—all of which treat this text at length, see also Erich Dinkler, "Eirene—The Early Christian Concept of Peace," in *The Meaning of Peace: Biblical Studies,* ed. Perry B. Yoder and Willard M. Swartley (Louisville: Westminster John Knox Pr., 1992), 164–212; Ulrich Mauser, *The Gospel of Peace: A Scriptural Message for Today's World* (Louisville: Westminster John Knox Pr., 1992), 151–65; Peter Stuhlmacher, "'Er ist unser Friede' (Eph 2,14): Zur Exegese und Bedeutung von Eph 2,14–18," in *Versöhnung, Gesetz und Gerechtigkeit: Aufsätze zur biblischen Theologie* (Göttingen: Vandenhoeck & Ruprecht, 1981), 224–45.

[2] Fittingly it receives attention, much in keeping with the treatment offered here, in Marlin E. Miller's "The Gospel of Peace," in *Mission and the Peace Witness: The Gospel and Christian Discipleship,* ed. Robert L. Ramseyer (Scottdale, Kitchener: Herald Pr., 1979), 15–19. See also, e.g., Donald Senior, "The Cosmic Scope of the Church's Mission in Colossians and Ephesians," in *The Biblical Foundations for Mission,* by Donald Senior and Carroll Stuhlmueller (Maryknoll: Orbis Bks., 1983), 203–4.

reconciliation in the one body of Christ and culminates in the worship of God. Second, mission is not *Christ*ian mission unless it addresses the whole of the human experience of brokenness—personal, religious, social, cultural. Third, such an understanding of peace is canonically rooted and connected, representing the peaceable work of the God operative from the beginning of the biblical story. Finally, God's work of peacemaking in and through Christ is none other than the kingdom of Christ and of God (Eph. 5:5).

Underlying this study is a conviction, which here can only be stated and not explored, that what is said of Christ has profound implications for those who are "in Christ." That is, what biblical writers say about Christ is invariably a claim on the quality of the church's life and the nature of its task. With respect to Ephesians, students of the letter invariably come away with a sense that what marks this letter more than any other in the New Testament is a highly exalted ecclesiology or understanding of the church. I could thus easily have concentrated instead on the exhortation to the church that marks the second part of Ephesians most especially. It is, however, entirely consistent with both the structure and the vision of Ephesians to reflect on the foundational event of peacemaking, God's peacemaking in and through Christ. Nowhere in Ephesians does this come to clearer and more concentrated expression than in 2:11–22. God's act of peace in Christ not only deals with enmity and hostility, but it brings into existence a community of peace—the "new human," the "body of Christ," a church made up of reconciled enemies. It thereby makes possible and inspires the peace-making of God's many reconciled peoples.

I will first explore Eph. 2:11–22, as well as some canonical threads that tie it to the rest of the Scriptures. I will then reflect on some of the implications of this text for the church's missional peacemaking, or conversely, the church's peaceable mission.

THE STRUCTURE OF EPH. 2:11–22

Biblical writers are often careful and deliberate not only about what they say, but about how they say it. Often the structure of their writings is meant to highlight the ideas they want to draw to their readers' attention. This is especially noticeable in the case of Ephesians. The letter consists of two halves or "panels" of roughly the same size.[3] The first panel, chapters 1–3, is a celebrative rehearsal of God's limitless bless-

---

[3] I am adapting the vocabulary of Ralph P. Martin, *Ephesians, Colossians, and Philemon,* Interpretation, a Bible Commentary for Teaching and Preaching (Atlanta: John Knox Pr., 1991), 46, which reflects the scholarly consensus about the shape and structure of Ephesians (see Yoder Neufeld, *Ephesians,* 19–21).

ings—captured and summarized in 1:10 as God's "gathering up all things in and through Christ."[4] The second half, chapters 4–6, consists of exhortation, summoning the readers to a grateful and worshipful response to God's mercy, love, and re-creating power.[5] The second half of chapter 2, located at the center of the first rhapsodic panel, celebrates Christ not only as bringing peace, but as himself being our peace, having reconciled enemies with each other and with God.

Not only does this peace text fit well into a carefully constructed first half of the letter, it is itself meticulously shaped to highlight the centrality of peace for our understanding and worship of Christ. At the center of 2:11–22 is a depiction of Christ as peace (vv. 14–16). It is the central pane around which are placed two sets of mirror-like panes.[6] The corresponding panes are of roughly equal size. The two outer panes are contrasting treatments of the theme of exclusion and inclusion of Gentiles, whereas the two inner panes depict Christ as one who has come preaching and making peace. Both artistry and theological focus can be easily discerned in the following manner. (I have supplied my own translation.)

> *[11]For this reason, remember that once you Gentiles in flesh, called "the uncircumcision" by those called "the circumcision" made by hand in flesh, [12]that you were at that time without Christ, alienated from the commonwealth of Israel and strangers to the covenants of promise, having no hope and being without God in the world.*

> *[13]But now in (or through) Christ Jesus you who once were far off have been brought near in (or by) the blood of Christ.*

> *[14]For he is our peace who made both into one and [who] broke down the dividing wall of the fence—the enmity— in his flesh, [15]having abolished the law of command- ments in regulations, in order that he might create the two in him[self] into one new*

---

[4] The NRSV captures the Greek well. The term ἀνακεφαλαιώσασθαι (*anakephalaiōsasthai*) is related to bringing things under one heading (cf. Yoder Neufeld, *Ephesians*, 51–2).

[5] The structure is typical of Paul's letters, and reflects what Perry Yoder calls the ancient "therefore pattern," in *Shalom: The Bible's Word for Salvation, Justice, and Peace* (Newton: Faith & Life Pr., 1987), 71–5.

[6] Instead of "panes" we might call them "frames." This device, also called *chiasm* or *chiasmus* is found frequently in the Bible, but seldom as dramatically as here. For a fuller discussion, see Yoder Neufeld, *Ephesians*, 20–1, 107–8.

> human, making peace, [16]and might reconcile
> both in one body to God through the cross,
> having killed the enmity in (through) it (or
> in himself).

[17]And when he came, he proclaimed the good news of peace to you who were far and peace to the near. [18]For through him we both have access in one Spirit to the Father.

[19]So then you are no longer strangers and aliens. You are, rather, co-citizens with the saints and members of the household of God, [20]built on the foundation of the apostles and prophets, Christ Jesus himself being the head- or cornerstone, [21]in (or through) whom the whole structure joined together grows into a holy temple in the Lord, [22]in (or through) whom you also are built together into a dwelling place for God in (or by) the Spirit.

First, then, the two outer panes. The first pane (vv. 11–12) depicts Gentiles as lost in the universe without God (cf. 2:1–2; 4:17–19; 5:3–7). What looks like Jewish stereotyping of Gentile existence, maybe even a bit of "ethnic backbiting,"[7] serves a particular purpose: to set the stage for the movement from alienation to reconciliation, from hostility and enmity to friendship and community, and most important, from being without God to being with God. In bold and explicit contrast to the first pane, the final one (vv. 19–22) shows those who were once strangers as now no longer strangers but members of God's family—more, they have now become an essential part of God's own home.

The basis for the movement from estrangement to integration, from enmity to reconciliation, is captured in the three inner panes. The two panes that immediately frame the central pane are again roughly equal in size (see v. 13 and vv. 17–18). By means of allusion to the great peace texts in Isa. 52:7 and 57:19, Christ is depicted as peacemaker in bringing home the exiles, "the far" (v. 13), and as messenger or evangelist of peace to both the far and the near, here intended to refer to Gentiles and Jews (vv. 17–18; more on Isaiah below).

The central pane is a hymnic celebration of Christ. He is now not only maker of peace (v. 15), not only an evangelist of peace (v. 17). He is himself our peace (v. 14). Ephesians 2:11–22 is then a highly concentrated inventory of divine peacemaking and a tantalizing glimpse of what that comprehensive divine peace looks like.

---

[7] Pheme Perkins, *Ephesians*, Abingdon New Testament Commentaries (Nashville: Abingdon Pr., 1997), 67.

A PEACE HYMN

With many other scholars, I believe that an early christological hymn praising Christ as God's peace has been employed in verses 14–16.[8] Before being modified to fit its present context it would have focussed on Christ as peace in a general, even cosmic sense. "Both" in verse 14 might then have referred to realms of reality at war with each other: God and creation, heaven and earth. The new body in verse 16 could then have been understood as the cosmos healed. In short, much like a psalm this poem would have expressed the mystery in 1:10, namely, "to gather up all things in [Christ], things in heaven and things on earth." Such a hymn would have expressed that peace lies at the core of Christ's identity and task. We might even say that in this poem peace is personified as Christ himself. "Peace" becomes a christological attribute and title.[9]

The euphoric poetry of praise is vulnerable to losing touch with reality. So, lest Christ's peace be allowed to drift off into the far reaches of the cosmos, this christological peace hymn has apparently been adapted to bring it into immediate and direct relationship, first, with the specifics of the gospel Paul and his associates preached, and second, with the enmity they struggled with daily, the longstanding hostility between Jews and Gentiles.[10]

There is no firm agreement on the exact shape of the hymn and the additions, but we can get a rough sense of its original shape and its contextualization (additions or adaptations are presented in bold font).

> [14]*For he is **our** peace*
> > *who made both (neuter plural) into one*
> > *and broke down the dividing wall **of the fence***
> > > *—the enmity—**in his flesh***
> > [15]***having abolished the law of commandments in regulations,***
> > > *in order to create the two **in him[self]** into one **new human**,*
> > > > *making peace,*
> > > > [16]*and might reconcile both (masculine plural; "both **groups**") in*
> > > *one body **to God through the cross**,*
> > *having killed the enmity **in (through) it (or: in him[self])**.*

---

[8] Yoder Neufeld, *Ephesians*, 112–13; see also, e.g., Barth, *Ephesians*, 261–2; Gnilka, *Epheserbrief*, 147–52; Lincoln, *Ephesians*, 127–30; Jack T. Sanders, *The New Testament Christological Hymns: Their Historical and Religious Background*, Society for New Testament Studies Monograph Series, no. 15 (Cambridge: Cambridge Univ. Pr., 1971), 88–92; Stuhlmacher, "'Er ist unser Friede,'" 337–58; but see in contrast, e.g., Best, *Ephesians*, 247–50; Schnackenburg, *Ephesians: A Commentary*, 107, 112.

[9] Yoder Neufeld, *Ephesians*, 129–30.

[10] This point is made frequently, and specifically drawn attention to also by Senior, "The Cosmic Scope of the Church's Mission," 203.

"CHRIST IS OUR PEACE"

If we are correct in seeing the underlying hymn as celebrating the cosmic implications of confessing Christ as peace, then the additions point to a number of special emphases we are meant to notice and then ponder.

First, Christ is *our* peace. Christ's peace is directly related to the enmities those singing the hymn know all too well. Further, this use of "our" anticipates the fruit of Christ's peacemaking. Notice that whereas "we" initially stands over against "you," implying the hostility laden distinction between us Jews and you Gentiles, in verse 18 "we" has come, as a result of Christ's work of peace, to mean "we both." The church made up of "us both" is in its essence a community of peace, or, to use the language of the hymn, the body of the one who is *our* peace.

Second, Christ has broken down the wall of division between humans and between them and God. Here this wall is identified as "the fence." We should not be surprised if such an image would have evoked memories for some Jewish and perhaps knowledgeable Gentile believers of the wall in the Jerusalem temple that separated the court of the Gentiles from holier precincts.

More likely, the fence would have been understood as referring to the law in its function of deliberately erecting a barrier between the people of God and those who are not.[11] The law is here specifically identified as the law "of commandments in regulations." This may well point not to the law in general as God's will. After all, there is a positive and explicit reference to the law in 6:2 and less direct allusions to holiness and righteousness in 4:24 and 5:3–5, which any Jew would have recognized as referring to living in accordance with the law of God. The fence should thus not be taken to refer to the law per se, but to specific laws and interpretive traditions that nurtured a sense of otherness from outsiders—the Gentiles.[12] It is law as a device for driving a wedge into humanity that has been abrogated by Christ.

The abrogation of such law rests, finally, not in a critique of the law as such, nor in a critique of the need in past history for separating God's

---

[11] See here in particular Deuteronomy 4, where in language similar to what we find here (see vv. 1, 5, 8, 40) the law serves to set the people apart and over against the nations, or Gentiles. See also the oft-quoted second-century B.C.E. *Letter of Aristeas* 138–42: "To prevent our being perverted by contact with others or by mixing with bad influences, [the legislator; 139] hedged us in on all sides with strict observances connected with meat and drink and touch and hearing and sight, after the manner of the Law (142)."

[12] Yoder Neufeld, *Ephesians*, 115–19. See also Calvin J. Roetzel's nuanced and careful discussion of this text, "Jewish Christian–Gentile Christian Relations: A Discussion of Ephesians 2,15a," *Zeitschrift für neutestamentliche Wissenschaft und die Kunde der Älteren Kirche* 74 (1983): 81–9.

people from the Gentiles, but in a conviction that to confess Jesus to be the Christ is to proclaim that the great ingathering of the nations has begun. That is a thoroughly Jewish eschatological hope (see, e.g., Zech. 8:20–23).[13] Drawing on one of the great prophecies of the past (Jer. 31:31–34), Paul elsewhere celebrates that this new day will be a time in which the law will be experienced as no law at all, precisely because it is written onto (or into) the hearts of the people (2 Cor. 3:3–6). We should thus be careful, against many commentators, not to see this as a rejection of law as such.

Even so, one should be careful not to remove the shock of this passage, which asserts that peace is made by demolishing the carefully constructed and religiously reinforced wall. This wall is, after all, a boundary around which the identity of who "we" are has been nurtured—and with it enmity toward "you." What makes this a peaceable rehearsal of a profoundly disturbing event is that the fence has been torn down, the wall has been broken down by *our* Messiah. More, it has been demolished from *within* the boundaries of identity and security. "Our" Christ has broken down the impediment to "your" access to "our" God.

Third, peace is purchased at great cost. As we have just seen, it is costly to us who are used to knowing who we are by cherished lines of self-definition and habits of fidelity that mark us off from those without. Intense resistance to paying this price lay at the heart of the struggles Paul had with fellow Jewish believers in Jesus.

Peace is costly even more because it costs the life of the peacemaker. In contrast to the "peace of this world" (John 14:27) or the Pax Romana, which purchased peace through the death of the enemy, Christ kills enmity with his own blood (v. 13) on the cross (v. 16). True, Christ's death was seen by all New Testament writers as a brutal miscarriage of justice, symptomatic of resistance to his peace evangelism. He clearly paid the price of speaking and making peace in a hostile world. His was the death of a victim, and biblical writers narrate it as such. But they view Jesus' death just as much or more even as God's decisive intervention to stop the cycle of alienation. As much as Jesus' death was violence against him, it was also God's peace offering to the perpetrators. Here in Ephesians 2, his death is described not as the fate of a victim, but as his act—even an act of aggression. Through his death on the cross, through his act of ultimate self-giving, Christ murders the enmity between insiders and outsiders and their God (v. 16).

---

[13] See Ben C. Ollenburger, "Peace As the Visionary Mission of God's Reign: Zechariah 1–8," in this volume, 97–120.

Fourth, the vocabulary of destruction—breaking down the wall, killing enmity, death in the flesh on the cross—ironically serves to highlight the vocabulary of construction and creation. The costly act of peace is intended not only to kill enmity but to "create a new human." Hymn writer Brian Wren captures this perfectly when he refers to Christ as the carpenter of new creation.[14]

We are struck in regard to this point, first, by the assertion that this new human is none other than Christ himself, recalling the new Adam of Rom. 5:12–21 and 1 Cor. 15:45–50 (cf. 2 Cor. 5:17). It is in the self-giving one that humanity is recreated to be what God intended from the outset (cf. Eph. 2:10; 4:24). Second, recreated humanity is made up of those who were once at enmity with each other—Jews and Gentiles, God's-people and those who were once not-God's-people, the near and the far, we and you.

An individualistic reading of the gospel, of the work of Christ, or of having peace with God, cannot possibly accommodate this hymn.[15] There can be no doubt that Paul's mission called individuals to faith; there is equally no doubt that they were given a new corporate identity. Having said that, members of the new human do not, for all their newfound unity in Christ, forget where they came from. Our passage begins with a deliberate summons to remember (v. 11). Christ creates a new human made up of individuals and groups with different but now shared memories: you (Gentiles) and we (Jews) are now the new "we"— the new human in Christ. It is useful to continue to use the singular "human" (ἄνθρωπος | anthrōpos), however, if for no other reason than to tie this new reality of peaceable creation inextricably to the one true anthrōpos, Christ, in whom all "boths" find their unity (v. 15; cf. also 4:1– 16). It is in Christ that the many find their new identity even as they retain their memories, and thus their histories.[16] That is why God is said in 3:14 to be father of *all* families.

---

[14] Stanza 3 of "God of many names," in Brian Wren, *Piece Together Praise: A Theological Journey* (Carol Stream: Hope Publishing Co., 1996), 8.

[15] Cf., in this regard, e.g., John Howard Yoder's repeated emphasis in his various treatments of this and other Pauline texts, notably 2 Cor. 5:17; *He Came Preaching Peace* (Scottdale, Kitchener: Herald Pr., 1985), 111–12; *For the Nations: Essays Evangelical and Public* (Grand Rapids: Eerdmans, 1997), 39–41; *The Politics of Jesus,* 2nd ed. (Grand Rapids: Eerdmans, 1994), 218–23. See also Croatian theologian Miroslav Volf's reminder of the importance of the transformed self nurtured in the culture of a peaceable community, in *Exclusion and Embrace: A Theological Exploration of Identity, Otherness, and Reconciliation* (Nashville: Abingdon Pr., 1996), 20–2.

[16] John Howard Yoder refers to the church's "bicultural history" in *For the Nations*, 39–40. Volf writes in *Exclusion and Embrace* of the body of Christ as "a complex interplay of

Fifth, the horizon of Christ's peacemaking extends beyond the reconciliation and re-creation of humanity. I suggested earlier that a hymn celebrating the cosmic peace of Christ has been adapted to celebrate the peace Christ has brought to divided humanity, and adapted in a way that highlights the divisions most palpably experienced daily by the readers. Interestingly, the hymn has not been altered so thoroughly that it obscures the earlier cosmic reach of the vision, and I think deliberately so. I translated τὰ ἀμφότερα *(ta amphotera)* in verse 14 as "both"; the NRSV translates it as "both groups," and most others simply as "the two" (e.g., NIV, NJB). A neuter plural can refer to persons or groups, but it need not. In verses 16 and 17 the author employs the less ambiguous masculine οἱ ἀμφότεροι *(oi amphoteroi)*, obviously refer-ring to groups, in this case Gentiles and Jews. We should allow for the possibility that the neuter plural has been deliberately retained from the original hymn to make the point that the abolition of human enmity is but one part of Christ's reconciling all things (τὰ πάντα | *ta panta*) in the cosmos (cf. 1:10). God's designs for reconciliation and re-creation encom-pass finally all things in heaven and on earth (1:10; see also 4:6). Here lies an important reminder not to be quick to set limits to the mission and peace agenda of the church. Indeed, we discover here an important foothold for bringing the contemporary concern for ecology within the missiological horizon. The reach of God's concern to save and to recon-cile extends to the edges of God's creation.

HE CAME PREACHING PEACE

We must return briefly to the panes that frame this great hymn in verses 14–16. Verse 13 identifies Christ as the one who brings near those who are far off. This verse finds an echo in verses 17–18 where the evangelist of peace emerges again, announcing the gospel of peace to both the far off and the near. In the present setting, the reference is clearly to far-off Gentiles and near Jews. As a result of Christ's peacemaking and re-creation of humanity we both are now equally free to enter the abode of God as members of the court, more, with the sovereign boldness and freedom (παρρησία | *parrēsia*) of daughters and sons of God. Standing in the holy presence of God with boldness is not hubris, but a breathtaking measure of God's endlessly gracious peace initiative toward broken and hostile humanity. The community of erstwhile enemies standing together in the presence of God is visible proof of the extent of God's grace. It is both the premise and the fruit of evangelism on the grandest

---

differentiated [and] interrelated . . . *discreet members*" (48), and of the new identity of the people of God as a "hybrid identity" (54–5).

scale, "so that in the ages to come [God] might show the immeasurable riches of his grace" (Eph. 2:7).

We come now to the final pane, which, in full contrast to the first (2:11, 12), reflects the extent of the movement from alienation to inclusion made possible by Christ. This pane also expands on what it means to have access to God in one Spirit (v. 18). "You" are strangers no more. You are now building blocks in the temple of God. God has found a home among reconciled enemies.

The structure of this text makes abundantly clear that the mission of peace is movement from somewhere to somewhere. Peacemaking as practiced by Christ responds to enmity by creating a new humanity fit to provide a home for God. The ultimate goal of peace is the worship of God. To state it differently, the motive for mission is cohabitation with erstwhile enemies in the house of God. In short, peacemaking is about the creation of a people God can inhabit. The most holy space—the temple—is constituted by the reconciliation of enemies.

CANONICAL THREADS

It is instructive to bear in mind that when it was first put into writing this text was not produced with the consciousness of writing Scripture. Perhaps because of that, we sense a deep conviction underlying this text that its vision of peace has a taproot that runs down to the earliest designs of God for peace as witnessed to in Scripture. God's intentions to gather up all things in Christ (1:10), specifically also lost and hostile sons and daughters (2:1–10), predate the foundation of the cosmos (1:4; 3:11). At the same time, this ancient mystery has now been revealed to the apostles and prophets in and through Jesus Christ. There is thus a conscious rootedness in the Scriptures, even as there is a radical openness to reflect on the implications of the revelation of God's eternal purpose as realized in the surprising event of Christ. If the majority of scholars is correct in discerning in Ephesians the inspired and creative hand of Paul's student(s),[17] then we can also see a deep appreciation not only for the Scriptures, but for the apostolic "deposit," to use the vocabulary of the pastoral letters (1 Tim. 6:20; 2 Tim. 1:12, 14). We are thus invited to take note of the canonical threads that come together in this richly woven tapestry of peace.

Connections to and echoes of other Pauline writings

Readers of Paul's letters will find many points of connection with concepts that lie at the center of Paul's prophetic message of good news,

---

[17] Yoder Neufeld, *Ephesians*, 24–8; 341–44; 359–62.

the gospel of peace. Given the concentrated nature of Eph. 2:11–22, we can only point to a few of the most important echoes:

> *Christ's death is God's offer of peace (Romans 5; 1 Corinthians 1) to rebellious and alienated humanity (Romans 1, 2).*
>
> *The cross is not only a sign of Christ's brutal humiliation at the hands of "ignorant" power (1 Cor. 2:8), but, bizarre as it seemed to Paul's contemporaries, God's strange power to save (1 Cor. 1:17–25).*
>
> *Reconciled Gentiles are a part of God's temple (1 Cor. 3:17; 6:19).*
>
> *Christ is the "sphere" in which old divisions are broken down (Gal. 3:28; Col. 3:11).*
>
> *The law is both gift and problem in the process of reconciling humanity (Romans 7–8; Galatians 3–6).*
>
> *God's designs for reconciling and re-creating humanity encompass all of humanity—both Jews and Gentiles (Romans 9–11).*

What emerges in a comparison of Eph. 2:11–22 with other Pauline treatments of these themes is that Paul's thinking regarding the effect of the cross is both expanded to "all things" and drawn into specific relationship to the reality of human suspicion and enmity. No doubt the cross has implications for the individual believer, but Ephesians 2 reminds us that Christ's cross intends to heal divisions that are culturally, socially, and even religiously experienced and nurtured. The messenger or evangelist of peace—Christ—addresses the good news not only to individuals who have run afoul of God, but to peoples at enmity with each other, and thus with the God who is father of every family. This comprehensive vision of peace and salvation is for all that no less rooted in the specifics of cross and flesh, and thus in the Jesus of Galilee tortured and killed by his contemporaries.[18]

Scriptural allusions, connections, and echoes

First, 1 Peter was likely written at about the same time as Ephesians, and the two letters display striking similarities. Salvation, new birth (1:3), means the integration of erstwhile rejects into the building of God's home as living stones; those who were once no people have become God's people (2:4–10). Note the immediate proximity of this motif to that of Christ as cornerstone or headstone in vv. 6–7, much as in Eph. 2:19–22.

---

[18] Comprehensiveness regarding the agenda of peacemaking necessarily includes the highly conflictual struggle with the powers. Ephesians itself contains one of the most trenchant calls to such divine warfare in 6:10–20. The motif is not central to the text presently under discussion, and so, for reasons of space, I have not treated it here. For fuller discussion, see my *Put on the Armour of God: The Divine Warrior from Isaiah to Ephesians*, JSNT Supplement Series 140 (Sheffield, England: Sheffield Academic Pr., Ltd., 1997), 94–153, as well as *Ephesians*, 290–316; 353–59 (see extensive discussion of literature there). For a trenchant treatment, see Marva J. Dawn, *Powers, Weakness, and the Tabernacling of God* (Grand Rapids: Eerdmans, 2001).

For this image of the cornerstone, both letters draw on Isa. 28:16, radically recasting a prophecy of judgment into an offer of peace to those who were hitherto themselves rejected stones (cf. also Rom. 9:33, where Paul retains the role of Isa. 28:16 as a text of judgment).

We observe this blend of dependency on Scripture, on the one hand, and recasting of familiar texts in light of God's surprising of humanity with the good news of peace, on the other, in other allusions to Isaiah in Eph. 2:11–22.[19] Two texts from Isaiah are particularly important:

> How beautiful upon the mountains
>   are the feet of the messenger who announces [lit. "evangelizes"] peace,
> who brings good news,
>   who announces salvation,
>   who says to Zion, "Your God reigns." (Isa. 52:7 NRSV)
>
> Peace, peace, to the far and the near, says the LORD. (Isa. 57:19 NRSV)[20]

First, by alluding to the Isaianic evangelist of peace, Eph. 2:13 and 17 provide a foothold for recalling Jesus' activity as an evangelist of the peaceable kingdom, the reign of God, as elaborated in the Gospels. This foothold, however slim, is of critical importance for holding together Jesus' proclamation in word and deed and his death on the cross. We might buttress this observation by drawing attention to Peter's speech to Cornelius in Acts 10:34–43, the only other place where the phrase "preaching peace" is employed in the New Testament (10:36). God is said to have come preaching the gospel of peace, "evangelizing" through Jesus' ministry in word and deed, culminating in Jesus' death and resurrection and the offer of forgiveness to all who believe.

Second, the double allusion to the evangelist of peace in 52:7 who announces peace, salvation, and the reign of God, and to YHWH himself as the proclaimer in 57:19, connects the peaceable proclamation of Jesus with God's regal intervention to make peace. Christ's peacemaking in word, death, and creation is nothing other than God's announcing and making peace with lost and alienated humanity. The proclaimer is no less also the proclaimed: Christ is our peace!

Of great importance is, third, how Isa. 57:19 is creatively reapplied to the recipients of Ephesians. In Isaiah, the far are those who were taken into exile, the near those left at home in Judah. In Isaiah, the far are exiles, "us" away from home. In Ephesians, the far are Gentiles who

---

[19] For specific studies of the use of the Old Testament more broadly, see, in addition to the commentaries, Markus Barth, "Traditions in Ephesians," *New Testament Studies* 30 (1984): 3–25.

[20] We might add the "Prince of Peace" from Isa. 9:6 to our brief inventory of Isaianic texts; so, e.g., Mauser, *The Gospel of Peace*, 152–3; Schnackenburg, *Ephesians: A Commentary*, 107, 112.

were alienated outsiders, not insiders taken off into exile. Employing Isaiah 52 in this manner effectively reclassifies Gentiles as "us" in exile.

It is not an overstatement to say that this reclassification is itself an act of peace. It asserts a common bond and identity between insiders and outsiders even before the one created by Christ (see also 2:1–3). The proclamation of peace to the far becomes thus a search for alienated and lost family members—for "us away from home." This startling welcoming home of exiles comes to its fullest expression in verses 21–22 in the description of Gentiles as building blocks of God's own holy home.

The generosity expressed in such use of Scripture must not be missed. It is a generosity learned with both excitement and pain by the followers of Jesus. Generous hospitality, or, to translate Paul's words in Rom. 12:13 literally, "pursuing the stranger with love," was seen as emerging out of the heart of Jesus' own proclamation and self-giving. Regrettably, this generosity would be tragically betrayed, as the guests who were welcomed into the family would drive out the hosts.[21] The new human would soon be limping badly, with terrible consequences, as the past century of Jewish experience attests. We thus see that the missional embrace has been from the beginning inherently fraught with great risk.[22] Without risk, it is not the embrace of enemies, nor is it the peace of Christ. The cross is the shape of God's risky embrace of hostile humanity.[23]

Indirect canonical threads

The strangely ironic phrase "killing the enmity" in verse 16 contains echoes of the ancient tradition of the divine warrior found everywhere in the Scriptures.[24] Indeed, the close proximity of killing to creation in

---

[21] See here Roetzel, "Jewish Christian–Gentile Christian Relations," 88. Yoder Neufeld, *Ephesians*, 130, 136–7.

[22] Volf, *Exclusion and Embrace*, 26–7, 140–7. Volf quotes Louis Smedes: "Grace is gamble, always" (147).

[23] Ibid., 154.

[24] The literature on the tradition of divine warfare is extensive. I mention here only a few relevant items. For fuller bibliography see the annotated bibliography in Gerhard von Rad's classic, *Holy War in Ancient Israel*, trans. Marva J. Dawn (Grand Rapids: Eerdmans, 1991), and in my *Put on the Armour of God*, 23, n.25. See, among many works, Theodore Hiebert, *God of My Victory: The Ancient Hymn in Habakkuk 3*, Harvard Semitic Monographs, no. 38 (Atlanta: Scholars Pr., 1986); Waldemar Janzen, *Still in the Image: Essays in Biblical Theology and Anthropology*, Institute of Mennonite Studies Series, no. 6 (Newton, Winnipeg CMBC Pubns., 1982); Millard Lind, *Yahweh Is a Warrior: The Theology of Warfare in Ancient Israel* (Scottdale, Kitchener: Herald Pr., 1980); Ben C. Ollenburger, *Zion, the City of the Great King: A Theological Symbol of the Jerusalem Cult*, JSOT Supplement Series 41 (Sheffield,

verses 15 and 16 contains faint echoes of ancient traditions of the conquest of chaos as an essential component of creation. The motif of divine warfare is more obviously present elsewhere in Ephesians (1:21; 4:8; and especially 6:10–20), but its presence at the core of this peace text should not be overlooked. While use of warfare traditions in Ephesians always involves a certain irony, their presence here reflects also the un-ironic insight that salvation is not without conflict, that the birth of the new humanity is accompanied by pain, and more generally, that struggle lies at the core of peacemaking. As Paul says unforgettably in Rom. 16:20: "The God of peace will shortly crush Satan under your feet!" In Eph. 2:14–16 this "violence" is related to the "act" of dying on the cross; in 6:10–20 it finds expression in the struggle of the messianic community with the powers (6:12).

So, much as in later parts of the book of Isaiah, themes of restoration, homecoming, intimacy with God, and divine warfare are indissolubly related to the themes of peace and salvation. This hymnic celebration of Christ's work is thus at the center of the canonical tradition(s).

THE KINGDOM OF GOD

One of the strings holding this collection of essays together is the intra-canonical exploration of the relation of peace and mission to the kingdom or reign of God. Ephesians says little directly about the kingdom of God. There is one explicit if somewhat cryptic reference to the "kingdom of Christ and of God" in 5:5. It is mentioned as part of a warning not to practice the "works of darkness" and thereby forego participation in that kingdom.

Does Eph. 2:11–22 then relate to this part of our shared task in this volume of studies? I think it does. The reign of God is present just behind the curtains in the allusion to Isa. 52:7 (see above). The announcing of peace is in Isaiah 52 the proclamation that God reigns. If βασιλεία (basileia) is translated dynamically as "rule" or "reign" rather than more spatially as "kingdom," then our hymn and the panes that frame it represent a climactic celebration of both the scope of God's reign and how and by whom it is realized. The kingdom of God is then expressed in Ephesians as the mystery now revealed in the gathering up of all things in and through Christ (1:10; cf. 3:3–11), and as the peace of God secured through the death of Christ and perfected in the re-creation of humanity in Christ (2:14–16). Christ is none other than the sovereign king who sits enthroned above "all rule and authority and power and

England: Sheffield Academic Pr., Ltd., 1987); Devon Wiens, "Holy War Theology in the New Testament and Its Relationship to the Eschatological Day of the Lord Tradition" (Ph.D. diss., University of Southern California, 1967).

dominion, and above every name that is named, not only in this age but also in the age to come" (1:21). More, in 2:4–7 it is once dead but now liberated and resurrected humanity that participates in the reign of that Christ. The language is nothing short of breathtaking:

> ⁴*But God, who is rich in mercy, out of the great love with which he loved us* ⁵*even when we were dead through our trespasses, made us alive together with Christ—by grace you have been saved—*⁶*and raised us up with him and seated us with him in the heavenly places in Christ Jesus,* ⁷*so that in the ages to come he might show the immeasurable riches of his grace in kindness toward us in Christ Jesus. (NRSV)*

Ephesians 2:11–22 is a rehearsal of how God in Christ has injected that peaceable yet costly reign into the hostilities marking human existence. The specific vocabulary of the kingdom or reign of God may not be present in abundance in Ephesians, and is absent from our text, but on any useful account of the semantic import of the reign of God its content is abundantly and creatively present.

MUSINGS

Peace and mission: One agenda

This text illustrates forcefully the inextricable link between the core of mission, proclamation, and peacemaking. The one who came preaching peace is none other than the one who is, himself, God's peace. And as much as God's peace comes to expression in the person and work of Christ, its resultant scope knows only the limits of God's creation. Christ as peace is thus none other than God's endlessly "multivaried wisdom" (3:10) in and through whom all things are being gathered up (1:10) so that God might be all in all (1:23; 3:19; 4:6).

Consequently, we can make several observations. First, as long as people keep saying, "Jesus is Lord," the germ of a radical and encompassing peace position is present. The genie is in the bottle, so to speak, waiting for the bottle to be massaged, even in traditions that have buried an explicit peace position. The memory is there, waiting to be awakened. This text reminds us that there is no evangelical and missional way of speaking of Christ that is worthy of him that does not come to terms with the radical spiritual, social, and even cosmic dimensions of peace. Were it not for the fact that we see it all around us in churches great and small, we would find it inconceivable that one could come to know the peace of God without being drawn into the costly making of peace in our world.

Second, if remembering Christ but forgetting peace is a terrible truncation of the gospel, so also is remembering peace while forgetting the Christ who is our peace. Such forgetfulness results in losing touch with the core of peace, its roots, and its pedigree. Peace thus becomes divorced from the mission of reconciling people not only with each other but with God. Worse, the proclamation of Christ as peace is viewed as exclusivistic and arrogant, as maintaining or erecting new walls when they should be coming down.

For Christians to speak and make peace without anchoring it in the teaching, work, and person of Christ is to want the fruit without growing it from the root. Such peace loses its moorings in the vision that integrates wholly the spiritual and the physical, the personal and the social, the micro and the macro, a vision able to understand suffering as an act of creative peacemaking. In the end, such a peace runs the risk of becoming a peace that is no peace (John 14:27; Jer. 6:14; 8:11; Ezek. 13:10, 16; Mic. 3:5). It is satisfied with having stemmed a particular skirmish, addressed a particular issue of deprivation or oppression, but no longer appreciates that such oppression and conflict has its roots in alienation from God. It thus has little to say to the myriad of issues that arise in "peacetime." War is necessarily on the agenda of mission, but peace must have something to say equally to those no longer at war. Abuse is a real peace concern. But the gospel of peace is not exhausted when the abuse ends. Poverty is real and necessarily an objective of mission (cf. 2 Corinthians 9; cf. Luke 1, 4; Matthew 11). But anyone who does not live in poverty knows that selfishness, greed, license, and callousness to the needs of others rear their head more starkly than ever in times of abundance. The one who is peace must continue to be able to address those no longer poor with words of judgment, hope, the promise of new birth, and the summons to become engaged in the divine project of reconciling all people and all things to God in Christ.

Our text celebrates the cessation of hostility, the shattering of the wall. But it identifies the means of peace specifically and pointedly as the Christ who with flesh and blood gives his life and creates a new humanity in himself. However exclusive that identification might sound in our day, it is ironically that specific memory of Christ—more, such an identity in Christ—that will create a community that views walls as an affront to the God of all (4:6), and that will recover, retain, and nurture a commitment to demolishing them. That such a community will have markers of belief and confession, boundaries of behavior and worship, is essential to honing such a vision of demolition and construction (see chapter 5!; cf. the implicit notion of holy and bounded space in the notion of temple and home in 2:20–22). Such boundaries and practices are faithful to the one who is peace only if they engender a passion to overcome division, to break down walls, and build a home for us, for our enemies, and for God. Otherwise, a community that is a result of embrace and inclusion becomes a community of exclusion and self-satisfaction. Peace is betrayed. The voice of the announcer of peace is subverted and in the end silenced. God is driven from home.

Conversely, where the church is made up of reconciled enemies—erstwhile enemies of each other and reclaimed enemies of God—then its very existence becomes proclamation, a living word of gospel that reconciliation is real and can be experienced and celebrated in human existence, individually and collectively.[25] Church planting then becomes participation with Christ in the re-creation of the new human. Mission is in its fullest sense peacemaking.

Unity and identity: "We" and "you" make up the new "we"

"Remember . . ." marks the beginning of our text (2:11). Even as a new identity is born in and through Christ, the old identities are present in a recollection sparked by grace and gratitude. In these verses a strong sense of identity and orientation is retained even as the hymn throws open the arms of the church's embrace. The new humanity is a community that remembers where it came from—a community of recollection and rehearsal of God's peace. "We" remind "you" of where you have come from; "you" have become part of "us"; "we" are now a community of both "you" and "us." In Ephesians 2, Gentiles and Jews have in Christ become one new humanity, but their memories are intact with respect to the particular histories they merge into the new identity. Those once excluded retain a clear sense of who they were and of what they have become a part. And those long a part of the community of divine privilege are not asked to forget who they are and have been, even as that memory no longer serves to exclude.

An important point of reflection for mission and peace is that while the church's "we" is always inclusive of "you," the memory of the old we and the old you is erased only at the cost of the identity of the church as the one new human made up of discreet members, whether they are individuals, groups, cultures, or peoples.[26] The new human is bicultural (John Howard Yoder) and hybrid (Miroslav Volf),[27] and not the average

---

[25] This is what Yoder means when he refers to the new humanity as both "pulpit and paradigm" (*For the Nations*, 37, 41).

[26] Cf. Paul's argument regarding Jews and Gentiles in Romans 9–11.

[27] See note 14 above. Miroslav Volf is helpful in reflecting on the missiological and peace dimensions of this text, especially as they relate to issues of identity, memory, exclusion, and embrace of the other. Mennonites should heed Volf's critique of tribalism, as well as his call for a re-centering in Christ as the necessary condition of a true embrace of the other. That leaves the question of identity always and necessarily in a state of flux, not at its center but at its edges.

of all those enclosed in the embrace of peace. The new human is the melding into one of families (plural; 3:14) who now have access together with one breath (Spirit) to their divine parent (2:18). Peaceable arms embrace those hitherto beyond reach, but it is an embrace no less, an enclosing, a bringing near. The movement of peace is from the inside out, and then both a drawing in and a redrawing what is in and what is out. The precincts of the holy temple of God are widened beyond the horizon, perhaps, but they are precincts no less, bounded by grace, reconciliation, re-creation, and holiness (see, e.g., 5:1–21; cf. 1 Cor. 3:16–17).

Thus, for a missional and peaceable community the definition of identity must always remain problematic or at least open to redefinition, given the reach of the creator's embrace. Stated more carefully, all familial identities are relativized by finding their ultimate point of reference in the Christ who fuses those discreet identities into one "multivaried" human, to borrow a word from 3:10. Deep respect and love for the diversity of the people(s) of God who find their unity in Christ lie at the heart of the biblical vision of peace and mission.

Suffering and the mission of peace
Suffering, sacrifice, and death are essential to the movement of peace in this text. It may be that peacemaking and mission entail suffering in the conventional sense in which peacemakers can expect opposition from others. But that is not the issue in Ephesians 2. Here the struggle and conflict have to do with the self-giving and self-sacrificing of the peacemaker in the process of removing the impediments to full access to God, to participating in the family of God, to exercising hospitality toward God. Peace comes about through the death of the peacemaker; peace comes about through the destruction of the dividing/defining wall between us and you, and between both of us and God.

In imitation of that Christ, or as participation in the new human, peace also comes about through the sacrificial self-giving of "us" who welcome "you"—an opening of ourselves to becoming a new "us" profoundly reshaped by the embrace. This represents a costly but at the same time life-giving challenge for all communities, for all tribes— Christian or not—who would like to protect their identity via exclusion. At the same time, remembering where we all have come from is important so that the suffering and self-giving entailed in the process of becoming the new human is creative (2:15) and constructive (2:20–22). Forgetting where "we" and "you" have come from can lead to victimization and even elimination of either the once far (as has happened too often in mission efforts) or the near (the fate of Jewish followers of Jesus in the first decades and centuries of the church).

CONCLUSION

Ephesians 2:11–22, as much as any other text in the Bible, shows that the agendas of peace and mission are indivisible, however much for strategic purposes only we might want to sort out different agendas around different gifts. Too often, what need have been no more than a division of task regarding mission and peace has provided the ground for tearing asunder what God never meant to come apart. To state it differently, a wall of division has been erected that betrays both the center and the circumference of God's peace. For the church to be faithful to the call to peace and mission will require that that wall be demolished first.

13 | *Reign of God, mission, and peace in 1 Peter*

M Y ENDURING FASCINATION WITH 1 PETER[1] IS IN PART
the result of my perception that the epistle deals holistically
with issues of mission and peace. How the people of God are
to witness and serve in the world is inextricably linked with who they
are and are to become. I have come to read this biblical document
essentially as a letter calling the churches to be followers of Jesus Christ
in loving the enemy and blessing those who curse them. This
discipleship is to be lived out in concrete situations in which believers
are falsely accused, experiencing physical mistreatment and abuse, and
even suffering persecution for bearing the name of Christ. Discipleship is
at the heart of the church's calling to bear witness to the world.

To early Anabaptists, 1 Peter was a significant source of guidance
and strength when they suffered for their faith.[2] However, 1 Peter came
to be neglected in New Testament studies until in a recent renewal of
interest many new commentaries have been written on it. I view 1 Peter
as relevant for the contemporary church, which lives in a society in
which violence and abuse are prevalent. This New Testament tract calls
the church both to mission and to peace, both to evangelism and to
activism, explicitly and implicitly, recognizing both the current and
future reign of God as ultimate context.

For this essay I choose to focus on 1 Peter 3:8–12. In this choice I
have been influenced by John Piper's article "Hope As the Motivation of

---

[1] See my Believers Church Bible Commentary on 1 Peter (Scottdale, Waterloo: Herald Pr., 1999).

[2] Thieleman J. van Braght, *The Bloody Theater or Martyrs Mirror,* trans. Joseph F. Sohm (Scottdale: Herald Pr., 1968; originally published in Dutch in 1660), is a major but not sole resource to support this observation. See Eldon T. Yoder and Monroe D. Hochstetler, *Biblical References in Anabaptist Writings* (Lagrange, Ind.: Pathway Pubs., 1969).

Love: 1 Peter 3:9–12" and Mary H. Schertz's "Nonretaliation and the Haustafeln in 1 Peter."[3]

In the NRSV this passage reads as follows:

Finally, all of you, have
    unity of spirit,
    sympathy,
    love for one another,
    a tender heart, and
    a humble mind.
Do not repay evil for evil or abuse for abuse;
but, on the contrary, repay with a blessing.
It is for this that you were called—that you might inherit a blessing.

Then, to help define and motivate this calling, the author quotes and adapts Ps. 33:13–17 (LXX):[4]

For
"Those who desire life
    and desire to see good days,
let them keep their tongues from evil,
    and their lips from speaking deceit;
let them turn away from evil and do good;
    let them seek peace and pursue it.[5]
For the eyes of the Lord are on the righteous,
    and his ears are open to their prayer.
But the face of the Lord is against those who do evil."

THE REIGN OF GOD AS THEOLOGICAL CONTEXT

While the phrase "kingdom of God" does not occur in 1 Peter, the concept of a God who reigns is pervasive. The nature and character of that reign needs to be discerned through careful reading of the biblical text. Only a few dimensions of the concept "reign of God" in 1 Peter can be identified in this chapter.

First Peter is addressed to scattered Christian congregations residing in five provinces of Asia Minor, namely, Pontus, Galatia, Cappadocia, Asia, and Bithynia. Recent biblical scholars have probed deeply and

---

[3] John Piper, "Hope As the Motivation of Love: 1 Peter 3:9–12," *New Testament Studies* 26 (1980): 212–31; Mary H. Schertz, "Nonretaliation and the Haustafeln in 1 Peter," in *The Love of Enemy and Nonretaliation in the New Testament*, ed. Willard M. Swartley (Louisville: Westminster John Knox Pr., 1992), 258–86.

[4] Ps. 34:12–16 in English Bible.

[5] Emphasis added.

helpfully the sociological backgrounds of 1 Peter.[6] However, many clues within the biblical text itself indicate that for the author the active presence and reign of God in the people's experience was the ultimate context.

The designation θεός (*theos*) occurs thirty-nine times in the 105 verses. Moreover, θεός is not a distant or benign reality but is involved in the past and current experiences of both the author and the readers. This one is both present and active, not only as an observer but as one who initiates and intervenes. θεός is not only one to be worshiped (2:5; 4:11) but one who can be trusted (1:21; 4:19; 5:7) and also one to be reckoned with (1:17; 2:23; 4:5, 17) as the final arbiter and creator of justice.

In 1 Peter it is God who chooses and destines people (1:2). Not only is God creator (4:19) but the one in whom the people of God find their origin and destiny as a community of faith. God begets them to a living hope through the resurrection of Jesus Christ (1:3). God judges humanity impartially and justly (1:17; 2:23), and is sovereign over God's people (2:9–10). God is, indeed, to be glorified and feared (2:12, 19; 4:11; 5:11).

God is the one who waited patiently in the days of Noah (3:20). God is also the one to whom the pledge of a good conscience is to be made at baptism (3:21) and at whose right hand the risen Jesus Christ is seated with angels, authorities, and powers made subject to him (3:22).

God has given "good news" (4:6, 17–18), so that believers may experience deliverance (salvation). God humbles and exalts people (5:5–6), cares for us (5:7), and in due time, in grace, restores and establishes God's people (5:9–10). For the writer, the reign of God includes creation, the calling out of a community of faith, the redemption and judgment of that community, and its final salvation, restoration, and establishment.

Whatever may be the particular geographical, social, and political circumstances of the readers, from the perspective of the writer they are in God's world, a domain in which God has reigned, now reigns, and will reign. The author not only assumes that this world view is valid but also that his readers share it. He does not consider it necessary to persuade them to believe in the reign of God. He proceeds to give encouragement and counsel within the framework of this theological context.

The reign of God perspective is implicit throughout our core text, but becomes explicit in v. 12,

---

[6] John H. Elliott, *A Home for the Homeless: A Sociological Exegesis of 1 Peter, Its Situation and Strategy* (Philadelphia: Fortress Pr., 1981); David L. Balch, *Let Wives Be Submissive: The Domestic Code in 1 Peter* (Chico, Calif.: Scholars Pr., 1981).

"For the eyes of the Lord are on the righteous,
 and his ears are open to their prayer.
But the face of the Lord is against those who do evil."

This verse is part of a didactic passage in which the psalmist seeks to instruct people to walk in the fear of the Lord (LXX: φόβον κυρίου |*phobon kyriou*). Here God is "the Lord" in whose presence the appropriate inward posture is reverent fear. Reverence, for the psalmist as well as for the writer of 1 Peter, calls for moral rectitude (1:17).

Notable here is the imagery used to represent the divine in anthropomorphic terms (eyes, ears, face). Even more important is the perspective of a divine lordship in which the relationship between the divine and the human involves ethical dimensions, namely, the linkage of righteousness and prayer and the resistance to and judgment of evil. While the psalmist originally was speaking of Yahweh as Lord, some scholars continue to debate whether 1 Peter is already intending to mean that "Jesus is Lord" and here infers that meaning in the Old Testament text.[7]

The writer of 1 Peter, exhibiting a high Christology, speaks of Jesus as Lord without special pleading. In 1:3 he speaks of God as "the Father of our Lord Jesus Christ." In 3:15 he instructs his readers, "In your hearts sanctify Christ as Lord." The word translated "sanctify" means to make holy or to recognize as holy. Here the author's intent is to enjoin his readers inwardly to acknowledge that Jesus Christ is indeed Lord, the one to whom reverence and obedience are due. Moreover, the careful differentiation the author makes between the status of the emperor and God in instructing readers to "fear God" and "honor the emperor" (2:17) indicates congruence with the early Christian confession that Jesus Christ, not Caesar, is Lord.[8]

In either case, whether specific references point back to Yahweh or more immediately refer to Jesus, the reign of God perspective explicitly includes a moral dimension for human attitudes and behaviors. This perspective with its ethical implications pervades the entire letter of 1 Peter.

Essentially the thematic development in 1 Peter is embedded in the following outline:

1:1–2   *The opening greeting*
1:3–12   *The celebration of Christian hope and its impact*

---

[7] J. Ramsey Michaels, *1 Peter*, Word Biblical Commentary, vol. 49 (Waco: Word Bks., 1988), offers a lively discussion on this question (181–2).

[8] κύριος (*kyrios*) occurs eight times in 1 Peter, four times drawing on Old Testament passages (1:25; 3:6; and 3:12), twice clearly referring to Jesus Christ (1:3; 3:15), and twice with room for debate about whether the writer meant Yahweh (God) or Jesus Christ (2:3, 13). For the author the lordship of Christ is a dimension of the reign of God.

1:13–2:3	*The changed life style of hope*
2:4–10	*The community of hope, the church*
2:11–3:12	*Christian witness in hostile society*
2:11–12	*True witness of maligned believers*
2:13–17	*Witness as citizens under a hostile state*
2:18–25	*Witness as mistreated servants following Jesus*
3:1–7	*Christian witness in marriage*
3:8–12	*Witness of the united Christian community*
3:13–4:19	*Christian response to suffering for righteous living*
3:13–25	*In the light of Christ's suffering*
4:1–19	*In view of coming judgment*
5:1–11	*Leadership and loyalty in the suffering church*
5:12–15	*Concluding explanations and greetings*

For 1 Peter, then, God's world is a domain in which God's saving presence and work are operative and a realm in which a moral response on the part of the people of God becomes significant. In this world both righteousness and unrighteousness exist and are discernable. People do good or they do evil. Moral choices have consequences. God is both holy and just, loving and righteous, and has given Christian believers a hope that enables them to know and do God's calling for them. As John Piper has written, "Hope becomes the 'motivation' for love which in turn empowers 'good' and 'right' action."[9]

THE MISSION OF GOD'S PEOPLE IN GOD'S WORLD

The mission of God's people, according to 1 Peter, is to be a people of hope (1:3), declaring to others the mighty acts of God (2:9), proclaiming and following Jesus Christ as the ground of their hope (2:21–25; 3:15–16). This mission includes responding to mistreatment and other forms of evil in the pattern and the power of love, even and especially when suffering for doing the noble, the right, or the good (2:12; 3:13–17; 4:19).

In the larger literary context, God's people are sanctified for obedience to Jesus Christ (1:2); as children of a holy God, to be obedient in conduct (1:14–15); as a holy priesthood to offer spiritual sacrifices of praise and service (2:5); and as God's own people, to declare God's wonderful deeds (2:9–10). They are to maintain good conduct among the nations so that these may come to glorify God at the time of visitation, possibly by the nations' conversion to Christian faith (2:11–12). They are to honor the dignity of every created being, including civil authorities (2:13–14), and silence ignorant talk by serving God as free people (2:15–16). Mistreated servants are to respond as those aware of God's presence and as followers of Jesus in suffering (2:18–25). Freed from their sins, they are to live for righteousness as a healed people (2:24). Wives of un-

---

[9] Piper, "Hope As the Motivation for Love," 1.

believing husbands are to witness without words through inner beauty, possibly to win their unbelieving husbands to faith (3:1). Christian husbands are to deal so considerately with their wives that the men's prayers may be unhindered (3:7). As disciples of Jesus Christ they are to live with nonretaliating love (2:21; 3:9), suffering "for doing what is right" (3:14) and always ready to give a reason (ἀπολογία | *apologia*) for their hope in Jesus Christ (3:15–16) when they are asked. As a community of mutual love, they are to practice hospitality (4:8–9) and be good stewards of God's grace, speaking and serving for mutual benefit and God's glory (4:10). Under the pressure of persecution, even for bearing the name of Christ, they are to keep on doing what is noble, right, and good (2:11; 3:17; 4:19). Church elders are to lead by example rather than by wielding authority (5:3), and all, as humble people of God, are to trust God (5:7) and resist the devil steadfastly (5:9).

Within the narrower boundaries of our core text, 1 Pet. 3:8–12, they are called to become the kind of loving community that practices forgiving love, that rejects retaliation, and that thus blesses others even as it experiences the blessing of its own calling. To be this kind of community is one dimension of the church's mission in the midst of a hostile society.

Sequentially, 3:8–12 follows directly the address to mistreated servants in 2:18, the word to wives of non-Christian husbands (3:1), and the admonition to Christian husbands (3:7). Some have argued that this is the extent of its exegetical linkage.[10] In thought structure, however, the passage is linked with the larger passage that begins with 2:11 so that this core passage can be read as a kind of summary of what has been said from 2:11–3:7. This indicates that what has been said to mistreated servants and disadvantaged (possibly mistreated) wives is actually to be embraced by all members of the Christian community. I agree with Mary Schertz who writes, "This image of the new reality [envisioned here] provides the grounds and motivation of the central point the author is trying to make in the larger unit about how the community of believers should relate to the outside world."[11]

The believers' life together is to embody unity of spirit (ὁμόφρονες | *homophrones*). Literally this is "same-mindedness," recalling for us Paul's word in Phil. 2:5 when he encourages his readers to keep their minds moving in the same direction until they have "the same mind that was in Christ Jesus." Their thinking and their striving are to move toward the same goal, found in Jesus Christ, rather than toward some

---

[10] Balch, *Let Wives Be Submissive*, 88.

[11] Schertz, "Nonretaliation and the Haustafeln in 1 Peter," 273.

other cause. Neither individualistic self-actualization nor some schismatic social vision is to replace the reign of God.

Sympathy (συμπαθεῖς | *sympatheis*), named next, sometimes translated "compassion," may be understood in the light of Rom. 12:15, which speaks of rejoicing with those who rejoice and weeping with those who weep. While sympathy and empathy are not identical qualities, both may be embraced here in the thought of the writer.

A central quality, however, is love for one another (φιλάδελφοι | *philadelphoi*), literally "love for others who come from the same womb." This is a quality assumed previously (1:22), where the call was to supplement and transform it with ἀγάπη (*agapē*). Likewise in 4:8 the author speaks again of ἀγάπη as the bonding power in the Christian community. The term φιλάδελφοι however accents the mutuality of love in the Christian community under the image of a family.

A fourth quality commended is a tender heart (εὔσπλαγχνοι | *eusplanchnoi*). This word is rendered by Edward Gordon Selwyn as "good hearted."[12] Leonhard Goppelt suggests that it means "that inner turning of one's attention to one's neighbor in which one not only gives something but gives one's self" to others.[13]

The fifth quality is a humble mind (ταπεινόφρονες | *tapeinophrones*). This Greek word is used only here in the New Testament, but it reflects directly the mood and attitude of Jesus in Matt. 11:29. It denotes an appropriate rather than an inflated assessment of oneself in relation to God, to others, and to the cosmos. First Peter later reminds us that God humbles the proud and exalts the humble (5:5–6).

In 1 Peter these qualities are important in the loving Christian community not only to make it durable, but in this context, to be a faithful witness in the world. This may recall for us John 13:35 where Jesus says, "By this everyone will know that you are my disciples, if you have love for one another."

In becoming the kind of Christian community 1 Peter envisions, the church is both witness and servant in the world. It becomes the sign of the reign of God. It speaks of what can be, of what God intended to be, and of what God, by grace, has made possible.

This positive description of the Christian community is further expanded by indications of what its members are to avoid. They are not to return evil with evil or abuse with abuse. In short, 1 Peter proscribes

---

[12] Edward Gordon Selwyn, *The First Epistle of St. Peter* (1946; reprint, Grand Rapids: Baker Bks., 1981), 189.

[13] Leonhard Goppelt, *A Commentary on 1 Peter*, ed. Ferdinand Hahn, trans. and aug. John E. Alsup (Grand Rapids: Eerdmans, 1993), 253.

retaliation or any kind of violent verbal or physical response to evil. Here the call to mission seems to merge into the call to peace.

THE CALL TO SEEK PEACE AND PURSUE IT

We have observed how 1 Peter has first emphasized that, living in God's world, the believers have a living hope through the resurrection of Jesus Christ. This new reality has an impact on their life style, now characterized by holy love, and thus makes it possible for them to be a community of hope, a "spiritual house." Now they are proclaiming the gracious and mighty acts of God as people who have been called out of darkness into light (2:9). As the focus shifts from relationships within the Christian community to relationships between the community and the hostile world, the concern shifts from maintenance to mission. Given the circumstances, how does the church witness in the midst of a society rife with hostility, abuse, and violence? In response to this question, the concern for mission merges into a concern for peace. In 1 Peter, Christians are simultaneously missionaries and peacemakers.[14]

In our reading of 1 Peter the teaching of Jesus to love enemies and to practice nonretaliation is a background for understanding 2:11–3:12, which we have called "Christian witness in hostile society." One strand of this teaching is the call to honor or reverence the dignity of every created being, including those in civil government (the emperor and kings), masters, whether gentle or cruel, and spouses in marriage, whether or not they also believe in Christ. Another strand breaks the cycle of hostility, of mistreatment, of abuse, of violence.[15]

While the word εἰρήνη (eirēnē, "peace") appears only three times in 1 Peter (1:2, 3:11, and 5:14), the theme is pervasive, interwoven with the call to mission. The word is used in the opening and closing greetings. In the opening greeting it is joined with grace, and in the closing greeting it stands alone. In these passages εἰρήνη is viewed as a gift, as something

---

[14] For rigorous argument that living in peace and making peace are central in New Testament ethics, see William Klassen, "'Pursue Peace': A Concrete Ethical Mandate (Romans 12:18-21)," in *Ja und Nein: Christliche Theologie im Angesichts Israels, Festschrift zum 70. Geburtstag von Wolfgang Schrage,* ed. Klaus Wengst and Gerhard Saß (Neukirchen-Vluyn: Neukirchener Verlag, 1998), 195–207. See also Ulrich Mauser, *The Gospel of Peace: A Scriptural Message for Today's World* (Louisville: Westminster John Knox Pr., 1992), and Richard B. Hays, *The Moral Vision of the New Testament: Community, Cross, New Creation: A Contemporary Introduction to New Testament Ethics* (San Francisco: HarperCollins Pubs., Inc., 1996).

[15] This interpretation builds on the perspectives of J. Ramsey Michaels, Paul J. Achtemeier (*1 Peter: A Commentary on First Peter,* Hermeneia—A Critical and Historical Commentary on the Bible, ed. Eldon Jay Epp [Minneapolis: Fortress Pr., 1996]), and others contra older emphases on "subjection, submission, or subordination."

to be received. In this paper, however, we focus on its use in 3:11 as part of our core passage. Here εἰρήνη is something to be sought and pursued.

The language of seeking and pursuing peace connotes desiring peace eagerly, even passionately. It indicates an attitude that is translated into action. It tends to go beyond a passive image of what peace is to how to move toward it in life. On the surface this call to action seems to be in tension with the counsel of 2:21–23. There the believer is called to follow in the steps of Jesus, who "when he was abused, he did not return abuse; when he suffered, he did not threaten; but he entrusted himself to the one who judges justly." Some have read this passage as a call to quietism and passivity and have used it to support the pacifism of the quiet in the land.

William Klassen in "Pursue Peace" wrestles with various interpretations of the meaning of peace and various ways in which we are to seek and pursue it. He notes the interpretation of New Testament scholar Raymond Brown, for whom the pursuit of peace "has nothing to do with the absence of warfare . . . nor with an end to psychological tension, nor with a sentimental feeling of well-being. The peace of Jesus is a gift that pertains to man's salvation. . . . It is another way of saying 'eternal life.' . . . Peace is the same as joy. . . . In Johannine realized eschatology peace is enjoyed by Christians even during this life."[16] In contrast to this inward oriented and more passive view of peace, Klassen notes the interpretation of peace in the New Testament by Rudolf Schnackenburg, who writes,

> *The rule of God announced by Jesus is already begun. For in Jesus himself, in his person, and his actions, in his struggles, suffering and dying the meaning of the rule of God, what it can be and should be is clearly ear-marked: service for others, love to the uttermost. And everywhere where people follow him in his way, a portion of God's rule is realized, the strength for peace grown, and peace emerges triumphant over all hatred, clash of weapons, and tumults of war. Whoever has once comprehended the absolute will of Jesus toward peace, which nourishes itself on the peaceful disposition of God, can and must affirm and receive all human, earthly, socio-political efforts toward peace, all small initiatives and large organizational measures. Out of the message of Jesus, that God will eventually grant humankind the last perfect peace, such a person will never be disillusioned or discouraged. This is the power of Christian peace efforts and peace work.[17]*

---

[16] Raymond Brown, *The Gospel According to John (XII-XXI)*, The Anchor Bible, vol. 29A (Garden City, N.Y.: Doubleday, 1970), 653–5.

[17] Rudolf Schnackenburg, "Macht, Gewalt und Friede nach dem Neuen Testament," in *Maßstab des Glaubens: Fragen heutiger Christen im Licht des Neuen Testaments* (Freiburg in Breisgau: Herder, 1978), 248, quoted in Klassen, "'Pursue Peace,'" 201.

The perspective in 1 Peter lies somewhere between the spiritualized view of peace described by Raymond Brown and the more socially and politically active view of peacemaking described by Rudolf Schnackenburg.

But are these interpretations of the peace God intends mutually exclusive? In a reign of God perspective each has an appropriate place and neither should exclude the other.

The call to nonretaliation becomes explicit in 3:9, "Do not repay evil for evil or abuse for abuse; but, on the contrary, repay with a blessing." Here we hear a clear echo of the teaching of Jesus in Matt. 5:38–48 and Luke 6:27–36. In 1 Peter the instruction continues the thread of his counsel to mistreated slaves in 2:18–23 where the author makes clear reference to physical abuse and invokes the nonretaliating spirit and model of Jesus. It also parallels Rom. 12:17a: "Do not repay anyone evil for evil."

While the teaching of nonretaliation may have both Hellenistic and Jewish roots, it is most closely associated with the Jesus tradition, including both teaching and behavior. The specific form of the texts in 1 Peter (2:23 and 3:9) reflects an even closer relationship to Paul (Rom. 12:17, 1 Thess. 5:15, and 1 Cor. 4:12).[18]

The counsel that proscribes retaliation calls for alternative positive and active response. Mistreatment and abuse are not simply to be ignored or met with silence. The response commended is to repay with a blessing. Christians are themselves called for this purpose, that they may inherit a blessing.

First Peter has already identified their inheritance in 1:4; they are assured a living hope through the resurrection of Jesus Christ. Thus their blessing, in essence, is not one that is earned through a faithful practice of nonretaliation. Rather, 1 Peter is reminding them that the blessing they have received by grace, an inheritance that has both present and eschatological dimensions, now enables them to bless others, including enemies. Achtemeier helpfully suggests that "by flouting the behavior appropriate to that inheritance, they may jeopardize their eternal entrance into it."[19] He further notes that the application intended in 1 Peter is not limited to the community of believers but includes those who are still outside the circle of Christian faith.[20] John Piper deals most

---

[18] For fuller scholarly treatment of this theme in 1 Peter, see Gordon M. Zerbe, *Non-Retaliation in Early Jewish and New Testament Texts: Ethical Themes in Social Contexts* (Sheffield, England: JSOT Press, 1993), 270–90.

[19] Achtemeier, *1 Peter*, 224.

[20] Ibid., 225.

thoroughly with the exegetical and theological issues in this text. He concludes that 1 Peter intends to tell us that hope is indeed the motivation for love, including love of enemies, and that this hope is grounded in what Christ has already done and also on the anticipation of God's future just judgment.[21] Gordon M. Zerbe also emphasizes the christological and eschatological grounding of the call to nonretaliation in this passage, against the view that 1 Peter is concerned pragmatically to help the believers of Asia Minor get along with their neighbors and thus help them survive in a hostile environment.[22]

The notion of blessing others moves beyond verbal responses, beyond speaking well of those who speak ill of believers. The practice of blessing and its counterpart, cursing, is common in the Old Testament. Some form of εὐλογέω (*eulogeō*, "bless") appears no less than 450 times. Blessing had to do with more than speaking certain words. It had to do with attitude and action as well. The emphasis in 1 Peter on doing good (2:12; 3:11; 4:19) is congruent with Paul's call to overcome evil with good (Rom. 12:20–21). Both the word of grace and the work of grace are to be shared with an unbelieving and abusive world. This mission focus indicates that blessing (3:9) likely points forward to speaking truth (3:10), as well as doing good and seeking peace (3:11). These positive, active dimensions of response to abuse and evil go well beyond the passivity and quietism which has sometimes become oppressive to employees who are mistreated or women who are told to submit quietly to cruel or abusive husbands. It is particularly important that 1 Pet. 3:1–6 not be used abusively either by Christian husbands or by congregations.

The meaning of 3:8–9 becomes clearer as we examine 3:10–12, which is based on Ps. 33:13–17 (LXX). This Old Testament quotation helps explicate the meaning of the counsel given, and motivate compliance.

Using the style of proverbial wisdom, the psalmist declares that one who longs for life and wants to see good days (presumably now and eternally) should refrain from mouthing evil and from speaking deceit. Desiring life and good days is here linked with inheriting a blessing (3:9).

---

[21] Piper, "Hope As the Motivation for Love," 224–9.

[22] Zerbe, *Non-Retaliation*, 286–9. Zerbe notes that the supporting ὅτι (*hoti*) of 3:9b could be read either as pointing backward to the previous counsel and the ἵνα (*hina*) as pointing forward to the eschatological blessing promised, or the εἰς τοῦτο (*eis touto*) points forward to the ἵνα clause, emphasizing that Christians are called to receive eschatological blessing. Zerbe opts for the former (287). In short, the passage looks both ways, being both christological and eschatological, grounding the call to nonretaliation in the Christian community's special relationship to Jesus Christ rather than in some general ethic of social wisdom.

The call to disciplined speech is linked to the verbal dimensions of nonretaliation: desisting from reviling those who revile.

Instead, the psalmist enjoins that they turn away from evil and do good. Here the psalmist moves beyond verbal response to response in action. Word and deed are both important for a wise person seeking life. As Michaels notes, "appropriate speech must be accompanied by 'doing good,' clearly a central theme of the whole epistle."[23] As already suggested, the linkage between speaking evil and speaking guile would indicate a counterpart of speaking what is true. Blessing (3:9) implies more than kind words. It also implies speaking true words, recalling for us the admonition to the Ephesians to speak truth in love (4:15). The author may well be including here the prophetic word that confronts evil but with redemptive purpose. Steven Richard Bechtler offers the intriguing thesis that 1 Peter provides its readers "a legitimation of their symbolic universe." These early Christians needed to resolve the tension between their earthly experiences living in hostile society and the promise of glory they anticipated at the coming of Jesus Christ. Peter's words to them about "living hope" are intended to help them see their suffering not as an occasion for shame but as a participation in the glorious and ultimately victorious suffering of Jesus Christ. This perspective not only helps them bear their suffering, it also helps them see eternal meaning in it.[24]

Further, the psalmist enjoins those who long for life to seek peace and pursue it. Goppelt considers this "the core of his paranesis" in 1 Peter, and Michaels agrees.[25] In Rom. 12:18 Paul likewise enjoins, "If it is possible, so far as it depends on you, live peaceably with all." For 1 Peter, as for Paul, this injunction embraces peace with neighbors, enemies, and fellow members in the family of faith. It is anchored in Jesus' teaching: "Blessed are the peacemakers, for they will be called children of God" (Matt. 5:9).

1 Peter changes the verbs "seek" and "pursue" to third person from the second person form in the Septuagint; these actions are part of the mission of the people of God. The pursuit of peace expresses their living hope and their participation in the new people of God. This call is congruent with Heb. 12:14, "Pursue peace with everyone, and the holiness without which no one will see the Lord," and with Rom. 14:19, "Let us then pursue what makes for peace and for mutual upbuilding."

---

[23] Michaels, 1 Peter, 180.

[24] Steven Richard Bechtler, Following in His Steps: Suffering, Community, and Christology in 1 Peter (Atlanta: Scholars Pr., 1998).

[25] Goppelt, A Commentary on 1 Peter, 237; Michaels, 1 Peter, 180–1.

First Peter 3:12, noted earlier in this essay, grounds further the call to abjure retaliation and pursue peace within the reign of God perspective. God's eyes are on the righteous, who in this context are those who reject retaliation and pursue peace. God hears their prayers. God's face is against those who do evil. The author shows restraint in describing the fate of evildoers, omitting from his quotation the psalmist's description of divine judgment: "to cut off the remembrance of them from the earth" (Ps. 34:16).

First Peter anticipated that in their pursuit of peace Christian believers will experience suffering. In such experiences they are to remember that it is better to suffer for doing good than to suffer for doing evil (3:17). They are to remember how Jesus Christ also suffered innocently and vicariously (3:18). Even if they are persecuted because they bear the name Christian, they are to "entrust themselves to a faithful Creator, while continuing to do good" (4:19). This outlook is possible as they remain aware of the reign of God, God's will, which envelops this letter.

THE FUSION OF MISSION AND PEACE IN 1 PETER

While for purposes of analysis we have separated the themes of reign of God, mission, and peace, the longer one reads 1 Peter, the more one sees these themes as interwoven and blended together.

Out of their living hope, grounded on God's act of raising Jesus, not only salvation but nonretaliating, peacemaking love has become possible. Their mission begins with becoming a community of hope in the midst of a hostile world, a community of forgiving love in a violent world, and a community of witness and service in the midst of those who misunderstand, misinterpret, and mistreat them. They are not to remain silent or inactive in such a world but are to speak, to proclaim, to confront evil with truth and love, even as they turn from it. They live and witness in a spirit and manner that is congruent with the nonretaliating, peacemaking love of Jesus Christ.

The reign of God perspective, including its eschatological dimensions, grounds and nurtures Christian hope. First Peter helps us understand the missional and peace-pursuing implications of that hope by making its application concrete in encounter with an unredeemed world.

Although Ronald F. Thiemann was not writing directly from a study of 1 Peter, he summarizes well some perspectives of its author:

> *The fundamental witness of the Christian faith is that the destiny of humankind is inextricably tied to the destiny of Jesus. . . . To believe the Christian gospel is to enter into a life of discipleship following the crucified and risen Christ. Such discipleship calls the followers to a ministry in behalf of those to whom Christ ministered—the poor, the outcasts, those on the margins of society. Followers of the crucified are called to identify with those who*

suffer, but as they do they are also called to proclaim the good news that the crucified has risen, that suffering and despair are not the final judgment upon God's creation. Those who enter the life of discipleship are thus called to exemplify a 'cruciform hope' within a world too often plagued by despair and cynicism.[26]

---

[26] Ronald F. Thiemann, "Faith Seeking Understanding," *Harvard Divinity Bulletin* 27, no. 2/3 (1998): 25–6.

14 | *Leaning toward consummation*
Mission and peace in the rhetoric of Revelation

LOREN L. JOHNS

O ASK ABOUT THE INTERSECTION OF MISSION AND PEACE in the Apocalypse of John is, on the surface at least, to ask an odd question. What, after all, does the Apocalypse have to do with mission *or* with peace? If we define "mission" as inviting unbelievers to make a decision for Christ, and if we define "peace" as an absence of conflict, then the Apocalypse appears to have little to say on either account. On the contrary, the Apocalypse appears to hunker down into a survivalist pessimism about the possibility of repentance on the one hand,[1] and to revel in bloody violence on the other.

But if "mission" refers to the church's call to live out an alternative way of life in the world in a way that invites others—indeed, the whole creation—to join in the life of redemption, it may be appropriate to see the Apocalypse as missional in orientation. This is, after all, part of the rhetorical appeal of the New Jerusalem. As J. Nelson Kraybill has put it, "Identification with Jesus-centered Christian community—a place of healing and welcome—is the missiological strategy of Revelation."[2]

Revelation is irrelevant to mission only if one holds to a reductionistic view of mission. But if "mission is about calling people to a new political and spiritual allegiance," as Kraybill suggests,[3] then Revelation

---

[1] Revelation 22:11 seems most pertinent here: "Let the unjust continue to do injustice, and the filthy continue in their filth, and the just continue in being just, and let the holy still be holy." Recalling Ezek. 3:27 and Dan. 12:10, and ultimately, Isa. 6:9–13, this verse cannot be interpreted apart from a careful diachronic study of the theological and sociological function of "obfuscation" texts. For a helpful discussion of various efforts to deal with the theological challenges posed by this verse, see G. K. Beale, *The Book of Revelation: A Commentary on the Greek Text*, The New International Greek Testament Commentary (Grand Rapids: Eerdmans, 1999), 1131–4.

[2] J. Nelson Kraybill, "The New Jerusalem As Paradigm for Mission," in *Mission Focus: Annual Review* 2 (1994): 123.

[3] Kraybill, "New Jerusalem," 125.

clearly emerges as a missional document. If mission is understood as contextualization, then Revelation itself is an affirmation that God has turned toward the world, because God makes all things new.[4] If mission is concerned only with individualistic or existential realities, then perhaps not; but if suffering is a "normal element of faithful Christian witness"[5] or if the gospel seeks to transform institutions as well as individuals, then perhaps the Apocalypse is a missional document. And what about peacemaking, vulnerability, economic justice, worship, symbol, or life in the community of faith?[6] Are these elements of the church's mission in the world or are they at best tangential?

Revelation begins and ends with a blessing on those who keep the words written in this book:

Blessed are those who . . . keep what is written in it (1:3).
Μακάριος . . . οἱ . . . τηροῦντες τὰ ἐν αὐτῇ γεγραμμένα
Makarios . . . oi . . . tērountes ta en autē gegrammena

Blessed is the one who keeps the words of the prophecy of this book (22:7).
Μακάριος ὁ τηρῶν τοὺς λόγους τῆς προφητείας τοῦ βιβλίου τούτου
Makarios ho tērōn tous logous tēs prophēteias tou bibliou toutou

What does it mean to "keep" the words of prophecy? The blessing is an invitation to respond in a certain way—to allow the vision developed in this book not only to reinforce values held by the community of faith in the seven churches of the province of Asia, but also to make specific ethical decisions in their common life. The ethical calls of this book are most explicit in chapters 2–3, but the invitation to maintain certain allegiances and to give up certain allegiances pervades the book.

Is it valid to treat as mission an ethical call to faithfulness that is addressed not to unbelievers outside the church, but to believers within the church? I think that it is. The Apocalypse was not written for outsiders, but for insiders—for the seven churches in Asia. It is a call for the

---

[4] Cf. the effort to rethink the definition of mission in David J. Bosch, "Elements of an Emerging Ecumenical Missionary Paradigm," in *Transforming Mission: Paradigm Shifts in Theology of Mission*, American Society of Missiology Series, no. 16 (Maryknoll: Orbis Bks., 1991), 368–510.

[5] Kraybill, "New Jerusalem," 127.

[6] All of these are themes considered by Kraybill in "New Jerusalem," 123–31. For a brief overview of the relationship between apocalyptic and mission, see the article by Christopher Rowland, "Apocalyptic and Mission," in *Dictionary of Mission: Theology, History, Perspectives*, ed. Karl Müller, American Society of Missiology Series, no. 24 (Maryknoll: Orbis Bks., 1997), 30–3; and the older essay by Oscar Cullmann, "Eschatology and Missions in the New Testament," trans. Olive Wyon, in *The Theology of the Christian Mission*, ed. Gerald H. Anderson (New York: McGraw-Hill, 1961), 42–54. However, Cullmann has little to say about Revelation, and his working definition of missions is reductionistic.

church to be the church—to reject the idolatry of emperor worship and the various social-cultural entanglements that emperor worship involved and to live up to a higher calling. In making his appeal, the author uses the literary conventions of apocalypticism.

Revelation's invitation to engage in nonviolent resistance against the idolatry of empire is central to this book and is missional at its core.[7] The Lamb Christology of Revelation directly supports its ethic of non-violent resistance. Revelation is not simply a pastoral letter intended to provide comfort. It is a biblical prophecy written to empower resistance against an idolatry accepted as commonplace in the larger society. It is an invitation to view the world in different terms, as fellow pilgrims on the way of protest against imperial politics wedded to religion.[8] This is engagement literature, not escapist literature.[9] I would say that Richard Hays is fully justified when he goes so far as to claim that "Revelation can be read rightly only by those who are actively struggling against injustice."[10]

---

[7] For a striking interpretation of Revelation as a protest against empire with great potential significance for people living in the United States, see Wes Howard-Brook and Anthony Gwyther, *Unveiling Empire: Reading Revelation Then and Now* (Maryknoll: Orbis Bks., 1999).

[8] See Allan A. Boesak, *Comfort and Protest: Reflections on the Apocalypse of John of Patmos* (Philadelphia: Westminster, 1987), 11, *et passim*.

[9] Besides the works of Howard-Brook, Gwyther, and Boesak cited above, see also Christopher Rowland, "The Apocalypse: Hope, Resistance and the Revelation of Reality," *Ex Auditu* 6 (1990): 129–44; John H. Yoder, "Ethics and Eschatology," *Ex Auditu* 6 (1990): 119–28; Richard Bauckham, *The Theology of the Book of Revelation*, New Testament Theology (New York: Cambridge Univ. Pr., 1993), esp. 159–64; C. Freeman Sleeper, *The Victorious Christ: A Study of the Book of Revelation* (Louisville: Westminster John Knox Pr., 1996), esp. 56; Elisabeth Schüssler Fiorenza, "Visionary Rhetoric and Social-Political Situation," chap. 7 in *The Book of Revelation: Justice and Judgment* (Philadelphia: Fortress Pr., 1985), 181–203; Loren L. Johns, *The Lamb Christology of the Apocalypse of John: An Investigation into Its Origins and Rhetorical Force*, Wissenschaftliche Untersuchungen zum Neuen Testament, 2nd series, no. 167 (Tübingen: Mohr Siebeck, 2003), 127, 187–8; Klaus Wengst, *The Pax Romana and the Peace of Jesus Christ*, trans. John Bowden (Philadelphia: Fortress Pr., 1987), 118–35; and Walter Wink, *Engaging the Powers: Discernment and Resistance in a World of Domination*, The Powers, vol. 3 (Philadelphia: Fortress Pr., 1992), esp. 87–104. For an overview of Revelation's contribution to the question of war and peace, see Willard M. Swartley, "War and Peace in the New Testament," in *Aufstieg und Niedergang der römischen Welt* II.26.3 (Berlin: de Gruyter, 1996), 2301–408. See esp. pp. 2369–74, which treat Revelation specifically. See also Fleming Rutledge, "The Apocalyptic Foundations of Peacemaking," *St. Luke's Journal of Theology* 34 (1991): 145–55, and the excellent chapter on Revelation in Richard B. Hays, *The Moral Vision of the New Testament: Community, Cross, New Creation: A Contemporary Introduction to New Testament Ethics* (San Francisco: Harper San Francisco, 1996), 169–85.

[10] Hays, *Moral Vision*, 183.

Lesslie Newbigin sees the consummation as "the goal of history, that which makes possible responsible action in history, . . . something which heals the dichotomy between the private and public worlds which death creates."[11] This is a healing vision in which all of the positive contributions of history and culture are brought into the city (21:24–26), while that which is common, abominable, or unclean will be excluded (21:27). "John does not write to individual Christians who have withdrawn from public life, or to groups of Christians in retreat centers, but to churches in seven large cities."[12] The high point in humanity's realization of human community is portrayed as a city.

The Lamb Christology of Revelation is directly related to its ethical call. Jesus' resistance to the point of death is clearly treated as a model for the believers—a paradigm for their own faithful, nonviolent resistance, which may well lead to death, just as Jesus' own faithful witness led to his death (see esp. Rev. 3:21; 12:11).

The Apocalypse of John has been perhaps the most influential book in the history of the West in terms of informing and empowering the sort of imagination that undergirds an ethical vision. It is also arguably the most dangerous book in the history of Christendom in terms of the history of its effects.[13] It has inspired Münsters[14] and Wacos.[15] Thus, any attempt to consider the contribution of the Apocalypse for understanding mission, peace, and the reign of God today must deal with the book's contribution to the problem of ethics and responsibility for the world.

This essay will consider first the mixed record of the Apocalypse regarding the history of its effects. Then, following an introduction to the rhetoric of the Apocalypse, it will examine one particular vehicle of that rhetoric, the rhetoric of "coming" in the Apocalypse, which reaches its climax in the last chapter of the book. The essay will conclude with a

---

[11] Lesslie Newbigin, *The Gospel in a Pluralist Society* (Grand Rapids: Eerdmans, 1989), 115.

[12] M. Eugene Boring, *Revelation,* Interpretation: A Bible Commentary for Teaching and Preaching (Louisville: John Knox Pr., 1989), 219.

[13] See Johns, *Lamb Christology,* 5, and the discussion there on 1–14.

[14] In 1534–35, certain Anabaptists seized control of the city of Münster and named it a "New Jerusalem," the "kingdom of God," the "new Zion." See Cornelius Krahn, "Münster Anabaptists," in *The Mennonite Encyclopedia: A Comprehensive Reference Work on the Anabaptist-Mennonite Movement* (Scottdale: Herald Pr., 1957), 3:777–83.

[15] In 1993 in Waco, Texas, David Koresh and the Branch Davidians were tragically killed in a confrontation with federal authorities. See Craig L. Nessan, "When Faith Turns Fatal: David Koresh and Tragic Misreadings of Revelation," *Currents in Theology and Mission* 22 (June 1995): 191–9; Peter Steinfels, "Bible's Book of Revelation Was Key to Waco Cult," *New York Times* 142 (1993): 16; James D. Tabor and Eugene V. Gallagher, *Why Waco?: Cults and the Battle for Religious Freedom in America* (Berkeley: Univ. of California Pr., 1995).

brief consideration of some of the promises and challenges this book represents for a biblical theology of peace and mission.

THE APOCALYPSE AND THE ETHICS OF ENGAGEMENT: GOOD NEWS OR BAD?

Although the Apocalypse has inspired in some readers both fear and violence, it has provided for other readers significant hope, peace, comfort—and even grounds for nonviolence. In his book, *Irenic Apocalypse: Some Uses of Apocalyptic in Dante, Petrarch, and Rabelais*, Dennis Costa argues that to see the Apocalypse as supporting a violent world view or ethic is essentially to misappropriate the text. Although the book is full of violent images, its aim is to liberate a people and leave them at peace. This irenic function is often missed in today's discourse, according to Costa. Even Dante, who drew on the most violent of Revelation's images, found in apocalyptic language a means of resolving his own political and spiritual aspirations nonviolently. Costa does not go so far as to suggest that the Apocalypse articulates a nonviolent ethic. Rather, his point is that the vision is essential irenic—that whatever the means to the goal, the goal actually is an irenic paradise, not cataclysmic destruction or violence for its own sake.[16] Whatever the violence encountered along the way, the goal of the Apocalypse is an irenic paradise.

Allan Boesak has articulated a different sort of hopeful vision. Boesak has found in the Apocalypse significant support for active protest—a message of hope and nonviolent resistance to evil.[17] It is here, in the Apocalypse, that we encounter the "deepest questions about human history." It is here that "we are present with the struggle to understand the meaning of history . . . and the inexplicable chasm and relationship between God's promises and Israel's lot."[18] A word of comfort? Yes, but not comfort through escapism. Rather, the comfort offered in the Apocalypse is a comfort in and for engagement in the world, generated by a vision of the ultimate victory of God—a victory that comes through protest, active witness, resistance to evil, and martyrdom.[19]

---

[16] Cf. Dennis Costa, *Irenic Apocalypse: Some Uses of Apocalyptic in Dante, Petrarch, and Rabelais* (Saratoga: Calif.: Anma Libri, 1981), 1–3, 44–5; cf. also R. E. Kaske, "Dante's DXV," in *Dante: A Collection of Critical Essays*, ed. John Freccero (Englewood Cliffs: Prentice Hall, 1965), 122–40.

[17] Allan A. Boesak, *Comfort and Protest*, esp. 34–9. It is not clear to me whether in Boesak's perspective, resistance to evil that is consistent with the apocalyptic vision is *essentially* nonviolent, or whether it simply needed to be nonviolent in light of the historical contingencies of the seven churches of the Apocalypse.

[18] Ibid., 16–17.

[19] Ibid., 17.

For this reason, the Apocalypse has occasionally been seen as quite subversive in a this-worldly sort of way. Boesak notes that in the Japanese occupation of Korea during World War 2, the Japanese were wary of the subversive power of the Apocalypse. It undercut the authority of the occupying powers. As a result, they prohibited Korean preachers from preaching from the Apocalypse.[20]

What is odd about contemporary readings of the Apocalypse is the gaping divide between those who hold that the Apocalypse is literature's greatest betrayal of the ethical vision[21] and those who hold that the Apocalypse informs and upholds a just and empowering ethical vision. For Jack Sanders, the Apocalypse represents a type of Christianity that is at odds with what the gospel is really about. He says that it is the Apocalypse's "retreat from the ethical dimension that is the basic evil of the Apocalypse." Furthermore, "it is unfortunate that we are today experiencing a revival of just the kind of Christianity found in Revelation."[22]

---

[20] Ibid.

[21] Examples here would include D. H. Lawrence, who found the Apocalypse "annoying," "ugly," even "detestable" (*Apocalypse* [1931; reprint, Harmondsworth: Penguin Bks., 1974]; see esp. 5–9); C. H. Dodd, who hated its "eschatological fanaticism" and considered the Apocalypse a "relapse into a pre-Christian eschatology" (*The Apostolic Preaching and Its Developments*, 2nd ed. [London: Hodder and Stoughton, 1944], 41 and 40, respectively); Harold Bloom, who says, "Resentment and not love is the teaching of the Revelation of St. John the Divine. It is a book without wisdom, goodness, kindness, or affection of any kind. Perhaps it is appropriate that a celebration of the end of the world should be not only barbaric but scarcely literate. Where the substance is so inhumane, who would wish the rhetoric to be more persuasive, or the vision to be more vividly realized?" (*The Revelation of St. John the Divine*, Modern Critical Interpretations [New York: Chelsea Hse. Pubs., 1988], 4–5); and Tina Pippin, who says that misogyny, which is deeply writ in the Apocalypse, ultimately destroys any liberating vision the author may have intended (*Death and Desire: The Rhetoric of Gender in the Apocalypse of John*, Literary Currents in Biblical Interpretation [Louisville: Westminster John Knox Pr., 1992], 47). Even Rudolf Bultmann mostly ignored the Apocalypse in his theology of the New Testament, a work Heikki Räisänen says is still regarded as "the unrivalled classic in the field" (Heikki Räisänen, *Beyond New Testament Theology: A Story and a Programme* [Philadelphia: Trinity Pr. International, 1990], xi). Bultmann called the thought of the Apocalypse "a weakly Christianized Judaism" (Rudolf Bultmann, *Theology of the New Testament*, trans. Kendrick Grobel [New York: Charles Scribner's Sons, 1951–55], 2:175).

[22] Jack T. Sanders, *Ethics in the New Testament: Change and Development* (Philadelphia: Fortress Pr., 1975), 114–15. In contrast to Sanders, Pheme Perkins argues that Revelation "is really a work about justice." See Pheme Perkins, "Apocalyptic Sectarianism and Love Commands: The Johannine Epistles and Revelation," in *The Love of Enemy and Nonretaliation in the New Testament*, ed. Willard M. Swartley, Studies in Peace and Scripture (Louisville: Westminster John Knox Pr., 1992), 287–96; see esp. 293.

Sanders was influenced by scholars like Albert Schweitzer, Martin Dibelius, and Philipp Vielhauer who, all in different ways, buried the ax deep between eschatology and ethics. Typical of this approach was the denial that apocalyptic literature had any interest in ethics or in the concrete applications of the Law in light of the imminent end of this age. It was claimed that apocalypticists, like Gnostics, knew no ethic. Ethicists presupposed an unbroken world that should be preserved, or a curable world that should be renewed. Apocalypticists had no such presuppositions.[23]

Philipp Vielhauer's highly influential "Introduction to Apocalypses and Related Subjects" in Hennecke-Schneemelcher's two-volume *New Testament Apocrypha* did much to perpetuate a dichotomy between the this-worldly, national eschatology found in rabbinic texts and the other-worldly eschatology found in the apocalypses.[24] In this article, Vielhauer essentially equated apocalyptic thought with pessimism, determinism, and temporal dualism (this age vs. the age to come). The result of this approach was a near consensus that apocalyptic thought is essentially escapist, pessimistic, sectarian, and conservative—even survivalist.

This generally negative consensus about the ethical stance of apocalyptic thought continued in biblical studies until the 1960s and 1970s, when a number of significant studies of apocalyptic literature appeared that cast apocalyptic literature in a new light. In 1964, D. S. Russell published his book, *The Method and Message of Jewish Apocalyptic*, which accelerated the rehabilitation of apocalyptic literature among biblical scholars.[25] More influential on the continent was Klaus Koch's little 1970 volume, *Ratlos vor der Apokalyptik*, which appeared in English as *The Rediscovery of Apocalyptic*, but whose title would more faithfully be translated as "perplexed with [or embarrassed by] apocalyptic."[26] Since then, apocalypticism has come into its own as a subdiscipline, marked by

[23] For an excellent discussion of this era and of the relation of ethics and eschatology in Jewish apocalyptic literature, see Christoph Münchow, *Ethik und Eschatologie: Ein Beitrag zum Verständnis der frühjüdischen Apokalyptik mit einem Ausblick auf das Neue Testament* (Göttingen: Vandenhoeck & Ruprecht, 1981).

[24] Philipp Vielhauer, "Apocalypses and Related Subjects: Introduction," revised by Georg Strecker, in *New Testament Apocrypha*, rev. ed., ed. Wilhelm Schneemelcher and Edgar Hennecke, trans. Robert McL. Wilson (Louisville: Westminster John Knox Pr., 1992), 542–602.

[25] D. S. Russell, *The Method and Message of Jewish Apocalyptic: 200 BC–AD 100*, The Old Testament Library (Philadelphia: Westminster Pr., 1964). Ernst Käsemann's work in the 1950s remains an important precursor to Russell's work theologically.

[26] Klaus Koch, *The Rediscovery of Apocalyptic: A Polemical Work on a Neglected Area of Biblical Studies and Its Damaging Effects on Theology and Philosophy*, trans. Margaret Kohl, Studies in Biblical Theology (London: SCM Pr., 1972).

such significant studies as Paul Hanson's *The Dawn of Apocalyptic*[27] and John J. Collins's *The Apocalyptic Imagination: An Introduction to Jewish Apocalyptic Literature.*[28]

Nevertheless, despite recent gains in the study of apocalypticism among biblical scholars, such terms as "apocalypse," "apocalyptic," and "apocalypticism" retain in popular use connotations of catastrophe, chaos, horror, despair, and violent cosmic meltdown. Even among some scholarly disciplines, it remains acceptable to define apocalyptic discourse and apocalyptic rhetoric phenomenologically in terms of a presumably stable "apocalyptic myth" that perceives salvation as "collective, terrestrial, imminent, total, and miraculous."[29] Such writers deal with Hal Lindsey and the author of the Apocalypse, for instance, not in terms of the content of their thought or message, however similar or disparate they may be, but in their common dependence upon apocalyptic discourse as their mode of communication.

The recent works of Stephen O'Leary[30] and Catherine Keller,[31] for all of their brilliance, ultimately assume too much about the deep structure of apocalypticism within the human soul. They imagine too easily what apocalypse "is," regardless of whether their readings are faithful to the rhetorical strategy of *John's* Apocalypse. As a biblical scholar, I would appeal to John's right to object to what later became of the discourse to which he contributed.

Like O'Leary and Keller, Elisabeth Schüssler Fiorenza also attempts a rhetorical reading strategy. However, Fiorenza's rhetorical method honors the historical specificity of the Apocalypse more than do O'Leary's and Keller's. Fiorenza's rhetorical method aims at "reconstructing both Revelation's rhetorical world of vision and the rhetorical and sociopolitical situations in which this imagery can be understood to have developed as an active and fitting response."[32] As such, Fiorenza's

---

[27] Paul D. Hanson, *The Dawn of Apocalyptic: The Historical and Sociological Roots of Jewish Apocalyptic Eschatology*, rev. ed. (Philadelphia: Fortress Pr., 1979).

[28] John J. Collins, *The Apocalyptic Imagination: An Introduction to Jewish Apocalyptic Literature*, 2nd ed. (Grand Rapids: Eerdmans, 1998).

[29] See, e.g., Norman Rufus Colin Cohn, *The Pursuit of the Millennium: Revolutionary Millenarians and Mystical Anarchists of the Middle Ages*, rev. ed. (New York: Oxford Univ. Pr., 1970), 15; and Stephen D. O'Leary, *Arguing the Apocalypse: A Theory of Millennial Rhetoric* (New York: Oxford Univ. Pr., 1994), 6.

[30] Ibid.

[31] Catherine Keller, *Apocalypse Now and Then: A Feminist Approach to the End of the World* (Boston: Beacon Pr., 1996).

[32] Elisabeth Schüssler Fiorenza, *Revelation: Vision of a Just World*, Proclamation Commentaries (Minneapolis: Fortress Pr., 1991), 22.

rhetorical method forces the modern reader to take seriously the conventions of communication current in first-century Asia Minor. Fiorenza's method takes seriously the historical task of interpretation without privileging one particular form of historical criticism. Rhetorical criticism asks questions like "What is going on in the text?" and "What is the force of this discourse?" and "What persuasive techniques is the author using and to what end?" These questions are too often passed over or their answers simply assumed in popular approaches to the Apocalypse.

THE RHETORIC AND ETHICS OF THE APOCALYPSE

The Apocalypse of John is an example of epideictic rhetoric. Deliberative rhetoric seeks to effect certain kinds of decisions and thus focuses on the future. Juridical rhetoric seeks to establish the legitimacy of decisions previously made and thus focuses on the past. In contrast, epideictic rhetoric is concerned primarily with values, with world view, with the constitutive vision of its audience. It therefore focuses on the present. In the case of the Apocalypse, the language of the future functions to inform and energize a world view designed to transform the present. There is certainly a deliberative edge to this rhetoric, since the author is eager for the audience to remain "faithful unto death" (2:10; cf. 1:5; 2:13; 3:14; 17:14; 19:11), and there is admittedly overlap between deliberative and epideictic rhetoric.[33] But the primary rhetorical mode of the Apocalypse is that of epideictic.

According to Robert M. Royalty Jr., epideictic rhetoric is designed, first, to "affect an audience's view, opinions, or values. . . . Second, epideictic rhetoric includes speeches of praise (encomium, panegyric, *laudatio*) and blame (ψόγοι, *vituperatio*) of persons and cities. . . . Third, epideictic rhetoric is distinguished by its amplification (ἐργασία, *amplificatio*) of topics and imagery; vivid description (ἔκφρασις); and compassion (σύγκρισις). All three of these characteristics are prominent features in Revelation."[34]

In the case of the Apocalypse, the author's aim is to mold or re-shape the world view and values of the audience. The Apocalypse seeks

---

[33] Cf. George A. Kennedy, *Classical Rhetoric and Its Christian and Secular Tradition from Ancient Times to Modern Times* (Chapel Hill: Univ. of North Carolina Pr., 1980), 74.

[34] Robert M. Royalty Jr., "The Rhetoric of Revelation," in *Society of Biblical Literature 1997 Seminar Papers*, Society of Biblical Literature Seminar Papers Series, no. 36 (Atlanta: Scholars Pr., 1997), 601–2. For a further consideration of the rhetoric of the Apocalypse, see Johns, *Lamb Christology*, 155–8; and Loren L. Johns, "The Lamb in the Rhetorical Program of the Apocalypse of John," in *Society of Biblical Literature 1998 Seminar Papers*, Part 2, Society of Biblical Literature Seminar Papers Series, no. 37 (Atlanta: Scholars Pr., 1998), 762–84.

to effect a world view consistent with the understanding of Jesus' slaughter as the key to God's victory over evil. This understanding necessarily entails an ethic of nonviolent resistance to any world view, social influence, or political power that would challenge such a gospel. The rhetorical tools of praise and blame[35] figure prominently in the author's persuasion technique.

Epideictic rhetoric is sometimes considered politically neutral or even essentially conservative, because it often serves to shore up the status quo, reaffirming traditional values in a nonthreatening way. Nevertheless, epideictic rhetoric can also be revolutionary. As I have argued elsewhere, "The inculcation of values is not politically neutral or inherently conservative; rather, by focusing on values, epideictic rhetoric not only 'messes with the mind' of the readers, both individually and collectively; it also represents a socially significant act. John used the tools this sort of rhetoric provided not only to criticize the prevailing values of the seven churches, but also to suggest the sorts of values that were in keeping with the new order being revealed by God."[36]

MISSION AND PEACE AS PARTICULARISTIC UNIVERSALISM

There is a strong universal thrust in the Apocalypse. In one sense, Revelation is the most conspicuously nonsectarian book in the New Testament. It is akin to the Zion theology of Isaiah or Micah, but one in which the one sitting on the throne and the Lamb replace the temple as the magnet that draws all nations into the orbit of the worship of Yahweh. The whole universe is pictured as being under the lordship of God. Not content rhetorically with identifying simply "everyone" or "all people," this vision encompasses "every tribe and language and people and nation" (5:9; cf. also 7:9; 10:11; 11:9; 13:7; 14:6; 17:15). But it is even larger than that because more than people are involved. "*Every creature* in heaven *and* on earth *and* under the earth *and* in the sea, *and* all that is in them" join in praise of the one seated on the throne and of the Lamb (5:13).[37]

---

[35] Sometimes praise and blame are expressed directly, as in the hymns of praise or the funeral celebration of the fall of the whore. Sometimes they are expressed obliquely through the use of names and sobriquets. See Johns, "The Lamb in the Rhetorical Program," 764–5; and Edith M. Humphrey, "On Visions, Arguments and Naming: The Rhetoric of Specificity and Mystery in the Apocalypse" (paper presented at the annual meeting of the Society of Biblical Literature, San Francisco, November 1997).

[36] Johns, "The Lamb in the Rhetorical Program," 762.

[37] The book's aural nature should be kept in mind here. This was a book intended to be read aloud (1:3). Aurally, repetitions like "tribe and language and people and nation" would have carried a pulse that emphasized the universality of vision's scope. This

But to claim that the Apocalypse teaches universalism requires that one carefully define the term. Vernard Eller discusses this thorny issue in his commentary.[38] Eller concludes that given the ambiguity on this issue in the text, the modern interpreter should leave the theological problem open—or leave it to God. In a similar way, M. Eugene Boring sees the particularism and universalism in the Apocalypse as an intentional dialectic that should not be resolved prematurely.[39] Harrington agrees with Boring that there is tension and paradox in the Apocalypse's treatment of limited vs. universal salvation. For Harrington it is crucial to note that death and evil are destroyed, rather than punished eternally, suggesting that the only eschaton envisioned in the Apocalypse is a positive one.[40]

Eller is correct in saying that *if* the Apocalypse teaches universalism, it is an odd type of universalism. The author does not consider the possibility of salvation apart from Jesus Christ, or apart from justice. There is no cheap grace here. The author certainly cannot be accused of underestimating the power of evil, nor does he undermine the necessity or the urgency of decision. What the author does is leave open what Eller calls "the universalistic possibility."[41]

The Apocalypse does not speak the language of postmodern pluralism. It does not seek to comfort its audience with the acceptability of a broad-minded pluralism. The Apocalypse represents no generic utopian vision that can be accepted or rejected on the basis of one's religious preferences. There is a particularity in its universalism that is quite specific.

If the Apocalypse sounds at points as if all will be saved, it may be expressing the conviction that all are invited on the same basis to drink the water of life freely, and the hope that all will indeed do so. But all will also be judged by the same criterion—the criterion of works (20:12;

---

universal impulse is not a novel contribution of the Apocalypse, however. The repetition of "peoples, nations, and languages" is a pulse within the Book of Daniel, occurring at 3:4, 7, 29; 4:1; 5:19; 6:25; and 7:14. Cf. also 4 Ezra 3:7; 9:3.

[38] Vernard Eller, *The Most Revealing Book of the Bible: Making Sense out of Revelation* (Grand Rapids: Eerdmans, 1974), 202–5.

[39] See especially his excursus, "Universal Salvation and Paradoxical Language," in Boring, *Revelation*, 226–31; cf. also M. Eugene Boring, "Revelation 19–21: End Without Closure," *Princeton Seminary Bulletin* Supplementary Issue, no. 3 (1994): 57–84.

[40] See the excursus, "Positive Eschaton Only: Revelation and 'Universal Salvation,'" in Wilfrid J. Harrington, *Revelation*, Sacra Pagina, vol. 16 (Collegeville, Minn.: Liturgical Pr., 1993), 229–35.

[41] Vernard Eller, *The Most Revealing Book*, 204.

22:12).[42] This is indeed the sort of vision that can energize and sustain mission.

The Apocalypse envisions consummation, not escape. Its theology of salvation is significantly different from prophetic remnant theologies. At the final judgment before the great white throne, some will be invited to enter the New Jerusalem freely, while others will be thrown into the lake of fire. The author of the Apocalypse does not conceive of a salvation that does not include judgment. However, the image is not that of a small, beleaguered remnant that has successfully survived by the skin of their teeth. Rather, the saints will participate in a new creation (21:1–2) that is full of the glory of God (21:3–22:5). And they will reign on earth (5:10; 20:4, 6; 22:5).

Furthermore, although the consummation includes judgment, the saints apparently enjoy no ethnic commonalities. The Lamb is considered worthy to take the scroll in the central scene precisely because he was slaughtered and because he ransomed humanity in all its diversity:

> You are worthy to take the scroll
>   and to open its seals,
> for you were slaughtered and by your blood you ransomed for God
>   saints from every tribe and language and people and nation;
> you have made them to be a kingdom and priests serving our God,
>   and they will reign on earth. (Rev. 5:9–10)

Rhetorically, the universalistic vision serves to empower the vulnerable Christian community in its ethic of nonviolent resistance to a world power that does not recognize the sovereignty of God or of the king of kings.

This universal thrust is thus a universalism of invitation: all are invited to come. The author of the Apocalypse writes as one who is conscious about his audience.[43] The work begins with a blessing on "the one who reads (aloud) the words of the prophecy," and on "those who hear and who keep what is written in it" (1:3). The audience of this work is thus inscribed within the book as readers/hearers to whom the author

---

[42] Contra Stephen Goranson, "The Text of Revelation 22.14," *New Testament Studies* 43 (1997): 154–7, there is no anti-Pauline polemic in the Apocalypse on the question of salvation by grace through faith vs. salvation by works.

[43] I use the term "audience" intentionally here to underscore that the book was originally read aloud to a series of churches in worship, not read individually by unconnected individuals.

occasionally makes direct appeals.[44] It is not just Jesus who comes: the thirsty are invited to come as well (22:17).

The Apocalypse is a call to action from beginning to end.[45] Although this call to action is couched in an epideictic rhetoric in which praise of God and of the Lamb is central—along with vituperation against the beasts and the whore of Babylon—the author makes clear that this book is a book of prophecy that is to be "kept" or "observed" (1:3; 22:7, 9). This call to action is buoyed along not only by the admonition to "keep" the words of this prophecy, but also by the invitation to "come."

THE RHETORIC OF COMING IN THE APOCALYPSE

The multivalence of "coming" in the Apocalypse is fascinating. God is presented as the one who was, who is, and who "is to come" (ὁ ἐρχόμενος | *ho erchomenos*) in 1:4, 8; 4:8. God is not limited by time: God owns the future as much as the past and present. So "coming" refers to the future in a general sense (in this connection, cf. also 17:10).[46] But "coming" also refers to the apocalyptic coming of the Son of Man in 1:7; 2:25; 3:3, 11 (where ἔρχομαι | *erchomai* and ἥξω | *hēxō* seem to be used interchangeably). Jesus is presented as one who is "coming with the clouds" in Rev. 1:7, an attribution lifted from Daniel's description of the Son of Man in Dan. 7:13 (cf. also Rev. 16:15). Sometimes this coming is seen as an act of judgment, as in 2:5, 16; sometimes whether in judgment or grace is unclear (2:25).

The coming of the synagogue of Satan to worship at the feet of the Philadelphians is portrayed as an ironic act of judgment (3:9). The coming of the wedding is announced in 19:7. Similarly, plagues will come on Babylon in one day of judgment (18:8, 10). Jesus also threatens to come to the seven churches in judgment (2:5, 16; cf. also 3:10, where the subject is the hour of testing). Other characters in the story come in judgment, such as the four equestrians (6:1, 3, 5, 7), the "great day of their wrath" (6:17), the hour of God's judgment (14:7), the hour of harvest (14:15), angels (8:3; 17:1; 21:9), or the second and third woes (9:12; 11:14, 18).

---

[44] These direct appeals include the sevenfold "Let anyone who has an ear hear what the Spirit is saying to the churches" (2:7, 11, 17, 29; 3:6, 13, 22). Cf. also Rev 1:1, 3, 9–11; 13:9, 10, 18; 14:12–13; 22:6, 10.

[45] Cf. Boring, *Revelation*, 225.

[46] That some word play is meant by the author's use of ἔρχομαι (*erchomai*) seems likely, since the future participle of εἰμί | *eimi* (ἐσόμενοι | *esomenoi*) was available to the author: "the one who will be"; cf. David E. Aune, *Revelation 1–5* (Dallas: Word Bks., 1997), 32.

In the heavenly throne scene in Rev. 5:7, Jesus did not just take the scroll, he "came" (ἦλθεν | *ēlthen*, from ἔρχομαι | *erchomai*) and "took" (εἴληφεν | *eilēphen*, from λαμβάνω | *lambanō*) the scroll. In 15:4 the coming of the nations to worship before the Lord is celebrated in the praise song of Moses and of the Lamb. The coming of the wedding day of the Lamb is celebrated in 19:7.

"Coming" is also seen as an act of the faithful. Thus, in the proleptic scene of paradise, where the great multitude is praising God, who is seated on the throne, and the Lamb, the elder asks who the praisers are and "where have they *come* from?" The answer is that these are the ones "who have *come* out of the great ordeal" (7:13–14). In other words, the faithful are those who have come, who have passed, through martyrdom.

This theme of coming is developed further in Revelation 22. In v. 17 we read,

> Both the Spirit and the bride say, "Come" (ἔρχου | *erchou*, from ἔρχομαι).
> And let everyone who hears say, "Come" (ἔρχου, from ἔρχομαι).
> And let everyone who is thirsty, come (ἐρχέσθω | *erchesthō*, from ἔρχομαι).
> Let anyone who wishes, take (λαβέτω | *labetō*, from λαμβάνω) the water of life freely.

But to whom are these petitions addressed? Who is being asked to come here? Three suggestions have been made: (a) the unbelieving world; (b) the church; and (c) a combination, with the first two imperatives addressed to Christ and the third to the church.[47]

R. H. Charles, George Eldon Ladd, Robert H. Mounce, and Philip E. Hughes argue for the first interpretation: this is an altar call to the world.[48] Although it may seem as if the first part of the verse is an invitation to Jesus, the first half should be interpreted in light of the second half, which is addressed to "the world," according to Ladd. Charles says that "the Spirit" (τὸ πνεῦμα | *to pneuma*) in the Apocalypse is consistently the Spirit of Christ. It is Christ who speaks in the prophetic oracles to the seven churches (chaps. 2–3), when the audience is encouraged to listen to what the πνεῦμα is saying to the churches. So

---

[47] Although Frederick J. Murphy recognizes and discusses the problem, he remains noncommittal: Fredrick J. Murphy, *Fallen Is Babylon: The Revelation to John* (Harrisburg, Pa.: Trinity Pr. International, 1998), 439.

[48] Cf. R. H. Charles, *A Critical and Exegetical Commentary on the Revelation of St. John*, The International Critical Commentary (Edinburgh: T. & T. Clark, 1920), 2:179; George Eldon Ladd, *A Commentary on the Revelation of John* (Grand Rapids: Eerdmans, 1972), 294–5; Robert H. Mounce, *The Book of Revelation*, The New International Commentary on the New Testament, vol. 17 (Grand Rapids: Eerdmans, 1977), 395; and Philip Edgcumbe Hughes, *The Book of the Revelation: A Commentary* (Grand Rapids: Eerdmans, 1990), 240.

whoever is the addressee of the petition, it must be understood that the speakers are "Christ and the church in the heavenly Jerusalem."[49] According to Charles, it is therefore most natural, even without the clarification of the third and fourth petitions, to see the addressee of all four as the "world of men that were still thirsting for life and truth or were willing to accept them."[50]

G. B. Caird prefers the second interpretation: this petition is addressed "not to Christ but to all comers."[51] It is both an invitation to communion and an invitation to join the ranks of the conquerors. G. K. Beale agrees: all three petitions are addressed to the church. In fact, according to Beale, who follows G. H. Lang and Jan Fekkes in this regard, "Isaiah's three imperatives to 'come' are probably the model for the three imperatives to 'come' here in Rev. 22:17."[52] Robert Wall argues for a slightly modified version of the second interpretation: this petition and the entire book are addressed not to the church as such, but specifically to the embattled church, which is being invited to embrace fully the word of the gospel.[53] The last petition is not meant as a word of grace for those who need to be justified; rather, it is a word of grace for those believers who need to be sanctified.[54] If the church generally were the object of this imperative, he says, we would expect the final petition to offer a symbol of comfort, rather than grace, as the reward.

Beasley-Murray argues for the third interpretation: the first two petitions are directed toward Christ, the third to the "hearers of the book," and the fourth to the unbelieving world.[55] Along the same vein,

---

[49] Charles, *Revelation,* 2:179.

[50] Ibid., 2:180.

[51] George B. Caird, *The Revelation of St. John the Divine,* 2nd ed., Black's New Testament Commentaries (London: Adam & Charles Black, 1984), 286. Cf. also Ray Summers, *Worthy Is the Lamb: An Interpretation of Revelation* (Nashville: Broadman Pr., 1951), 218.

[52] G. K. Beale, *Book of Revelation,* 1149. Although he admits that "this is a difficult issue," Grant R. Osborne ultimately sides with Beale in arguing that Christ is the speaker of all of the invitations to come in Rev. 22:17 (*Revelation,* Baker Exegetical Commentary on the New Testament [Grand Rapids: Baker Bks., 2002], 793). Leonard L. Thompson agrees that *people* are being invited to come in this verse, not Jesus (*Revelation,* Abingdon New Testament Commentaries [Nashville: Abingdon Pr., 1998], 188).

[53] Robert W. Wall, *Revelation,* New International Bible Commentary, no. 18 (Peabody, Mass.: Hendrickson Pubs., Inc., 1991), 267.

[54] Ibid., 267–8.

[55] G. R. Beasley-Murray, *The Book of Revelation,* 2nd ed., New Century Bible Commentary (Grand Rapids: Eerdmans, 1978), 342. Cf. also John Sweet, *Revelation,* TPI New Testament Commentaries (Philadelphia: Trinity Pr. International, 1990), 137, 139; Jürgen Roloff, *The Revelation of John,* A Continental Commentary, trans. John E. Alsup (Minneapolis: Fortress Pr., 1993), 252–3; and Richard L. Jeske, *Revelation for Today: Images of Hope* (Philadelphia:

Beckwith refers to the shift in the implied addressees as a "sudden turn," and claims that such a sudden shift to directly addressing the audience is also seen in 13:9f. and 14:13f.[56]

The context of v. 17 within the chapter seems to support Beasley-Murray's interpretation. No less than three times in this chapter do we have the assurance of Christ, "Behold, I am coming quickly" (ἰδοὺ ἔρχομαι ταχύ | *idou erchomai tachy*, v. 7; ἰδοὺ ἔρχομαι ταχύ, v. 12; ναί, ἔρχομαι ταχύ | *nai erchomai tachy*, v. 20). The last of these is met with the prophet's answer, ἀμήν, ἔρχου κύριε ᾽Ιησοῦ | *amēn, erchou kyrie Iēsou*, "Amen! Come, Lord Jesus!" (v. 20). The theme of the imminent coming of Christ seems to run through this chapter as a grounding bass note.

The immediate context for v. 17 is set in v. 16, where ἐγώ (*egō*, "I") is repeated twice in reference to Jesus. "I, Jesus, have sent my angel. . . . I myself am the root and offspring of David, the bright morning star." Immediately after that the Spirit and the bride join to say, "Come!" So the most logical character implied in the imperative ἔρχου of v. 17 is Jesus.

In v. 7 we read, "See, I am coming soon!" (ἰδοὺ ἔρχομαι ταχύ). The subject of the verb is Christ. The nearness of Christ's coming is the basis for the macarism that follows: "Blessed is the one who keeps the words of the prophecy of this book."[57] Because of the nearness of Christ's coming, the reader/hearer who keeps the words of the prophecy of this book will be blessed. In v. 12 the ideas expressed in v. 7 are repeated. Here again we read, "See, I am coming soon!" (ἰδοὺ ἔρχομαι ταχύ), and again the implication of this nearness is expressed in ethical terms: "My reward is with me, to repay according to everyone's work." Finally, in v. 20, the promised imminent coming of Christ is repeated one more time:

Fortress Pr., 1983), 123. This interpretation is implied in Boesak, *Comfort and Protest*, 138; Boring, *Revelation*, 225; and Christopher Rowland, *Revelation*, Epworth Commentaries (London: Epworth Pr., 1993), 161. David E. Aune also seems to support this interpretation. For him the problem of the inconsistency of implied referent is at least partially resolved in the recognition that "come" functions here as a transitional catchword. See David E. Aune, *Revelation 17–22*, Word Biblical Commentary, vol. 52c (Nashville: Thomas Nelson, Inc., 1998), 1227.

[56] Isbon T. Beckwith, *The Apocalypse of John: Studies in Introduction, with a Critical and Exegetical Commentary* (New York: Macmillan, 1919), 778; cf. also Henry Barclay Swete, *The Apocalypse of St. John: The Greek Text with Introduction, Notes, and Indices*, 3rd ed. (New York: Macmillan, 1909), 310, who calls this "a remarkable change of reference."

[57] See Virgil P. Cruz, "The Beatitudes of the Apocalypse: Eschatology and Ethics," in *Perspectives on Christology: Essays in Honor of Paul K. Jewett*, edited by Marguerite Shuster and Richard A. Muller (Grand Rapids: Zondervan Publishing Hse., 1991), 269–83, for a succinct argument on how the beatitudes or macarisms reflect the essential unity of eschatology and ethics in the Apocalypse.

"Surely I am coming soon." This time the author bows the knee in invitation to Christ: "Amen. Come, Lord Jesus!" (v. 20).

The Spirit and the bride, which is the church, join in one voice to pray, "Come." But this invitation is not just for some distant narrative voice in space and time. The invitation is brought home to the audience in the second line of v. 17 as the author explicitly invites the audience to join in the invitation: "Let everyone who hears say, 'Come.'" As with the first invitation, the object of the invitation is again Christ, but here the audience is invited by the author to join in the invitation. Finally, in the third line of this verse, the invitation shifts dramatically into a direct address to the audience as the author speaks the eschatologically pregnant word of invitation directly to the reader: "And let everyone who is thirsty come."

What is going on here? Is the author attempting to subtly shift the audience's understanding of "coming" from an apocalyptic coming of the Son of Man to a more existential coming of the individual believer? Is John finally showing his hand as he subtly demythologizes Jewish apocalypticism in one small stroke? Probably not.

Mitchell G. Reddish agrees with the mixed-addressee interpretation. He says, "In contrast to the first two invitations that are issued to Christ, this invitation is addressed to people to come and partake of God's offer of salvation. . . . These words are an 'evangelistic invitation' to everyone who thirsts for God to come and be satisfied. The water of life that provides salvation, wholeness, and healing is God's gift to creation."[58] That the water of life was a symbol of salvation in both the Jewish and Christian literature of Early Judaism is widely acknowledged.[59] This interpretation suggests that for John the author, the ultimate purpose in writing his Apocalypse was to call his reader/hearers to salvation—that realm of faithful witness and consistent resistance that elsewhere in the New Testament is called the kingdom of God. And when they do, the kingdom of the world becomes the kingdom of the messiah.[60]

Roloff also agrees with the mixed-addressee interpretation. However, he sees the double invitation as intentional and natural within its liturgical context. The one invitation is the eschatological "maranatha" addressed to Christ. The second is the invitation to the Lord's Supper,

---

[58] Mitchell G. Reddish, *Revelation,* Smyth & Helwys Bible Commentary (Macon, Ga.: Smyth & Helwys Publishing, Inc., 2001), 429.

[59] For examples drawn from Deutero-Isaiah, the Dead Sea Scrolls, and rabbinic literature, see David E. Aune, *Revelation 17–22,* 1229.

[60] Rev. 11:15; cf. also 1:6, 9; 5:10; 12:10; 16:10; 17:12, 17–18 for other occurrences of βασιλεία (*basileia*).

addressed to the believer. He says: "Precisely this double meaning is . . . intended here. . . . In this cry, which every hearer of the reading of Revelation is to join, the entire fulfillment of salvation, which is promised for the future in 21:1–22:5, is transposed into the personal sphere and brought together with the present coming of Jesus in the Lord's Supper. . . . Thus, John is not content with pointing to a temporally imminent future dawning of salvation (cf. 1:3; 22:10); rather, he indicates where salvation can be discovered and experienced in the present."[61]

The interplay between the *maranatha* cry of the early church and the invitation to the Lord's Supper can be seen in Didache 10:6, where we have a similar phenomenon. There we read,

> Let grace[62] **come** (ἐλθέτω | *elthetō*)
> and let this world **pass away** (παρελθέτω | *pareltheto*).
> Hosanna to the God of David.
> If anyone is holy,
> let him **come** (ἐρχέσθω | *erchesthō*).[63]
> If anyone is not,
> let him repent.
> μαρανα θα (*marana tha*, "Our Lord, **come!**") Amen!

Although the Didache concludes with a short apocalyptic section (chap. 16), the author does not identify himself as living in the last days. As Vielhauer and Strecker have shown, everything is schematized. The author is concise and organized. In other words, even the so-called apocalyptic section of the Didache is concerned not with traditional apocalyptic rhetoric, but with catechism, with church order.[64] Though the topic is eschatology, eschatological urgency is missing from the rhetoric.

It is not as if the eschatological tension is relaxed entirely in the Didache. In commenting on this verse in the Didache, Oscar Cullmann states that "this connection between present and future reality (a rela-

---

[61] Roloff, *The Revelation of John*, 252–3. Cf. also Catherine Gunsalus González and Justo L. González, *Revelation* (Louisville: Westminster John Knox Pr., 1997), 146–7; and Harrington, *Revelation*, 223, 225–6, who hold a similar view on the close relationship between the double meaning in the Apocalypse and the nature of the eucharistic celebration in the early church.

[62] "Grace" here may be a title for Christ. Cf. Cyril C. Richardson, ed. and trans., *Early Christian Fathers*, Library of Christian Classics, vol. 1 (Philadelphia: Westminster Pr., 1953), 176, n. 57. Cullmann notes that the Coptic has "the Lord," which he thinks is perhaps original. See Oscar Cullmann, *The Christology of the New Testament*, rev. ed., trans. Shirley C. Guthrie and Charles A. M. Hall (Philadelphia: Westminster Pr., 1963), 210, n. 2.

[63] Or, "let him keep coming."

[64] Philip Vielhauer, "Apocalypses and Related Subjects," 591.

tionship which was of course lost with the passing of time) represents the peculiar character and greatness of the early Church's worship."[65] The invitation to come to the Lord's Supper is an invitation to "proclaim the Lord's death *until he comes*" (1 Cor. 11:26).

However, the rhetorical interests of these two writings are quite different. In contrast to the Didache, Revelation 22 leans on tiptoe toward the consummation. This is not a consummation premised on the demise of the present order, or on the ignoring of the present order. Rather, it is a consummation premised on God's judgment of the present order. In a satire addressed to Domitian, the Roman emperor who may have been in power during the writing of the Apocalypse, Martial wrote:

> *Thou, morning star,*
> *Bring on the day!*
> *Come and expel our fears,*
> *Rome begs that Caesar*
> *may soon appear.*[66]

If Revelation 22 is read in light of Martial's satire, the promise of Christ to come soon and the invitation of the author welcoming him take on political significance. The author is saying that Christ, not Caesar, is the morning star.[67] If we stay with a more conservative interpretive strategy, in which we look first to the Hebrew Scriptures and second to the traditions within Early Judaism for the symbolic referents, we see in v. 16 a direct appeal to the messianic traditions developing in Early Judaism.[68] In any case, the invitation to come (ἔρχομαι) and take (λαμβάνω) freely the water of life in v. 17 recalls the scene in chap. 5, where the Lamb came (ἔρχομαι) and took (λαμβάνω) the scroll from the right hand of the one sitting on the throne.

Jesus *acted* in the crucial scene in heaven. Jesus' nonviolent resistance to evil, his "consistent resistance" (Schüssler Fiorenza's apt translation of ὑπομονή | *hypomonē*)[69] led to his execution. The resulting slaughter of Christ is seen in the Apocalypse as the key to his victory and the

---

[65] Cullmann, *The Christology of the New Testament*, 211.

[66] Boesak, *Comfort and Protest*, 137. Boesak says he got this from Stauffer. Neither Boesak nor Stauffer is very good about bibliographical specificity.

[67] Morning star was, in Second Temple Judaism, a developing messianic symbol. Cf. Rev. 2:28; Num. 24:17; Isa. 14:12; 60:3; Matt. 2:2, 10; *Testament of Levi* 18:3; *Testament of Judah* 24:1; Cairo Genizah copy of the *Damascus Document* 7.18–20; *Milḥamah* 11.6; y.Ta'anit 68d.

[68] To speak of "messianic traditions developing" is already somewhat risky, because these traditions were neither monolithic, nor did they develop in a linear fashion. For a helpful overview of the evidence, see John J. Collins, *The Scepter and the Star: The Messiahs of the Dead Sea Scrolls and Other Ancient Literature* (New York: Doubleday, 1995).

[69] Fiorenza, *The Book of Revelation*, 4, 182.

image of Christ as vulnerable lamb (ἀρνίον | *arnion*) becomes the central, controlling image of Christ in the Apocalypse.[70] Just as Christ overcame through *his* nonviolent resistance unto death, so are the believers to overcome through *their* nonviolent resistance unto death (cf. esp. 3:21). The victories of both through the same means enable both to sit on God's throne and to reign (cf. 3:21; 5:10; 11:15, 17; 20:4, 6; 22:5). And just as Christ came and took the scroll from the hand of the one seated on the throne (5:7), so the reader is invited at the end of the vision to come and take the water of life freely (22:17).

CONCLUSION: THE PROMISES AND CHALLENGES OF THE APOCALYPSE

The goal toward which the Apocalypse moves is the vision of the restoration of creation, including the proper worship of God, suggested especially by Trito-Isaiah and Ezekiel. In this final eschatological vision, paradise merges not with some idealized return to the garden, but with a city to which the nations come for healing (cf. Ezek. 47:12; Rev. 5:9). It is therefore forward-looking; it leans toward consummation, but not in an escapist sort of way.

The sovereignty of God is what sustains mission (22:13). The Revelation is a revelation of what God is doing and how God's people are to respond; it is not a program of hope conceived or initiated by humans (22:6). To the extent that this vision is pessimistic, it is a pessimism about humanity's ability to bring this consummation to realization. Only God can do this. Still, the human response is critical. The believing community's role is to resist consistently and nonviolently, to "follow the Lamb wherever he goes" (14:4). Thus, the power of the Apocalypse lies in recalling the traditions of the past (both Jewish and Jewish-Christian) in a way that unleashes the power of eschatology (a vision of the future) for an ethical stance in the present.

This book is an invitation—to the altar of decision, yes, but more fundamentally to a "vision for the church as an alternative community pitted in conflict with the powers that be."[71] It is an invitation to the peace of justice with a profound sense of the underlying moral orderliness of the universe.[72] As such, Revelation represents the biblical high point in the intersection of mission and peace in the New Testament as it envisions life as it ought to be under the lordship of Christ, and calls all comers to that vision.

---

[70] Christ is referred to as ἀρνίον 28 times in the Apocalypse—more often than any other title or designation.

[71] Hays, *Moral Vision*, 173.

[72] Ibid., 172.